Teach Yourself®
Microsoft® Windows®
Me Millennium
Edition

Teach Yourself®
Microsoft® Windows®
Me Millennium
Edition

Brian Underdahl

IDG Books Worldwide, Inc.
An International Data Group Company

Foster City, CA • Chicago, IL • Indianapolis, IN • New York, NY

Teach Yourself® Microsoft® Windows® Me Millennium Edition

Published by

IDG Books Worldwide, Inc.

An International Data Group Company

919 E. Hillsdale Blvd., Suite 400

Foster City, CA 94404

`www.idgbooks.com` (IDG Books Worldwide Web site)

Library of Congress Control Number: 00-104428

ISBN: 0-7645-3488-2

Printed in the United States of America

10 9 8 7 6 5 4 3 2 1

1V/QU/QY/QQ/IN

Distributed in the United States by IDG Books Worldwide, Inc.

Distributed by CDG Books Canada Inc. for Canada; by Transworld Publishers Limited in the United Kingdom; by IDG Norge Books for Norway; by IDG Sweden Books for Sweden; by IDG Books Australia Publishing Corporation Pty. Ltd. for Australia and New Zealand; by TransQuest Publishers Pte Ltd. for Singapore, Malaysia, Thailand, Indonesia, and Hong Kong; by Gotop Information Inc. for Taiwan; by ICG Muse, Inc. for Japan; by Intersoft for South Africa; by Eyrolles for France; by International Thomson Publishing for Germany, Austria, and Switzerland; by Distribuidora Cuspide for Argentina; by LR International for Brazil; by Galileo Libros for Chile; by Ediciones ZETA S.C.R. Ltda. for Peru; by WS Computer Publishing Corporation, Inc., for the Philippines; by Contemporanea de Ediciones for Venezuela; by Express Computer Distributors for the Caribbean and West Indies; by Micronesia Media Distributor, Inc. for Micronesia; by Chips Computadoras S.A. de C.V. for Mexico; by Editorial Norma de Panama S.A. for Panama; by American Bookshops for Finland.

For general information on IDG Books Worldwide's books in the U.S., please call our Consumer Customer Service department at 800-762-2974. For reseller information, including discounts and premium sales, please call our Reseller Customer Service department at 800-434-3422.

For information on where to purchase IDG Books Worldwide's books outside the U.S., please contact our International Sales department at 317-596-5530 or fax 317-572-4002.

For consumer information on foreign language translations, please contact our Customer Service department at 800-434-3422, fax 317-572-4002, or e-mail rights@idgbooks.com.

For information on licensing foreign or domestic rights, please phone +1-650-653-7098.

For sales inquiries and special prices for bulk quantities, please contact our Order Services department at 800-434-3422 or write to the address above.

For information on using IDG Books Worldwide's books in the classroom or for ordering examination copies, please contact our Educational Sales department at 800-434-2086 or fax 317-572-4005.

For press review copies, author interviews, or other publicity information, please contact our Public Relations department at 650-653-7000 or fax 650-653-7500.

For authorization to photocopy items for corporate, personal, or educational use, please contact Copyright Clearance Center, 222 Rosewood Drive, Danvers, MA 01923, or fax 978-750-4470.

 is a registered trademark or trademark under exclusive license to IDG Books Worldwide, Inc. from International Data Group, Inc. in the United States and/or other countries.

ABOUT IDG BOOKS WORLDWIDE

Welcome to the world of IDG Books Worldwide.

IDG Books Worldwide, Inc., is a subsidiary of International Data Group, the world's largest publisher of computer-related information and the leading global provider of information services on information technology. IDG was founded more than 30 years ago by Patrick J. McGovern and now employs more than 9,000 people worldwide. IDG publishes more than 290 computer publications in over 75 countries. More than 90 million people read one or more IDG publications each month.

Launched in 1990, IDG Books Worldwide is today the #1 publisher of best-selling computer books in the United States. We are proud to have received eight awards from the Computer Press Association in recognition of editorial excellence and three from Computer Currents' First Annual Readers' Choice Awards. Our best-selling ...*For Dummies®* series has more than 50 million copies in print with translations in 31 languages. IDG Books Worldwide, through a joint venture with IDG's Hi-Tech Beijing, became the first U.S. publisher to publish a computer book in the People's Republic of China. In record time, IDG Books Worldwide has become the first choice for millions of readers around the world who want to learn how to better manage their businesses.

Our mission is simple: Every one of our books is designed to bring extra value and skill-building instructions to the reader. Our books are written by experts who understand and care about our readers. The knowledge base of our editorial staff comes from years of experience in publishing, education, and journalism — experience we use to produce books to carry us into the new millennium. In short, we care about books, so we attract the best people. We devote special attention to details such as audience, interior design, use of icons, and illustrations. And because we use an efficient process of authoring, editing, and desktop publishing our books electronically, we can spend more time ensuring superior content and less time on the technicalities of making books.

You can count on our commitment to deliver high-quality books at competitive prices on topics you want to read about. At IDG Books Worldwide, we continue in the IDG tradition of delivering quality for more than 30 years. You'll find no better book on a subject than one from IDG Books Worldwide.

John Kilcullen
Chairman and CEO
IDG Books Worldwide, Inc.

Eighth Annual
Computer Press
Awards 1992

Ninth Annual
Computer Press
Awards 1993

Tenth Annual
Computer Press
Awards 1994

Eleventh Annual
Computer Press
Awards 1995

Credits

Acquisitions Editors
Ed Adams, David Mayhew

Project Editor
Paul Winters

Technical Editor
John Preisach

Copy Editors
Lane Barnholtz, Marti Paul

Project Coordinator
Amanda Foxworth

Graphics and Production Specialists
Amy Adrian, Brian Drumm,
Clint Lahnen, Gabrielle McCann,
Jacque Schneider, Rashelle Smith

Book Designers
Daniel Ziegler Design
Cátálin Dulfu, Kurt Krames

Proofreading and Indexing
Laura Albert, York Production Services

About the Author

Brian Underdahl has written more than 40 computer-related titles on a broad range of topics, including Windows 95, Windows 98, Microsoft Office, and the Internet. His recent efforts include *Teach Yourself Windows 98, Teach Yourself Windows 2000 Professional, Teach Yourself Microsoft Office 2000, Windows 98 One Step at a Time, Internet Bible* 2nd edition, and *Small Business Computing For Dummies.*

I dedicate this book to the people who have taught me so much in life. My family, my friends, and, most of all, my wife have shown me that the world can be a wonderful place.

Welcome to
Teach Yourself

Welcome to *Teach Yourself*, a series read and trusted by millions for a decade. Although you may have seen the *Teach Yourself* name on other books, ours is the original. In addition, no *Teach Yourself* series has ever delivered more on the promise of its name than this series. That's because IDG Books Worldwide has transformed *Teach Yourself* into a new cutting-edge format that gives you all the information you need to learn quickly and easily.

Readers have told us that they want to learn by doing and that they want to learn as much as they can in as short a time as possible. We listened to you and believe that our new task-by-task format and suite of learning tools deliver the book you need to successfully teach yourself any technology topic. Features such as our Personal Workbook, which lets you practice and reinforce the skills you've just learned, help ensure that you get full value out of the time you invest in your learning. Handy cross-references to related topics and online sites broaden your knowledge and give you control over the kind of information you want, when you want it.

More Answers . . .

In designing the latest incarnation of this series, we started with the premise that people like you, who are beginning to intermediate computer users, want to take control of your own learning. To do this, you need the proper tools to find answers to questions so you can solve problems now.

In designing a series of books that provide such tools, we created a unique and concise visual format. The added bonus: *Teach Yourself* books actually pack more information into their pages than other books written on the same subjects. Skill for skill, you typically get much more information in a *Teach Yourself* book. In fact, *Teach Yourself* books, on average, cover twice the skills covered by other computer books — as many as 125 skills per book — so they're more likely to address your specific needs.

Welcome to Teach Yourself

...In Less Time

We know you don't want to spend twice the time to get all this great information, so we provide lots of time-saving features:

▶ A modular task-by-task organization of information: any task you want to perform is easy to find and includes simple-to-follow steps

▶ A larger size than standard makes the book easy to read and convenient to use at a computer workstation. The large format also enables us to include many more illustrations — 500 screen illustrations show you how to get everything done!

▶ A Personal Workbook at the end of each chapter reinforces learning with extra practice, real-world applications for your learning, and questions and answers to test your knowledge

▶ Cross-references appearing at the bottom of each task page refer you to related information, providing a path through the book for learning particular aspects of the software thoroughly

▶ A Find It Online feature offers valuable ideas on where to go on the Internet to get more information or to download useful files

▶ Take Note sidebars provide added-value information from our expert authors for more in-depth learning

▶ An attractive, consistent organization of information helps you quickly find and learn the skills you need

These *Teach Yourself* features are designed to help you learn the essential skills about a technology in the least amount of time, with the most benefit. We've placed these features consistently throughout the book, so you quickly learn where to go to find just the information you need — whether you work through the book from cover to cover or use it later to solve a new problem.

You will find a *Teach Yourself* book on almost any technology subject — from the Internet to Windows to Microsoft Office. Take control of your learning today, with IDG Books Worldwide's *Teach Yourself* series.

Teach Yourself
More Answers in Less Time

Search through the task headings to find the topic you want right away. To learn a new skill, search the contents, chapter opener, or the extensive index to find what you need. Then find — at a glance — the clear task heading that matches it.

Learn the concepts behind the task at hand and, more important, learn how the task is relevant in the real world. Time-saving suggestions and advice show you how to make the most of each skill.

After you learn the task at hand, you may have more questions, or you may want to read about other tasks related to the topic. Use the cross-references to find different tasks to make your learning more efficient.

Adding Toolbars to the Taskbar

You can make the Windows Me Taskbar even more useful by adding new toolbars to the Taskbar. These toolbars provide several very useful functions that may surprise and please you.

You're probably already familiar with one of the Taskbar toolbars — the Quick Launch toolbar. This toolbar contains icons that you can click to quickly view your desktop, browse the Internet, or check your e-mail. You may even have added some of your own shortcuts to the Quick Launch toolbar. But the Quick Launch toolbar is only one of the toolbars that you can add to the Taskbar.

The Address toolbar is one of the most useful of the toolbars that you can add to the Taskbar. If you know the URL of a Web page you'd like to visit, the quickest way to go directly to the site is to add the Address toolbar to the Taskbar. You can then enter the URL into the Address bar. After you type the address and press Enter, Internet Explorer opens and takes you directly to the Web site, bypassing any start pages that Internet Explorer normally opens first.

The Links toolbar provides you with one-click access to the links on the Internet Explorer Links bar. By clicking one of the links you can quickly visit the associated Web site.

The Desktop toolbar enables you to access anything that appears on your Windows Me desktop. You don't have to minimize the open windows to click a desktop icon because all of those icons appear in the Desktop toolbar.

▶ You may wish to expand the Taskbar to two rows before you add new toolbars.

❶ Right-click a blank space on the Taskbar to display the context menu.

❷ Select Toolbars ➪ Address to add the Address toolbar to the Taskbar.

❸ To use the Address toolbar, enter a Web page address and press Enter.

❹ Right-click a blank space on the Taskbar to display the context menu.

❺ Select Toolbars ➪ Desktop to display the Desktop toolbar.

▶ You may wish to remove the Address toolbar.

CROSS-REFERENCE
See "Moving and Hiding the Taskbar" earlier in this chapter.

258

Ultimately, people learn by doing. Follow the clear, illustrated steps presented with every task to complete a procedure. The detailed callouts for each step show you exactly where to go and what to do to complete the task.

Welcome to Teach Yourself

Go to this area if you want special tips, cautions, and notes that provide added insight into the current task.

The current chapter name and number always appear in the top right-hand corner of every task spread, so you always know exactly where you are in the book.

Who This Book Is For

This book is written for you, a beginning to intermediate PC user who isn't afraid to take charge of his or her own learning experience. You don't want a lot of technical jargon; you *do* want to learn as much about PC technology as you can in a limited amount of time. You need a book that is straightforward, easy to follow, and logically organized, so you can find answers to your questions easily. And, you appreciate simple-to-use tools such as handy cross-references and visual step-by-step procedures that help you make the most of your learning. We have created the unique *Teach Yourself* format specifically to meet your needs.

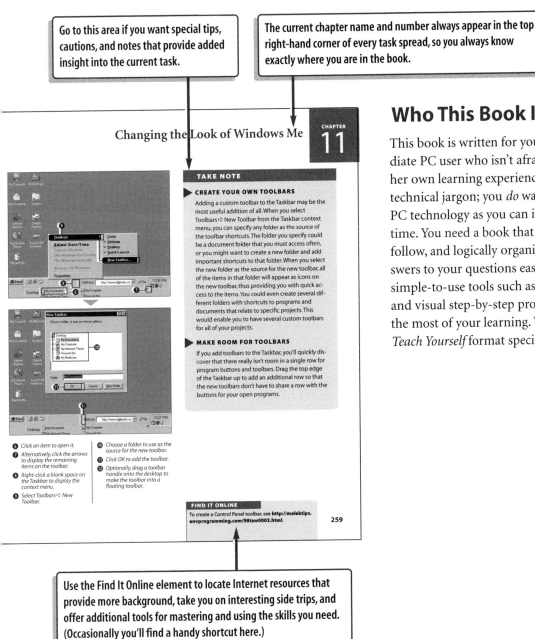

Changing the Look of Windows Me — CHAPTER 11

TAKE NOTE

CREATE YOUR OWN TOOLBARS

Adding a custom toolbar to the Taskbar may be the most useful addition of all. When you select Toolbars ⇨ New Toolbar from the Taskbar context menu, you can specify any folder as the source of the toolbar shortcuts. The folder you specify could be a document folder that you must access often, or you might want to create a new folder and add important shortcuts to that folder. When you select the new folder as the source for the new toolbar, all of the items in that folder will appear as icons on the new toolbar, thus providing you with quick access to the items. You could even create several different folders with shortcuts to programs and documents that relate to specific projects. This would enable you to have several custom toolbars for all of your projects.

MAKE ROOM FOR TOOLBARS

If you add toolbars to the Taskbar, you'll quickly discover that there really isn't room in a single row for program buttons and toolbars. Drag the top edge of the Taskbar up to add an additional row so that the new toolbars don't have to share a row with the buttons for your open programs.

⑥ Click an item to open it.

⑦ Alternatively, click the arrows to display the remaining items on the toolbar.

⑧ Right-click a blank space on the Taskbar to display the context menu.

⑨ Select Toolbars ⇨ New Toolbar.

⑩ Choose a folder to use as the source for the new toolbar.

⑪ Click OK to add the toolbar.

⑫ Optionally, drag a toolbar handle onto the desktop to make the toolbar into a floating toolbar.

FIND IT ONLINE

To create a Control Panel toolbar, see **http://malektips.envprogramming.com/98taw0003.html.**

259

Use the Find It Online element to locate Internet resources that provide more background, take you on interesting side trips, and offer additional tools for mastering and using the skills you need. (Occasionally you'll find a handy shortcut here.)

Personal Workbook

It's a well-known fact that much of what we learn is lost soon after we learn it if we don't reinforce our newly acquired skills with practice and repetition. That's why each *Teach Yourself* chapter ends with your own Personal Workbook. Here's where you can get extra practice, test your knowledge, and discover ideas for using what you've learned in the real world. There's even a Visual Quiz to help you remember your way around the topic's software environment.

Feedback

Please let us know what you think about this book, and whether you have any suggestions for improvements. You can send questions and comments to the *Teach Yourself* editors on the IDG Books Worldwide Web site at **www.idgbooks.com**.

> ## Personal Workbook
>
> ### Q&A
>
> **1** What will happen if you change the screen resolution setting but don't click the Yes button in the confirmation dialog box?
>
> _____
>
> _____
>
> _____
>
> **2** How can you make a hidden Taskbar pop up without moving the mouse?
>
> _____
>
> _____
>
> _____
>
> **3** How can you find a hidden Taskbar using the mouse?
>
> _____
>
> _____
>
> _____
>
> **4** What do you need to activate before you can use a JPEG image as your desktop wallpaper?
>
> _____
>
> _____
>
> _____
>
> **5** What can you do to restore order to the Start menu if items are no longer being sorted?
>
> _____
>
> _____
>
> _____
>
> **6** How can you reduce the size of the icons on the Start menu?
>
> _____
>
> _____
>
> _____
>
> **7** What is the fastest way to choose a desktop element on the Appearance tab of the Display Properties dialog box so that you can change the element's color?
>
> _____
>
> _____
>
> _____
>
> **8** How can you view the items in the Control Panel folder without opening the folder?
>
> _____
>
> _____
>
> _____
>
> ANSWERS: PAGE 396
>
> 262

After working through the tasks in each chapter, you can test your progress and reinforce your learning by answering the questions in the Q&A section. Then check your answers in the Personal Workbook Answers appendix at the back of the book.

Welcome to Teach Yourself

Another practical way to reinforce your skills is to do additional exercises on the same skills you just learned without the benefit of the chapter's visual steps. If you struggle with any of these exercises, it's a good idea to refer to the chapter's tasks to be sure you've mastered them.

Changing the Look of Windows Me

CHAPTER 11

Read the list of Real-World Applications to get ideas on how you can use the skills you've just learned in your everyday life. Understanding a process can be simple; knowing how to use that process to make you more productive is the key to successful learning.

EXTRA PRACTICE

1. Try out a different screen resolution setting.
2. Move the Taskbar to the left side of your screen.
3. Try one of the sample color schemes.
4. Sort your Start menu into alphabetical order.
5. Try several different refresh rates to see which produces the best display.
6. Add a toolbar that shows the contents of the My Documents folder to the Taskbar.

REAL-WORLD APPLICATIONS

✓ Your company has several PCs in public areas of your office. You add the company logo as wallpaper.

✓ You will be away from your desk for a few minutes, and you need to make certain that people won't be able to view the salary budget worksheet. You apply a password-protected screen saver to prevent unauthorized access.

✓ You have added several new programs to your PC, and your Start menu is a mess. You change to small icons and re-sort the menu to make your system easier to use.

✓ You use your PC a lot and have been experiencing headaches. You adjust your monitor refresh rate to correct the problem.

Visual Quiz

How can you display this dialog box? How do the controls on this tab interact?

_____

_____

_____

_____

_____

_____

Take the Visual Quiz to see how well you're learning your way around the technology. Learning about computers is often as much about how to find a button or menu as it is about memorizing definitions. Our Visual Quiz helps you find your way.

Acknowledgments

I have many people to thank for making this book a reality. Some of them include:

At IDG Books Worldwide

David Mayhew and **Ed Adams**, acquisitions editors, for all of their support and understanding.

Paul Winters, project editor, for helping me get this project done on time.

John Preisach, technical editor, for making certain you don't have to deal with technical errors.

The copy editors, production coordinator, and all the countless other wonderful people who work behind the scenes to make certain you get to read the best book possible.

At Microsoft

The Windows Me Millennium Edition development team for all the excellent help. Without these folks we wouldn't have Windows Me Millennium Edition and I wouldn't have been able to write this book.

Contents

Contents

Contents

Contents

Contents

Contents

Contents

Teach Yourself®
Microsoft® Windows®
Me Millennium
Edition

Contents of 'Desktop'

Name

My Computer

Network Neigh

Internet Explore

Microsoft Outlook

Recycle Bin

My Briefcase

3252-9

3259-6

3261-8

3262-6

3281-2

3286-3

DE Phone List

Device Manager

In

Iomega Tools

PART

I

Learning Windows Me Basics

This first part of the book provides you with an introduction to Windows Me. Here you learn about what you see on the Windows Me screen and how to use those items. You learn how to find your way around so that Windows Me will be much more comfortable and easy to use.

You don't have to be an expert to use Windows Me, nor do you have to spend hours learning new ways to do things. As you'll see in this part, it's even easy to find additional help when you really need it.

CHAPTER 1

MASTER THESE SKILLS

▶ Using the Start Menu
▶ Using Your Desktop
▶ Using My Computer
▶ Using My Network Places
▶ Using My Documents
▶ Using the My Pictures Folder
▶ Using the Quick Launch Toolbar
▶ Using the System Tray Icons
▶ Switching Between Programs

[ˌɪntəˈdjuːɪŋ]

Introducing Windows Me 介紹

Every computer needs an operating system — a set of services and commands that enable the computer to run programs, to work with devices such as printers, and that enable the user to interact with the computer. Windows Me is one such operating system and is a part of the Microsoft Windows family that includes Windows 95, Windows 98, and Windows 2000. Windows Me looks very much like those older versions of Windows but it includes significant improvements.

All versions of Windows provide you with access to all the parts of your computing environment — documents, files, applications, e-mail, and the Internet. From a user's standpoint, the basic tasks involved with using Windows are quite similar no matter which version you use.

As you can gather from the name, the Windows Me environment is heavily focused on *windows* — rectangular areas on the screen that present information. You open windows when you need them and close them when you don't need them. Individual windows can be resized and moved about the screen.

Windows Me uses small graphical *icons* — small pictures — on the desktop to represent objects such as documents, applications, folders, devices, Web pages, and other computers. Icons often also have text labels to help make their purpose a bit clearer. If you move the mouse over an object on the desktop or in a window and click the right mouse button, Windows Me displays a menu with the object's common commands. Many Windows applications use this same convention, called a *context menu* or *right-click* menu.

You can *select* objects in several ways. For most types of objects you *click* the object: you move the mouse cursor onto the object and then press the left mouse button once. A selected object is highlighted; its label is darkened and has a dotted line indicating that the selected object is ready to be chosen. You *choose* an object to activate its associated command. You choose the object by *double-clicking* its icon: you move the mouse cursor onto the icon and then press the left mouse button rapidly twice. If the object is a menu selection or command button, however, you choose it with a single click.

You can also move or copy objects using *drag and drop*. To drag and drop an object you move the mouse cursor onto the icon of the object to be dragged. Press and hold the left mouse button while you move the mouse cursor to the destination object's icon. Then release the mouse button.

You'll learn more about all these terms as you follow along and try out the tasks for yourself.

Using the Start Menu

At the lower left corner of your Windows Me desktop is the Start button. When you click this button, a list of options pops up — the Start menu. This menu provides you with access to most of your programs, to your most recent documents, to options that enable you to search for items, to the Windows Me help system, and to the settings options that control how your system operates.

The Start menu is similar to most other menus you will encounter while using Windows Me. It includes three different kinds of items — commands, cascading menus, and items that display dialog boxes.

Command selections run programs immediately when you select them. The Windows Update and Help commands in the figures on these pages are command selections. When you click the command, the application starts.

A small arrow next to the label indicates a cascading menu. These items display additional menus when you select them. Programs, Documents, Settings, and Search are cascading menu selections. If you move the mouse cursor to one of them, a submenu pops out. Cascading menus, in turn, can contain the same three selection types that the Start menu contains. In the first figure of this task, the Programs menu is open. Internet Explorer, an application program, is selected. If you click it once, Internet Explorer will run.

Three dots (. . .) next to the label indicate menu selections that open dialog boxes. The Run, Log Off, and Shut Down selections are dialog box selections. Dialog boxes are special boxes that appear on your screen to display messages or to accept input from you. The last figure of this task shows such a dialog box.

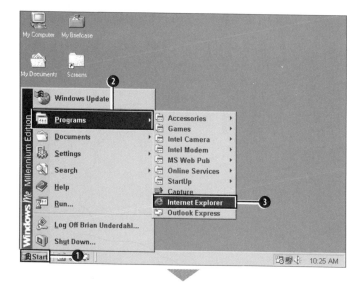

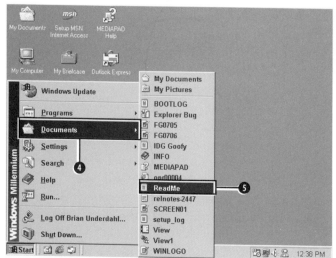

① Click the Start button to open the Start menu.

② Select Programs to open the Programs menu.

③ Click an application such as Internet Explorer to start the application.

④ Select Documents to open your list of recently used documents.

⑤ Click an item to open it.

CROSS-REFERENCE

See "Opening Items" in Chapter 2 for more information about opening programs that aren't on the Start menu.

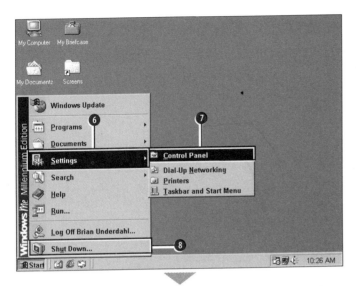

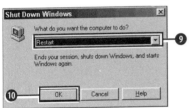

TAKE NOTE

WINDOWS ME HAS NO FAVORITES

If you've used Windows 98 in the past, you'll notice one big difference with Windows Me as soon as you open the Start menu — the Favorites list does not appear on the Windows Me Start menu. You can still use Favorites in Internet Explorer in Windows Me — they just don't appear on the Start menu. In Chapter 11 you learn how to add the Favorites selection to the Start menu.

STOP BY STARTING

It's important that Windows Me be shut down properly. Although it may seem that you need only turn off the switch when you're finished working, you'll damage your files and may lose some of your work if you don't close Windows Me correctly. Before you turn off your PC, always click the Start button and choose Shut Down.

PAUSE TO IDENTIFY START MENU ITEMS

If you briefly hold the mouse pointer over program items or documents on the Start menu, Windows Me will display a pop-up message showing the location of the item. The pop-up box will disappear when you move the mouse slightly.

⑥ Select Settings to open the list of settings options.

⑦ Click an item to open it.

⑧ When you're ready to shut down your computer, click Shut Down.

⑨ Choose the shut down option you want to use from the drop-down list.

⑩ Click OK to shut down your computer.

FIND IT ONLINE

See **http://support.microsoft.com/directory/** for the latest information on help for all versions of Windows.

Using Your Desktop

Your Windows Me desktop displays a number of small pictures — *icons* — that enable you to access your programs, files, documents, and other computers. The icons on your desktop may be neatly aligned or spread randomly across the desktop, but they work just the same regardless of their layout.

Five icons are almost certain to appear on your Windows Me desktop. My Documents provides access to the document files you create and save. My Computer provides access to the files, folders, disk drives, and so on that are on your PC. My Network Places provides access to the shared files and printers of other computers on your local network. Recycle Bin is where you place discarded items from the desktop and file folders. Internet Explorer provides access to the World Wide Web.

All of the icons on your desktop include both pictures and labels, so you should be able to determine their purpose quite easily. Most of the desktop icons are program icons that will run the associated programs when you click them. This is true even if the icon represents a document, because Windows Me generally knows which program to use to open most document files.

Many of the desktop icons have a small arrow at their lower-left corner to indicate that they are *shortcuts* to applications or documents. Shortcuts provide you with quick access to an item, but because shortcuts are only pointers to the real program or document, they save space and reduce the chance that you might accidentally delete an important item.

❶ Double-click an icon to open the item.

❷ Click the Close button to close the item you opened.

❸ Right-click an item to view its shortcut menu.

CROSS-REFERENCE

See "Configuring the Desktop" in Chapter 11 for more information on controlling how your desktop looks.

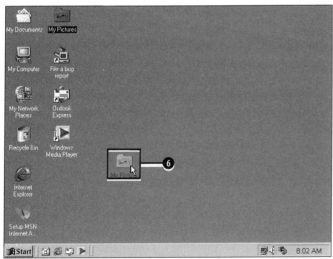

STRAIGHTENING UP YOUR DESKTOP

If your Windows Me desktop is a bit of a mess with icons scattered all over the place, you can tell Windows Me to automatically bring some order to the chaos. If you right-click a blank spot on the desktop and select Arrange Icons ➪ Auto Arrange, the icons will snap into orderly rows and columns. Any new icons that are added to your desktop will also move into place automatically. Alternatively, you can *drag* icons to new locations by pointing to the icon, holding down the left mouse button, and moving the mouse. When you release the left mouse button the icon will stay in the same general area where you dropped it (although if auto arrange is selected the icons will snap into the rows and columns).

USING YOUR MOUSE

If you find that it is confusing to remember when you need to click your mouse button once and when you need to double-click, you can change the way your mouse works. In Chapter 12 you'll learn more about using this option to enable you to open icons with a single click — very much the same way you select menu items and Web page links. But as you'll also learn, setting up your desktop to use single clicks can make it a bit harder to copy and move items.

④ To view the desktop shortcut menu, right-click a blank space on the desktop.

⑤ Select Arrange Icons ➪ Auto Arrange to align the icons in neat rows and columns.

⑥ To rearrange the desktop, point to an icon, hold down the left mouse button, and drag the icon to a new location.

SHORTCUT

See **http://search.support.microsoft.com/kb/c.asp** for the Windows Me knowledge base.

Using My Computer

Your PC stores information on *disk drives*. Double-clicking the My Computer icon on your Windows Me desktop opens a window that shows you the disk drives that are connected to your PC. Typically this display will include such things as a diskette drive, a hard disk, and a CD-ROM drive. Depending on your system configuration you may see additional drives. In the figures on these pages the PC has a total of three different disk drives. My Computer also includes an icon to open the Control Panel.

The icons in the My Computer window can represent not only your disk drives, but also folders, documents, data files, applications, shortcuts to devices and other PCs on the network, and so on. You can view the contents of a drive by double-clicking the drive's icon. You can also view the contents of a folder by double-clicking the folder's icon. Folders are subdirectories in the file system. To close a folder, click the Close button — the button with an X in the upper right corner of the open folder's window.

You can open documents by double-clicking the document's icon. When you do, Windows Me first opens the application that created the document, and then the document opens within that application. If you double-click an application, the application opens directly. If you attempt to open an object that Windows Me does not recognize, Windows Me will ask you to choose the application to use for opening the item. In most cases it is safest to open only those documents that Windows Me automatically recognizes.

The Control Panel in My Computer contains many icons that enable you to manage the configuration of Windows Me and your PC. For example, one of the icons in Control Panel opens the Add/Remove Programs

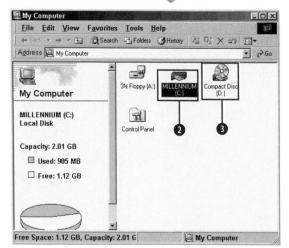

❶ Double-click the My Computer icon to open the My Computer window.

❷ Click an item to view its description on the left side of the window.

❸ Double-click an item to open it.

CROSS-REFERENCE

See "Controlling the View Detail Level" in Chapter 2 for more information about folder views.

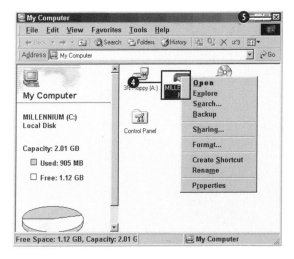

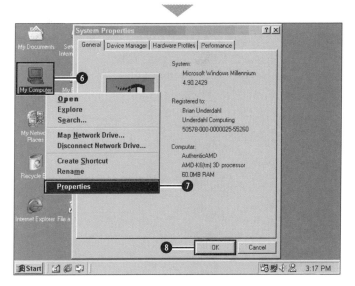

dialog box so that you can install new programs or remove old programs that you no longer need.

My Computer also contains links to your My Documents folder, to your My Network Places folder, and to the Dial-up Networking folder so you can easily access those folders. You will learn about each of these folders later.

TAKE NOTE

▶ VIEW OBJECT DETAILS

Select View ⇨ Details from the menu to see more information about each of the items in the My Computer window. Windows Me automatically provides a description of each item as it is selected, but changing to the Details view provides additional information about all items even when they are not selected.

▶ EXPLORE MY COMPUTER

To view the objects in My Computer using the standard Windows Explorer view, right-click My Computer and choose Explore. This is different from double-clicking the My Computer icon, which opens My Computer using the Open view as discussed in the figures and steps. You may find that it is easier to navigate My Computer in Explore view because you can use the folder tree to locate items. You may wish to try both methods to see which view you prefer.

④ *Right-click an item to view its shortcut menu.*

⑤ *Click the Close button to close My Computer.*

⑥ *Right-click the My Computer icon to view its shortcut menu.*

⑦ *Select Properties to display the System Properties dialog box.*

⑧ *Click OK to close the dialog box.*

FIND IT ONLINE

See **http://support.microsoft.com/directory/ directory/phonepers.asp** for Windows Me support phone numbers.

Using My Network Places

If your PC is connected to a network, clicking the My Network Places icon opens a window that displays the computers and shared printers in your network. Initially, the My Network Places window contains only two icons: Add Network Place and Entire Network. You can add icons to represent individual computers and printers on the network or to represent shared folders on the network.

Network resources such as shared folders and shared printers may not always act the same way local resources do. For example, someone may share a folder but may not allow you to do anything except read the files in the folder. Your System Administrator may also set up rules that specify who has access to specific network resources. You might need to change your user name and password to save files on the network or to use shared printers. In addition, you won't be able to see quite as much information about network folders as you can for local folders.

If you have a home network, you probably won't have the same level of restrictions as you might on a corporate network. This is especially true if all of the computers on your network use Windows Me, Windows 98, or Windows 95.

Networks are generally somewhat less responsive than what you may be used to. If you haven't browsed the network before, you may be surprised by the delays you encounter when you're browsing My Network Places. This is especially true if you view folders where someone else is making changes to the files. When you select a new folder, the view will reflect the current status of the folder, but you may find it necessary to select View ⇨ Refresh to see the changes.

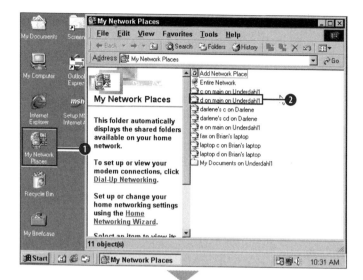

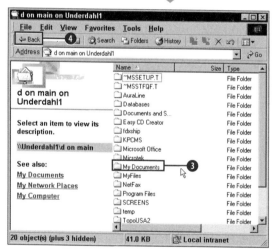

① Double-click the My Network Places icon to open the My Network Places window.

② Double-click a computer icon to view the shared resources on that computer.

③ Double-click a folder to open the folder.

④ Alternatively, click the Back button to return to the previous window.

CROSS-REFERENCE

See "Sharing Your Files" in Chapter 7.

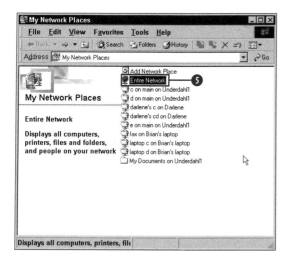

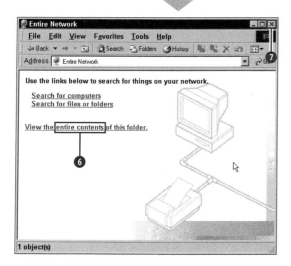

⑤ Double-click the Entire Network icon to view all the available computers in your workgroup.

⑥ Click the entire contents link to see the entire network.

⑦ Click the Close button to close the window.

FIND IT ONLINE

See **http://www.proxim.com/symphony/index.htm** for simple networking solutions.

Using My Documents

Whenever you create a document on your PC, you must store that document in a file if you want to be able to reopen the same document at a later time. If you don't save your work in a file, it will be lost when you turn off or restart your computer.

The My Documents folder is the default location that most Windows Me applications use when storing document files. By storing all of your documents in a central location you have not only the convenience of being able to easily locate those files, but also a single main folder to back up when you want to make a copy of all of your document files. You do not have to use the My Documents folder, but it's a very good idea to do so.

You may want to add a little extra organization by creating additional folders that are contained within the My Documents folder. You can then use these additional folders to store the files for individual projects. You'll still be able to locate your files quickly and easily simply by opening the My Documents folder and then opening the project folder. The figures for this task show you how to add new folders to the My Documents folder.

Although the My Documents folder is created automatically, in most ways it is a standard Windows Me folder. You could rename or move the My Documents folder, but be sure to see the Take Note section for special information on the best method for doing so. Because Windows Me supplies the name and location of the My Documents folder to applications, you'll want to make certain that the correct information is passed along.

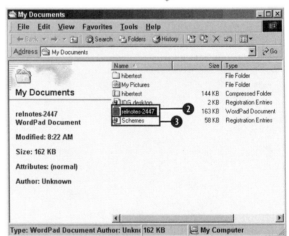

❶ Double-click the My Documents icon to open the My Documents folder.

❷ Click an item to display its description on the left.

❸ Double-click an item to open it in the application in which it was created.

CROSS-REFERENCE

See "Sending Objects to the Recycle Bin" in Chapter 6 for more information about deleting unneeded files.

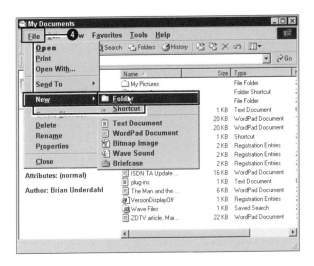

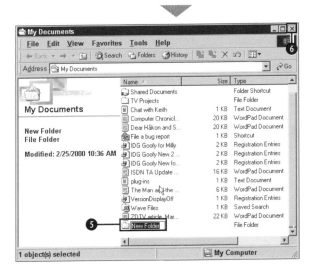

MOVING THE MY DOCUMENTS FOLDER

By default, Windows Me creates a folder on your
C drive named My Documents. If you'd rather save
your documents in a different location — such as on
your network — you can change the location of the
My Documents folder. Right-click the My Documents
icon, select Properties from the shortcut menu that
pops up, and specify a new location in the Target
folder location text box. If you can't remember the
exact name of the new location, click the Browse
button to find the folder you wish to use.

SAVING DOCUMENTS ON DISKETTES

If you save all of your document files in the My
Documents folder, you may also wish to make
backup copies of those files. But because most application programs remember the last file save location, saving your document files once in the My
Documents folder and once on a diskette may not
be very convenient. A better way to do this is to
save your documents in the My Documents folder
and then later open the folder. Right-click any files
that you wish to save on diskettes and choose Send
To ⇨ 3¹/₂ Floppy (A) from the context menu.

❹ To create a new folder within
the My Documents folder,
select File ⇨ New ⇨ Folder.

❺ Type a name for the new
folder and press Enter.

❻ Click Close to exit the My
Documents folder.

FIND IT ONLINE

See **http://officeupdate.microsoft.com/services/
drivewaycohome.htm** to learn about saving
documents on the Web.

Using the My Pictures Folder

Windows Me also has a special folder that is intended for storing graphic images on your computer. The My Pictures folder is a subfolder within the My Documents folder. Although you could store graphic images anywhere, storing them in the My Pictures folder enables you to quickly preview or print those images without opening a special graphics program.

Graphic images can be created from many different sources. If you have a digital camera, you can load the image files directly from your camera into the My Pictures folder. You can also use a scanner to scan printed photographs and store the resulting image files on your PC. Of course, you can download many different digital images from the Internet, too.

The My Pictures folder is a very special Windows Me folder. In addition to the various icon views that are used to identify files in other folders, the My Pictures folder includes a fifth type of view — thumbnail view. This special view shows small representations of the actual file contents rather than simply an icon representing the file type. Because of this, you can locate specific graphic images simply by opening the My Pictures folder and scrolling through the list.

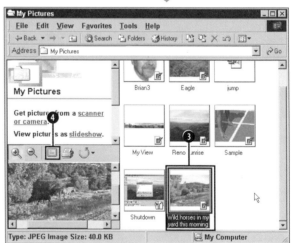

❶ Double-click the My Documents icon to open the My Documents folder.

❷ Double-click the My Pictures icon to open the My Pictures folder.

❸ Click an item to view it.

❹ To view the image in a full-screen window, click the Preview button.

CROSS-REFERENCE

See "Using Imaging for Windows" in Chapter 17 for more information about creating image files.

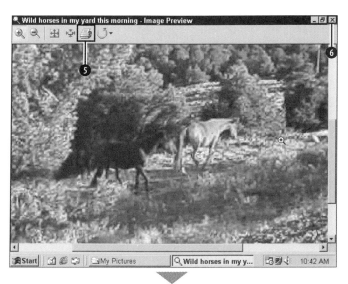

TAKE NOTE

▶ **PREVIEWING IMAGES**

The My Pictures folder can generate a preview of many types of image files but not every image file. Generally it is possible to generate previews of still images but not of video files. If you have video files in the My Pictures folder, you will see an icon that indicates the type of file rather than a preview of the file contents. Double-clicking a video file will usually open the file in a viewer such as Windows Media Player.

▶ **GRAPHIC IMAGE FORMATS**

Dozens of different file formats are used for graphic images. The most common types you will encounter are JPEG, GIF, TIFF, and BMP — all of which can be viewed using the My Pictures folder viewer. The JPEG and GIF formats are the most common image formats used on the Web, and most photos you download from the Web will be in JPEG format. If you use a digital camera you will likely find that JPEG is the default format used when saving your photos. Scanners often use the TIFF format. GIF is generally not suitable for photos, but works well for simpler images. BMP is an older format that is not as popular, because the file sizes for BMP files tend to be much larger than for other image formats.

⑤ *To print the image, click the Print button.*

⑥ *Click the Close button to close the Image Preview window.*

⑦ *Click the Close button to close the My Pictures folder.*

FIND IT ONLINE

See **http://www.microsoft.com/office/photodraw/ trial/default.htm** to download a trial version of PhotoDraw.

Using the Quick Launch Toolbar

Using the programs that are installed on your PC should be easy. As you have already seen earlier in this chapter, you can open applications by selecting them from the Start menu or by clicking their icon on your Windows Me desktop. In this section, you will learn about another way to access the programs that you use most often even more quickly.

If you look in the Windows Me Taskbar just to the right of the Start button, you will notice several icons in the *Quick Launch toolbar*. The Quick Launch toolbar normally has three buttons. The Show Desktop tool button minimizes all open windows to buttons on the taskbar so that you can view the desktop. The Launch Internet Explorer Browser tool button starts Internet Explorer. The Launch Outlook Express tool button opens Outlook Express — a program that provides e-mail and newsgroup services. If you move the mouse cursor over a button for a few seconds, the button's description will appear.

You have already seen that you can easily start your programs by clicking their desktop icons or by choosing them from the Start menu. Why, then, would you need the Quick Launch toolbar? One good reason is that the Quick Launch toolbar is visible whenever the Windows Me Taskbar is visible. An open window might cover your desktop icons, and opening the Start menu so that you can wade through several layers of menus may not be the most convenient way to start your favorite programs.

CROSS-REFERENCE

See "Moving and Hiding the Taskbar" in Chapter 11.

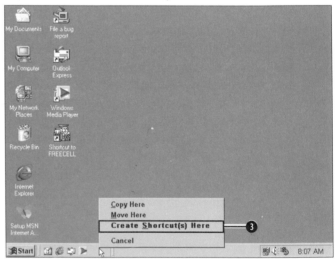

❶ To add an icon to the Quick Launch toolbar, select the icon.

▶ You can select items on your desktop or from Windows Explorer.

❷ Hold down the right mouse button and drag the icon onto the Quick Launch toolbar.

❸ Release the button and in the dialog box that appears select Create Shortcut(s) Here.

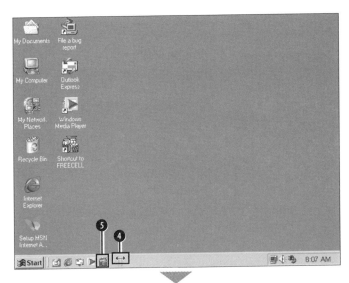

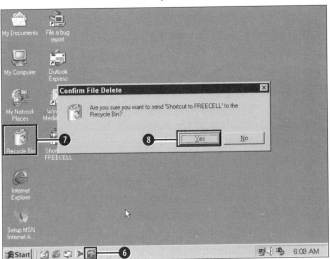

What really makes the Quick Launch toolbar useful, however, is that you can add your own programs to it and gain the ability to launch them quickly. You can also remove some of the existing icons from the Quick Launch toolbar. In these ways you can customize the Quick Launch toolbar and make it more useful. The figures in this task show you how to make these changes.

④ *If necessary, drag the edge of the Quick Launch toolbar so that you can see all the icons.*

⑤ *Click the icon to open the application.*

⑥ *To remove the icon from the Quick Launch toolbar, point to the icon and hold down the left mouse button.*

⑦ *Drag the icon onto the Recycle Bin and release the mouse button.*

⑧ *Select Yes to delete the icon. (You may not see this confirmation depending on your Recycle Bin settings.)*

FIND IT ONLINE

If your Show Desktop icon disappears, see
http://support.microsoft.com/support/kb/
articles/q190/3/55.asp.

19

Using the System Tray Icons

In addition to the Start button, the Quick Launch toolbar, and space for buttons that show what applications are currently running, the Windows Me taskbar has a small area on the right-hand side known as the *system tray*. The system tray usually contains several icons that vary depending on the software and hardware you have installed on your PC. You'll probably have at least three items in your system tray: the Task Scheduler icon, the Volume icon, and the Time display.

The Task Scheduler icon enables you to schedule important system maintenance items. The Volume icon launches the Windows Me Volume Control applet. The Time display enables you to constantly view the time of day. You can view the date by moving the mouse cursor to the Time display and waiting a few seconds.

The system tray may include additional icons as well. For example, if you use a laptop computer, your system tray may include an icon for PC Card status whenever a PC Card is inserted into one of the slots. Clicking this icon will give you the option of stopping the card so that you can safely remove it from your system without shutting down your computer. When you are connected to the Internet through a modem, the Modem icon flashes to show you when data is being sent or received.

If you're not sure of the purpose of a system tray icon, hold your mouse pointer over the icon for a few seconds. Windows Me will pop up a ToolTip that tells you about the icon. If you still aren't clear about an icon's purpose, try right-clicking the icon. This usually pops up a shortcut menu. You should be able to obtain additional clues about the icon's purpose from the shortcut menu items.

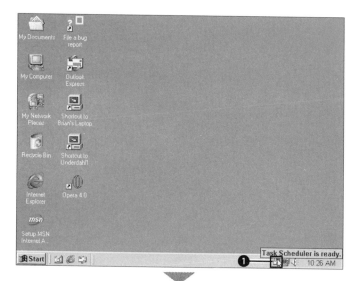

❶ Hold the mouse pointer over a system tray icon to view the ToolTip for the icon.

❷ Click the Volume control icon to display the master volume control.

▶ Alternatively, double-click the Volume control icon to display the more detailed volume control window.

CROSS-REFERENCE

See "Installing Programs" and "Uninstalling Programs" in Chapter 4.

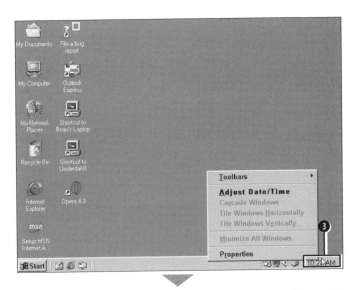

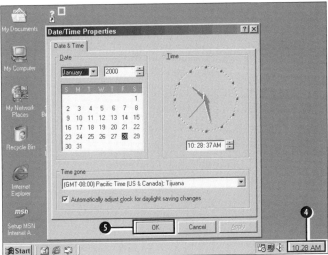

MODIFYING THE SYSTEM TRAY

It is generally not very easy to modify the system tray because Windows Me does not provide any tools for doing so. *PC Magazine* offers one tool, TrayManager, at **http://www.zdnet.com/pcmag/pctech/content/18/04/ut1804.001.html** that you can use to modify the system tray. The Windows 98 Resource Kit Sampler that was included on the Windows 98 CD-ROM included another tool, Quiktray, that may be on your system if you upgraded from Windows 98.

WATCH THE MODEM STATUS ICON

If you use a modem, you'll probably see a modem status icon on the system tray whenever the computer is connected. This icon has two spots that become bright blue when data is flowing to or from your PC. If both spots stay dark for a long time, your connection may be stalled, and you may wish to try reloading the current page or going to a different site. If neither works, you may need to restart your Internet connection. You can close your Internet connection by right-clicking the modem icon and choosing Disconnect.

---

❸ *Right-click a system tray icon to display the icon's shortcut menu.*

▶ *In this case the shortcut menu for the Time icon is displayed.*

❹ *Double-click the Time icon to display the Date/Time Properties dialog box.*

▶ *You can use this dialog box to adjust the system date, time, and time zone settings.*

❺ *Click OK to close the dialog box.*

FIND IT ONLINE

For tips on customizing the system tray, see **http://www.playernet.net/setup/win/tray.html**.

Switching Between Programs

Windows Me is a *multitasking* operating system. This means that you can have several different programs running at the same time — each in their own window.

Even though you can have several program windows open at the same time, only one of those windows is said to be *active* or to have the *focus*. The active window receives any keystrokes you type, and is usually the most recent window you opened or interacted with. An active window displays on top of the others and usually has a dark blue border — although the color may vary according to the color scheme that you are using.

You can change the focus to another window whenever you choose. Switching between open windows is easy. If you can see the window that you want to make active, simply click anywhere in it. If the window that you want to make active is not visible, you can use one of the methods that are shown in the figures.

If you prefer to use your keyboard, you will probably like the task list method best of all. Because you only need to press two keys — Alt and Tab — to use the task list, you can keep your hands right on the keyboard and never touch your mouse. Even if you don't mind using your mouse, you may find that the task list is a bit more convenient if you have a large number of windows open at the same time. That's because the Taskbar buttons can become too small to read unless you expand the Taskbar.

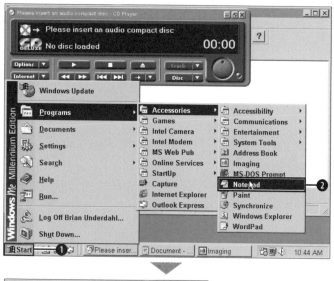

❶ Click the Start button.

❷ Open several programs, and then press Alt+Tab to display the task list.

❸ Press Tab until you have highlighted the window you wish to make active. Then release the Alt key.

CROSS-REFERENCE

See "Closing Programs" in Chapter 4.

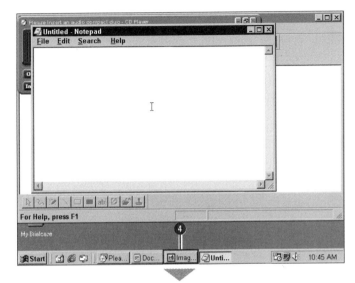

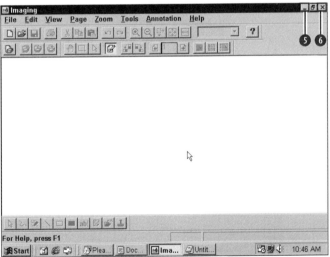

If you feel that using your mouse is a natural way to interact with your PC, you will probably prefer to click Taskbar buttons. Because Windows Me shows a button for each open window, a quick click on the appropriate button is a fast method to switch between windows. As you'll learn in Chapter 5, the Taskbar buttons are also convenient when you want to copy information from one window to another.

TAKE NOTE

► ALTERNATING BETWEEN TWO PROGRAMS

If you quickly press and release Alt+Tab, you'll return to the last open window. If you have several programs open, you can quickly switch back and forth between two of them by using this technique without waiting for the task list to display.

► CLOSING STALLED PROGRAMS

If you find that one of your applications stops responding, press Ctrl+Alt+Del and look for an item that says "Not Responding." Select the item and click the End Task button to close the item that has stopped working. In Windows Me you can often close a stalled program and continue working without restarting your system. Usually, though, it is safest to save your work, close all of your open programs, and restart Windows Me.

④ Alternatively, click a button on the Taskbar to switch to the associated window.

⑤ Click the Minimize button to hide the current window.

⑥ Click the Close button to close the current window.

FIND IT ONLINE

For additional ways to manage open programs, see
http://www.davecentral.com/sysauto.html.

Personal Workbook

Q&A

1 What are the three types of items that you will find on the Start menu?

_____

_____

_____

2 What do three periods following a menu item mean?

_____

_____

_____

3 What happens when you click an item on the Start menu that has a small arrow next to the item?

_____

_____

_____

4 What does a small arrow in the lower left corner of a desktop icon mean?

_____

_____

_____

5 How can you make the icons on your desktop align automatically?

_____

_____

_____

6 What is the purpose of the My Network Places icon?

_____

_____

_____

7 How can you quickly minimize all open windows to view your desktop?

_____

_____

_____

8 How can you quickly switch between two programs using your keyboard?

_____

_____

_____

ANSWERS: PAGE 389

EXTRA PRACTICE

1. Open the Control Panel using the Start menu.

2. Open a program's Properties dialog box using one of the desktop icons.

3. Use My Computer to determine the free space on Drive C.

4. Use the My Network Places to determine what computers you can access.

5. Use the Show Desktop button to view your desktop.

6. Open several programs and try switching between them using the task list and the Taskbar buttons.

REAL-WORLD APPLICATIONS

✔ You have been assigned the task of writing a report about a group project. To enable yourself to complete the report at home, you use the My Documents folder to copy the report to a diskette.

✔ You have two computers in your home. To make it easy for everyone to share a color printer, you use My Network Places and share the printer.

✔ You like to include spreadsheets in your reports to explain the financial aspects, so you keep your spreadsheet program and your word processor open at the same time. When you're working on a report, it's easy to switch quickly between the two programs using Alt+Tab.

Visual Quiz

How can you display this folder? What must you do to make the folder display the message shown here?

_____

_____

_____

_____

_____

_____

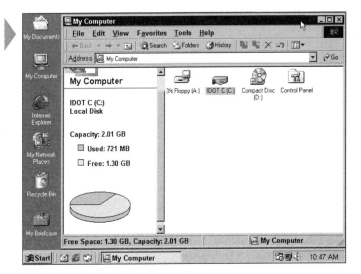

CHAPTER **2**

MASTER
THESE
SKILLS

▶ **Opening Windows Explorer**
▶ **Opening Items**
▶ **Copying and Moving Files**
▶ **Controlling the View Detail Level**
▶ **Viewing Thumbnails**
▶ **Sorting the File Listing**
▶ **Viewing Folders as Web Pages**
▶ **Controlling the Toolbars**
▶ **Customizing the Toolbars**
▶ **Using the Address Bar**
▶ **Using the History List**

Getting to Know Windows Explorer

Every computer needs a method for users to interact with the computer. That method may be something as simple as a command prompt, or it may be as complex as a *graphical user interface*—GUI. In Windows Me the most recognizable part of the GUI is Windows Explorer.

Windows Explorer shows you the contents of the folders that are available on your system. Whether these folders are on your local hard drive, on a removable drive, or even located somewhere on your network, Windows Explorer enables you to explore that folder structure. Folders are the directories and subdirectories that you use to store files on your disks. Folders are arranged in a hierarchical tree-like structure such that the set of folder and file names uniquely identify each file on a disk. Each folder can contain additional subfolders that branch off of it. These branches can extend several levels deep, but too many levels can make exploring your disk drives harder than necessary.

Windows Explorer displays information in *windows*—rectangular areas on the screen that present information. Individual windows can be resized and moved about the screen, and you can open and close them as necessary. You can even open several copies of Windows Explorer at the same time so that you can view the contents of different folders — perhaps to make it easier to copy or move files between those folders.

You have a number of options that you can choose to control how Windows Explorer displays information. You can see a simple group of icons, a more detailed view that shows file size and date information, or even a *thumbnail* view that enables you to preview the file contents before you open files. You can use Windows Explorer to customize the appearance of your folders so that they take on the appearance of Web pages — complete with background images and links that you can click to jump to other pages.

In this chapter, you will learn how to navigate in Windows Explorer, how to set Windows Explorer to display different types of information, and how to use it to copy and move files. You will learn how to use the Windows Explorer toolbars so that you can more easily control Windows Explorer with a few mouse clicks. The chapter also explains how to sort file lists and how to use the Address Bar and History list to work with specific files.

Opening Windows Explorer

Windows Explorer is extremely flexible, and this is reflected in the number of different ways you can open the program. Each of these methods gives you a slightly different way to view your files and folders. In this section you'll learn about a few of the more common ways to open Windows Explorer.

Of course, one problem with having so many different ways to start Windows Explorer is that it's easy to become confused and choose a method that does not exactly suit your needs.

An example is what happens when you right-click the Start button and choose Explore. Windows Explorer opens and displays the contents of the C:\Windows\Start Menu folder. This might seem a little confusing if you were expecting Windows Explorer to show you your entire hard drive.

If, on the other hand, you right-click the Start button and choose Open, Windows Explorer again opens and displays the contents of the C:\Windows\Start Menu folder, but this time the display will be very different. Rather than displaying the folder tree as the Explore command does, the Open command displays just the contents of the folder without providing the folder tree and its navigational controls.

If you open Windows Explorer from the Start menu, Windows Explorer will open in the C:\ folder. If you wish to view a different folder you must make a selection from the Folders Explorer Bar that appears in the left pane of the Windows Explorer window. You can then choose the folders that you wish to view. Notice,

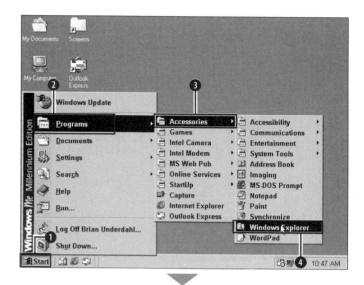

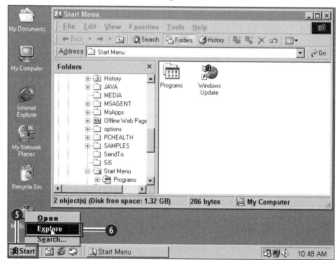

❶ Click the Start button to open the Start menu.

❷ Select Programs to open the Programs menu.

❸ Select Accessories to open the Accessories menu.

❹ Select Windows Explorer to open the program.

❺ Alternatively, right-click the Start button.

❻ Select Explore to explore your Start Menu folder.

CROSS-REFERENCE

See Chapter 1 for more information about using the Quick Launch toolbar.

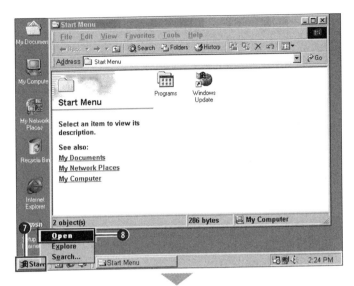

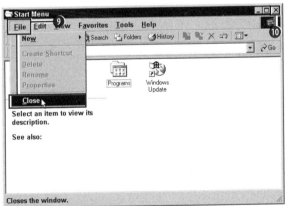

too, that the Windows Explorer Folders Explorer Bar has icons to take you directly to your desktop folder, your My Documents folder, the Control Panel, the My Network Places folder, and to the Recycle Bin.

TAKE NOTE

▶ CREATE A SHORTCUT TO FOLDERS

If you often explore a particular folder on your PC, you may want to use a Windows Explorer trick to make this task easier. While Windows Explorer is open, use the right mouse button to drag the folder onto your desktop. Choose Create shortcut here. Windows Explorer will place an icon for the folder on your desktop. Double-clicking the new icon will open the folder.

▶ CREATE A SHORTCUT TO WINDOWS EXPLORER

You may also wish to create a shortcut to Windows Explorer on your Quick Launch toolbar. This will enable you to quickly open Windows Explorer whenever the Windows Me Taskbar is visible. To add Windows Explorer to your Quick Launch toolbar, open the Windows folder in Windows Explorer and use the right mouse button to drag the Explorer application to the Quick Launch toolbar. Choose Create Shortcut(s) Here from the context menu. If necessary, drag the border of the Quick Launch toolbar so that all of the icons are visible.

⑦ *Alternatively, right-click the Start button.*

⑧ *Select Open to open the Start Menu folder.*

⑨ *With Windows Explorer open, Select File ⇨ Close to close the window.*

⑩ *Alternatively, click the Close button to close the Windows Explorer window.*

FIND IT ONLINE

Find a free add-on with info about drives and files at
http://fdl.msn.com/ pubshows/computingcentral/ windows95/ pplus165.exe.

Opening Items

In addition to simply using Windows Explorer to view the items on your disk drives, you can open programs, folders, and documents from within Windows Explorer. This enables you to open items that are located anywhere on your system — not just those that are found on your desktop.

The default Windows Explorer view includes two panes. The Folders Explorer Bar generally occupies the left-hand pane. The Folders Explorer Bar displays the hierarchical tree structure that is used for the folders on your disk drives. The Contents pane occupies the right-hand side of the Windows Explorer window. The Contents pane shows the files and folders that are contained within the currently selected folder. As you choose different folders in the Folders Explorer Bar, the Contents pane changes to show the items that are in the new folder.

Both the Folders Explorer Bar and the Contents pane use icons to represent the types of items that are being displayed. The same icons that appear on your desktop also appear in the Windows Explorer window — although not necessarily in the same sizes. You should be able to easily identify the items that are on your desktop in the Windows Explorer window.

The Folders Explorer Bar uses some special indicators to help you understand the status of the folders that are shown in the listing. An open folder icon shows the folder that is currently open. All of the other folders have icons that look like closed folders. Each folder's relationship to the other folders is shown by the vertical

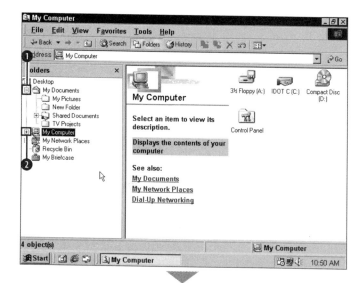

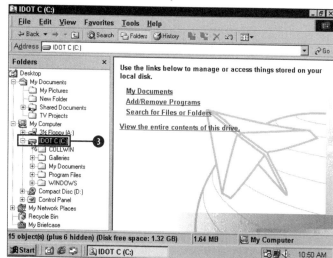

▶ If necessary, open Windows Explorer.

❶ Click a plus sign (+) to expand a folder.

❷ To collapse a folder, click a minus sign (–).

❸ Click the plus icon next to your C drive to expand the display so you can see the folder icons.

▶ The plus sign changes to a minus sign when you expand the display.

CROSS-REFERENCE

See Chapter 5 for more information about working with documents.

and horizontal dotted lines. If you follow the horizontal line to the left of a folder and then follow the vertical line up, you can see the *parent* folder — the folder that contains the folder where you started. Some folders have small boxes at the intersection of their horizontal and vertical lines. These boxes indicate that the folder contains additional folders. If the box contains a plus sign (+), you can click the box to see the additional folders. If the box contains a minus sign (−), all of the subfolders are already visible.

④ Click the icons to open the folders you wish to view.

▶ You may need to scroll to see all of the folder icons.

⑤ Double-click an application's icon to run the program.

▶ Alternatively, select an item to view its description.

⑥ Click the Close button to close Windows Explorer.

TAKE NOTE

▶ VIEW NETWORK FILES

If you click the My Network Places icon in the Folders Explorer Bar you can browse the shared resources that are available on your network. Only those items that have been shared will be visible, so if you cannot see anything on one of the computers on your network, this is a good place to start your troubleshooting. Chapter 7 shows you how to share files on a network.

▶ REFRESH THE VIEW

If necessary you can cause Windows Explorer to re-examine the drives and refresh the view by pressing the F5 key. You may have to do this to see changes on network drives.

FIND IT ONLINE

To control access to programs using a password, see http://www.winsite.com/info/pc/win95/desktop/acontrol.zip.

Copying and Moving Files

Y ou might want to copy or move files for many different reasons. Whatever your reason, Windows Explorer makes both very easy to do. In fact, there are even a couple of different methods that you can use depending upon which best suits your needs at the moment.

In Windows Me the Windows Explorer toolbar includes two buttons that you can use to copy or move files. The Move To button relocates the selected files to a different folder. The Copy To button adds a copy of the selected files to the new folder. If you are used to Windows 98, you may be surprised by the lack of a Paste button. In Windows Me this button is unnecessary because both the Move To and Copy To buttons handle the entire process — including specifying the destination for the selected files.

You can also use the drag-and-drop method to copy or move files. Using this method you first select the items that you wish to move, then you hold down the left mouse button, drag the selected items to the destination folder, and release the mouse button to move the selected items. To copy rather than move the selected items you can hold down the Ctrl key as you drag.

Finally, you can use the right mouse button to drag and drop the selection. When you use the right-button drag-and-drop method, Windows Explorer displays a context menu so that you can choose whether to copy or to move the items.

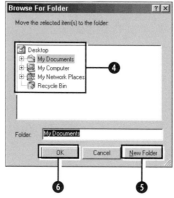

❶ Select the items that you wish to move or copy.

❷ Click the Move To button to move the items.

❸ Alternatively, select the Copy To button to make a copy of the items.

❹ Select the destination folder.

❺ Optionally, click the New Folder button to create a new destination folder.

❻ Click OK to place the item in the new folder.

CROSS-REFERENCE

See Chapter 5 for more information about dragging and dropping data within documents.

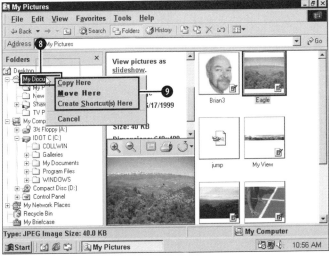

⓻ *Select an item to drag and drop.*

⓼ *Hold down the right mouse button and drag the item to the new folder.*

⓽ *Choose the option that you prefer from the context menu.*

TAKE NOTE

▶ NAMES MUST BE UNIQUE

No two files or folders can have exactly the same name. This is less of a problem than it might seem because the entire *pathname* — the name of the disk drive and the folders leading to the file's location — is a part of each file's name. You could, for example, have a file named Norway.GIF in a folder named C:\Photos1 and another file named Norway.GIF in a different folder named C:\Photos2. But you could not have two different files named Norway.GIF in the same folder. If you were to try it, Windows Explorer deals with this problem by asking if you wish to replace the existing file if you are moving a file or by adding "Copy of" to the beginning of the file name if you are copying a file.

▶ DRAGGING AND DROPPING BETWEEN DRIVES

Drag and drop works differently if you're dragging and dropping to a different disk drive. If you drag a file or folder to a different disk drive, the file or folder is copied if you use the mouse alone, and moved if you hold down the Shift key while you drag and drop. You may find that using the right mouse button is less confusing because that works the same regardless of the destination folder's location.

FIND IT ONLINE

To download FileWrangler, an alternate file management system, see **http://www.winsite.com/info/pc/win95/dskutil/fw32_32.zip**.

Controlling the View Detail Level

One of the biggest lies of the modern world is the phrase "one size fits all." As anyone who is taller, shorter, thinner, or heavier than average can tell you, people really do need different sized clothing. In many ways, computer programmers have taken a "one size fits all" approach to designing programs — if you wanted any variation from the way the programmer decided was the one best way to do things, you were out of luck.

Windows Explorer doesn't work like that. When it comes to viewing your files in Windows Explorer, you have a number of different options that you can choose to get just the view that you want. If you can't set up Windows Explorer to show the view that you want, you probably aren't trying hard enough!

In Windows Me, Windows Explorer has five different types of views you can select. The large-icon view displays folder contents using the same large icons you normally see on your desktop. In this view the icons are displayed in rows beginning in the upper-left corner of the screen. All the folders are shown first, followed by any files. The small-icon view is similar to the large-icon view except for the size of the icons. You can see many more files onscreen in the small-icon view than in the large-icon view. The list view uses the same small icons as the small-icon view but sorts the icons in columns rather than in rows. In details view you can see the icon, the file or folder name, the file size, the object type, the

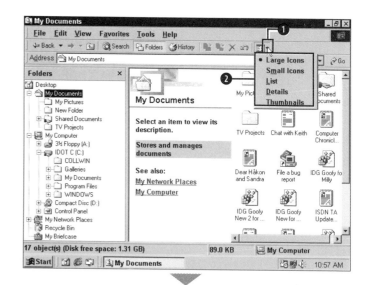

① Click the down arrow at the right of the Views button.

② Select the type of view from the drop-down list.

▶ The currently selected view is indicated by a dot.

③ Select Tools ⇨ Folder Options to display the Folder Options dialog box.

CROSS-REFERENCE

See Chapter 6 for more information about finding files.

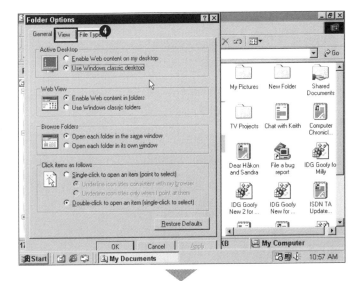

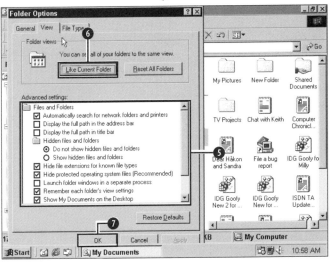

date the file was last modified, and, optionally, the file's attributes. The final view, thumbnails view, is covered in detail in the next task.

To provide you with even more control, Windows Explorer has a number of optional settings that you can set on the View tab of the Folder Options dialog box.

TAKE NOTE

▶ LEAVE SOME FILES HIDDEN

It is a good idea to make certain that the *Hide protected operating system files* checkbox on the View tab of the Folder Options dialog box is selected. Because these files are vital to making certain that your PC runs properly, keeping them hidden offers some protection against accidentally moving or deleting these important files.

▶ SHOW THE FULL PATH

Selecting either the *Display the full path in the address bar* or the *Display the full path in title bar* checkbox causes Windows Explorer to fully identify selected files. This can help you avoid mistakes in copying or moving files by reducing the possibility that you will accidentally select files in the wrong folder. Only one of these options needs to be selected because they serve essentially the same purpose.

---

④ Click the View tab.

⑤ Select the view options that you prefer.

⑥ Optionally, click the Like Current Folder button to apply the current settings to all folders.

⑦ Click OK to complete the task.

FIND IT ONLINE

See **http://tucows.servint.com/files4/aipicx.zip** to download a program that can handle more graphics file types than Windows Explorer.

Viewing Thumbnails

Windows Explorer uses different icons to represent the various applications used to create files. This feature helps you to identify different types of files by simply looking at the icon. From the icon you can tell which document files are Word documents and which ones are Excel spreadsheets, for example. But simply identifying the file type isn't very useful when you are trying to locate specific files based on their content.

To help you identify files based on their content, Windows Explorer attempts to display a preview of each file as it is selected. This preview, which appears between the Folders Explorer Bar and the file listing, can give you a pretty good idea of each file's content. Unfortunately, locating a specific file by previewing every file in a folder can be pretty time consuming — especially if the folder contains a large number of files. Before you can see what is in each file you must first select the file and wait while Windows Explorer generates the preview. You may find yourself going back and forth as you need to compare the different files.

In Windows Me, Windows Explorer offers a far easier method of locating specific files based on their content. If you choose the thumbnail view, Windows Explorer will automatically show a preview of every file in the folder so you don't have to select individual files to preview one at a time.

If a folder contains several different types of files, you may find that it is useful to sort the file listing as discussed in the next task, "Sorting the File Listing." For example,

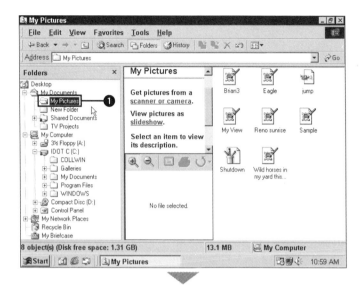

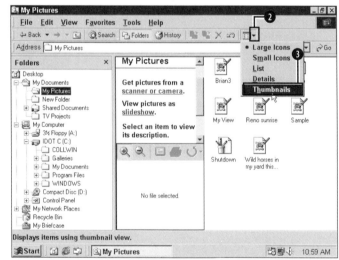

① Select the folder containing the document files you wish to view in thumbnails.

▶ Some folders use the thumbnail view by default.

② Click the down arrow at the right of the Views button.

③ Select Thumbnails from the drop-down list.

CROSS-REFERENCE

See Chapter 6 for more information about file types.

sorting the files by type will sort the files based on their *file extension* — the part of the file name that Windows Explorer uses to determine which program created a file. Remember, though, that there are many different file extensions that are used to identify certain types of files such as graphic image files. Sorting by type may result in several different groups of similar files.

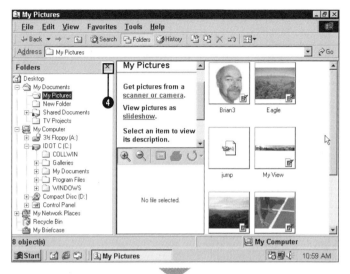

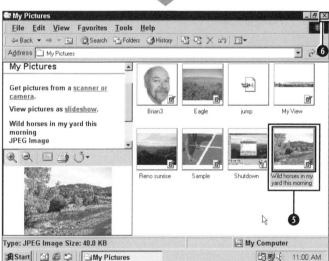

TAKE NOTE

▶ NOT ALL FILE TYPES HAVE THUMBNAILS

Although Windows Explorer attempts to generate a preview for most types of files, not all files can generate a thumbnail preview. Generally speaking, thumbnails can be generated for most *document* files — image files, word processor documents, spreadsheets, and so on. If Windows Explorer cannot generate a thumbnail for a file, the correct file type icon will be shown in place of the thumbnail.

▶ HIDE THE EXPLORER BAR

Thumbnails require far more space in the Windows Explorer window than do icons. If you want to make the best use of the thumbnail view, you may want to hide the Folders Explorer Bar so there is more room for your thumbnails. You can still navigate to different folders by using the toolbar buttons or by entering the destination folder path in the Address bar.

④ *Optionally, click the Close button to close the Folders Explorer Bar.*

▶ *You can choose View ⇨ Explorer Bar ⇨ Folders to redisplay the Folders Explorer Bar.*

⑤ *Double-click an item to open it.*

⑥ *Click the Close button to complete the task.*

FIND IT ONLINE

To download a free utility that lets you easily change default Windows icons, see **http://fdl.msn.com/ pubshows/computingcentral/pcutilities/acticn21.zip**.

37

Sorting the File Listing

If you have ever gone looking for a book in a library or a bookstore, you probably noticed that the books were arranged in a specific order. Organization is absolutely vital if you want to locate specific books — especially if the collection contains more than just a few titles. Arranging items in a specific order is also known as *sorting* the items.

Your computer probably contains thousands of files on its hard disks. Trying to find a specific file among all those files would be no easier than finding that gem in a bookstore full of unorganized piles of books. Of course there are several tools at your disposal to make the task somewhat easier. You already know that Windows Me creates a My Documents folder so that your document files aren't mixed in with hundreds of other types of files. Simply using the My Documents folder is a very good step towards making your documents easier to locate. But the My Documents folder is not a complete answer, because you may need to find other types of files than just document files, and there's no rule forcing you to use the My Documents folder anyway.

Windows Explorer can sort file listings several different ways. You can choose the method that will be most effective in helping you locate specific files. You might want to use a date sort to help you find those files that were created during a specific time period — such as the week that you were on vacation. You might choose to

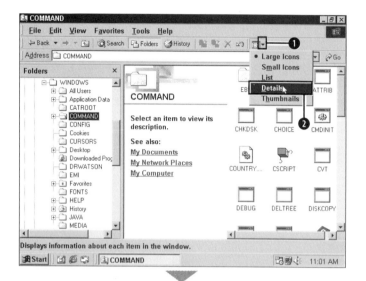

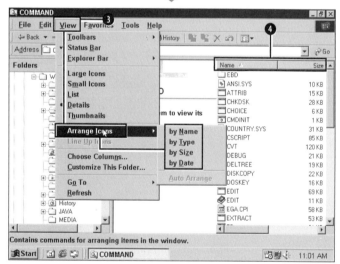

❶ Click the down arrow at the right of the Views button.

❷ Select Details as the type of view from the drop-down list

❸ Select View ➭ Arrange Icons and choose the sort order.

❹ Alternatively, click a column heading to sort the file listing in order of the values in the column.

▶ Click the column again to sort the listing in reverse order.

CROSS-REFERENCE

See Chapter 6 for more information about how to search for files.

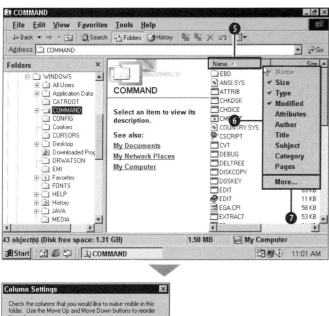

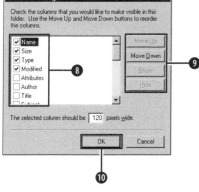

sort by file type to help you locate any text files that provide special configuration information to make certain that your programs are properly set up.

It is best to select the details view before sorting the file listing. Although you can use the View menu options to sort the files in other types of views, you will probably find that sorting by name is the only useful option in any view except for the details view.

TAKE NOTE

▶ SORT BY ADDITIONAL FILE CHARACTERISTICS

As the figures show, you can add additional columns to those that are displayed in the default details view. For example, if you include the attributes column, you can click the Attributes column header and sort the listing by file attributes. You might find this alternative useful, especially if you want to locate all the files with the "A" attribute, which shows which files have not been backed up.

▶ FOLDERS APPEAR SEPARATELY

No matter which sort order you choose, Windows Explorer always separates the files and folders into two groups. The folders may appear first or last — depending on the sort order you selected — but they are never mixed in with the files.

⑤ *Right-click the column headings to display the context menu.*

⑥ *Choose the columns to show in the view.*

⑦ *Alternatively, choose More to select additional columns.*

⑧ *Select additional columns here.*

⑨ *Choose the display order options for the selected columns.*

⑩ *Click OK to complete the task.*

FIND IT ONLINE

See **http://fdl.msn.com/pubshows/computingcentral/ pcutilities/File/folsi10.zip** to download a utility that displays the tree size and folder size of each folder.

Viewing Folders as Web Pages

Windows Explorer displays certain folders a bit differently than other folders. For example, if you click on the \Windows folder in the Folders Explorer bar, you will see a message telling you that the folder contains files that are needed to keep your system working properly, and that there is no need to modify the folder's contents. Windows Explorer can display folders differently by displaying them as if they were Web pages, thus enabling folders to have unique appearances and to display customized messages.

You can customize the appearance of many of your folders to control how they look in Windows Explorer. By far the easiest appearance change you can make to your folders is to display a background image. When you add a background image to a folder, Windows Explorer places the image behind the file icons.

You aren't limited to simply adding a background image. You can also add any of the items you might see on a Web page — such as colored text or links that you can click to jump to another location. If you want to get fancy you can use sound or video files, too, but those types of elements will require some heavy-duty programming that is well beyond what can be covered in this book. That doesn't mean your folders can't be pretty impressive, though. As the figures show, the Customize This Folder Wizard includes several templates you can use without doing any programming.

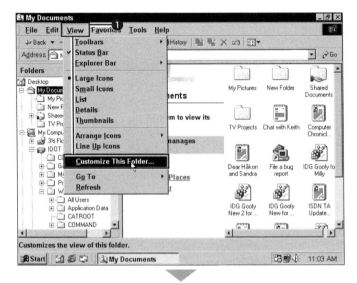

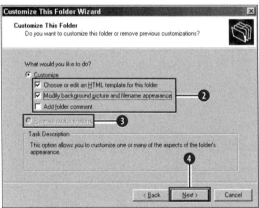

❶ Select View ➪ Customize This Folder to open the Customize This Folder Wizard.

▶ Click Next on the first Customize This Folder Wizard page to continue.

❷ Choose the ways you wish to customize the folder.

❸ Alternatively, choose Remove Customizations to return the folder to the default appearance.

❹ Click Next to continue.

CROSS-REFERENCE

See Chapter 12 for more information about changing the appearance of folders.

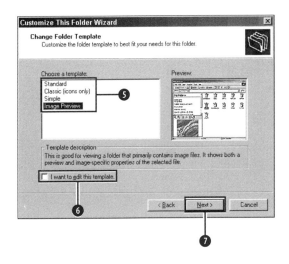

▶ USE THE TEMPLATES

The Customize This Folder Wizard includes several different templates you can choose to modify the appearance of your folders. You may be surprised when you see how sophisticated some of those templates are. For example, the image preview template includes tools that enable you to zoom in or out so that you can view graphic image files more easily.

▶ MODIFYING THE TEMPLATES

Web pages are HTML (Hypertext Markup Language) documents. If you choose to add a template to a folder, you can modify the HTML code in the template if necessary. To do so you must first attach a template to the folder using the Customize This Folder Wizard. Once a template has been attached to a folder the *I want to edit this template* option becomes available and you can then edit the HTML code. You will find that the sample templates include a number of comments that may enable you to make simple changes without the necessity of learning a lot about HTML programming. If you make a mistake you can always rerun the Customize This Folder Wizard and remove the folder customizations.

⑤ Optionally, choose a template.

⑥ To edit the template's HTML code, select the I want to edit this template check box.

⑦ Click Next to continue.

⑧ If desired, choose a background image.

⑨ Click Next to continue.

▶ Complete your modifications and click the Finish button to complete the task.

FIND IT ONLINE

See **http://www.camalott.com/html/htmltutor/** to learn a bit more about HTML.

Controlling the Toolbars

Toolbars make using your PC far easier. With a single click of your mouse you can complete tasks that would take many individual steps to accomplish using menu commands. Instead of wading through the menus trying to find what you need, you simply point, click, and you're done. Windows Explorer has several different toolbars that can help you use the program.

The Standard toolbar includes navigation tools that will be very familiar to anyone who has spent any time browsing the Internet. You'll find a Back and a Forward button as well as an Up button to move you around through your folders. This toolbar also includes three buttons that quickly switch among the Search, Folders, and History Explorer Bars. Further to the right you'll find File and View management buttons.

The Address toolbar serves two primary purposes. The first is informational — the toolbar shows the currently active folder. The second purpose is navigational. You can either enter a folder address or click the down arrow and choose a destination folder from the list box.

The Links toolbar contains a number of interesting Web page links. The Links toolbar includes a Customize Links button you can use to design your own set of links.

The Radio toolbar is the newest of the toolbars. If you have a fast Internet connection, you can use the Radio toolbar to listen to radio stations all around the world while you work. You can get the latest news, many different styles of music, and even talk radio. Of course, you can only listen to Internet radio stations while you are actually connected to the Internet, so this may not be

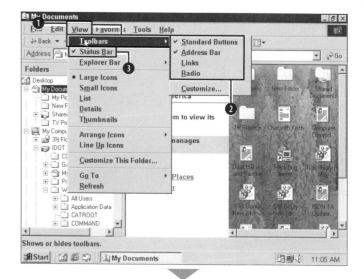

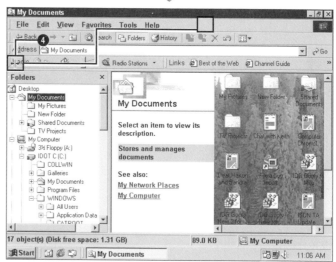

❶ Select View ⇨ Toolbars to display the toolbar selections.

❷ Click any of the toolbar options to change the display.

❸ Optionally, deselect Status Bar to hide the Status bar.

❹ Optionally, drag a toolbar to a new location.

CROSS-REFERENCE

See Chapter 12 for more information about adding toolbars to the Windows Me Taskbar.

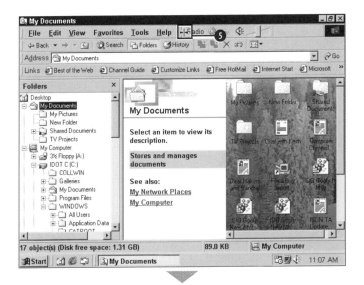

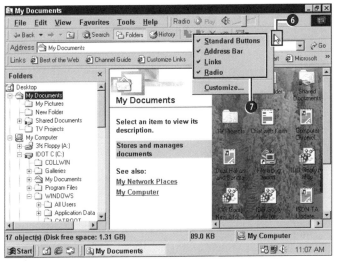

a practical option if your modem shares your voice line because you won't be able to make or receive calls while you are listening.

The Windows Explorer toolbars may be quite useful, but they can also eat up quite a bit of space. Fortunately you can easily control the toolbar layout and even choose which toolbars are displayed on your screen.

Although the Status bar — which appears at the bottom of the Windows Explorer window — is not really one of the toolbars, it is another Windows Explorer element that you can choose to display or hide. If you need the absolute maximum of usable space in the Windows Explorer window, you may want to consider hiding the status bar.

TAKE NOTE

MOVE YOUR TOOLBARS

The toolbars can eat up a lot of space. You can regain some of that space by stacking the toolbars. You can drag the toolbars onto the same row as another toolbar, and you can resize them to make them more useful.

SHRINK THE TOOLBARS

Before you decide to remove toolbars that you find useful, consider removing the text labels as discussed in "Customizing the Toolbars" next in this chapter.

⑤ Drag the border of a toolbar to resize the toolbar.

⑥ Right-click one of the toolbars.

⑦ Select the toolbars you want to appear.

FIND IT ONLINE

See **http://www.microsoft.com/windows98/using windows/internet/tips/advanced/CustomizeLinksBar .asp** to customize the Links toolbar.

Customizing the Toolbars

Adding additional toolbars is not the only way to get added Windows Explorer toolbar functionality. You can also customize the Standard toolbar to add or remove buttons as you see fit. Although you can't really duplicate the full set of Windows Explorer toolbars by customizing the Standard toolbar, you can make a number of changes you may find useful.

As one example of a change you might make, suppose that you use several different PCs, and some of them are still running Windows 98. The standard toolbar in Windows 98 shows the Cut, Copy, and Paste buttons, while in Windows Me it shows the Move To and Copy To buttons. Moving back and forth between the two could be a little confusing. But because you cannot customize the Windows 98 toolbar, you'll have to customize the Windows Me toolbar if you want both toolbars to work the same.

As you customize the toolbar, keep in mind the only modifications you can make to the first two sections on the left side of the toolbar are to choose the size of the icons and how any text labels are displayed. Even with small icons and no text labels these portions of the toolbar take about as much room as eight buttons. You'll want to make certain you add only those buttons that are truly useful — especially if you intend to make another toolbar share the same row. Also remember that you can use the Move Up and Move Down buttons in the Customize Toolbar dialog box to rearrange the button order.

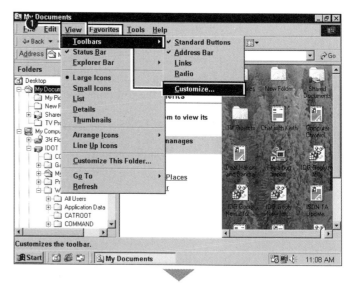

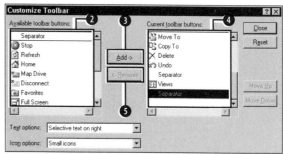

① Select View ➪ Toolbars ➪ Customize to display the Customize Toolbar dialog box.

▶ You can also right-click a toolbar and choose Customize.

② Choose the buttons you wish to add.

③ Click the Add button to add the selected buttons to the toolbar.

④ Optionally, choose buttons that you don't need.

⑤ Click the Remove button to remove the selected buttons.

CROSS-REFERENCE

See Chapter 7 for more information about network drives.

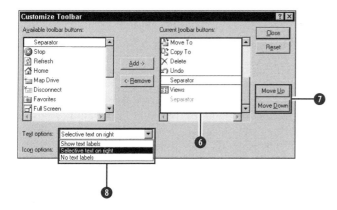

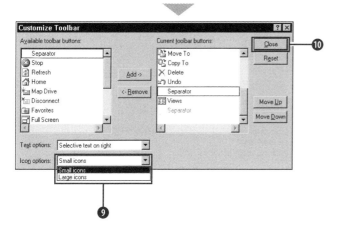

SHRINK YOUR STANDARD TOOLBAR

The text labels increase the amount of space that is needed for the toolbar. Once you have learned the purpose of the various toolbar buttons you can choose to remove the text labels so that the toolbar requires a bit less space. Because Windows Me will pop up a description of a button if you hold the mouse pointer over a button for a short while, you will still get the reminders you need if you aren't certain which button to select. After you remove the text labels you may even find that another tool-bar can share the same row as the standard toolbar.

USING THE NETWORK DRIVE BUTTONS

If you add the Map Drive button to the toolbar, you can connect to a shared folder on the network us-ing a drive letter. Most programs are perfectly happy using a folder anywhere on the network, but you may find that it is just a bit easier to refer to a deeply buried folder by using a single drive letter rather than a long pathname. You may also want to add the Disconnect button to remove the drive let-ter substitution when you no longer need the connection.

⑥ *Optionally, choose buttons you wish to move.*

⑦ *Use these buttons to move the toolbar buttons.*

⑧ *Choose the label text option you prefer.*

⑨ *Choose the icon size option you prefer.*

⑩ *Click the Close button to apply your changes and complete the task.*

FIND IT ONLINE

For even more control over your screen, see
ftp://ftp.cmp.com/dist/wm/wmfiles/1998/9811nov/twekui98.exe.

Using the Address Bar

I f you have done any Web browsing you are probably quite familiar with the purpose of the Address bar that appears in Internet Explorer. If so, you will quickly understand the Address bar in Windows Explorer, because it serves essentially the same purpose as the one you see in Internet Explorer.

You can type a folder address into the Address bar or choose a folder from the drop-down list box that appears when you click the down arrow at the right side of the Address bar. If you type in an address you must then press Enter or click the Go button to make the new folder the active folder. If you choose a folder by clicking in the Folders Explorer Bar, the Address bar will change to show the new folder's address.

You can choose to show the entire path or only the current folder name in the Address bar. Showing the entire path offers one rather subtle but very useful advantage — you can right-click the address and choose Copy from the context menu to make an accurate copy of an address without the possibility of making a typing error. You can then paste this address into a document or into a dialog box as needed. You might, for example, keep a text file with the addresses of important files so you can easily access each of them as necessary in the future. You could later copy the addresses from the text file into the Address bar to quickly locate the important files. You'll find this especially useful for files that are buried under many layers of nested folders or that are located on another computer on your network.

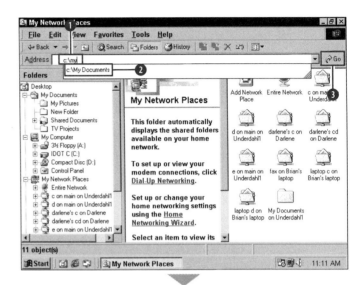

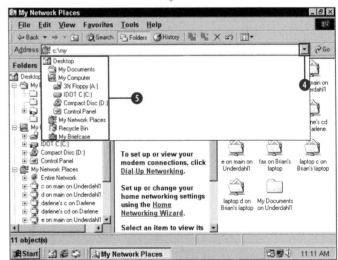

❶ Type an address in the Address bar.

❷ If the correct address appears in the drop-down box, you can select it to save typing.

❸ Click the Go button or press Enter.

❹ Alternatively, click the down arrow to display the drop-down address list box.

❺ Click the icon of the new folder that you wish to display.

CROSS-REFERENCE

See Chapter 9 for more information about Internet addresses.

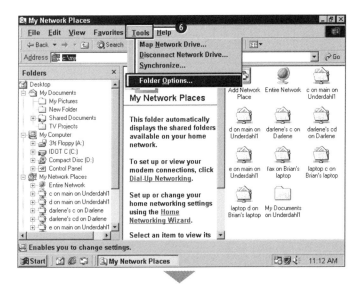

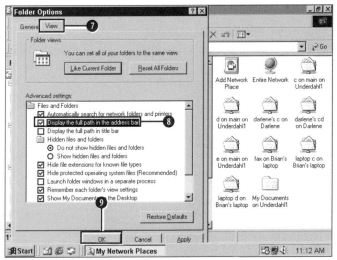

⑥ *Select Tools ⇨ Folder Options to display the Folder Options dialog box.*

⑦ *Click the View tab.*

⑧ *Select the Display the full path in the address bar check box.*

⑨ *Click the OK button to apply your changes and complete the task.*

TAKE NOTE

▶ NETWORK ADDRESSES

If you want to access computers on your network using the Address bar, it is important to understand the correct format for network addresses. Each computer in a workgroup or a domain has a unique name. In the Address bar, the computer name is preceded by two backslashes as in \\Darlene. Following the computer name is the name assigned to a shared resource, such as \Darlene's C. This is followed by the pathname, such as \My Documents. Thus the complete address for the folder would be \\Darlene\DARLENE'S C\My Documents.

▶ INTERNET ADDRESSES

You can also access folders on the Internet by entering the correct address in the Address bar. Internet addresses look quite similar to network computer addresses although there are some important differences between the two. Because the Internet is based on rules that were developed for Unix-based computers, the address separator is a forward slash (/) rather than a backslash (\) as used on Windows-based PCs. Also, Internet addresses cannot contain spaces, so an underscore is often used in place of a space.

FIND IT ONLINE

See **http://www.microsoft.com/windows98/usingwindows/work/tips/advanced/addressbar_run.asp** for more information on using the Address bar.

Using the History List

The history list is a record of the local HTML documents and Web pages you have visited recently. By clicking a link in this list you can quickly reopen the document or Web page without searching for the correct address.

Because both your local HTML documents and the Web pages you have visited are shown in the same list, finding a specific document in the history list takes a bit of understanding. If you want to revisit a local document, for example, you must first locate the My Computer icon in the history list. That icon will lead you to links for the local documents contained in the history list.

The history list is displayed using the History Explorer Bar. Unless you choose one of the optional views, documents and Web sites are listed by date. This can make it difficult to locate a specific document or Web site if you don't remember the exact date you last used the document or visited the Web site. You may want to choose one of the optional views to make it easier to find things in the history list.

The History Explorer Bar shows the history list using a series of folders. Each folder represents the main or *root* folder of the Web site. In the case of local documents, that folder is My Computer. When you click a folder to open it you will see links for each of the documents or Web sites you visited. Clicking one of those links returns you to that same location—if the Web page or document is still accessible. Remember, though,

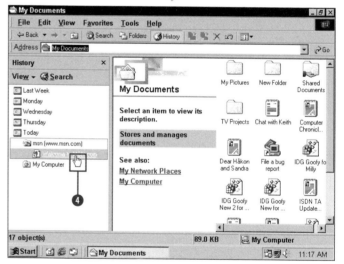

1 Click the History button to display the History Explorer Bar.

2 Click a folder icon to open the folder.

3 Click a link to open the Web page or local document.

4 Hold the mouse pointer over a link to view a description of the link.

CROSS-REFERENCE

See Chapter 7 for more information about sharing files on a network.

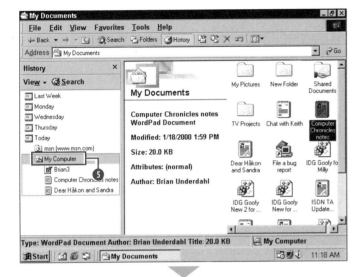

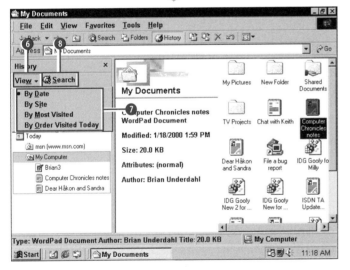

that Web pages may quickly disappear and that local documents can be deleted, renamed, or have their sharing status changed. Any of these things can prevent you from reopening the document or Web page.

TAKE NOTE

▶ CONTROL THE HISTORY LENGTH

By default, the history list maintains links to folders and Web pages for the preceding three weeks. If you would prefer to specify a different time length, you must make the change from within Internet Explorer, not Windows Explorer. You can either open the Internet Options icon in Control Panel or choose Tools ⇨ Internet Options when Internet Explorer is open to access the Internet Properties dialog box. On the General tab use the *Days to keep pages in history* spin control to set the number of days of historical links to maintain.

▶ CLEARING THE HISTORY

If you want to hide the fact that you've been using certain documents, you can clear the history list by clicking the Clear History button on the General tab of the Internet Properties dialog box. This will not, however, clear the Documents list nor the recently used file lists that are maintained in many application programs.

⑤ Open the My Computer folder to view the local HTML document history list.

⑥ Click the View button to choose a different sort order.

⑦ Choose a sort order from the drop-down list.

⑧ Alternatively, click the Search button to search for a document or Web site.

FIND IT ONLINE

See **http://www.microsoft.com/Windows/ie/Features/ history.asp** for more information on the History bar.

Personal Workbook

Q&A

1 How can you display your Start menu items when you open Windows Explorer?

_____

_____

_____

2 How can you run a program that doesn't appear on your Start menu?

_____

_____

_____

3 What will happen if you click the History button?

_____

_____

_____

4 How can you preview the contents of graphics files without opening them?

_____

_____

_____

5 How can you make Windows Explorer display file previews in place of file type icons?

_____

_____

_____

6 How can you locate all of the Web pages you visited last week?

_____

_____

_____

7 Which Windows Explorer toolbar can you use to listen to music over the Internet?

_____

_____

_____

8 Which Windows Explorer toolbar can you use to visit the "Best of the Internet" Web site?

_____

_____

_____

ANSWERS: PAGE 390

Getting to Know Windows Explorer

1. Open Windows Explorer and explore your Desktop folder.

2. Compare the differences between the Move To and Copy To buttons.

3. Use the drag-and-drop method to copy a file.

4. Sort the view of the My Documents folder so that you can find your oldest files.

5. Customize one of your folders by adding a background image.

6. Use the history list to find the Web pages that you visited yesterday.

✔ You install a program but then don't find it listed anywhere on your Start menu. You use Windows Explorer to locate and run the program.

✔ You're working on a project on your office PC and realize you need to take the file with you on a business trip. Using Windows Explorer, you make a copy of your data file on a diskette.

✔ You have a new digital camera and you've downloaded a large number of images to your PC. You use thumbnail view to preview the images to decide which ones to keep and which ones to discard.

✔ You suddenly realize that a Web site you visited last week had information you need. You use the History bar to find the site again.

Visual Quiz

How does this view differ from the standard Windows Explorer view, and how can you make Windows Explorer display image previews like this?

_____

_____

_____

_____

_____

_____

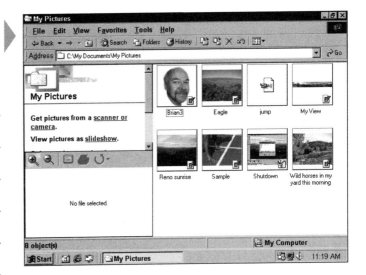

CHAPTER 3

MASTER THESE SKILLS

- ▶ Opening Windows Me Help
- ▶ Searching for Topics
- ▶ Copying and Printing Topics
- ▶ Using the Troubleshooters
- ▶ Getting More Help on the Web

Using Windows Me Help

Windows Me is a very complex operating system. No one book — no matter how comprehensive — can possibly answer every question someone may want to ask about Windows Me. Eventually there will be something you need to do in Windows Me that will require a bit of extra help. Knowing how and where to look for that extra help can save you hours of frustration.

The Windows Me help system is intended to provide the additional information that may solve a problem. Because the Windows Me help system is right there on your computer, it should be one of the first places that you turn to when you need more help.

In addition to providing answers to many of the questions that users commonly ask, the Windows Me help system includes a series of powerful troubleshooters. When you encounter problems that keep you from making full use of your system, these troubleshooters can lead you through a series of steps that may well solve the problem in just a few minutes. In this way minor problems don't grow into major ones, and your PC runs the way that it should.

In this chapter you'll learn how to find the answers that you need in the Windows Me help system. You'll see how you can search for specific topics and then copy or print out the information so that it is convenient to use. You will see that it often helps to get a little creative in trying to understand where the information that you need might be hidden within the hundreds of available help topics. You may need to play a little guessing game at times, but if you are persistent enough you'll be rewarded with most of the answers that you need.

You will also learn how to obtain the absolute latest available information by accessing Windows Me help resources on the Web. Often these resources will include answers to questions that didn't even exist when the original Windows Me help system files were created.

Once you know how to make the best use of the help system, you will find that using Windows Me will be far less frustrating. Rather than wondering how to accomplish the tasks that you need to do, you will know where to find the answers to help you become a bit more successful.

Opening Windows Me Help

When you need help, the last thing that you want is trouble finding it. That's why the Windows Me help system is so easy to open and navigate. You wouldn't want to have to use a help system that compounds your problems.

If you are used to Windows 98, you have probably found that some of the familiar things you knew in the past seem to have disappeared. In some cases this is true, but in reality most of the missing items are still there someplace. Some things have been renamed, while others have been combined into new, more powerful tools.

Some help topics are simple enough that you can understand the subject after reading it through the first time. Many other help topics, however, are much more complex. You may need to refer to these topics several times in order to obtain their full value. In some cases you may wish to print out a help topic, as discussed later in this chapter, so that you can refer to the topic as many times as necessary.

The Windows Me help system was really designed to help ordinary users — not just those who already know almost everything about computers. That is pretty clear when you first open the help system and notice that many common issues already appear as a list of links that you can click to focus on just the help you need.

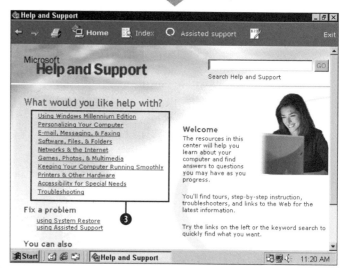

❶ Click the Start button to open the Start menu.

❷ Select Help to open the online help system.

❸ Click a link to display the topics.

CROSS-REFERENCE

See Chapter 1 for more information about using the Start Menu.

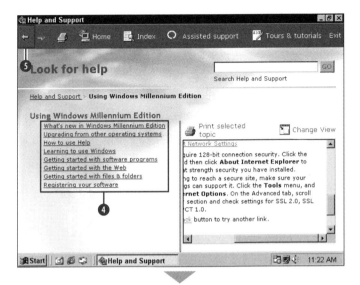

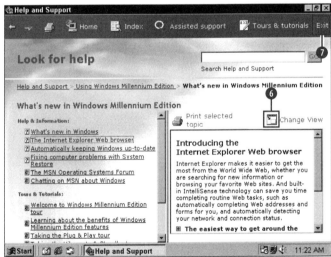

④ Continue to choose topics until you narrow down to the information you need.

▶ Notice that the selected topics are shown above the list of topics.

⑤ Optionally, click the Back button to return to the previous level.

⑥ Click here to show only the content area.

▶ Compressing the help system down to the content area may enable you to view the help topic while you work.

⑦ Click Exit to close the help system.

TAKE NOTE

▶ USE HELP TOURS AS A LEARNING TOOL

The Windows Me help system includes a number of items listed under the topic *Tours & Tutorials*. These topics are an excellent way to learn more about Windows Me at your own pace. Note, however, that many of the tours and tutorials will only work if your PC can access the Internet. If Internet access is necessary but unavailable when you try to use one of the tour or tutorial topics, the help system will display a message telling you that the page cannot be accessed. To correct this, make certain your computer is connected to the Internet and then click the Refresh link on the message page.

▶ DRILL DOWN TO FIND HELP

Many of the links in the Windows Me help system lead to additional links. That is, when you click a link such as *Networks & the Internet*, you will see a more focused set of links dealing with topics that only relate to networking or the Internet. In most cases you will need to click additional links as you *drill down* to find your specific topic. In some cases you may discover that you have taken a path that clearly is not going to answer your question. If so, click the Back button on the Help system toolbar to step back one level and try a different topic.

FIND IT ONLINE

For Microsoft's frequently asked questions online, see **http://support.microsoft.com/directory/faqs.asp?**.

Searching for Topics

Have you ever tried to find a relatively obscure type of product by looking in the yellow pages of your local telephone directory? If you have, you know that different people may use different names for the same thing. For example, suppose your sister asked you to take care of her horse while she went on a trip around the world. Two days after she left, the horse started limping and you discovered it had lost one of its horseshoes. Would you know to look under Farriers to find someone who could fix the problem?

This same difficulty can occur in any online help system. Sure, the help system includes a whole list of help topics in the contents list, but will you always know where to begin looking? Would you think of looking under the *Personalizing Your Computer* category to learn how to adjust your PC's time setting? No matter how careful the developer is in setting up the help system categories and list of topics, there will still be occasions when you know that the topic is there someplace, but you just can't figure out where.

The Windows Me help system includes both an index and a search box that you can use to locate topics. At first glance it may seem as though the two items perform similar functions, but this is really not the case at all. The index displays topics that have been *indexed*—linked to specific subjects by someone who felt they were relevant to the subject. The search box displays any topic where

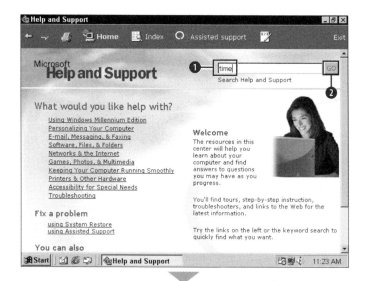

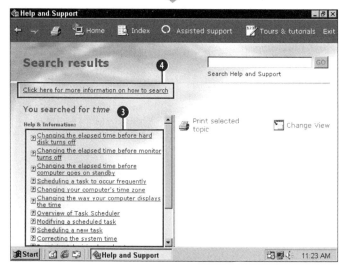

❶ Type the word or phrase you wish to find.

❷ Click Go.

❸ Choose the appropriate topic.

❹ Optionally, click here for help on searching.

CROSS-REFERENCE

See "Copying and Printing Topics" later in this chapter for information about printing out topics.

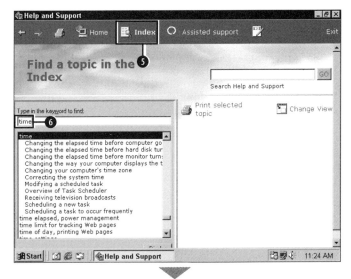

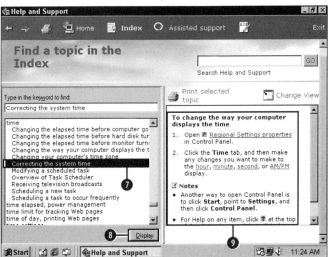

the *keyword* that you type appears. Both items are useful in finding topics. You may want to see the Take Note section to learn more about the effectiveness of each.

Even when you are searching for help topics, it pays to have an open mind. If your search doesn't produce the results that you are seeking, try the creative approach. See if you can think of a different name for the topic, and also look for the *Related Topics* link at the bottom of many help topics.

5 *Click Index on the toolbar.*

6 *Type the keyword.*

7 *Select the topic.*

8 *Click Display to view the topic in the content area.*

9 *Read the help topic here.*

FIND IT ONLINE

For frequently asked questions about Windows Me, see
http://support.microsoft.com/ directory/faqs.asp.

Copying and Printing Topics

Onscreen help is great, but there are times when nothing beats a printed copy. For example, you probably wouldn't remember all of the steps to setting up and configuring a new network connection, so if you were using the Windows Me onscreen help system, you would probably find yourself switching back and forth a whole bunch of times trying to get it all correct. Rather than doing that, why not simply print out a copy of the instructions so that you can go right through the process without stopping?

If you are creating a document that contains user instructions for performing various Windows Me tasks, there's no reason to type out everything by hand. You can copy help topics into your documents as discussed in the Take Note section. Remember, though, that the material in the Windows Me help system is copyrighted, and you must be careful to respect that copyright if you wish to avoid legal problems. You aren't likely to have problems if you copy something for personal use, but you will need permission to use the copied material commercially.

When you copy help topics and then paste them into a document, the topics will be pasted as HTML rather than as plain text. You can use the Edit ⇨ Paste Special command if you wish to paste the topic as plain text. Or you can paste the topic into a Notepad document because all Notepad documents are plain text.

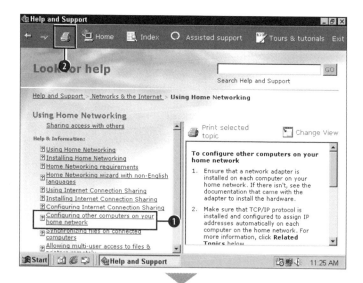

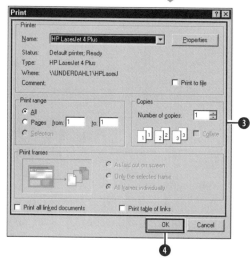

❶ Select the topic to print.

❷ Click the Print button.

❸ Choose the printing options you prefer.

❹ Click OK.

CROSS-REFERENCE

See Chapter 5 for more information about printing documents.

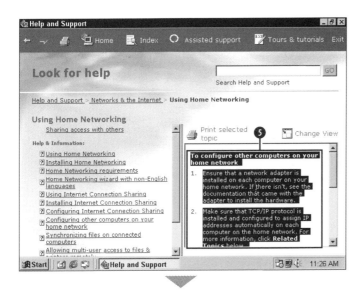

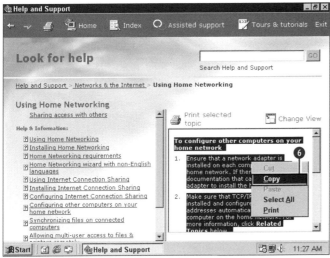

5 Drag your mouse across a topic.

▶ Alternatively, select a topic and press Ctrl+A to select the entire topic.

6 Right-click the selection and choose Copy.

▶ Paste the material into a document before copying anything else to the Clipboard.

TAKE NOTE

▶ USE THE CONTEXT MENU

The Windows Me help system doesn't exactly make it easy for you to copy information for your own use. You won't find an Edit ⇨ Copy command or even a Copy button in the help window. The key is to use the right-click context menu and choose the Copy command from that menu to copy any selected material to the Windows Me Clipboard. You can use your mouse to first select part of a topic or you can press Ctrl+A to select the entire topic before you select the Copy command. Once you have copied a help topic to the Clipboard you can paste the material into a document using the Edit ⇨ Paste command or the Paste button in the application that you use to create the document.

▶ PRINTING THE CORRECT TOPIC

Many help topics lead to a series of related topics. When you drill down through the topics, clicking the Print button will print whichever topic is currently being displayed in the content area. If you have selected a new help topic from the index but have not yet clicked the Display button, you will print the old topic when you click the Print button. Make certain you have displayed the correct topic before clicking Print.

FIND IT ONLINE

For information on solving Windows problems, see
http://www.fixwindows.com/.

Using the Troubleshooters

There aren't too many things that are as frustrating as a computer that doesn't work correctly. Unfortunately, problems can occur on almost any system. That's one reason why companies often employ large computer staffs — so there will be someone whose job is to troubleshoot and correct problems.

The Windows Me help system also has a number of troubleshooters that are designed to help you discover the cause of certain types of problems and to resolve those problems. While these troubleshooters cannot solve every problem you might encounter, they are quite capable at fixing the most common problems.

The troubleshooters simply cannot resolve some types of problems. For example, if you attempt to run application programs that were not designed to run on Windows Me–based PCs, those programs may not be able to run correctly no matter what you do. This is especially true for older programs such as those designed for 16-bit versions of Windows. Many older games and other programs that attempt to directly access the hardware or that rely on older versions of important system files fall into this category.

One of the design goals for Windows Me was to greatly reduce the number of situations that would require you to restart your computer. Still, there are problems that cannot be resolved without restarting your system. To avoid unnecessary delays or even the potential for data loss, be sure to close all open applications before you begin working with the troubleshooters.

If the troubleshooters cannot solve your problems, you may want to refer to "Using System Restore" in Chapter 14. System Restore is a drastic step, but can often resolve the most stubborn problems.

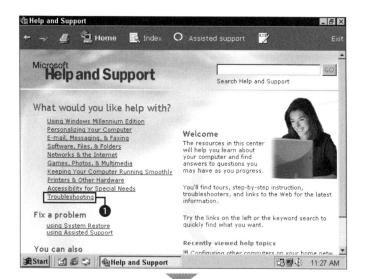

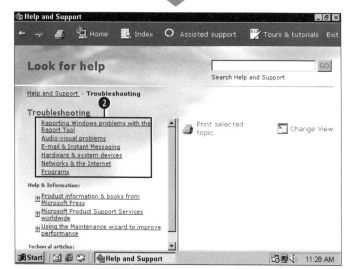

① Click the Troubleshooting link.

② Select the link that describes your problem.

CROSS-REFERENCE

See Chapter 12 for information about adding new hardware.

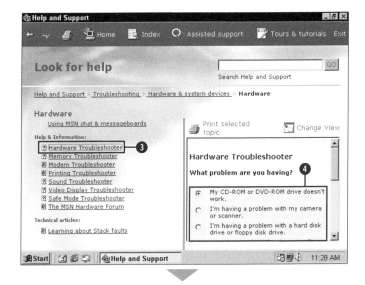

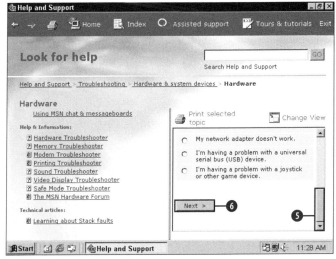

3 *Continue drilling down until the troubleshooter appears in the content area.*

4 *Select the type of problem you are having.*

5 *If necessary, scroll down to the bottom of the list.*

6 *Click the Next button to begin the troubleshooting process.*

▶ *Follow the steps to work through the problem.*

TAKE NOTE

▶ ### INTERACTIVE VERSUS PASSIVE TROUBLESHOOTERS

Some of the Windows Me troubleshooters are interactive — they lead you though the process step-by-step. These troubleshooters are generally easiest to use if your screen is set to a high enough resolution to see the troubleshooter at the same time as any dialog boxes or other windows that might be displayed during the troubleshooting process. The passive troubleshooters generally consist of a set of specific steps that you will need to follow to resolve a problem on your own. You will probably find that printing out the steps will make it easier to follow along with the passive troubleshooters.

▶ ### FIND THE RIGHT TROUBLESHOOTER

As the figures show, you may have to look in several topics to find the correct Windows Me troubleshooter. If you are having a problem and don't immediately see a troubleshooter that relates to the problem, be sure to look in the other topics of the Troubleshooting category. You may find that the help you need is buried within one of the related topics.

FIND IT ONLINE

For some online troubleshooting help, see
http://www.computing.net/.

Getting More Help on the Web

The Internet has changed modern life in many important ways. For the Windows Me PC user, one of the changes comes in the form of up-to-date help that is available 24 hours a day, every day of the year. If you happen to be a person who works at odd hours, you no longer have to wait until "normal business hours" to get assistance with your computer-related problems.

You can find many different types of help resources on the Internet. Some of the ones you may find useful include *FAQs*, the *knowledgebase*, and *forums*. FAQs are lists of frequently asked questions. The knowledgebase is a vast resource that covers thousands of different problems with suggested solutions or workarounds. Forums are places where people can ask questions online. Other users answer some forum questions, while an official tech support person may answer others.

When you access the Windows Me Support Web site, you may see an almost overwhelming series of options. In most cases the option that will be of the greatest benefit is the search option. When you choose this option, you will be able to enter a phrase that defines the problem and then look for related topics. When you enter multiple word search phrases, remember to enclose the phrase in quotation marks so that the search engine looks for the complete phrase rather than just the individual words.

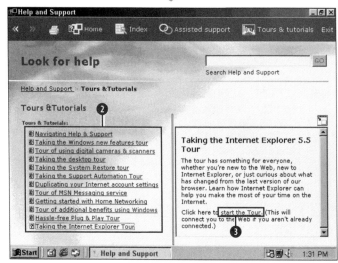

① *Click the Tours & Tutorials link.*

② *Choose a tour.*

③ *Click the start the Tour link.*

CROSS-REFERENCE

See Chapter 9 for information about finding things on the Internet.

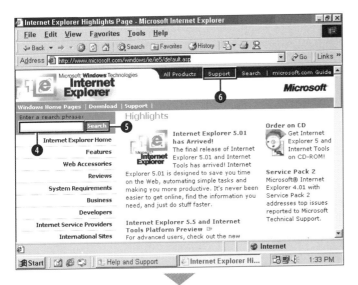

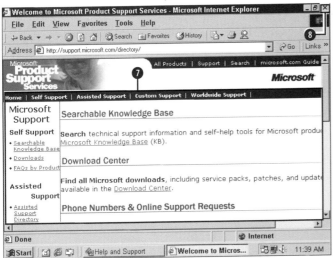

④ *Enter a search phrase to find a related help topic.*

⑤ *Click the Search button.*

⑥ *Alternatively, click the Support link.*

⑦ *Choose a support option.*

⑧ *Click the Close button to close Internet Explorer — you may need to confirm that you wish to disconnect.*

TAKE NOTE

▶ THE WEB CONSTANTLY CHANGES

You will likely notice quite a few differences in the appearance of the Windows Me support pages whenever you visit those pages. In fact, you will probably notice changes in those pages almost daily if you visit the Web site often. Don't let those changes throw you — they are a big part of what makes Web-based help so useful. Because Web pages can be updated so quickly and frequently, they are an ideal place to provide all of the latest information in a location that anyone can easily access.

▶ YOU NEED INTERNET ACCESS

Although it may seem obvious, you can only use the Web-based Windows Me help resources if you already have Internet access. As a result, you won't find this option very useful for resolving problems with your Internet connection. For these types of problems you will probably have to open the *Networks & the Internet* category on the Windows Me help system home page.

▶ VISIT IDG BOOKS

One of the best sources of Windows Me help on the Web isn't provided by Microsoft. On the IDG Books Worldwide site at **http://www.idgbooks.com** you'll find all sorts of useful resources that can make Windows Me easier to use. You can even subscribe to free newsletters and find daily tips in addition to looking for the latest titles by your favorite IDG authors.

FIND IT ONLINE

Register at **http://technet.microsoft.com/reg/ support/default.htm** for some special help resources you won't find elsewhere.

Personal Workbook

Q&A

1 How can you print a help topic?

_____

_____

_____

2 How can you copy a help topic?

_____

_____

_____

3 What is the Back button used for?

_____

_____

_____

_____

4 How can you find a topic the quickest way when you know the correct keyword?

_____

_____

_____

5 How can you find a topic if your keyword is not indexed?

_____

_____

_____

6 How can you toggle the display of the left side of the help window?

_____

_____

_____

7 Which help system component is intended to step you through solutions to problems?

_____

_____

_____

8 How can you get more help if you can't find the answer in the Windows Me Help system?

_____

_____

_____

ANSWERS: PAGE 390

EXTRA PRACTICE

1. Open Help and find out where the Active Desktop settings are in Windows Me.

2. Locate the help topic on setting the system clock.

3. Find the fourth topic under Sound in the index.

4. Copy that topic to a document.

5. Print the *Specifying sounds for Infrared Monitor events* topic.

6. Find the *Games & Multimedia* troubleshooter.

REAL-WORLD APPLICATIONS

✔ You install a modem but then can't use it. You use the troubleshooters to diagnose the problem.

✔ You're working on a document and realize that you need to add a recorded message to it. Using Windows Help, you learn how to use Sound Recorder.

✔ Your computer sometimes displays a "memory parity" error message. You use the Memory Troubleshooter to find out what the problem is.

✔ You want to buy a new scanner but aren't sure how to make it work with Windows Me. You use the help system to help to make the scanner work.

Visual Quiz

How would you display the topic shown in the figure? How would you print the topic?

_____

_____

_____

_____

_____

_____

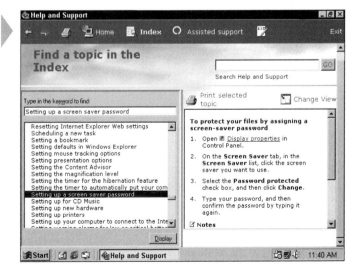

Contents of 'Desktop'

Name

My Computer
Network Neigh
Internet Explore
Microsoft Outloo
Recycle Bin
My Briefcase
3252-9
3259-6
3261-8
3262-6
3281-2
3286-3
DE Phone List
Device Manager
In
Iomega Tools

PART

II

Using Windows Me

Now that you have had an introduction to the basics of Windows Me, it's time to learn some of the ways to get even more out of your PC. In this part you learn how to use your favorite programs, how to work with your documents, how to open and save files, how to use your network, and how some special options may provide you with a bit of extra help when it is needed.

Most Windows Me programs work pretty much alike, so the skills that you learn in this part help you get more done with far less work and frustration in almost any program you use. You'll see that there are many ways Windows Me can help you become more efficient and productive.

CHAPTER 4

MASTER THESE SKILLS

- ▶ Installing Programs
- ▶ Uninstalling Programs
- ▶ Installing Windows Me Components
- ▶ Installing Program Shortcuts
- ▶ Starting Programs Automatically
- ▶ Adding a Program to the Start Menu
- ▶ Using Menu Bars
- ▶ Using Scroll Bars
- ▶ Using Dialog Boxes
- ▶ Closing Programs

Using Programs

The programs that you install on your PC are what make it so versatile and useful. With these programs you can surf the Internet, write a letter, calculate your taxes, track your investments, and play games. In fact, Windows Me enables you to use most of the popular software that is available today.

Because Windows Me is a *multitasking operating system* you can generally have many applications running at the same time — if your system has enough memory. This enables you to accomplish a lot more with your PC because you don't have to exit from one program before you start a different one. You simply load the programs you need and switch between them as necessary.

This chapter covers some program basics. It starts by showing you how to install new programs and how to uninstall them if necessary. It then explains how to make your programs easier to use.

You can, for example, easily set up programs so they automatically load whenever you start Windows Me.

You'll also learn how to use common elements such as the menus, dialog boxes, and scroll bars you'll find in most programs. Of course, this chapter doesn't show you how to use specific programs, but it explains what you need to know to at least open and navigate within programs.

Windows Me can run most Windows 98 and Windows 2000 compatible programs. In fact, because Windows Me was designed with consumers in mind, many programs will actually run better on Windows Me. For example, many newer games can take advantage of certain system services that simply weren't available in earlier operating systems. As a result, they will run more quickly and smoothly on a Windows Me–based PC.

Installing Programs

Installing most programs on your Windows Me PC is generally a pretty easy task. In most cases you'll probably find that once you've answered a few questions about where you want the program installed and which optional features you want, you'll just sit back and wait for the installation to complete. Windows Me registers the programs that you install so that you can later go back and change the installation or uninstall the program.

Programs you install from a CD-ROM often use *AutoPlay* to automatically launch their installation program. If you install a program that uses AutoPlay, you won't need to start the Add/Remove Programs window yourself. You can still use the Add/Remove Programs window to change the installation options after the program has been installed or to run the installation program if you canceled out of the installation the first time.

Although most programs are now distributed on CD-ROM, not all programs come that way. Applications distributed on a diskette cannot use the AutoPlay feature, and you must launch the application's setup program manually. Applications you download from the Internet typically arrive as a single executable file that expands into a setup configuration and then runs its own setup program. You can download and execute the installation file in one step, or you can download it, save it to disk, and manually execute it later.

The figures on these pages show you the first steps in installing a new program. This task continues on the following two pages.

Continued

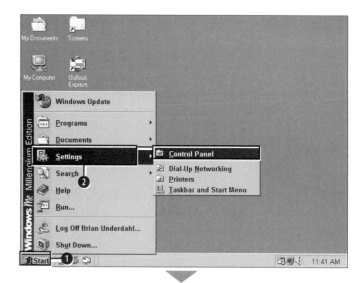

① Click the Start button to open the Start menu.

② Select Settings ➪ Control Panel to open the Control Panel.

③ Double-click the Add/Remove Programs icon.

CROSS-REFERENCE

See Chapter 3 for more information about troubleshooting program installation problems.

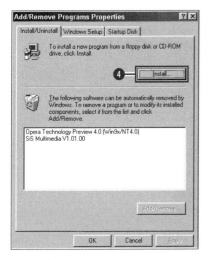

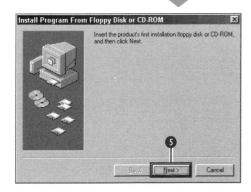

④ *Click the Install button.*

⑤ *Insert the installation disk in the drive and click Next to continue.*

PROGRAMS MUST BE INSTALLED

Although it might seem like the logical thing to do, you generally cannot install programs simply by copying them from another computer. Windows Me programs often share components so that they will use less disk space and consume less memory while they are running. In addition, most Windows Me programs add special settings to the *Registry* when they are installed. The Registry is a special Windows database that stores system and program settings. If you simply copy programs from another PC, the Registry will not be modified with the correct settings, and certain necessary shared files may be missed. These omissions will often cause errors that appear once you attempt to run the program and can usually be corrected only by doing a proper installation.

SOME PROGRAMS ARE NOT USER FRIENDLY

Although most Windows compatible programs will work just fine in Windows Me, some will not. The reason for this is usually that the installation program is ignoring the rules and attempting to install older versions of certain shared files. Windows Me will enable these programs to install, but will then replace the files that were incorrectly changed to older versions. This will prevent program installations from destroying your existing programs.

FIND IT ONLINE

See **http://www.pictureworks.com/support/ antivirus.html** for information on disabling antivirus software when installing programs.

Installing Programs

Continued

You will find that most program installations go pretty smoothly. Still, you'll probably have to answer several questions to get just the installation that you really want.

By default, most programs will offer to install themselves in a folder under the \Program Files folder located on the same disk drive as your Windows Me installation. This new folder will generally be named such that it indicates the name of the program that is installed in the folder. Some installation programs won't even offer you any options and will automatically choose the program folder. Fortunately, most programs will give you the choice of selecting a different destination.

You may choose to specify a different folder for your programs for any number of reasons. You might, for example, have more than one hard disk and you may want to place programs on the disk that has the most space available. Or perhaps you simply want to organize your folders in some other order that makes it easier for you to use your system.

Often you will be given the option to choose which program features are to be installed. If you choose a custom or advanced option you will have to make additional selections, but you can make certain that just the feature set that you need is installed.

Although Windows Me generally does not need to be restarted very often, it's usually a good idea to restart your PC after installing a new program. This is true even when the installation program does not prompt you to restart. Otherwise some configuration changes may not be completed properly.

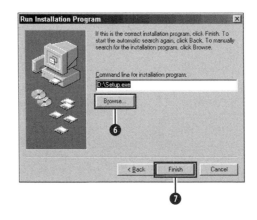

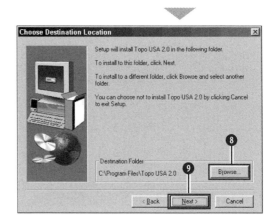

❻ *If the correct installation program is not shown in the Command line text box, click Browse and locate the correct program.*

❼ *When you've finished specifying the installation program, click Finish.*

▶ *Each installation program varies — follow the onscreen instructions to continue.*

❽ *Optionally, click the Browse button and choose a destination folder.*

❾ *Click Next to continue.*

CROSS-REFERENCE

See Chapter 1 for more information about different methods for starting programs.

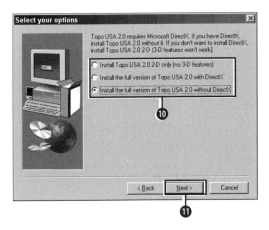

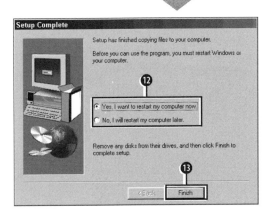

TAKE NOTE

▶ DUAL BOOT CONSIDERATIONS

If your PC is set up to run more than one operating system, you'll need to exercise a bit more than normal care when you install programs. It is generally considered safest to install different operating systems on different disk drives, or at least on different *partitions* of the same physical drive. If you use the same program in more than one of those operating systems, you may be tempted to use the same program folder for each operating system. While this may work, it is usually not a good idea. The program may need different versions of certain shared files for different operating systems, and this could mean the program will only work correctly on the last operating system for which it was installed.

▶ WATCH FOR PROBLEMS

One difficulty you may encounter after installing certain programs is that your other programs or maybe even your entire system may quit working properly. The reasons for this are many, but the end result can be frustration. To minimize the problems, install one program at a time and thoroughly test your system after the installation. If you have problems, see "Using System Restore" in Chapter 14 for information on returning your PC to normal operation.

⑩ *If you are given the option, choose the type of installation you want.*

⑪ *Click Next to continue.*

⑫ *If you are given the option, choose when you want to restart your system.*

⑬ *Click Finish to complete the installation.*

FIND IT ONLINE

See **http://malektips.envprogramming.com/ gen0029.html** for information on failing installation programs.

Uninstalling Programs

You will no doubt encounter some programs that really serve no useful purpose and are simply taking up space on your hard disk. This could be a result of finding a newer program that does a better job, or it could simply mean the old program just doesn't suit your needs. Whatever the reason, you will probably want to uninstall programs from time to time.

Even if you have plenty of spare disk space, there are still good reasons to uninstall old programs you no longer need. Windows Me programs often share certain types of files. These shared files are usually installed in one of the Windows Me *system* folders rather than in the individual program folders. In many cases there are Registry entries that load these files into memory even when they are not being used, and this can cause your system to lose performance. By uninstalling those old programs you may free up some memory and make your PC run a bit faster.

The task of removing unwanted programs often involves a few small snags. In some cases folders cannot be removed. This is usually due to data files that you have stored in those folders. You may want to make a copy of any such files before you manually delete the folders. A system restart is often necessary in order to complete the uninstall process.

One problem that can occur after uninstalling programs is that program icons may be left on your desktop or on the Start menu. If you click an icon for a program that has been uninstalled, Windows Me will display a waving flashlight to indicate that it is looking for the program. You can cancel the search and delete the icon.

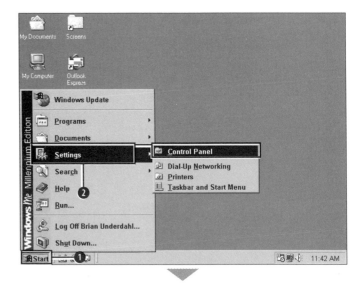

❶ Click the Start button to open the Start menu.

❷ Select Settings ➪ Control Panel to open the Control Panel.

❸ Double-click the Add/Remove Programs icon.

CROSS-REFERENCE

See Chapter 13 for more information about backing up files.

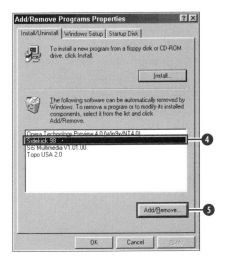

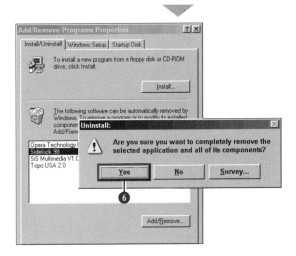

④ *Choose the program to remove.*

⑤ *Click the Add/Remove button to continue.*

⑥ *Click Yes to continue.*

▶ *Different programs will vary in the steps necessary to remove the program. Follow the onscreen prompts.*

FIND IT ONLINE

See **http://www.mijenix.com/easyuninstall2000.asp** for information on an alternative way to uninstall programs.

Installing Windows Me Components

Although most of the components of Windows Me that most users will ever need are installed automatically along with Windows Me, there are some additional optional components that you may have use for. These optional pieces provide additional services for many different tasks, including such things as sharing your Internet connection, additional desktop themes, and Web TV for Windows.

You may need your Windows Me CD-ROM to install these components from the CD-ROM. In some cases the optional components may already be stored on your hard drive so you will not have to insert the CD-ROM to install them.

As you will learn in Chapter 14, Windows Me uses another method to add new system files. This method, known as Windows Update, is not used to add optional components. Rather, it is used to make certain that the latest bug fixes and other system updates have been applied to your system.

You may need to browse several different categories of Windows Me components to learn what is and what is not already installed. One good way to determine if a category has components that have not been installed is to look at the category's check box. If the box is empty, none of the components are installed. If the box has a check and the background in the box is white, all of the components are installed. If the box has a gray background, only some of the components are installed.

Randomly adding the optional Windows Me components will not only waste disk space, but it may reduce your system performance as well. If you find that you have components installed that you never use, remove them to free up extra disk space.

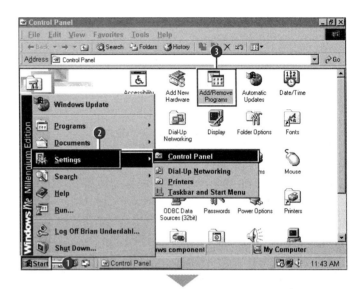

❶ Click the Start button to open the Start menu.

❷ Select Settings ➪ Control Panel to open the Control Panel.

❸ Double-click the Add/Remove Programs icon.

❹ Click the Windows Setup tab.

❺ Choose the component category to install.

❻ Click the Details button.

CROSS-REFERENCE

See "Installing Programs" earlier in this chapter.

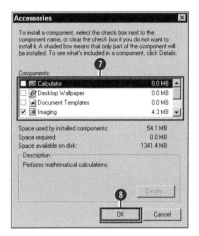

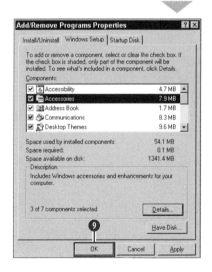

TAKE NOTE

LOOK IN WINDOWS HELP

It can be difficult to understand the usefulness of many of the optional Windows Me components from the very brief descriptions that are provided in the Add/Remove Programs dialog box. Fortunately, you will find most of the components covered within the Windows Me help system. If you aren't sure whether you need to add one of these components, look for the component name on the Index of the Windows Me help window.

YOU MAY NEED SPECIAL HARDWARE

You will probably find that some Windows Me components are not all that useful unless you have the correct hardware installed on your system. Specifically, Web TV for Windows is an example of a Windows Me component that is not too useful unless you have a video tuner installed. You can download local TV listings without installing a TV tuner, but you probably don't want to waste over 30MB of disk space for that. If you do want to receive TV broadcasts on your PC, you will need to install an ATI All-In-Wonder display adapter.

7 *Choose the individual items you wish to install.*

8 *Click OK.*

9 *Click OK to continue.*

▶ *Depending on the components you selected, you may need to insert the Windows Me CD-ROM to complete the task.*

FIND IT ONLINE

See **http://www.microsoft.com/enable/training/ windows98/accessoptions.htm** for information on installing the accessibility options.

Installing Program Shortcuts

You have most certainly noticed that your Windows Me desktop has icons that you can use for starting many of your programs. Often, using a desktop icon is much more convenient than wading through several levels of the Start menu. Clicking a desktop icon is certainly a lot faster than looking for an application in the Windows Explorer windows! Of course you can use whichever of these methods you prefer, but this task will show you how to add your own Windows Me desktop shortcuts.

You can create desktop shortcuts to any type of file, but application programs, document files, and folders are the most likely candidates for useful shortcuts. Each of these will do something that is actually useful when you click their shortcut icon. In most cases Windows Me will know what to do when these types of shortcuts are opened. The same may not be true if you create shortcuts to most other types of files.

In addition to the procedures shown in the figures on these pages, you can create desktop shortcuts very quickly by right-clicking an item and choosing Send To ⇨ Desktop (create shortcut) from the context menu. No matter which method you choose for creating desktop shortcuts, you may want to look at the program documentation to learn if there are any optional *startup parameters* you can add to the command line. These can often provide additional functionality that would otherwise be missing.

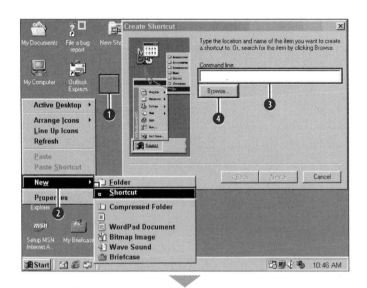

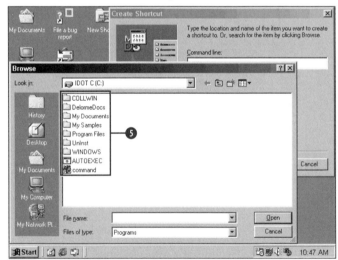

① Right-click a blank spot on the desktop.

② Select New ⇨ Shortcut.

③ Enter the command to start the program.

④ Alternatively, click the Browse button.

⑤ Locate the folder containing the item you wish to add to the desktop.

CROSS-REFERENCE

See Chapter 6 for more information about finding files.

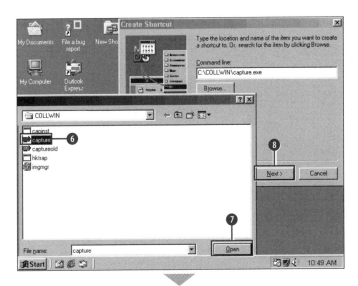

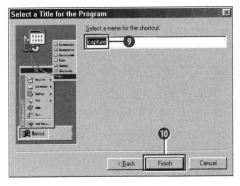

TAKE NOTE

USING DESKTOP ICONS

Even if you prefer to keep your desktop quite clean and to start your programs using the Start menu, there is one handy trick that may make you reconsider. Although Windows Me knows which application programs to use to open many different types of document files, you may sometimes want to open a document using a different program. You might, for example, want to use a particular graphics program to create some special effects in an image file even though the file's graphic format is associated with a different program. One of the easiest ways to open a document using a different application is to drag and drop the document onto the icon for the program that you wish to use. You can do this in Windows Explorer or by using desktop icons.

TAKE THE EASY WAY

When you install new programs on your system, you may be given the option of having an icon placed on your desktop. It's easier to go ahead and allow this desktop icon to be created than to create your own later. If you don't want to allow all your program icons to remain on your desktop, consider creating a new folder on your desktop and dragging the unwanted icons into the new folder.

6 *Select the file you wish to add.*

7 *Click the Open button.*

8 *Choose the Next button to continue.*

9 *Edit the name for the shortcut if you wish. This name will appear in the label of the icon.*

10 *Click Finish to complete the task.*

FIND IT ONLINE

To learn another way to control your desktop, see
**http://www.zdnet.co.uk/pcdir/content/may1998/
win98tips2/toolbars03.html.**

Starting Programs Automatically

You probably have a number of things that you do quite regularly with your PC. Some of these are tasks your computer can handle automatically — such as downloading your e-mail messages at regular intervals or perhaps alerting you to important changes in your stock market investments. To ensure these important tasks are running whenever your PC is running, you may want to make them run automatically when you start Windows Me. In this section you will learn an easy way to accomplish that goal.

The Windows Me Start menu includes an item called StartUp that is located on the Programs submenu. Anything appearing in the Startup menu will automatically load whenever you start Windows Me.

The Startup menu is actually a shortcut to the \Windows\Start Menu\Programs\StartUp folder. You can add items to the Startup menu by copying them to the folder, or you can add them directly to the menu. The figures for this task show you how to add them to the Startup menu. You can use the methods that you learned in Chapter 2 to copy the files to the Startup folder.

It is very easy to add shortcuts to the Windows Me Startup folder, but it is also easy to get carried away and add programs you only use occasionally. Even though Windows Me is a multitasking operating system, if you load every program you might ever use you will likely discover your PC starts to run very slowly. Unless your computer has enough memory for all of the loaded programs, some will have to be swapped out to *virtual memory* space on your hard disk. When this happens, switching between programs can be quite slow. It is far

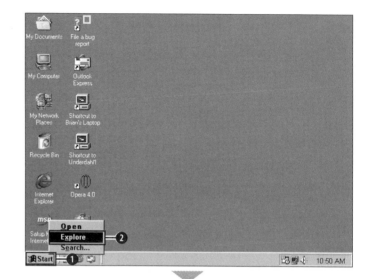

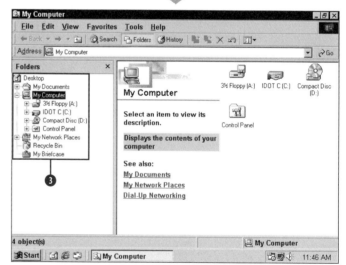

1 Right-click the Start button.

2 Click Explore on the context menu to open Windows Explorer.

3 Locate the folder containing the program you want to add to the Startup folder.

CROSS-REFERENCE

See "Installing Programs" earlier in this chapter for more information about adding new programs to your system.

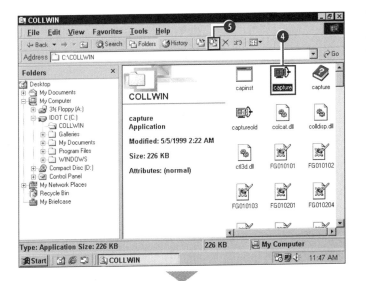

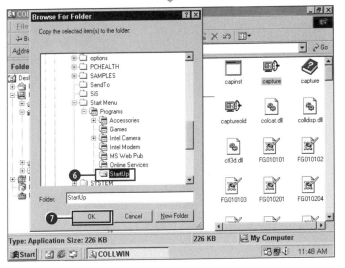

④ *Click the program to select it.*
⑤ *Click the Copy To button.*

⑥ *Select the Startup folder as the destination.*
⑦ *Click the OK button.*

better to only load the most important programs at startup, and then load other programs when you need them.

SOME THINGS DON'T USE THE STARTUP FOLDER

Although you use the Startup folder to automate the loading of applications, that's not the only method of automatically starting programs. It is also possible to start programs by making changes to the Windows Me Registry. This method is often used for programs that must be run automatically with no possibility of the user deleting them from the Startup folder.

PREVENT AUTOMATIC STARTUP

It is possible to prevent the items in the Startup folder from loading automatically. To do so you must hold down the Shift key after Windows Me completes the logon process but before the Startup programs begin to load. It may take some experimentation to discover the exact moment when to hold down the Shift key. It is generally easier to simply remove the shortcuts from the Startup folder than to try and prevent them from running using the Shift key. You can temporarily delete an item by sending it to the Recycle Bin as discussed in Chapter 6.

FIND IT ONLINE

For a utility to control startup options, see **http://www. winsite.com/info/pc/win95/sysutil/fastopen.exe**.

Adding a Program to the Start Menu

The Windows Me Start menu is probably the most convenient way to start most programs. No matter what you are doing, you can always display the Start menu by clicking the Start button, pressing the Windows key, or by pressing Ctrl+Esc. At least one of these methods is always available.

When you install new programs you will usually find the installation program automatically places an entry for the program on the Start menu. Even so, you may find there are program items that do not appear on your Start menu, but which you would like easy access to. In this section you will learn how to add these items to the Start menu yourself.

The accompanying figures show one of the methods you can use to add items to the Start menu. In Windows Me you can also use the drag-and-drop method to add items to the Start menu. In the drag-and-drop method, you drag a shortcut onto the Start button and wait for the Start menu to appear while you continue to hold down the mouse button. Then you drag the shortcut to the desired location and drop it. Placing a shortcut just where you would like it is a bit trickier than it sounds, and you may find yourself trying several times before you get the hang of it.

As you browse your PC looking for programs to add to your Start menu, keep in mind that some applications should not be run manually. Some items that are listed as applications in Windows Explorer are actually a part of another program. Although you usually won't do any harm by attempting to run these applications, there's no

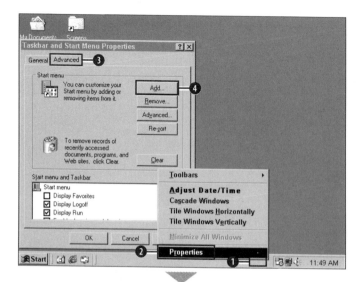

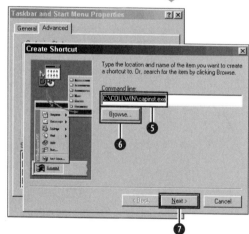

❶ Right-click a blank space on the Taskbar.

❷ Select Properties.

❸ Click the Advanced tab.

❹ Click the Add button.

❺ Enter the command to start the program.

❻ Alternatively, click the Browse button and locate the program you want to add to the Start menu.

❼ Click the Next button.

CROSS-REFERENCE

See "Starting Programs Automatically" earlier in this chapter.

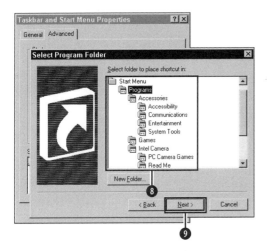

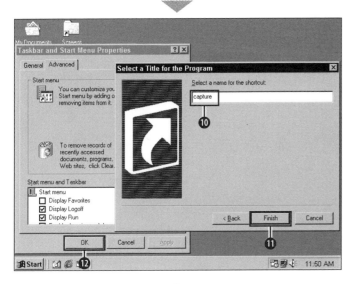

guarantee that it's safe to try to run an application you don't recognize. You should be able to recognize most of your programs by their file names, but, when in doubt, try right-clicking the application and selecting Properties. This should provide some additional clues about the program.

TAKE NOTE

▶ CORRECTING THE START MENU ORDER

If you make any changes to the Start menu, Windows Me will no longer automatically sort the menu items. The menu will instead remain in the same order in which you left it. You can drag-and-drop the menu items into whatever order you prefer. If you would like Windows Me to re-sort the Start menu, right-click the menu and choose *Sort by Name* from the context menu.

▶ USE SUBMENUS

Rather than just dumping everything into the Programs menu, organize your Start menu by creating several related submenus under the Programs menu. You will find it is far easier to deal with these smaller and simpler menus than to have one huge menu containing so many items that you end up scrolling through the menu to find your programs.

---

⑧ *Select the Start menu folder in which you want to place the new program item.*

⑨ *Click Next to continue.*

⑩ *Enter a name for the item.*

⑪ *Click Finish to add the item to the Start menu.*

⑫ *Click OK to complete the task.*

FIND IT ONLINE

To find programs you can add to the Start menu, see **http://pcwin.com/software**.

Using Menu Bars

Y ou will use menus quite often as you use Windows Me programs. Fortunately most of the programs you encounter follow certain rules that result in similar menus in most cases. For example, most programs display a menu bar just below the title bar at the top of the window. This menu bar generally includes a number of drop-down menus that organize commands into logical groupings. Different programs have different menus that fit the needs of the individual programs, of course, but most applications have File, Edit, and Help menus.

The File menu typically contains commands to open and close documents; print documents, open recently used documents, and exit the application. The Edit menu often contains cut, copy, and paste commands. Edit menus may also include commands for searching documents and for search-and-replace operations. If there is a View menu, it typically has commands to control the appearance of the program and documents. Most applications have a Help menu to provide access to online help information.

Menus all work the same way. You can use either your mouse or keyboard commands to open menus and to select commands. The end result is the same whether you point and click or use your keyboard to select.

Menu items often have an underline under one of the characters. For example, the F in the File menu is usually underlined. If you press the Alt key to activate the menu bar, you then press the underlined character to activate the associated menu or menu selection. Some menu

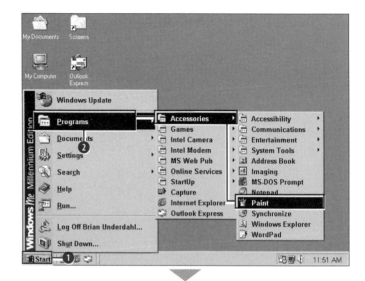

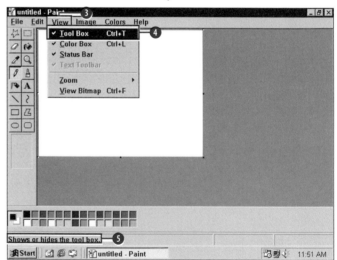

① Click the Start button.

② Select Programs ⇨ Accessories ⇨ Paint.

③ Click View to drop down the View menu.

④ Press the down-arrow to highlight the first choice.

⑤ Read the menu selection description in the status bar.

CROSS-REFERENCE

See Chapter 12 for more information on changing how your mouse works.

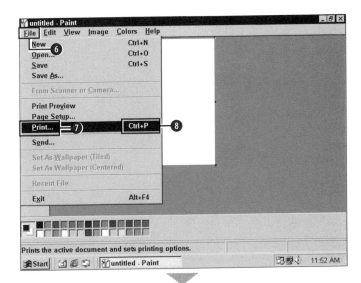

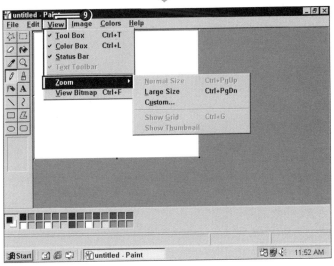

items also work with a shortcut or *hotkey* combination. Many of these hotkeys are common to a wide range of Windows Me programs. Ctrl+C is a common hotkey that copies a current selection to the Clipboard. Ctrl+Z usually selects Edit ⇨ Undo.

TAKE NOTE

▶ USE YOUR ARROW KEYS

If you're not certain which menu selection you need, click the menu name in the menu bar and then use your arrow keys to scroll down through the choices. Programs often provide menu item descriptions in either the title bar or the status bar, but only if the menu item is highlighted rather than clicked. You can highlight items using your mouse, but this can be a little tricky if you are in the habit of holding down the left mouse button while you scroll through the menu. If you release the mouse button the currently highlighted item will be selected. If you scroll using the arrow keys, items are only selected when you press Enter.

▶ MENUS USE SINGLE CLICKS

A single click of a mouse button always activates a menu selection. Cascading menus automatically open when you highlight them. You can then scroll over to the new window, highlight an item, and release the mouse button to select the item.

⑥ *Press Alt+F to open the File menu.*

⑦ *Click Print.*

⑧ *Alternatively, press Ctrl+P to print the document without opening the menu.*

⑨ *Select View ⇨ Zoom to display a cascading menu.*

FIND IT ONLINE

To learn more about menu bars, view **http://computingcentral.msn.com/guide/beginner/default.asp.**

Using Scroll Bars

When you open a large document file it's often impossible to view the entire document onscreen without the display being too small to be usable. In fact, it may be possible to only see a small part of the file at once. To view the rest of your file — whether it is a multiple page word processing document or a large graphic image — you may need to *scroll* the window vertically or horizontally. The easiest way to scroll most documents is to use the scroll bars. This section explains how to use the scroll bars in typical Windows Me programs.

You may not see any scroll bars when you first open a program. That's because the scroll bars often are hidden until they are needed. If the current view can display the entire document without scrolling, the scroll bars are unnecessary. If you zoom in so that the document is too large to view entirely or add more text so the document is too long to show, the scroll bars will appear.

Although using your mouse and the scroll bars is usually the easiest way to scroll through large documents, you can often scroll using the keyboard, as well. To scroll small distances with the keyboard, press the arrow keys to move in any of the four directions. When the cursor reaches the edge of the workspace, the window will move. To move one page at a time using the keyboard, press the PgUp and PgDn keys to page through the workspace vertically. In many applications you can also press Ctrl+PgUp and Ctrl+PgDn to page horizontally.

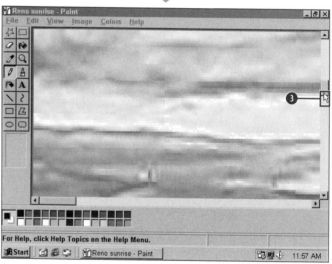

❶ If necessary, select a zoom percentage that activates the scroll bars.

❷ Click a blank space in the scroll bar to scroll one screen in that direction.

❸ Drag the scroll box in the direction you want to scroll.

CROSS-REFERENCE

See "Configuring Mouse Speed" in Chapter 12 for more information on controlling your mouse.

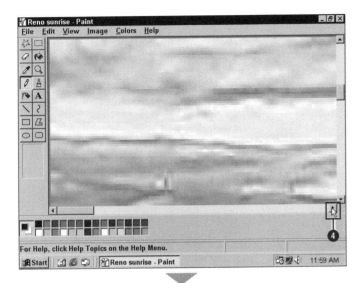

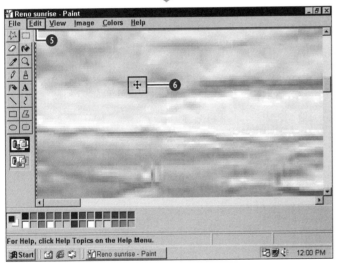

As the figures show, there are several techniques that you can use for scrolling with the scroll bars and your mouse. Clicking the arrows at the ends of the scroll bars generally scrolls by a smaller amount than clicking in the open space of the scroll bar. Dragging the scroll box is usually the fastest way to move large distances within the document.

TAKE NOTE

SCROLL BOXES ARE OFTEN PROPORTIONAL

In many programs the scroll bars contain scroll boxes whose size indicates the percentage of the total document that is visible. While this is not true in all programs, it is a fairly common convention.

SCROLLING WITH A WHEEL MOUSE

Some mice, such as Microsoft's Intellimouse, have a wheel between the two buttons. The wheel is used for scrolling. You can turn the wheel to scroll, and often you can hold down the wheel to power scroll in the direction you move the mouse. In some programs you can also zoom in or out if you hold down the Ctrl key while you turn the wheel. Not all programs work with the mouse scroll wheel.

④ *To scroll one line at a time, click the arrow at either end of a scroll bar.*

⑤ *Select Edit ⇨ Select All to select the entire image.*

⑥ *Point to the image, hold down the left mouse button, and drag the image to scroll.*

FIND IT ONLINE

For information on making your scrollbars easier to grab, see **http://www.goshen.edu/its/softw/win95tt/win12.shtml**.

Using Dialog Boxes

Another of the elements that you will encounter in most Windows Me programs is a dialog box. Dialog boxes are windows that are often used to set program options or to gather user input. Within dialog boxes you will find items such as command buttons, radio buttons, list boxes, text boxes, spin controls, and so on. These items are often referred to as *controls*.

Command buttons are controls that execute commands immediately. The OK button and the Cancel button are typical command buttons.

Check boxes are small square boxes that are either empty or contain a check mark. When the check box contains a check, the associated option is selected — otherwise it is deselected.

Radio buttons — which are sometimes called option buttons — are always located in groups of two or more. The selections in a group of radio buttons are mutually exclusive. When you choose one of the options in a group, the other options are deselected.

Text boxes are rectangular boxes in which you can enter text. User name and password boxes are typical text boxes.

List boxes are also rectangular boxes, but they include a small down arrow at the right side of the box. When you click the down arrow you can choose an option from the drop-down list.

Spin controls are boxes with small arrows pointing both up and down at the right edge of the box. You can enter an integer number in a spin control by typing a number or by using the up or down arrows.

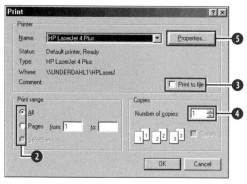

❶ Select a command, such as File ⇨ Print, that displays a dialog box.

❷ Click one of a set of radio buttons to select one of the options and deselect the others.

❸ Click a check box to select or deselect the option.

❹ Click an up or down arrow to change the value of a spin box.

❺ Click a button that displays another dialog box.

CROSS-REFERENCE

See Chapter 3 for more information on using the Windows Me help system.

Only one of the controls in a dialog box is active at any one time. A dotted-line box that surrounds the control usually indicates the active control. You can make another control active by clicking the new control or by using your keyboard. You can press the Tab key to move forward, or Shift+Tab to move backward through the controls. The up and down arrow keys change the selection in a list box or in a set of radio buttons.

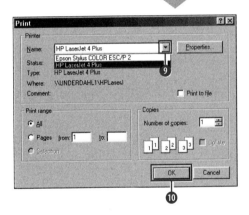

TAKE NOTE

▶ CANCEL DIALOG BOXES

If you discover that you don't want to make any of the changes in a dialog box, click the Cancel button. You can also cancel the dialog box by clicking the Close button (the X in the upper right corner). In addition, you can usually press Esc to back out of dialog boxes without entering any changes.

▶ GET SOME HELP

Dialog boxes often have a help button — a button with a question mark — near the right side of the title bar. If you're not certain what a dialog box control does, click the help button to change the mouse pointer into a question mark, and then click the question mark on the control. You'll see a quick help tip about the control.

⑥ Click a tab to view the options on that tab.

⑦ Make your selections in the dialog box and click OK to confirm your choices.

⑧ Alternatively, click Cancel.

⑨ Click the down-arrow at the right side of a drop-down list box to display the list box contents.

⑩ Click OK to print the document and close the dialog box.

FIND IT ONLINE

For more information on common Windows Me elements see **http://computingcentral. msn.com/ guide/mastercomputing/**.

Closing Programs

Closing programs properly is an important part of using your PC. If you don't use proper procedures you can end up losing your work. In extreme cases you could even prevent a program from working correctly in the future, although that outcome isn't very likely.

Windows Me programs will generally warn you if you have unsaved changes in an open document when you attempt to close the program. If you ignore the warning, any changes made since the last time the document was saved will be lost.

Most programs have a File menu, and most File menus have an Exit command. To close a program from the File menu, select File ⇨ Exit. In addition, most programs have a Close button at the right end of the title bar at the top of their main window. You can click the Close button to terminate the application. You can also press Alt+F4 to close a program or Ctrl+F4 to close a document window in a program that has multiple documents open. Of course, it is always a good idea to save your work first.

If you have a newer PC that supports *hibernation*— a new feature in Windows Me, you have another option rather than closing your programs. By using the hibernation feature you can simply tell your system to go to sleep. When you do, all of your open files are saved and your system shuts down. When it is powered up again, all of the programs and documents you had open are restored to their previous state. If your system supports the hibernation option you will find it as one of the options in the Shut Down Windows dialog box.

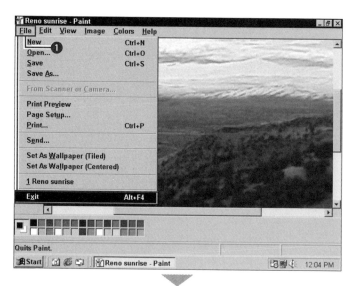

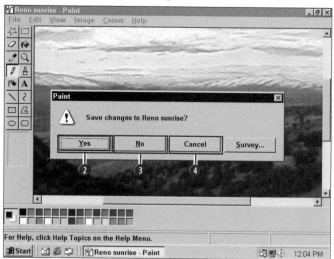

❶ Select File ⇨ Exit to begin an orderly shutdown.

❷ Click Yes to save any changes you've made.

❸ Alternatively, click No to abandon any changes and close the program.

❹ Alternatively, click Cancel to return to the program.

CROSS-REFERENCE

See "Switching Between Programs" in Chapter 1.

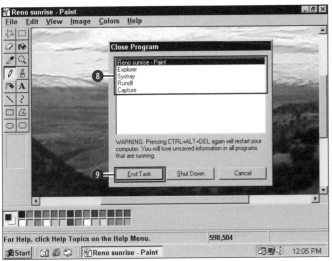

USING THE CLOSE PROGRAM DIALOG BOX

Windows Me uses the Close Program dialog box to control the applications that are running on your computer. The Close Program dialog box not only can terminate an application if necessary, it can also show you applications that have stopped responding, and can even initiate a system shutdown if required.

DON'T LEAVE YOUR SYSTEM UNSTABLE

It's not very likely that you'll ever need to use the Windows Me Close Program dialog box to end a nonresponding task. Still, if a program is not responding and must be shut down, the Close Program dialog box should be able to force it to do so. Although this may seem a little drastic, it makes it possible for you to save your work in any other open programs before restarting your computer. Restarting after closing an unresponsive program is always a good idea because your system could be unstable and prone to further crashing. Remember to save your work and properly close any other open programs before restarting to prevent loss of data.

⑤ *Click the system menu icon.*

⑥ *Select Close to close the application.*

⑦ *Alternatively, click the Close button.*

▶ *If an application has stopped responding, press Ctrl+Alt+Del.*

⑧ *Select the application that has frozen.*

⑨ *Click End Task to close the program.*

Personal Workbook

Q&A

1 If you have items you want to run automatically whenever you start Windows Me, where should you place them?

_____

_____

_____

2 How many options can you select at the same time from a group of radio buttons?

_____

_____

_____

3 Which Control Panel icon do you use when you want to install a new program?

_____

_____

_____

4 What does the size of the scroll box often indicate?

_____

_____

_____

5 What dialog box can you use to shut down a program that has quit responding?

_____

_____

_____

6 What are desktop shortcuts?

_____

_____

_____

7 What dialog box would you use to add Web TV for Windows to your PC?

_____

_____

_____

8 What will happen if you select No when Windows Me tells you that you are closing an application and haven't saved your work?

_____

_____

_____

ANSWERS: PAGE 391

Using Programs

CHAPTER 4

EXTRA PRACTICE

1. Install a new program using the Add/Remove Programs dialog box.

2. Add a shortcut to Paint to your desktop.

3. Set up Notepad to start automatically when you start Windows Me.

4. Experiment with the hotkeys on the WordPad menus.

5. Open the Print dialog box and try out the various controls.

6. Try the different methods of closing programs.

REAL-WORLD APPLICATIONS

✔ You get a CD-ROM that contains several programs, each in its own folder. To install each individual program, you use the Add/Remove Programs dialog box and browse for the correct installation programs.

✔ You depend on e-mail messages to keep in touch with your office. To make certain you get your e-mail frequently, you add your e-mail program to the Startup folder so that it starts whenever you run Windows Me.

✔ You've just tried a new program but you get errors whenever you try to use it. You use the Add/Remove Programs dialog box to uninstall the program so you won't have to deal with a faulty program.

Visual Quiz

How can you display this window? What can you tell about the installed status of the Accessories category?

_____

_____

_____

_____

_____

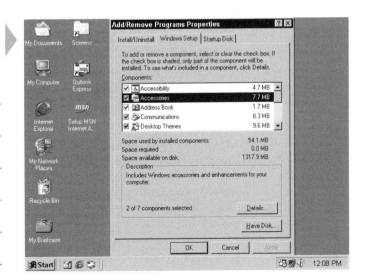

CHAPTER 5

MASTER
THESE
SKILLS

▶ **Opening Documents**
▶ **Opening Recently Used Documents**
▶ **Saving Documents**
▶ **Organizing Your Documents**
▶ **Changing the My Documents Location**
▶ **Selecting Text**
▶ **Cutting, Copying, and Pasting to the Clipboard**
▶ **Dragging and Dropping Data**
▶ **Setting Printer Properties**
▶ **Putting a Printer on the Desktop**
▶ **Printing Documents**

Working with Documents

Do you know what is the most valuable thing about your computer? Actually, the answer is an easy one. Your *documents* represent the time and effort that you have expended on your computer. Everything else — your monitor, your disk drives, your programs, and so on — are items that could be replaced or repaired quite easily. Your documents are unique and are therefore more important than any of these other items.

Windows Me makes it very easy to work with your documents. You can place them where you want, you can copy or move them easily, and you can open them without first figuring out which program you should use. This means that you can think about what you want to do rather than which tools you need. And because the same general techniques apply in most Windows Me applications, you can concentrate on results rather than procedures.

If you have used a Windows 98 or Windows 95 PC in the past, many of the techniques that you will use for working with your documents in Windows Me will seem quite familiar. You won't have to learn a whole new way of working to become productive in Windows Me. In fact, what you will find is that Windows Me is very adept at enabling you to get things done with very little fuss.

When you have documents rather than programs as your focus, it is far easier to manage your projects productively. For example, imagine how difficult it would be to plan a family picnic if you spent all of your time trying to figure out which mode of transportation each family member was going to use rather than what food everyone should bring. Because the ultimate goal is to put together the feast, why would you care if some family members came by bicycle, some by car, and others by bus?

The same principal applies to your documents. When you are working on a project you will find that it is far easier to keep all of the project documents together regardless of whether you used a word processor, a spreadsheet program, or a graphics editor to create those documents. Then you can think about the results, not the tools.

Opening Documents

When you want to work with one of your document files in Windows Me, you don't need to first figure out which program was used to create the document. That's because Windows Me *associates* document types with the application programs that create those types of documents. When you double-click a document file, Windows Me uses that association to open the document in the correct program. You don't have to first open the program and then open the document, because opening the document opens the correct program.

When you right-click a file in Windows Explorer, you open a context menu that displays a number of actions that you can perform. The item at the top of the context menu is the default action that Windows Me will perform if you double-click the file. In most cases the default action is to open the file. If the file is a document file, then Windows Me uses the associated program to open the document.

You can also open documents by first opening the program that you wish to use. Once the program is open you generally open documents using the File ⇨ Open command or by using the Open button on the program's toolbar. If you are already working on a document, it is usually far easier to use one of these methods to open additional documents than by returning to Windows Explorer.

Windows Me associates document types with specific programs by using the *file extension*. The file extension is the three characters that follow the file name. Common

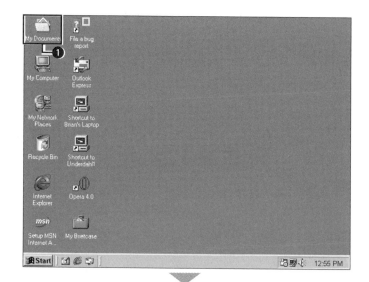

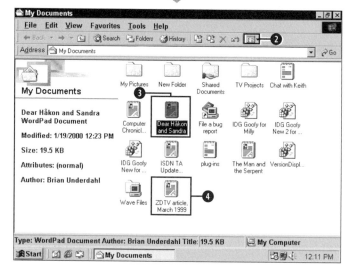

❶ Double-click the My Documents icon on your desktop to open the folder.

❷ If you want to change the way document files are displayed, click the Views button.

❸ Select a file to view its description.

❹ You can double-click a document to open it.

CROSS-REFERENCE

See "Opening Recently Used Documents" later in this chapter.

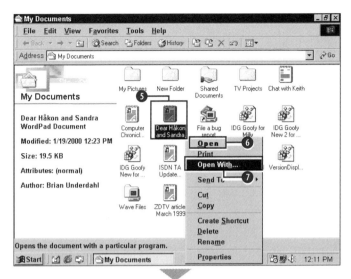

document file extensions include .doc for word processing documents, .xls for Excel spreadsheets, and .jpg for certain graphic image files.

You may not even realize that your Windows Me programs are using file extensions to designate their document files. Windows Me normally does not show the file extensions, and most programs automatically add the extensions after you indicate the file name that you wish to use.

TAKE NOTE

▶ VIEW THE FILE EXTENSIONS

If you want to see the file extensions for your files, you will need to change one of the default settings for Windows Explorer. To do so, first open Windows Explorer. Then select Tools ➪ Folder Options and click the View tab. Remove the check from the *Hide file extensions for known file types* check box. Click OK to close the dialog box. Be careful not to change any file extensions that are displayed.

▶ OPEN DOCUMENTS AS YOU LIKE

If you wish to open a document using a program other than the one that Windows Me associates with the document, right-click the document and choose Open With to display a cascading menu. You can then choose one of the programs that are listed, or you can select the Choose Program option.

⑤ Right-click a file to view the context menu.

⑥ Click Open to open the file using the default application.

⑦ Alternatively, select Open With to choose an alternate application to open the document.

⑧ Choose the application from the list of available programs.

⑨ Click OK to open the document.

FIND IT ONLINE

See **http://ois.unomaha.edu/casde/webshop/ 6%20hr%20WS/HowToExtensions.html** for information on file extensions.

Opening Recently Used Documents

Whenever you work on a document, Windows Me adds that document to a list that it maintains of the documents that you have opened recently. The list of your most recently used documents appears on the Start menu, and you can reopen one of the listed documents by selecting it from the list. This makes it easy to open those documents because you don't have to open the My Documents folder and search for them.

The Start menu Documents list shows the 15 most recently accessed documents. This list is made up of document shortcuts that are stored in the \Windows\Recent folder — a hidden folder. This folder may actually contain far more than 15 shortcuts, but only 15 will show on the Documents list.

If you work with a large number of documents in the course of a day, it's easy for important documents to get bumped off the Documents list. To keep this from happening you may want to manually delete unimportant documents from the list, as shown in the figures.

You can open any of the items on the Documents list by clicking the item. You can also open a shortcut menu for any of the items on the Documents list by right-clicking the item. This shortcut menu includes the same context-sensitive choices you'd see if you opened the item's shortcut menu in Windows Explorer. The items on the shortcut menu vary according to the type of object you've selected. You'll always see an Open choice, a Delete choice, and a Properties choice along with several

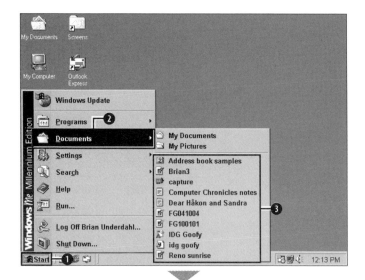

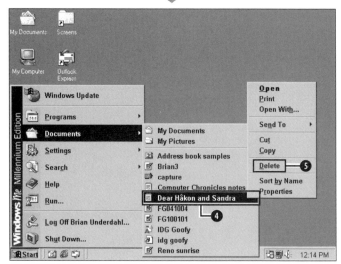

1. Click the Start button.

2. Select Documents to open the list of recently used documents.

3. Click a document to open the document file.

4. Right-click a document to open the context menu.

5. If you want to remove the shortcut, select Delete.

CROSS-REFERENCE

See "Sending Objects to the Recycle Bin" in Chapter 6.

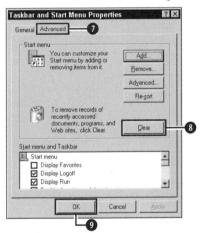

other choices. Open is always the first choice at the top of the shortcut menu, and selecting Open is the same as clicking the document. Use Delete to remove the shortcut without affecting the actual document file.

TAKE NOTE

▶ THE DOCUMENTS LIST CAN BE WRONG

Just because an item is on the Start menu's Documents list doesn't mean that you'll be able to open the document file by selecting it from the list. If you delete a document file, the shortcut may remain in the list for some time. If you move a document file without opening the file, the shortcut won't be corrected to point to the new file location.

▶ PROTECTING YOUR PRIVACY

Anyone who examines your Documents list can easily see which document files you've been using. Clearing the Documents list is an important first step in protecting your privacy, but it does not provide a complete solution. Most application programs also maintain a list of the documents you opened using the application, and if you use a program such as Microsoft Outlook, you may find that the Outlook Journal also records which documents you open. If you need to protect your privacy, you will probably want to prevent anyone from using your PC.

⑥ Right-click the Taskbar and select Properties to open the Taskbar and Start Menu Properties dialog box.

⑦ Click the Advanced tab.

⑧ Click Clear to delete the shortcuts to recently accessed documents.

⑨ Click OK to close the Taskbar Properties dialog box.

FIND IT ONLINE

To download a program that can view many different types of files, see **http://www.fineware.com/peep32a.htm**.

Saving Documents

Unless you like wasting your time redoing the same work each time that you work on a document, you will probably want to save your documents in files. Any program that you use to create documents will give you the option to save your work (although the save function may be disabled on trial versions of some software packages).

Most Windows Me programs follow certain conventions so that users will have an easier time using the software. One of the standard conventions followed by Windows Me programs is to include a File ➪ Save command so you can easily save your documents.

The first time that you save a new document you will have to supply a name for the file. Once you have saved the file, the same name will be used if you save the file again to incorporate any changes that you have made.

You can also save your work using a new file name by selecting the File ➪ Save As command. This command enables you to not only specify a different name, but also a different destination folder or even a different file format in most instances. One example of why you might use this option is if you need to convert a graphics file from one format to another — perhaps so that you can use the image on your Web site. Because only a few graphics file formats can be used on the Web, using File ➪ Save As and choosing one of the Web-compatible formats would enable you to use an image file that might not work otherwise.

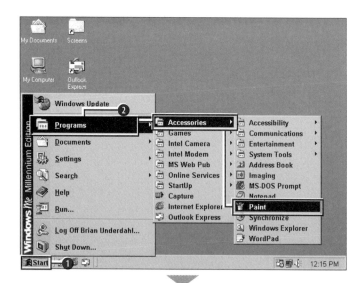

① Click the Start button.

② Select Programs ➪ Accessories ➪ Paint.

▶ You may wish to open an existing Paint document.

③ Select File ➪ Save As to open the Save As dialog box.

CROSS-REFERENCE

See "Copying and Moving Files" in Chapter 2.

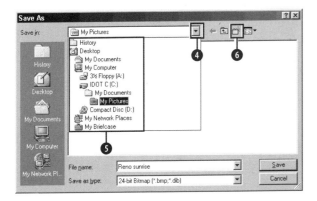

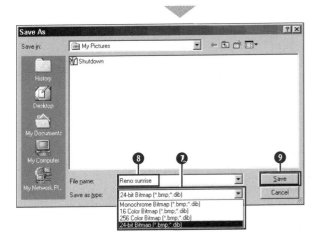

ADD THE CORRECT FILTERS

Programs often use add-in features that are called *filters* to convert files from one format to another. If you want to use File ⇨ Save As to save a document file in a different format you may need to install some extra filters that were not installed by default. In most cases you will need to use the application's install program and choose a custom or advanced option to select which of the filters are installed.

USE THE SEND TO OPTION

Many Windows Me programs remember the last location of opened or saved files, and they offer the same location when you save a new file. Although this practice is usually convenient, it can cause problems. For example, if you use the File ⇨ Save As command to save a copy of your document onto a diskette, you may see an error message if you later try to open a new file after the diskette is no longer in the drive. To avoid this you may want to always save your documents on your hard disk, and then use the right-click context menu Send To command to save a copy on the diskette.

④ Optionally, click the down-arrow at the right edge of the "Save in" list box to drop down the list box.

⑤ Select a location for saving the file.

⑥ Click here if you want to create a new folder to hold the file.

⑦ Optionally, select the file type from the "Save as type" list box.

⑧ Enter a name for the file here.

⑨ Click Save to save the file and close the dialog box.

FIND IT ONLINE

For a quick way to open documents, see **http://helpnet. ut.cc.va.us/MSoffice/GettingResults/013_4.htm**.

Organizing Your Documents

P roper organization can be the key to getting more done in less time. If you find that you simply cannot get everything finished, maybe you just need to be a little more organized.

You already know that most Windows Me application programs use the My Documents folder as the default location for saving document files. What you may not realize, though, is that this folder should be the starting point rather than the ending point as you organize your documents. If you use the My Documents folder as a base for creating new document folders, you can easily separate your documents by project so that each of your projects will be well organized.

Imagine that your boss has assigned you four different projects that you are to work on over the next several months. Each of those projects has some similar elements, but each also requires separate documentation. By creating four separate project folders under the My Documents folder you can keep each project's files together and you don't have to worry about using the same file name in two or more projects.

There's no reason why you can't take this concept a few steps farther. You can create new folders within other folders, so you might even want to add new folders to your project folders. Remember, though, that Windows Explorer sorts folder contents into two separate groups. Any folders that are contained within a folder are sorted together as one group, and all other files make up the second group. Shortcuts — even shortcuts to folders — are grouped with files rather than with folders.

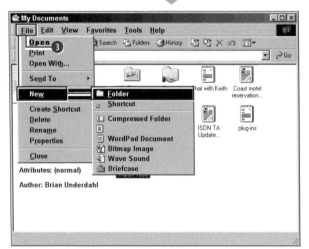

❶ Double-click the My Documents icon to open the folder.

❷ Select a document to view its properties.

❸ Select File ➪ New ➪ Folder to create a new project folder.

▶ Give the new folder a descriptive name so it is clear which project's files belong in the folder.

CROSS-REFERENCE

See "Finding a File" in Chapter 6.

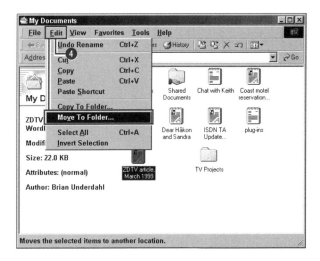

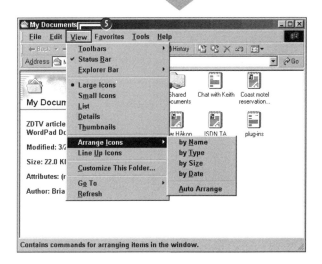

▶ REUSE DOCUMENTS

If you are working on several projects that will require you to create a number of similar documents, you can save some time by reusing some of those documents. For example, if each project requires a budget analysis, it's likely that most of the basic details will be quite similar in each budget analysis document. You can create a master document and then use the File ⇨ Save As command to save the individual copies in their separate locations. Then you can plug in the proper numbers and have the separate documents completed in no time.

▶ USE THE CONTEXT MENUS

The context menus that appear when you right-click an object in Windows Explorer are also available in the Save As and the Open dialog boxes. You can use these context menus for many different file management tasks including renaming files, deleting files, or copying files. Using the context menus in one of the dialog boxes can save you considerable time because you won't have to open Windows Explorer to handle these tasks. In most cases you can use the context menus to perform several actions without closing the dialog box.

▶ Select the project files that you wish to move to the new folder.

④ Select Edit ⇨ Move To Folder and choose the new folder for the project files.

⑤ Optionally, select the view options for the new project folder.

▶ You can select different options for organizing each project folder.

FIND IT ONLINE

For updates for Microsoft Office products, see
http://officeupdate.microsoft.com/.

Changing the My Documents Location

In most ways the My Documents folder functions just like any other folder on your PC. You can add files and folders to it, you can clean out old items that you no longer need, and you can view the My Documents folder using Windows Explorer.

Even with these important similarities to the other folders on your hard drive, the My Documents folder is just a bit different from most other folders. Because My Documents is the default location where most Windows Me programs save document files, you have to be a little careful about renaming or moving the folder. The reason for this is simple — you want to make certain that your programs can locate the folder both for saving new files and for opening your existing documents.

As the figures show, you use the My Documents Properties dialog box to move or rename the My Documents folder. By using this dialog box you record the changes in the Registry so that your programs will also be informed of any changes. This will also enable new programs that you install later to locate the new folder.

If your PC has more than one hard disk, you may want to move the My Documents folder to the disk with the most free space. You may also want to consider using a network drive as your document storage location — especially if your network has a file server that is backed up automatically.

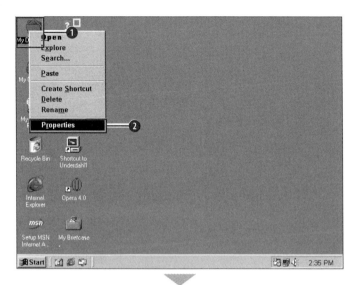

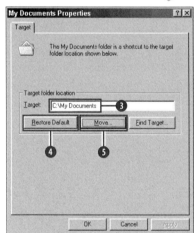

① Right-click the My Documents icon to open the context menu.

② Select Properties to display the My Documents Properties dialog box.

③ To specify a new folder, type the folder name here.

④ To revert to the original My Documents folder location, click the Restore Default button.

⑤ Alternatively, click the Move button to browse for a new location.

CROSS-REFERENCE

See "Sharing Your Files" in Chapter 7.

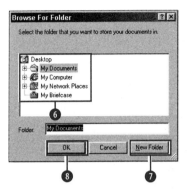

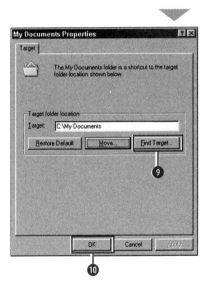

6 Select the new folder.

7 Alternatively, click the New Folder button and specify a name and location to create a new folder.

8 Click OK to continue.

9 Optionally, click the Find Target button to specify a different folder.

10 Click OK to complete the task.

Selecting Text

When you work with documents there's a very good chance that you'll need to select text so that you can move, copy, or delete words or phrases. Once you have selected text you can store it on the Windows Me Clipboard so that it can be added to another location in the same or another document.

Selecting text is generally pretty easy, although it might take some practice to become comfortable with the techniques that you need to use. If you have still not made peace with your mouse, now is definitely the time to learn. While you can select text with the keyboard alone, using the mouse is far faster and simpler. Here is a comparison of the two techniques:

To select a block of text with the mouse, move the cursor to the first character of the block. Next, press and hold the left mouse button and drag the cursor to the last character of the block. As you move the mouse, the text is highlighted to indicate the range of the selected block. When you have selected the text block that you want, release the mouse button.

To select text using the keyboard, use the arrow keys to move the cursor to the first character of the block. Next, press and hold the Shift key and move the cursor with the arrow keys. The highlight indicates which text has been selected.

Most programs make it somewhat easier to select text with the mouse by using *automatic word selection*. When automatic word selection is enabled, you don't have to start at the beginning of a word. Instead, you can start dragging the pointer anywhere within the first word of

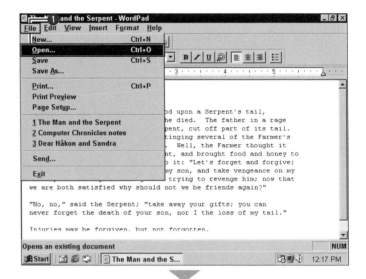

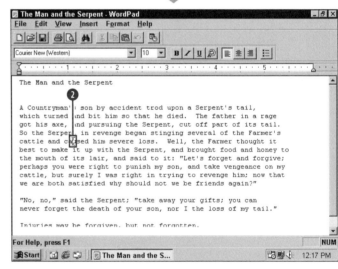

▶ Open WordPad or your word processor.

❶ Select File ⟳ Open and open a document that you can use to practice selecting text.

❷ Move the mouse pointer over the middle of a word.

CROSS-REFERENCE

See "Cutting, Copying, and Pasting to the Clipboard" later in this chapter.

your selection; the selection automatically expands to select complete words as soon as you drag the pointer onto a new word. Automatic word selection usually does not work when you are selecting text using the keyboard.

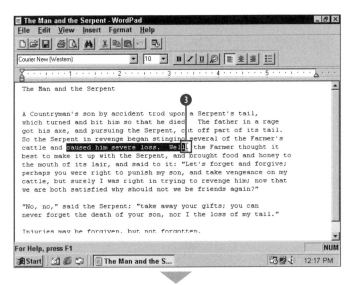

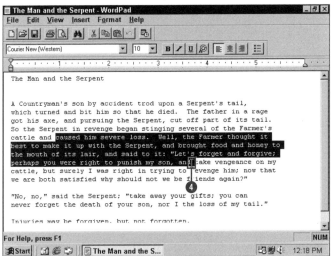

❸ Hold down the left mouse button as you drag the mouse pointer across several words.

▶ The selection automatically expands one word at a time as you continue dragging.

❹ Continue holding down the left mouse button and drag the pointer down several rows.

▶ As you extend the selection downward, it includes all words from the first to the last selected word.

TAKE NOTE

▶ REDUCE TYPING ERRORS

To reduce the chance of making a typing error — especially in something that must be absolutely perfect such as a Web page address — select the text and copy it to the Clipboard rather than retyping it.

▶ SELECT ALL TEXT

You can usually select all the text in a document by clicking Edit ➪ Select All. Most programs use Ctrl+A as a shortcut for this command. In Windows Explorer you use this shortcut to select the entire contents of a folder.

▶ SELECT WORDS AND PARAGRAPHS

To select a word you can double-click within the word. To select an entire paragraph at once you can generally triple-click within the paragraph. If you accidentally select more text than you intended, click outside the selection and try again. You can also extend a selection by holding down the Shift key and clicking the new end point.

FIND IT ONLINE

See **http://www.sunysuffolk.edu/~mandias/tips/clipboard.html** for more on these commands.

Cutting, Copying, and Pasting to the Clipboard

Once you have selected something you can copy or cut the selection to the Clipboard. Copying leaves the original selection in place, whereas cutting removes the original selection. If you wish to make a duplicate without removing the original selection, use copy. If you wish to move the selection to another location, use cut.

Once you have data on the Clipboard, you can paste the data to a new location in the same or in another document. As long as the original data remains on the Clipboard you can paste as many copies of the data as you like.

Although the examples here use text, you can actually copy, cut, and paste many different types of data. Of course, you can only paste data that is compatible with the destination document type. You would not, for example, be able to paste a graphic image into a plain text document.

You can use several methods to copy or cut data. Once you have selected the data, you can use the Edit ⇨ Copy or Edit ⇨ Cut commands on the program's menu, the Copy or Cut buttons on the toolbar, or the Copy or Cut commands on the right-click context menu. Regardless of the option that you choose, a copy of the selected data will be placed onto the Clipboard.

Before you paste Clipboard data into a document, make certain that the insertion point — generally the cursor — is at the point where the inserted data should begin. The easiest way to do this is usually to click the mouse pointer where you want to place the data.

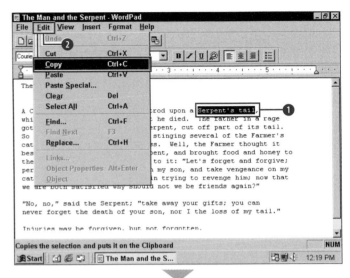

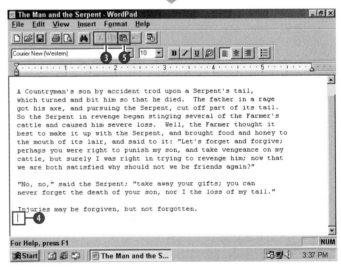

① Select the text you want to copy or cut.

② Select Edit ⇨ Copy to copy the text to the Clipboard.

③ Alternatively, click the Copy or the Cut button to move the selection to the Clipboard.

④ Move the insertion point to the place where you'd like to insert the data.

⑤ Click the Paste button to paste data from the Clipboard.

CROSS-REFERENCE

See "Dragging and Dropping Data" later in this chapter.

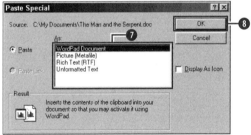

You can also replace existing data with the data from the Clipboard. To replace existing data rather than simply inserting the new data, select the data that you want to replace before you paste.

Data on the Clipboard can exist in several different formats. When you paste the data into a document, it is pasted using whichever format contains the most information about the data that is compatible with the document. If you'd like more control over how the data is pasted into the document, choose the Edit ▷ Paste Special command. You will then be able to choose the paste format.

6 Alternatively, select Edit ▷ Paste Special.

7 Select the data format to paste into the document.

8 Click OK to paste the data and complete the task.

FIND IT ONLINE

See **http://www.injurytracker.com/clipboardswitcher/ index.htm** for a better Clipboard replacement.

Dragging and Dropping Data

Although the commands that use the Clipboard — copy, cut, and paste — can be pretty handy, there is a more direct way to copy or move data. Drag and drop is a visual method of accomplishing the task using your mouse. Using drag and drop, you select data in a document and then drag and drop it into another location — even one in another document or application.

You may find that using drag and drop can be a little confusing initially. You must first select the data and then release the mouse button. Then you point to that selected data and hold down the left mouse button while you drag the mouse pointer to the destination location. You must wait for the mouse pointer to return to the standard arrow pointer after first selecting the data — otherwise you won't be able to move the selected block, because you'll end up changing the selection instead of dragging the data to the new location. Usually it's best to select the data, release the mouse button, move the mouse slightly, and then point to the selection before you press and hold the left mouse button to initiate the drag.

While you are dragging data it is important to remember that you must not release the mouse button until you are pointing to the intended destination. As soon as you release the mouse button the data will be dropped in the current location. If you make a mistake, select Edit ⇨ Undo or click the Undo button in the destination

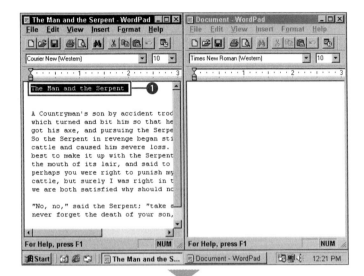

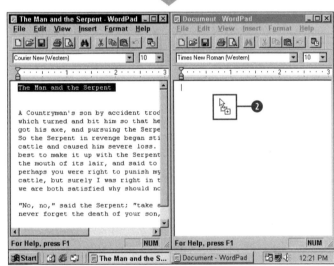

① Select the text you want to drag and drop.

② Point to the selected text, hold down the left mouse button, and drag the pointer to the desired location.

▶ Dragging and dropping between two applications copies the data unless you hold down Alt while you drag and drop.

CROSS-REFERENCE

See "Configuring Mouse Speed" in Chapter 12.

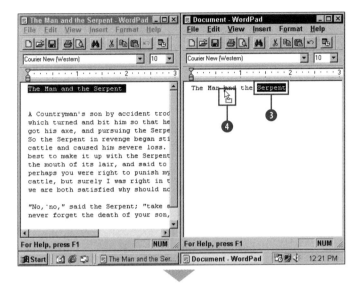

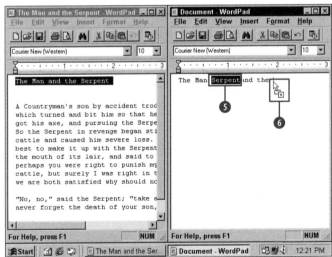

window. Do not use any other commands before selecting Edit ⇨ Undo or you may not be able to reverse the drag-and-drop action.

Dragging and dropping between two documents doesn't work in quite the same way as it does within a single document. Within a single document, the data is moved unless you hold down the Ctrl key; if you hold the Ctrl key the data is copied rather than moved. If you drag and drop between two documents, the data is always copied unless you hold down the Alt key; in that case the data is moved rather than copied.

TAKE NOTE

▶ **DRAGGING AND DROPPING BETWEEN TWO WINDOWS**

If you wish to drag and drop data into a document window that is not currently visible, you need to take a two-step approach. First drag the data onto the Taskbar icon for the destination window, but do not release the mouse button. Wait for the destination windows to open and then move the mouse pointer to the destination location before releasing the mouse button.

▶ **DRAGGING AND DROPPING FILES**

Drag and drop works the same way in Windows Explorer as it does in documents, and it is often the easiest method of copying or moving files.

---

❸ Select the text you want to move.

❹ Point to the selected text, hold down the left mouse button, and drag the pointer to the destination location.

▶ Dragging and dropping between locations within one document moves the data unless you hold down Ctrl while dragging and dropping.

❺ Select the text you want to copy.

❻ Point to the selected text, hold down the left mouse button, hold down Ctrl, and drag the pointer to the destination location.

FIND IT ONLINE

See **http://www.canyonsw.com/index.htm** for a selection of drag-and-drop shareware programs.

Setting Printer Properties

In spite of the predictions that we would all soon be enjoying the paperless office, it's pretty clear that printing is a big part of working with documents in today's world. Printing documents is typically not a difficult task, but there are several things that you should know in order to obtain the best possible output.

The first step towards putting your documents onto paper is making certain that your printer is set up properly. Printers have a number of properties such as resolution and color settings that you can adjust to get the desired type of output.

The settings that you choose may represent a compromise between the highest quality of printing and speed, or between the cost per page of output and the purpose of the document you're printing. You might, for example, choose to use a draft setting to quickly produce proof copies of a report and then switch to a high-quality setting to print the final report. The higher-quality setting might take several times as long to print and could also cost several times as much per page for toner or color ink. For day-to-day printing you might decide on a combination of settings that falls in the middle of these two extremes.

You can access the properties of your printer in a number of ways. You usually have access to more properties when you use the Printers folder as your starting point as shown here. If you prefer to set your printer options from the Print dialog box, look for a Properties button or an Advanced button.

Different types of printers will have different options that you can select. For example, color printers will generally include settings that adjust items such as color

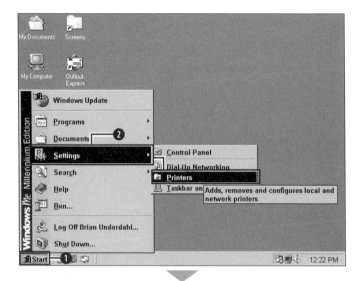

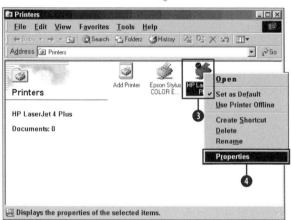

❶ Click the Start button.

❷ Select Settings ➪ Printers to display the Printers folder.

❸ Right-click the printer whose properties you wish to set.

❹ Select Properties.

CROSS-REFERENCE

See "Sharing a Printer" in Chapter 7.

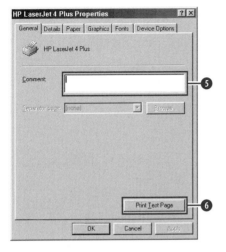

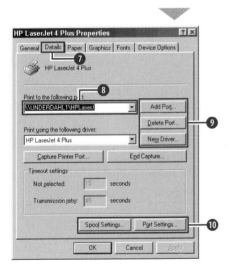

balance. Printers that can automatically print on both sides of the paper usually have settings that relate to duplex printing.

The figures on these pages show how you can access some printer properties. This task continues on the next two pages where you will learn about additional settings.

Continued

Continued

TAKE NOTE

▶ **FINDING YOUR PRINTER PROPERTIES**

Depending on how your PC is configured, selecting Settings ⇨ Printers from the Start menu may display either the Printers folder or the expanded list of the items in that folder. In Chapter 11 you will learn how to control this behavior. If you find that selecting Settings ⇨ Printers displays the printers rather than the Printers folder, you can right-click the printer in the menu to display the context menu so that you can select Properties.

▶ **PRINT A TEST PAGE**

Be sure to print a test page whenever you install a new printer driver. Printing a test page not only ensures that your printer is working properly but also provides you with a list of the printer drivers that are currently in use.

---

5 *Optionally, specify a comment for the printer.*

▶ *The comment will be visible to other people on your network when they share your printer.*

6 *Click Print Test Page to make certain the printer is working correctly.*

7 *Click the Details tab.*

8 *Select the correct printer connection.*

9 *Use these buttons to add, remove, or configure the connection.*

10 *Use these buttons to select the way data is sent to your printer.*

FIND IT ONLINE

See **http://windowsupdate.microsoft.com** for printer driver updates.

Setting Printer Properties

Continued

Because printers often have a large number of optional settings, you may find setting up your printer somewhat confusing. Often it is best to stick with the default settings for most items and only change one or two items at a time so you can see how those items affect the printed output.

You may not be familiar with a few of the printer settings that are shown in the figures. For example, the Unprintable Area button on the Paper tab can be used to prevent your printer from being sent data that simply disappears instead of being printed. Most printers have a small margin along the edges of the paper that cannot be used for printing. In laser printers this is typically on the order of 1/4 inch.

The Graphics settings typically control the detail level that will be shown when printing graphics. Higher resolution and finer *dithering* settings will produce better looking printed output, but will generally slow down your printing as well.

The font settings control the quality of text output. Downloading text as soft fonts generally speeds printing, but printing text as graphics enables you to use certain special effects such as *watermarks*.

Although there is not room to show this in the figures, you can also click the More Options button to obtain access to printer settings such as page layout for two-sided printing.

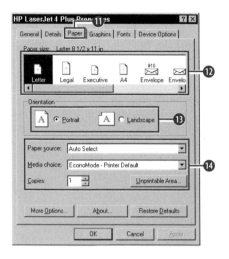

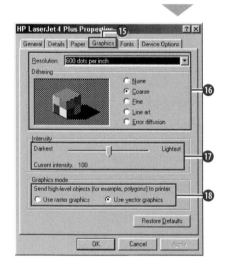

⑪ *Click the Paper tab.*

⑫ *Choose the paper size.*

⑬ *Select the paper layout.*

⑭ *Select additional paper options if they are available for your printer.*

⑮ *Click the Graphics tab.*

⑯ *Select the resolution and dithering options.*

⑰ *Select the darkness of the printing.*

⑱ *Choose the graphics mode.*

CROSS-REFERENCE

See "Sharing a Printer" in Chapter 7.

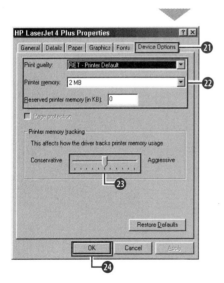

SELECTING A GRAPHICS MODE

The Graphics tab has two options for how objects are sent to the printer. In most cases you should se-lect the *Use vector graphics* option because this will result in images being printed much faster. If you encounter problems with different objects not lin-ing up properly in the printed output, try the *Use raster graphics* option. The raster graphics option sends the entire image as one complete picture rather than as a series of individual objects, and this generally resolves image printing problems.

SETTING MEMORY TRACKING

Laser printers are *page printers* — the entire page to be printed is assembled in the printer's memory be-fore any printing begins. This means that your laser printer must have enough memory for the entire print image or it will not be able to complete the entire page. Of course this means that higher reso-lution or larger-sized images will require far more printer memory than simple text pages. The *Printer memory tracking* setting on the Device Options tab controls how closely Windows Me tracks the avail-able memory in comparison to each page being printed. Too conservative a setting may result in Windows Me refusing to even try printing complex pages. Too aggressive a setting may result in a memory *overflow* in your printer, and the necessity of manually resetting the printer to continue your print job.

---

⑲ *Click the Fonts tab.*

⑳ *Select your font settings as available for your printer.*

㉑ *Click the Device Options tab.*

㉒ *Choose the print quality options that suit your needs — these will vary according to your printer.*

㉓ *Choose the memory tracking setting.*

㉔ *Click OK to complete the task.*

FIND IT ONLINE

See **http://mrdriver.hypermart.net/Devices/Printers/Windows/** for links to printer manufacturers.

Putting a Printer on the Desktop

Your Windows Me desktop is a handy place. You can place all sorts of shortcuts on your desktop so that you have quick access to your programs, documents, or folders. In this section you will learn that placing a shortcut on your desktop for your printer can be very handy, too.

Desktop shortcuts to your printers serve several purposes. Using the shortcut enables you to quickly check the status of the print queue or to pause a noisy printing job when you receive an important phone call. You can also do something very interesting with a desktop shortcut to a printer — you can print documents by dragging and dropping them onto the shortcut. There is no need to first open the document or the application that created the document, because Windows Me will automatically open and close these as necessary.

The printer dialog box that appears when you open a desktop shortcut to a printer provides quite a bit of information about your printer. You can see the names of any documents that are waiting to be printed, the current status of each print job, the name of the person who sent the document to the printer, the number of pages, the file size, the time that the print job was started, and which printer port was used. This information might be useful to help you plan for adding more paper or changing your printer's ink cartridges.

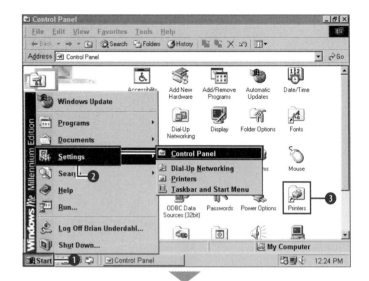

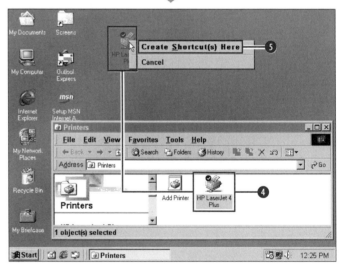

❶ Click the Start button.

❷ Select Settings ⇨ Control Panel.

❸ Double-click the Printers icon.

❹ Point to the printer icon, hold down the right mouse button, and drag it onto your desktop.

❺ Select Create Shortcut(s) Here from the context menu.

CROSS-REFERENCE

See "Adding New Hardware" in Chapter 12.

116

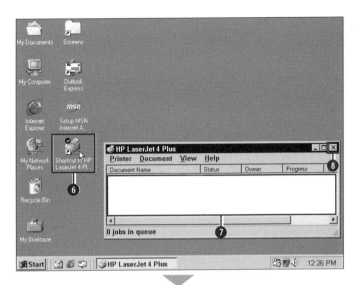

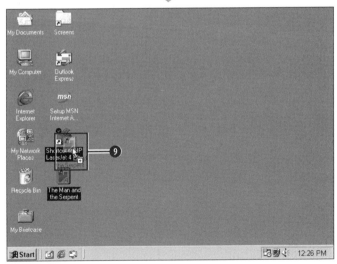

TAKE NOTE

USING THE PRINT QUEUE

The print queue is the list of documents that are waiting to be printed. If necessary you can control the print queue. You might, for example, note that a huge print job you sent to your printer is ahead of a more important document in the print queue. If you select the documents that are ahead of the one you wish to print first, you can use the Document ⇨ Pause command to prevent those documents from printing. Once the important document is completed don't forget to use Document ⇨ Resume to allow the paused documents to print.

YOU MUST HAVE THE RIGHT PROGRAM

A desktop shortcut makes it easy to print documents because you can print simply by dragging the document icon and dropping it onto the printer icon. But this technique works only if you have the correct application program installed on your PC. You must have the application that created the document, and that application must be one designed for Windows Me. If you do not have the application that created the document installed on your system but you do have another program that is associated with that type of document, the program that you do have will probably be able to handle the printing task without a problem.

6 Double-click the printer icon to open the printer status dialog box.

7 View the current print queue here.

8 Click the Close button to close the dialog box.

9 Drag and drop a document onto the printer icon to print the document without needing to open it.

FIND IT ONLINE

See **http://www.cs.wisc.edu/~ghost/ for Ghostscript**, a program that enables PostScript printing on any printer.

Printing Documents

Even though a desktop shortcut to your printer is handy for quickly printing a copy of an existing document, in most cases you will probably print documents while you have them open. When a document is open in an application, you have the option to change the print settings — something that you have no chance to do when you drag and drop a document onto the desktop shortcut to the printer. Besides, when the document is already open you don't need to hunt for it.

Most programs include a Print command on the File menu. In many cases you will also find Print (or Page) Setup and Print Preview commands on the File menu. In some cases you may need to be a little creative in determining where to find the print preview and setup options. Often these can be found somewhere in the Print dialog box.

You may also see a Print button on the toolbar. Typically this button will print a single copy of the entire active document using the current default settings. If you want to make any changes from the defaults, be sure to select File ⇨ Print rather than using the Print button.

Although the default settings of individual programs vary, most programs enable you to specify certain page setup options. Typically, these options include the orientation of the printing — portrait or landscape — along with the paper size and the margin settings. When you adjust the page setup options, the onscreen view of the document will likely change to reflect the new settings. If you're trying to control the final document appearance, it's best to make the page setup changes before you begin formatting your document.

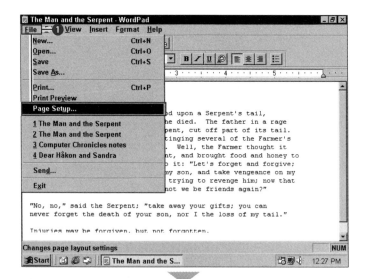

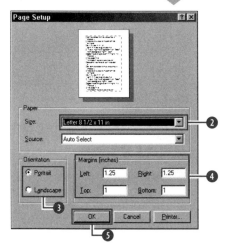

① Select File ⇨ Page Setup to display the Page Setup dialog box.

② Select the correct paper size.

③ Select the proper page orientation.

④ Adjust the margin settings as necessary.

⑤ Click OK to close the dialog box.

CROSS-REFERENCE

See "Opening Documents" earlier in this chapter.

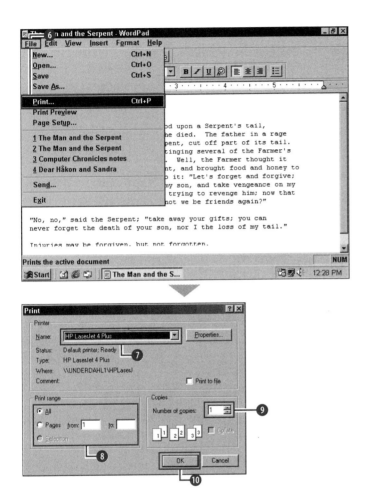

You can use the Print dialog box to select a different printer, change the printer properties, select the page range you wish to print, and choose the number of copies to print.

Correct page setup depends on the printer. Different printers have different features that affect the page layout, so if you have more than one printer installed, select the printer before trying to change the page settings. Otherwise, you may find that the page settings change when you select the correct printer.

TAKE NOTE

USE THE NUMBER OF COPIES OPTION

To print multiple copies of the same document, it's usually more efficient to select the number of copies in the Print dialog box than to issue several print commands.

CHOOSE MARGIN SETTINGS CAREFULLY

Printers often have limits to how close they can print to the edge of a page. If you set the print margins too small, you may get a warning from the application program, or there may be no warning and your document may be printed minus the characters closest to the edges of the page. For example, many printers cannot print within .25 inch of the edge of the paper.

⑥ Select File ➪ Print to display the Print dialog box.

⑦ Select a printer.

⑧ Select the range that you want to print.

⑨ Select the number of copies you want to print.

⑩ Click OK to print the document.

FIND IT ONLINE

See **http://www.tcisoft.com/techtalk/v30/30ts78.htm** for information on installing multilanguage support.

Personal Workbook

Q&A

1 What happens when you drag and drop data between two different documents without holding down any keys?

_____

_____

2 What is likely to happen if you specify 0 margins for a document?

_____

_____

_____

3 How can you control the format of data you paste from the Clipboard?

_____

_____

_____

4 What command can you use to copy selected text to the Clipboard?

_____

_____

_____

5 What happens to data that you've copied to the Clipboard when you copy additional data to the Clipboard?

_____

_____

_____

6 What is the best way to print multiple copies of the same document?

_____

_____

_____

7 How can you temporarily pause printing?

_____

_____

_____

8 If you are unable to open a document that appears on the Documents list, what might be the cause?

_____

_____

_____

ANSWERS: PAGE 392

EXTRA PRACTICE

1 Remove a document from the Documents list.

2 Copy some text to the Clipboard and then paste it into a new location in your document. Examine the Documents list to see your most recently used documents.

3 Copy some new text to the Clipboard and paste it to confirm that the original text is no longer available.

4 Open the printer Properties dialog box for your printer and print a test page.

5 Print three copies of the same document using a single print command.

6 Change the paper orientation for your printer to landscape and print another copy of the same document from the previous step.

REAL-WORLD APPLICATIONS

✔ You have a standard form that you print frequently, so you create a copy of the document on your desktop. Now you can easily print a copy simply by dragging and dropping the document onto your desktop printer icon.

✔ You're creating a report that includes a document file you created in Word and a photo you've retouched in Paint. After you complete work on the different pieces, you drag and drop them into one document to consolidate them.

✔ You are creating a new brochure to promote your company's new product line. To have the brochure printed professionally, you create a print file that works with the PostScript printers at your local print shop.

Visual Quiz

How can you display this dialog box? How can you change the number of copies to be printed?

_____

_____

_____

_____

_____

_____

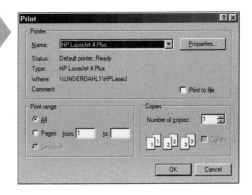

CHAPTER 6

Working with Files and Folders

Keeping track of the folders and files on your computer can be a major task. It is likely that there are hundreds of different folders that contain thousands of files. You need to learn effective ways to manage all of them and avoid the problems that could arise. This chapter shows you how to do that.

Certain file management functions are extremely important in maintaining your files. Two of the most important are being certain that you can locate specific files when you need them and getting rid of junk that is simply clogging things up. These two tasks are really somewhat related, because finding what you need is far harder when you have to sift through tons of trash. It is also far more likely that you'll accidentally delete something you need if you aren't sure where it is.

Windows Me makes finding things on your PC pretty simple. It has a search tool that enables you to look for items based on very simple to very complex search criteria. You can look for files and folders based on their names, or you can look for files that exhibit very specific content or dates.

Because no hard disk has unlimited space, you must eventually remove old files that are simply eating into your storage space. But unfortunately, anyone can make a mistake. If that mistake involves deleting a file and then discovering that you really did need it, you will be happy to learn that the Windows Me Recycle Bin can give you a second chance. When you delete files, Windows Me temporarily stores those files in the Recycle Bin. With this feature, you may be able to recover accidentally deleted files, which could otherwise cost you hours of work to reproduce.

Because your Recycle Bin is your safety net, controlling your Recycle Bin so that it protects you when you need it is important, too. Because there is only so much space on a hard drive, only the most recently deleted items can be saved for future recovery. But as you'll learn, there are some things that you can do to insure that the Recycle Bin protects you from major disasters.

Finding a File

I f you have ever lost track of just where you saved some of your files, you know that it can be easy to get confused. You know that you saved your work somewhere, but you just can't find it when you need it again. Virtually anyone who uses computers knows the frustration that results when you simply didn't pay close attention to the name or location of that one important file. To make matters worse, the lost file always seems to be one that would be hard to duplicate.

The file names you use can be an important factor in keeping track of your files. In the early days of personal computing it was pretty easy to misplace files because you were limited to 11 characters for the complete file name. Of those 11 characters, only the first eight were really available because the other three were the file extension. Coming up with something that fit into eight characters was often a real challenge.

Now, of course, you can use descriptive names for your files. If you want to name a file "Letter to my boss asking for a raise," you can, and this ability should make it far easier to determine the file contents without even opening the file. But see the Take Note section on the following two pages for some additional considerations.

Unfortunately, long file names can also complicate the search for lost files. Long file names are a problem for one very simple reason. When Windows Me searches for files or folders it uses the search criteria that you specify as alternate conditions that can be met and still satisfy your requirements. That is, if you search for *region budget for* in the hopes of finding the budget files

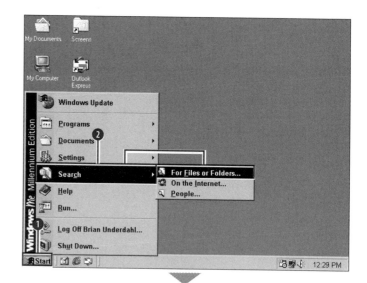

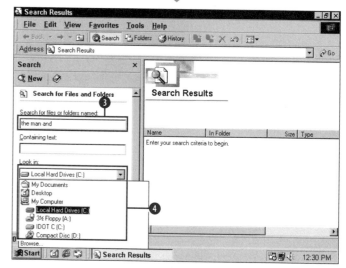

① Click the Start button.

② Select Search ⇨ For Files or Folders.

③ Enter the file name.

④ Optionally, choose a drive to limit the search area.

CROSS-REFERENCE

See "Searching for Web Sites" in Chapter 9.

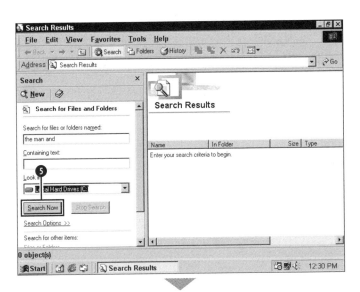

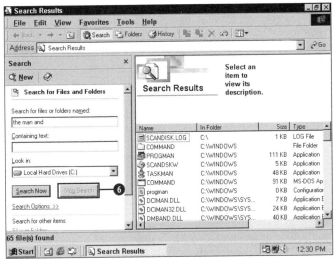

⑤ Click the Search Now button to begin the search.

⑥ Because the search is not producing the desired results, click Stop Search so you can refine the search.

for all regions no matter what year, Windows Me will look for any file that contains region, budget, or for in the file name. The figures illustrate this problem.

As you can see in the figures, the search results in this case probably won't be what you want. One solution is shown in the next (continued) task.

Continued

TAKE NOTE

WINDOWS ME VS INTERNET SEARCHES

If you're used to searching on the Internet, you may be surprised to discover that searches in Windows Me don't work quite the same way. On the Internet you can enclose a phrase in quotes to search for that phrase, but this technique does not work quite the same in Windows Me. To learn a method that you can use to control your Windows Me file searches more closely, see "Specifying a Wildcard Search" later in this chapter.

NARROW YOUR SEARCH

One way to speed up a search is to narrow the scope of the search. Use the "Look in" list box to limit the search locations to include only those drives on which the file might reasonably exist, and the search will take far less time.

FIND IT ONLINE

See **http://www.microsoft.com/Windows98/ usingwindows/work/articles/908Aug/ usabilitytips.asp** for help finding files.

Finding a File
Continued

A file search can produce results that aren't really what you wanted. This is because it is easy for Windows Me to understand your search phrase differently than you expected. Rather than looking for the file using the complete file name that you specified, Windows Me looked for any file that had any of the words anywhere in its name.

There are several useful solutions to this sort of problem. One of the possible solutions is to use the method shown in the figures on these pages. Because you know some of the text that is contained within the file you are seeking, you can add a condition that says that only those files meeting both the file name and text specifications can meet the criteria.

Of course, even solutions to problems can introduce new problems. Unless you are absolutely certain that the text really is in the file, specifying text to search for can bypass the file that you really want to find. For example, if the file that you are seeking uses the term "rain" instead of "precipitation" you might not find the file that you want.

Another way to reduce the number of incorrect results is to limit the area that is searched. For example, if your PC has several hard drives, you might specify the drive where you are confident the file will be found. You might also limit the search to specific folders such as the My Documents folder. Including fewer places in the search will also tend to make the search conclude far faster.

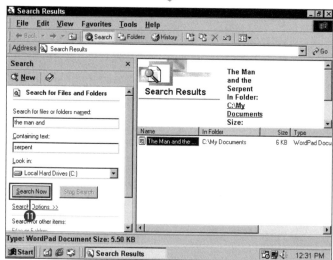

7 Click the New button to begin a new search.

8 Enter the file name.

9 Enter text that you know is contained in the file.

10 Optionally, choose a drive to limit the search area.

11 Click the Search Now button to begin the search.

CROSS-REFERENCE

See "Specifying a Date Search" later in this chapter.

When you've found a file that was hiding in an unexpected location, you can use the Open Containing Folder command to see what else you may have saved there. Before using this command, you must right-click the file in the list of found files.

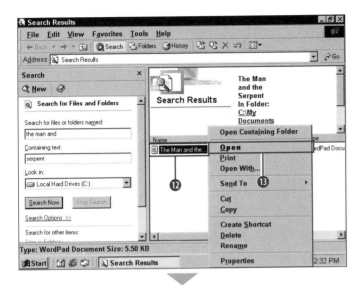

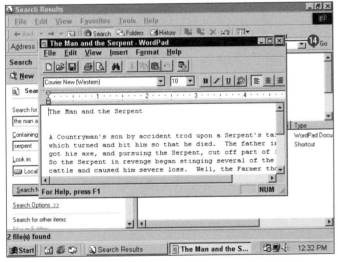

⑫ Right-click a found file to open the context menu.

⑬ Select Open to verify that you have found the correct file.

⑭ Click the Close button to complete the task.

TAKE NOTE

▶ KEEP SPACES OUT OF FILE NAMES

Because Windows Me assumes that words separated by spaces in search phrases are separate search phrases, you can eliminate a lot of search problems by not including spaces in your file names. You could, for example, use an underscore (_) between words rather than a space when you name files. You can also eliminate the problem by simply running the words in the file name together.

▶ SAVE YOUR WAYWARD FILES

If you discover that a lost file was saved in an out-of-the-way folder, you may want to move the file to a better location — such as your My Documents folder. To move the file to My Documents, right-click the file and choose Send To ▷ My Documents from the context menu. If you want to move the file to a different folder, use the Move To button in Windows Explorer.

FIND IT ONLINE

See **http://www.microsoft.com/windows98/using windows/work/articles/811Nov/WRKfoundation2.asp** for more on viewing your computer's contents.

Specifying a Wildcard Search

O nce you have tried finding files that include several different words in their file names, you'll begin to realize that the process has certain limitations. Sure, you can include additional conditions to narrow the search — such as specific text that you believe is in the file, but even that may not always produce the most useful results. In fact, it is more likely that you either won't find anything or that you will find far too many matches.

To refine your search methods you may wish to try using *wildcards* to filter the search criteria so that the results may be more acceptable. Wildcards are characters that Windows Me interprets in special ways.

Windows Me recognizes two wildcard characters, the asterisk (*) and the question mark (?). You use an asterisk to take the place of any number of characters in a text string. You use a question mark to take the place of a single character. For example, BU*.TXT would find any files that start with the letters BU and use the TXT extension. BU??.TXT would also find any files that start with BU and use the TXT extension, but would limit the search to filenames that were exactly 4 characters in length. Each question mark in a wildcard specifies that there must be a character in that position.

You can also use wildcards in the *Containing text* box. You might find this option useful if you were certain about only a part of the file name but knew that the file contained two or more words in a certain sequence. In

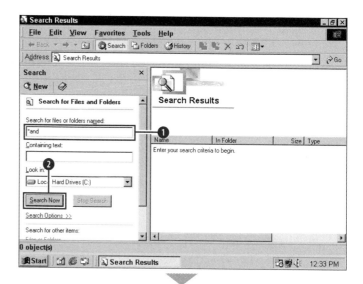

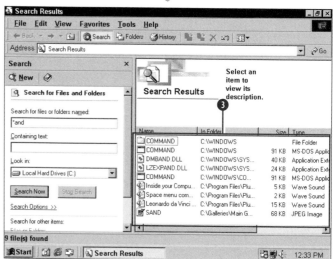

❶ Enter the file name using wildcards.

❷ Click the Search Now button to begin the search.

❸ View the search results to determine if the wildcards are producing the expected results.

▶ In this case the list was not quite as expected because the search found only files ending in "and."

CROSS-REFERENCE

See "Finding Specific File Types" later in this chapter.

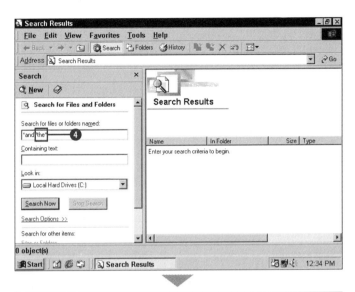

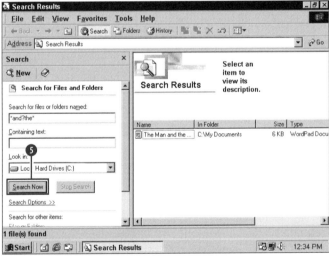

most cases, though, you will probably have better results if you try to limit the search criteria to a single field in the Search Explorer Bar.

④ *Add additional wildcards and words to refine the search.*

▶ *In this case the search phrase was changed to include "?the*" to find files where "the" followed "and".*

⑤ *Click the Search Now button to redo the search.*

▶ *With combined wildcards the search produced the correct file.*

FIND IT ONLINE

See **http://www.microsoft.com/windows98/using windows/work/articles/811Nov/WRKfoundation3.asp** for more information on organizing files and folders.

Specifying a Date Search

As useful as wildcard searches may be, there are likely to be times when a wildcard search just doesn't produce the best results. One very good example of this would be when you have no idea what file names might have been used. In this case you need to use one of the alternate search methods that Windows Me offers. In this section you learn how to conduct a search based on the date the file was created, modified, or last accessed.

Searching for files based on dates can produce results you might not easily duplicate using other search methods. You can, for example, discover which files were changed or added when you installed a new program so that you could troubleshoot a problem that developed later. You can also determine which files someone was snooping in while you were on vacation. Finally, you might want to find all of the files that were used during the time you worked on a big project. These are just a few examples of how searching for files using dates can be very useful.

When you specify a date search, you can also specify whether you're searching for the time the file was created, modified, or last accessed. For document files, you'll likely want to look for files that were modified within a time period. In that way you can tell which files were changed as well as find those that were originally created during the specified date range.

When you specify dates, be sure the period that you specify is large enough. It's always possible that you could be off a day or two, and such a miscalculation could affect your results.

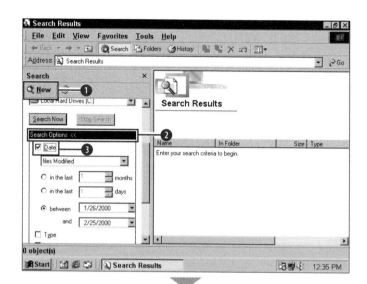

❶ Click the New button.

❷ Click Search Options to display additional options.

❸ Click the Date check box to display the date options.

❹ Click the "between" radio button.

❺ Enter the start date.

▶ When you click the date list box down arrow, Windows Me displays a calendar so that you can choose a date.

❻ Enter the end date.

CROSS-REFERENCE

See "Saving Documents" in Chapter 5.

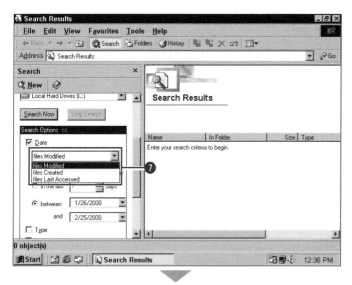

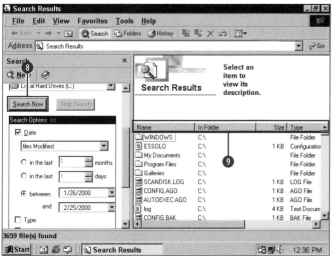

START WITH A FRESH SEARCH

Unless you're attempting to build a complex search based on multiple conditions, be sure to click the New button to clear the old search before you begin. Otherwise, Windows Me keeps any existing search conditions, and your search probably won't find the files you expect.

BUILD ON YOUR SEARCHES

You don't have to limit yourself to making simple searches that use a single search condition. You could, for example, specify that you wanted to find all documents created in the past two weeks that contain the word *budget* in their file name. A complex search that specifies more than one search condition narrows the results list considerably, but you must use care in setting up a complex search. Remember that each one of the search conditions must be satisfied. A good way to search effectively is to start with a simple search and then add additional conditions one at a time to narrow the results. Just remember to not click the New button when you add extra search conditions.

⑦ Select the type of date you're specifying.

⑧ Click the Search Now button to start the search.

⑨ If you want to sort the results, click a column header to sort by that column.

FIND IT ONLINE

See **http://www.wugnet.com/shareware/99/week156/** for a utility that enables you to compare and synchronize folders.

Finding Specific File Types

Most of the time you probably know what type of file you want to find before you even begin looking. In most cases you will probably be looking for a specific type of document file, certain types of multimedia sound files, or perhaps graphic images in a particular format. You aren't likely to be too interested in locating the various types of nondocument files that are used to keep Windows Me or your application programs running. By narrowing the scope of your search to specific file types you will likely find that it is far easier to locate the files you really want.

One way to limit your searches is to use the file type selection in the Windows Me search options list. You can then search for all files of a specific type, or use some of the techniques covered earlier in this chapter to further narrow the results list.

To search for files by file type, you use the Type check box that appears in the list of search options. When you select this option, Windows Me displays a list box that includes entries for every file type that is registered on your system. You can select a specific file type from this list and the search results will only show that one type of file.

When you search for files by type, be sure to select a file type that will actually be useful. It makes little sense to do a search for most of the items in the list of file

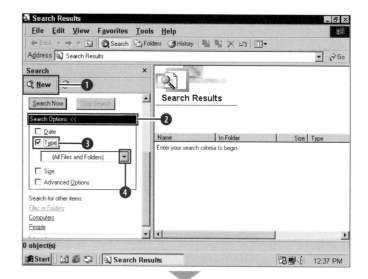

❶ Click the New button.

❷ Click Search Options.

❸ Click the Type check box.

❹ Click the down arrow at the right edge of the type list box.

❺ Use the scroll bar or the arrow keys to see the available file types.

❻ Choose the type of file you wish to find.

CROSS-REFERENCE

See "Saving a Search" later in this chapter.

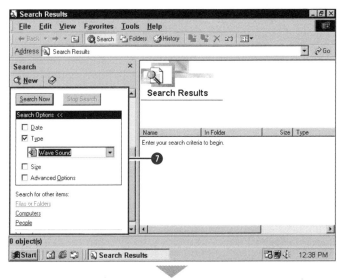

types because the majority of them are not files that you can safely open, and messing around with certain important files could render your system inoperable.

⑦ *Optionally, select any additional search conditions that you wish to apply.*

⑧ *Click the Search Now button to start the search.*

Saving a Search

You may soon discover that saving a complex search that you have created can be very useful. That is because it's likely that you will want to perform the same type of search at some future time. By saving the search you can reuse the same set of criteria without having to set up the whole search all over again.

You might want to reuse a search that you have saved for several reasons. For example, suppose you want to copy all of your modified files to a backup tape drive once a week. You could set up a search for files that were modified during the past week, select all of the files that appear in the results list, and copy them to the tape. If you make this a part of your Friday afternoon routine, you can have your weekly backup done in just a few minutes with very little fuss. You might also use a saved search to locate all of the files relating to a specific work project — even if several people were working together on the project.

You should know one very important thing about saving a search that you have created in Windows Me. Until you actually execute a search you cannot save the search. In fact, when you first open the search program you won't even find the Save Search command on the File menu. The command will appear once you have clicked the Search Now button or when you have opened a previously saved search. Also, you must click the Search Results pane before the command will be made available.

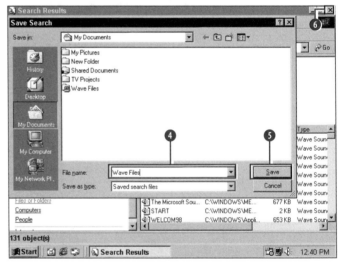

❶ Click the Search Now button to start a previously specified search.

❷ Click the Search Results pane.

❸ Select File ➪ Save Search.

❹ Specify a name for the saved search.

❺ Click the Save button.

❻ Click the Close button to close your search.

CROSS-REFERENCE

See "Specifying a Date Search" earlier in this chapter.

When you save a search, Windows Me creates an icon in the My Documents folder so you can later perform the same search by double-clicking the icon. The icon will have the name that you specify when you save the search. For example, saving a search for Windows Me sound files might result in a desktop icon named "Wave Files." You can save as many different searches as you like. Each one will have a different name, although if you save multiple copies of the same search the names will differ only by having a number appended to the icon name.

⑦ *Click the Start button.*

⑧ *Click Documents.*

⑨ *Click the saved search to reopen the same set of search criteria.*

⑩ *Click the Search Now button to start the search.*

TAKE NOTE

RESULTS ARE NOT SAVED

When you save a search, Windows Me only saves the set of criteria that you specified — not the results of the search. This enables you to click the Search Now button to quickly execute the same search again.

ORGANIZE YOUR SAVED SEARCHES

If you save a large number of searches, you may want to create a new folder named "Search" in your My Documents folder. You can then drag all the saved searches into the Search folder and reduce the clutter.

FIND IT ONLINE

See **http://coverage.cnet.com/Content/Features/ Dlife/Search/ss06.html** for tips on searches.

Synchronizing Files

If you often use more than one computer you have probably been faced with the challenge of keeping your document files synchronized on the different systems. You might start a report on your desktop PC and then take the file along on your laptop when you go on a business trip. When you later return to your office you need to make certain that you update any files on your desktop system that were modified on the laptop.

Of course you could just try to remember which files need updating, but Windows Me provides an automated way for you to keep your files in synch when you use more than one system. As the figures show, this automated method uses the Windows Me My Briefcase folder to store all of the files that you use on more than one computer.

Although My Briefcase can synchronize the changes between two copies of the same file, it is not intended as a means of coordinating changes made by multiple users at the same time. That is, you should not attempt to send copies of My Briefcase to several different people and expect to be able to synchronize the changes made by each of them. If you must combine the input from a number of people, make one copy of My Briefcase and route that copy to each person in turn. When each person concludes their changes and updates the My Briefcase files, they can send the copy of My Briefcase to the next person in the distribution list. When the copy returns to you, use it to bring your original copy up to date. You may then want to send the updated copy to the entire distribution list.

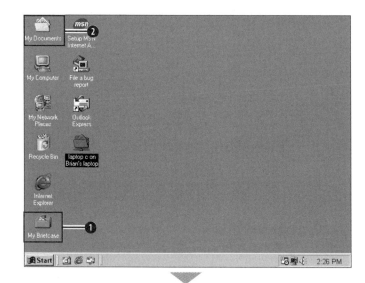

❶ Double-click My Briefcase to open the folder.

❷ Double-click My Documents to open the folder.

❸ Drag the documents you wish to synchronize into the My Briefcase folder.

❹ Click the My Documents Close button.

❺ Click the My Briefcase Close button.

❻ Click the Start button and choose Programs ⇨ Accessories ⇨ Windows Explorer.

CROSS-REFERENCE

See Chapter 7 for more information on using networks.

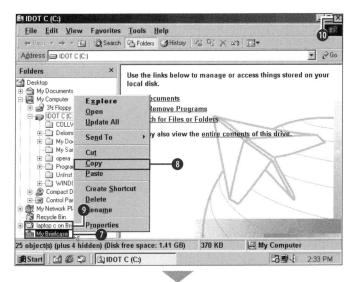

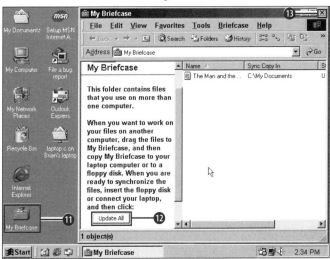

BE CAREFUL ABOUT SPLITTING FILES

When you add document files to the My Briefcase folder, Windows Me maintains a relationship between all copies of those files. That relationship enables Windows Me to automatically synchronize the different copies so that all copies contain the latest changes. If you select Briefcase ⇨ Split from Original from the My Briefcase menu, the file you selected becomes an *orphan* file and can no longer be synchronized with the file outside of My Briefcase. To restore the association between the copies of the file you must drag a new copy of the original into My Briefcase.

USE ANY CONNECTION

To synchronize document files using My Briefcase you must have a physical connection to the My Briefcase folder. This does not mean, however, that the two computers must be connected on a network. You can also use a direct cable connection or simply transfer the My Briefcase folder to a removable disk. If the files you wish to synchronize are small enough you may even be able to use a diskette for transferring My Briefcase.

⑦ *Right-click My Briefcase.*

⑧ *Select Copy.*

⑨ *Right-click the destination computer and choose Paste.*

⑩ *Click the Close button.*

⑪ *To update the files, double-click My Briefcase.*

⑫ *Click Update All.*

⑬ *Click the Close button to close My Briefcase.*

FIND IT ONLINE

See **http://windowsupdate.microsoft.com/nt5help/ Enterprise/bfc_update_status.htm** for information on checking the status of files in My Briefcase.

Sending Objects to the Recycle Bin

I f you have ever accidentally deleted a file, you know how easy it is to make that error. A couple of clicks, and hours of work could be lost. Of course the file you accidentally deleted will almost always be the one you cannot easily replace, too. That's why the Recycle Bin is so important. The Recycle Bin protects you by temporarily storing most of the files that you delete so that you can get them back if it turns out that you made a mistake.

When you delete a file, Windows Me does not really erase the file from your hard drive. In most cases it simply temporarily moves the file to the Recycle Bin. If you realize your mistake while the file is still in the Recycle Bin you can restore the deleted file — fully intact — to its original location with just a few quick clicks.

You don't have to do anything special to use the Recycle Bin. Files that you delete are automatically sent to the Recycle Bin unless you make a special effort to prevent that. When you consider that you probably wouldn't purposely delete files if you knew that you were going to need them in the future, it's easy to understand why the Recycle Bin is so easy and automatic to use. You wouldn't want to have to depend on guessing when it might be important to preserve a file that you were about to delete, would you?

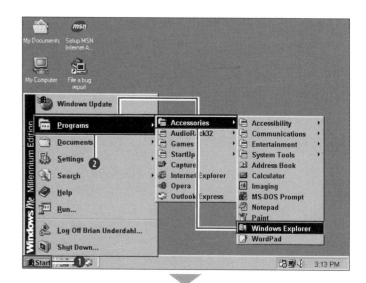

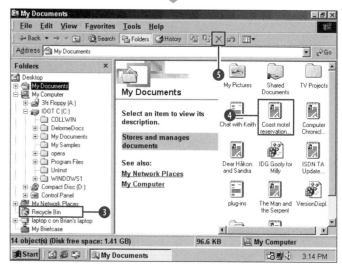

❶ Click the Start button.

❷ Select Programs ⇨ Accessories ⇨ Windows Explorer.

❸ Drag and drop an object from wherever it is onto the Recycle Bin.

❹ Alternatively, first select the object.

❺ Then click the Delete button, or hit the Delete key on your keyboard.

CROSS-REFERENCE

See "Setting Recycle Bin Properties" later in this chapter for information about controlling how the Recycle Bin works.

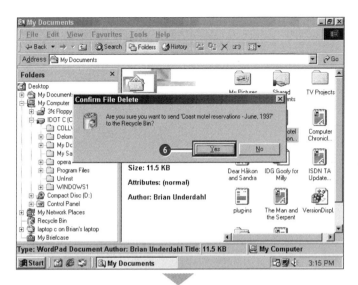

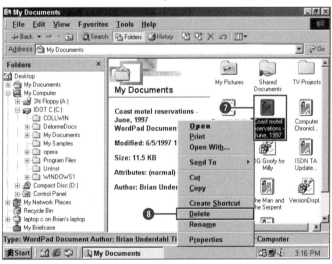

6 Click Yes to send the file to the Recycle Bin.

7 Alternatively, right-click the object.

8 Select Delete from the context menu.

TAKE NOTE

USING THE RECYCLE BIN IN WINDOWS EXPLORER

In addition to the Recycle Bin icon that appears prominently on your Windows Me desktop, another Recycle Bin icon appears in the Windows Explorer window. Both icons enable you to access the same Recycle Bin folder. The one that you choose to use is simply a matter of convenience.

HEED THE RECYCLE BIN WARNINGS

When you delete files, Windows Me will display a dialog box that asks you to confirm the deletion (unless you have configured the Recycle Bin so this message does not appear). Be sure to make note of the message that appears in this dialog box. In most cases the message will ask you to confirm that you want to send the files to the Recycle Bin. In some instances, however, the message will ask you to confirm that you want to delete the files. This difference is important because you can only recover files that were sent to the Recycle Bin — not those that were deleted. The delete confirmation message will appear when you delete files from diskettes, if you hold down the Shift key while you delete the files, or if you configure your PC to bypass the Recycle Bin. In each of these cases the Recycle Bin is not used, and deleted files are really gone.

FIND IT ONLINE

See **http://www.microsoft.com/Windows98/ usingwindows/work/articles/912Dec/RecycleBin.asp** for more on the Recycle Bin.

Viewing and Restoring Recycle Bin Contents

The Recycle Bin provides a great safety net when you accidentally delete files. But because Windows Me has no way to know which files you might later want to restore, it simply sends any file you delete from your hard disk to the Recycle Bin. As a result, your Recycle Bin may end up storing hundreds of different files in addition to the few that are important to you. Fortunately, you don't have to restore the deleted files on an all-or-nothing basis. Otherwise you might end up having to decide whether it was more trouble to re-create that one important file or to put up with having all those other deleted files returned, too.

Fortunately, once you've deleted files or folders, you can choose specific files or folders to restore or to delete permanently. You can also choose to restore or remove all the files at once.

The Recycle Bin actually has two different icons that tell you whether the Recycle Bin is full or empty. The empty Recycle Bin icon looks like an empty wastebasket. Once the Recycle Bin contains files or folders, its icon looks like a wastebasket full of papers.

The Recycle Bin has an important difference from the other folders on your hard disk. The Recycle Bin is the only place where two files or more can appear to have the same name. In reality, though, there is more to this than you might notice at first glance. In the Recycle Bin, files include their name, their original location, and the time that they were deleted in their description. It is this complete description that is unique — not just the file name on its own.

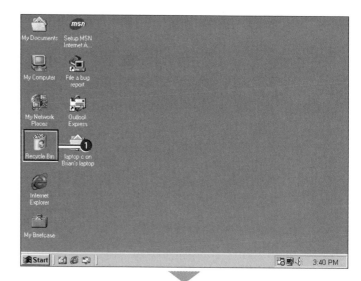

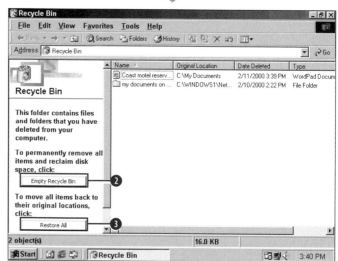

❶ Double-click the Recycle Bin icon on the desktop to open the Recycle Bin.

❷ Click Empty Recycle Bin to permanently delete everything from the Recycle Bin.

❸ Alternatively, click Restore All to return all objects to their original locations.

CROSS-REFERENCE

See "Emptying the Recycle Bin" later in this chapter for information about making the Recycle Bin more manageable.

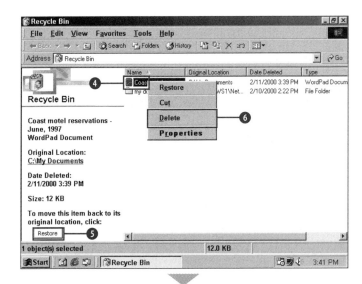

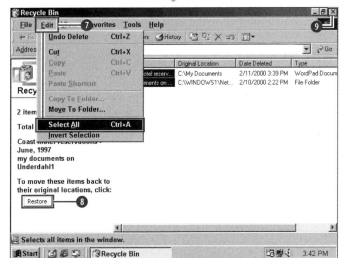

You may be surprised to discover that Windows Me doesn't have a Recycle Bin for files you delete from diskettes. That's because the Recycle Bin stores the deleted files on the disk, and there isn't enough room to enable deleted files to remain on the diskette. Windows Me does warn you of this when you delete files from diskettes, but the warning simply comes in the form of slightly different wording in the confirmation dialog box.

TAKE NOTE

▶ NO NETWORK RECYCLE BIN

If you delete files from another computer on your network, make certain you won't want to recover those files later. Because there is no Recycle Bin for network drives, files you delete on the network are erased immediately once you confirm the deletion. If you want a second chance, always delete only those files that are on your own hard drives.

▶ THE RECYCLE BIN REMEMBERS FILE ORIGINS

Fortunately, the Recycle Bin remembers each file's origin, so you can more easily determine which copy of the file you wish to restore by looking in the Original Location column.

④ Click an object to view its description.

⑤ Click Restore to return the selected object to its original location.

⑥ Alternatively, right-click the item and select Delete to permanently delete the file.

⑦ Alternatively, select Edit ⇨ Select All to select all objects in the Recycle Bin.

⑧ Click Restore to return all objects to their original locations.

⑨ Click the Close button.

FIND IT ONLINE

See **http://www.execsoft.com/undelete/about/ undelete.asp** to learn about Emergency Undelete.

Emptying the Recycle Bin

The Recycle Bin can generally hold quite a few files, but it does not have unlimited space available. If you allow the Recycle Bin to become too full, Windows Me uses the *first in, first out* method of automatically removing items from the Recycle Bin. This means that the items that have been in the Recycle Bin the longest are deleted first to make room for new items. This arrangement prevents the Recycle Bin from completely filling up your hard disk. Letting Windows Me handle the Recycle Bin contents automatically may not be the best idea, however.

By default, Windows Me sets the size of your Recycle Bin to 10 percent of the size of your hard disk. On a 2GB hard disk, this means that 200MB of disk space might be set aside to hold the Recycle Bin contents. Depending on the size of the typical files on your system, this amount of space could represent hundreds or even thousands of files. It could also be completely used up by a few or possibly even one very large file.

You can choose to remove all of the Recycle Bin contents in one step; or if you prefer you can select individual objects to delete (or restore). Remember, though, that there's no Recycle Bin for the Recycle Bin. Once you delete items from the Recycle Bin, they're gone forever and can't be restored. The Undo button does not restore a file that was deleted from the Recycle Bin. The Recycle Bin gives you a second chance, but there's no third chance. If you have any doubts, don't empty the Recycle Bin.

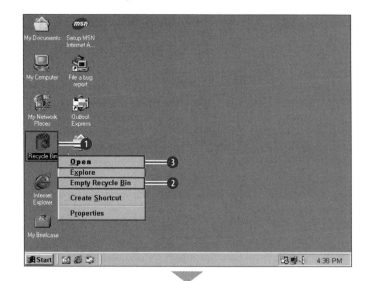

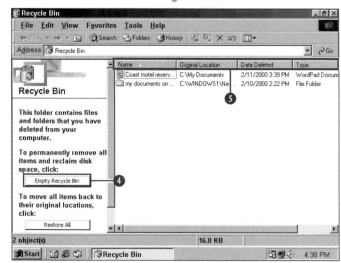

➊ Right-click the Recycle Bin icon on the desktop to open the context menu.

➋ Click Empty Recycle Bin to permanently delete everything from the Recycle Bin.

➌ Alternatively, click Open to view the Recycle Bin contents.

➍ Click Empty Recycle Bin to permanently delete everything from the Recycle Bin.

➎ To sort the listing according to one of the criteria, click a column heading.

CROSS-REFERENCE

See "Setting Recycle Bin Properties" (next) for information about controlling the Recycle Bin.

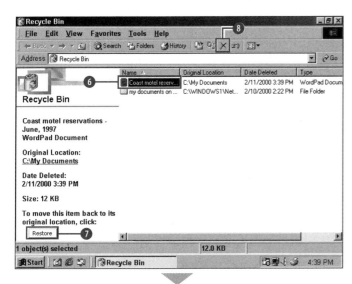

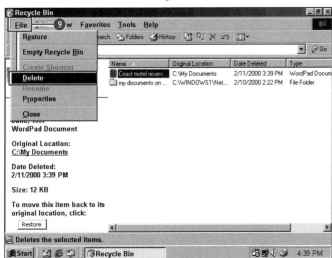

You may want to sort the Recycle Bin file listing to help determine which files to delete and which ones to restore. The easiest way to sort the file listing is to click one of the column heads to sort using the selected column. Click the column again to sort the items in reverse order.

MAKING A FAST SELECTION

When you first open the Recycle Bin you have the option of completely emptying it by deleting all the objects. If you'd rather save some of the items in case you might need them in the future, the best course is to select the files and folders you want to keep, choose Edit ⇨ Invert Selection, and then delete the selected files. Inverting the selection deselects the objects you selected and adds all the others to the selection. This technique makes it easy to remove objects you won't ever need from the Recycle Bin.

CHOOSING THE CORRECT FILE

Because the Recycle Bin can contain several files with similar names, it is important to make certain you select the correct files to restore or to delete. Make use of the information in the Original Location and Date Deleted columns to help you identify the correct files.

⑥ Click an object to view its description.

⑦ Click Restore to return the selected object to its original location.

⑧ Alternatively, click the Delete button to permanently delete the selected file.

⑨ Another way to permanently delete the file is to select File ⇨ Delete.

Setting Recycle Bin Properties

The Recycle Bin includes default settings that dictate how the Recycle Bin works. These settings include such things as the amount of space that is used by the Recycle Bin, the messages Windows Me displays when you use the Recycle Bin, and the option to choose whether the Recycle Bin is used at all. You can change any of these settings to better suit your needs. For example, you might choose to limit the size of the Recycle Bin on one of your disks if you are running low on disk space. Or you might decide that you don't want to save any of the files deleted from one of your drives.

Even if you do decide to use the Recycle Bin, you may not always want to confirm that you want to send files to the Recycle Bin. Sure, the first few hundred times you see that message you may not mind it, but eventually you will probably get tired of confirming that you really do want to send files to the Recycle Bin. In that case, you can change a setting and thereafter skip the dialog box. Then when you delete an object, Windows Me will send it straight to the Recycle Bin without asking for your permission.

Windows Me normally uses the same Recycle Bin settings for all of your hard disks. In most cases there is little reason to change this, but you might have reason to if you've set aside one hard disk for a special purpose and need to make certain you have enough space available. If you need to dedicate an entire hard disk to the project, you might be concerned about running out of space if

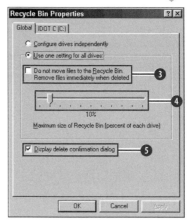

① Right-click the Recycle Bin icon on the desktop to open the context menu.

② Click Properties to view the Recycle Bin Properties dialog box.

③ Check here to delete files without using the Recycle Bin.

④ Drag the slider to adjust the size of the Recycle Bin.

⑤ Remove this check to skip the confirmation dialog box that appears each time you delete a file.

CROSS-REFERENCE

See "Sending Objects to the Recycle Bin" earlier in this chapter for information about skipping the Recycle Bin.

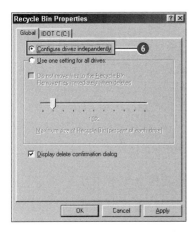

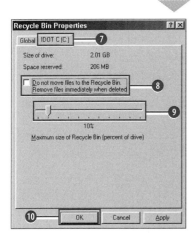

the Recycle Bin uses up disk space. You might also want to increase the Recycle Bin size on a separate hard disk that you have set aside for your document files to provide additional protection for those files.

TAKE NOTE

▶ BE SAFE NOT SORRY

You can choose to skip the Recycle Bin and delete files directly. It's hard to make a good case for using this option, because it eliminates any chance to recover from an accidental file deletion. Rather than choose to skip the Recycle Bin, it's better to eliminate the dialog box that confirms your deletions. If you like, you can combine this with reducing the Recycle Bin size to the minimum effective size, which is 1 percent of your hard disk space.

▶ CHOOSING YOUR CONFIRMATION SETTING

Even if you choose to use different Recycle Bin settings for each of your hard drives, you can choose only one setting for the delete confirmation dialog box. The delete confirmation dialog box will either appear for all of your drives or for none of them. This uniform setting is intended to reduce confusion and the possibility of errors.

---

⑥ *Click here to configure each drive separately.*

▶ *This is useful only if you have more than one hard drive installed.*

⑦ *Click the tab for the drive you want to configure.*

⑧ *Click here to delete files from this drive without using the Recycle Bin.*

⑨ *Drag the slider to adjust the size of the Recycle Bin for this drive.*

⑩ *Click OK to complete the task.*

FIND IT ONLINE

See **http://www.microsoft.com/windows98/using windows/maintaining/tips/beginner/diskcleanup.asp** for information on clearing up disk clutter.

Personal Workbook

Q&A

1 What will happen if you don't click the New button between searches?

_____

_____

_____

2 How can you specify that you want to limit your search to files larger than a certain size?

_____

_____

_____

3 How can you temporarily bypass the Recycle Bin and delete a file permanently?

_____

_____

_____

4 Why is it more dangerous to delete files from diskettes than from hard disks?

_____

_____

_____

5 How can you change the Recycle Bin sort order?

_____

_____

_____

6 What steps must you take before saving a search for future use?

_____

_____

_____

7 How can you reuse a search you've saved?

_____

_____

_____

8 How can you find a file if all you know is two words that occur together somewhere in the file name?

_____

_____

_____

ANSWERS: PAGE 392

EXTRA PRACTICE

1. Find all the files *created* in the past month.

2. Search for all the Bitmap image files on your hard disk.

3. Select and restore one of the files in the Recycle Bin.

4. Prevent the delete confirmation dialog box from appearing when you delete files.

5. Create and save a search that finds all your word processor document files for the past two weeks.

6. Find all the files that are more than 750KB.

REAL-WORLD APPLICATIONS

✔ You do a lot of work on your PC. To make it easy to back up your files, you create and save a search that locates all the files you've created each day.

✔ You suspect that someone modified your files while you were away from the office for a few days. You do a search for files created or modified during that time so that you can see if they changed any critical information.

✔ You've been assigned to prepare a confidential report that must not appear on your hard disk. After you make a backup on a diskette, you hold down the Shift key when you delete the file from your hard disk so that it is not saved in the Recycle Bin.

Visual Quiz

How do you display this dialog box? Which part of the dialog box do you use to control how much disk space the Recycle Bin uses? What would you do if you didn't want to confirm that deleted items should go to the Recycle Bin?

_____

_____

_____

_____

_____

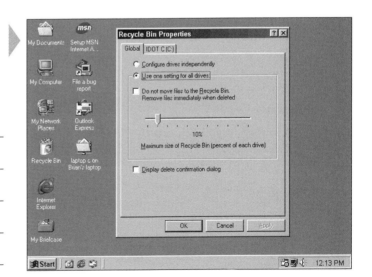

CHAPTER 7

**MASTER
THESE
SKILLS**

▶ **Finding Computers on Your Network**

▶ **Adding Network Places**

▶ **Sharing Your Files**

▶ **Finding Files on Your Network**

▶ **Sharing a Printer**

▶ **Monitoring Your Network Connections**

▶ **Adding an Internet Connection**

▶ **Sharing an Internet Connection**

Mastering Local Networks

Computer networks are becoming common. They are no longer only found in office settings, but have now become very important in many homes, too. Windows Me has everything you need to set up your network, and it makes connecting your PCs a very easy prospect.

You don't even have to be running Windows Me on all of the PCs on your network. The Windows Me Home Networking Wizard can help you set up all of the Windows-based PCs even if they are running older Windows versions.

Even if you don't have several computers connected in a local network, you will likely make use of the biggest network of all — the Internet. This chapter shows you how to make a connection from your PC to the Internet, and how to share that connection with the other PCs that are on your network. You will also learn how to monitor your network connection. Using this feature you can see who else on your network is using the files on your system.

Before starting on this chapter you should make certain that your network is completely installed and that it is working correctly. If you are having problems making your network function properly you may want to refer to Chapter 3 for more information on using the Windows Me troubleshooters before you continue.

Even if you don't yet have a network, you'll probably want to browse through this chapter. Seeing the examples may make it easier for you to determine whether a network would offer you enough benefits to make it worthwhile. Installing a network is generally not too difficult as long as you are careful to follow the directions.

If you haven't used a network before, you're in for a pleasant surprise. It is amazing how much easier it can be to get things done when you can share network resources without ever leaving your chair. If you need to use the fancy color printer that is in the next room, or want to play a game with someone on your network, you can do so with a few clicks of your mouse. That's a lot more convenient than copying things to diskettes and running down the hall to borrow someone's PC!

Finding Computers on Your Network

One of the first things you will probably want to do once you have a network is find out what other computers you can find on your network. If you are using Windows Me on a home network, you probably already know what you expect to see, so this will be a good confirmation that things are working the way you expect them to.

New network users are often surprised when they access their network for the first time. That's because initially nothing may appear when you click the My Network Places icon. This icon enables you to locate and view the shared resources on the network. These can include the files, folders, drives, or printers that have been made available for your use on the network. But initially nothing is shared, so nothing will be available in My Network Places until some items are shared. That is, you must explicitly share the items that you want someone to be able to access through the network. If everyone on your network is selfish, then no one will be able to use anything except what is on their own computer.

If all of the PCs on your network use Windows Me, Windows 98, or Windows 95, your network will have a *workgroup* that all of the computers are a part of. Some networks use *domains*—a more secure form of network organization that generally requires at least one PC running Windows 2000 or Windows NT. For a small home or office network it is generally best to use a single workgroup, because this reduces the complications involved in accessing network resources.

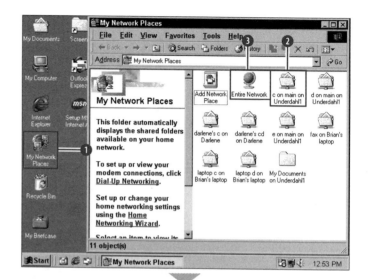

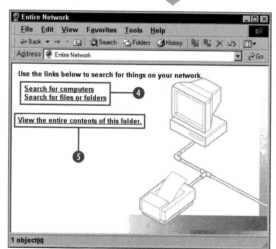

① Double-click the My Network Places icon to open the My Network Places folder.

② Double-click an item to open it.

③ Alternatively, double-click the Entire Network icon.

④ Click one of these links to search the network.

⑤ Alternatively, click the entire contents link to view the workgroups on the network.

CROSS-REFERENCE

See "Sharing Your Files" later in this chapter.

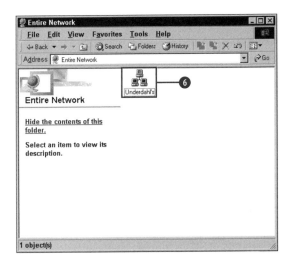

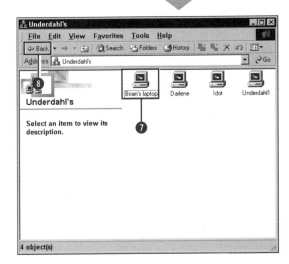

USE THE FOLDERS EXPLORER BAR

You may find that locating specific computers or folders on your network in the My Network Places window is a little confusing. To make the process a bit easier you may want to click the Folders button in the toolbar to display the Folders Explorer Bar. When the Folders Explorer Bar is displayed, use it to open the computer or folder that you wish to use. You can then click the Folders Explorer Bar Close button to regain the space that the Folders Explorer Bar used so that you can view more items in the contents pane.

TROUBLESHOOTING NETWORKS

One of the most common problems people encounter with their small network is the inability to see the shared resources on other computers. To resolve this problem, start by making certain that something has actually been shared on each computer. If this does not solve the problem, try restarting each of the networked PCs one at a time. Don't restart all of them at the same time — you want each computer to be able to see other operating computers when they restart. This is especially true if you have changed any network settings.

⑥ *Double-click a workgroup icon to view the computers in the workgroup.*

⑦ *Double-click a computer icon to view its shared resources.*

⑧ *Alternatively, click the Back button to return to the previous folder.*

Adding Network Places

As you use your network, it's likely that you use some of the same things quite often and others hardly at all. For example, if you have a shared folder where everyone stores certain document files, you will probably find that you want to open that folder far more often than many of the other shared folders. You can make the task of opening the items that you need to use often a bit easier by adding them as *network places*. A network place is simply a quick shortcut that takes you directly to a computer or a folder somewhere on your network. You can also use network places as shortcuts to folders on the Internet — such as Web folders or FTP sites.

Once you have added a folder as a network place, an icon for that folder will appear in the My Network Places window and in Windows Explorer. You can then use the icon to quickly open the shared folder without navigating through several different levels to reach your destination.

If you create a network place icon that is a link to an FTP site — a *File Transfer Protocol* site where you can upload or download files — you will also have to specify how to log on to the site. In most cases FTP sites use an anonymous logon. If a site requires a specific logon, you should obtain the proper user name and password before you attempt to set up a network place icon for the site.

The easiest way to locate folders that you want to add as network places is usually to click the Browse button as shown in the figures. Then open the workgroup and select the folders on a specific computer.

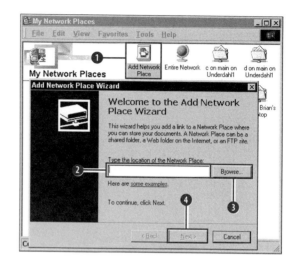

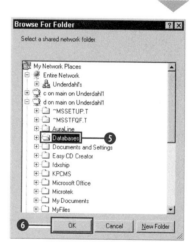

❶ Double-click the Add Network Place icon to open the Add Network Place Wizard.

❷ Type the network place address.

❸ Alternatively, click the Browse button to view the servers on the network.

❹ If you typed the address, click Next to continue.

❺ Select the shared folder you wish to use.

❻ Click OK to continue.

CROSS-REFERENCE

See "Finding Files on Your Network" later in this chapter.

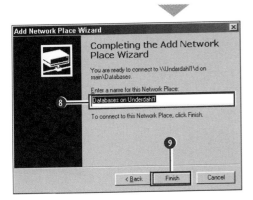

ADDING NETWORK FOLDERS

When you are setting up network places you can select only those folders that have been specifically shared. When folders are shared, any subfolders contained within those folders are also available on the network. If someone shares a master folder that contains a number of other folders, you can open the master folder and select any of the subfolders as a network place. You can create the network place, and then by using it you will not have to navigate the entire network to get to the correct place within a folder or its subfolders. Remember, though, that you cannot create a network place for a folder that has not been shared.

NETWORK COMPUTER NAMES

If you type in the location of a network folder rather than browsing for the folder, remember to use two backslashes (\\) in front of the computer name. Follow this with another backslash and the name of the shared folder, as in \\Brian's laptop\laptop C. If you browse for network places, Windows Me automatically enters the correct computer name.

⑦ *Click Next to continue.*

⑧ *Optionally, enter a new name for the new network place.*

⑨ *Click Finish to continue.*

▶ *Once you have added a new network place, Windows Me opens the folder.*

FIND IT ONLINE

For an FTP site that makes a great network place, see
ftp://ftp.microsoft.com/softlib/MSLFILES/.

Sharing Your Files

Sharing is the essence of networking. Without sharing there is really no reason to have a network. *Sharing* is the process of enabling other people access to files, folders, and printers. Initially, nothing on the network is shared — you must initiate sharing explicitly for each resource that you want to be available on the network.

If your PC is part of a network that includes file servers, you may find that the network administrator has already set up a limited amount of sharing on those servers. You, however, will probably have to set up any folders you wish to share on your PC. Of course, if you are responsible for your own network, you must set up sharing yourself on all of the PCs.

Windows Me file sharing is done at the folder level. If you want to share a set of files you do so by sharing the folder containing those files. If you wish to restrict the access to certain files, you can place those files into a different folder and change the passwords that are used to access those folders. For example, you can set up certain folders to contain files that can be read but not changed. You can set up other folders for more complete access. Some application programs also enable you to specify passwords for access to specific documents.

You can use several access settings. You can enable *read-only* access so that visitors can open or copy a file but cannot delete, modify, or create a file. *Full* access enables a visitor to do anything that you can do. *Depends on Password* access enables someone with the correct password to read or to modify a file, depending on the password they enter.

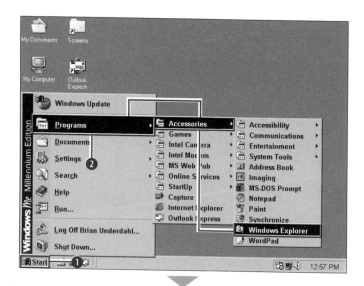

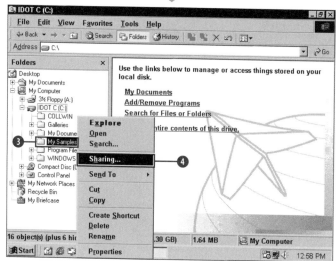

❶ Click the Start button.

❷ Select Programs ➪ Accessories ➪ Windows Explorer.

❸ Right-click the folder you wish to share.

❹ Select Sharing from the context menu.

CROSS-REFERENCE

See "Finding Files on Your Network" later in this chapter.

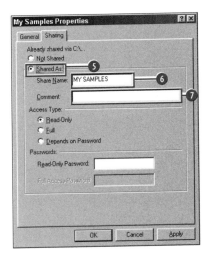

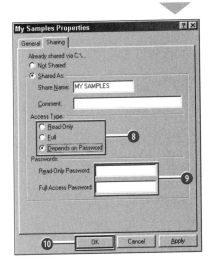

UNDERSTANDING NETWORK ACCESS

When you share a folder, Windows Me provides, by default, read-only access to anyone who can access the folder on your network. If you have a need for freer access on your network, you must use the access type controls to set up the access that is granted to users. Windows Me does not enable you to restrict access except through the use of passwords.

CONTROLLING WHAT YOU SHARE

When you share a drive or a folder, everything contained in it is also shared. You can restrict access to a folder on a shared drive or to a folder contained within a shared folder, but you must do so explicitly. So, for example, if your \My Documents folder contains a folder named "Resume" and you share \My Documents, anyone on the network can access \My Documents\Resume unless you specifically restrict the access to the \My Documents\Resume folder. For this reason it is generally better to explicitly share specific folders rather than to share your entire hard disk.

⑤ *Click Shared As to enable sharing.*

⑥ *Optionally, enter a share name for the folder.*

⑦ *Optionally, enter a comment for the folder.*

⑧ *Select the type of access you want to enable.*

⑨ *Optionally, enter access passwords.*

⑩ *Click OK to apply your changes.*

FIND IT ONLINE

For more information on how to set up a simple network, see **http://www.users.dircon.co.uk/ ~tbrown/network/**.

Finding Files on Your Network

The techniques you learned in Chapter 6 for searching for files on your computer are similar to the ones you can use to find files on your network. Even so, there are some important differences that you need to be aware of when you are looking for files on a network. In this section you learn how to quickly locate what you need on your network.

One of the important differences you may encounter when looking for files on your network is that computers may not always be available. A computer may be turned off, the network connection may have been disrupted, or the owner may simply have decided to stop sharing their files. Any of these events can occur without any notice, and they can easily prevent you from finding files that you are quite sure are really there.

Just as when you're searching your PC, you can narrow the search by specifying the starting folder rather than searching the entire drive. This is often a good idea because it reduces network traffic and speeds the search. Depending on the speed of your network, the network traffic level, and the number of files that are contained in the folders being searched, a network file search can take considerably longer to complete than a search on your own PC.

Windows Me needs a means to identify the computers on a network so that it can specify the exact location of files on the network. On your computer Windows Me uses the drive letter, a colon, and a backslash to identify the drive where files can be found. This approach isn't

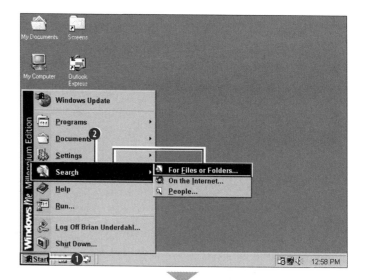

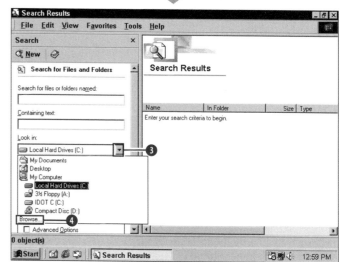

❶ Click the Start button.

❷ Select Search ➪ For Files or Folders.

❸ Click the down arrow at the right side of the Look in list box.

❹ Select Browse.

CROSS-REFERENCE

See "Finding Computers on Your Network" earlier in this chapter.

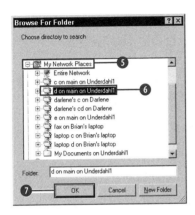

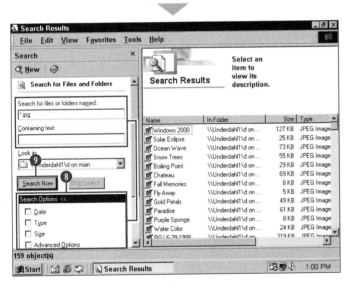

practical on the network because there would be no way to discern whether C:\ referred to drive C on your local PC or to drive C on one of the other computers on the network. To remedy this problem, Windows Me uses *UNC*—Universal Naming Conventions—to designate computers that are on the network. For example, if a computer is named Brian, on the network that computer would be referred to as \\Brian.

TAKE NOTE

▶ ONE AT A TIME

When you are looking for files on the network you can search only one computer at a time. You cannot search the entire network at once, so if you aren't sure where a file is located you may end up searching several times before you are successful.

▶ NETWORK PLACES ICONS REMAIN

If you have created network places icons, those icons will remain even if the folder they refer to is no longer available. As a result, you may receive an error message telling you that the network place is no longer accessible, if you click on the icon. If you receive this type of error message, check your network connection by trying to access other places on the network

⑤ Click My Network Places.

⑥ Select the folder you wish to search.

⑦ Click OK to continue.

⑧ Enter the search criteria.

⑨ Click Search Now to complete the task.

FIND IT ONLINE

For easy networking kits, see **http://computingcentral. msn.com/topics/networking/newsletter2.asp.**

Sharing a Printer

If you have a home network to connect several PCs, one of the biggest advantages may be your ability to share your printers on the network. You probably don't need a printer connected to every PC, but it sure can be convenient to be able to print directly from any of your computers by using a network-connected printer. Of course, by sharing a printer it is probably a bit easier to afford a higher quality printer, too, because one really good printer will probably cost less than a couple of poorer quality ones.

In order to use a network printer, you must have the correct printer drivers installed. This is really no different than using a printer connected directly to your PC. Because your application programs rely on Windows Me to control the printer, Windows Me must know the correct commands to use for your printer — no matter where it is located. The only real difference between installing a local printer and a networked printer comes when you specify the *printer port* — the place where the printer is physically connected. The port is simply the address to which your PC sends the print commands. When you select a network printer, you are sending those commands across the network to the PC connected to the printer. That PC then forwards the commands to the printer.

When you share your printer on the network you are allowing other people on your network to print their documents on your printer. This can mean that you will use far more paper and other printer supplies than you might if you were the only user of that printer. Be prepared to service a shared printer more often.

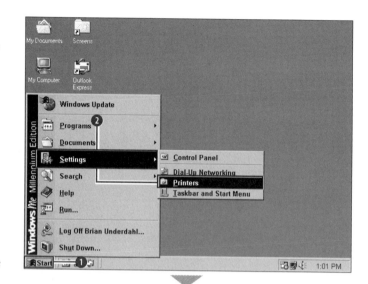

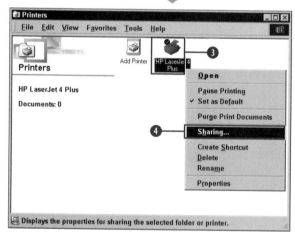

① Click the Start button.

② Select Settings ➪ Printers.

③ Right-click the printer you wish to share.

④ Select Sharing from the context menu.

CROSS-REFERENCE

See "Adding New Hardware" in Chapter 12.

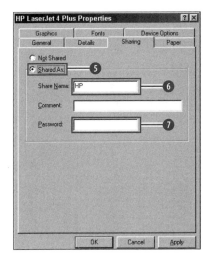

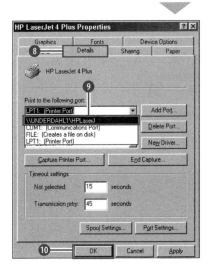

USE THE NETWORK EFFECTIVELY

Adding a second printer to a PC is certainly possible, but it is not always the easiest task to successfully accomplish. In most cases you will have to locate an open expansion slot in your PC, and you may encounter problems with system conflicts, too. But because virtually all PCs already include one printer port as standard equipment, you can avoid these problems by spreading extra printers around your network and sharing them. You eliminate the hassle and expense of adding extra hardware, and you spend far less time dealing with configuration issues, too.

INSTALL LOCAL PRINTERS FIRST

Be sure to first install the printer on the *print server* — the computer connected to the printer — and then share the printer before you attempt to install it on the other computers. Otherwise, you may see error messages when the printer cannot be found on the network. In fact, other people on the network will not even be able to set up the network printer unless you already have it installed and set up to be shared.

⑤ Select the Shared As button.

⑥ Optionally, enter a share name for the printer.

⑦ If you want to require a password to use this printer, enter it in the Password box.

⑧ Alternatively, click the Details tab.

⑨ Select the network printer to which you wish to connect.

⑩ Click OK to complete the task.

FIND IT ONLINE

For information on home automation, see
http://www.homeautomation.org/.

Monitoring Your Network Connections

One of the biggest problems with sharing your computer's resources on your network is the fact that other people are sharing your computer. Those other people who are accessing your system across the network are tapping some of your computer's power and performance.

Normally you aren't likely to notice much performance degradation when other people are accessing your PC, but sometimes you may not want to risk any problems. For example, if you are creating a CD-R or CD-RW disc, it is possible that the process could be interrupted or even aborted if someone else on the network tries to modify or copy the files you are writing to disc. This could also be a problem if you are backing up your files and have chosen to back up the same files that someone tries to access from their PC. Or maybe you are working on a sensitive project and simply don't want to risk having someone accessing data that they shouldn't see. Whatever the reason, you can monitor and control the network access to your Windows Me PC.

Net Watcher enables you to monitor and control network connections to your PC. As the figures show, you can choose to monitor the connections in several different ways. The default view shows who is connected. You can also choose to see which folders or files are being accessed. When you select the folders view, you can modify the sharing properties for the shared folders. You could, for example, temporarily allow full access to a folder that normally has just read-only access. Full access enables a visitor to create, modify, or even delete files in the shared folder.

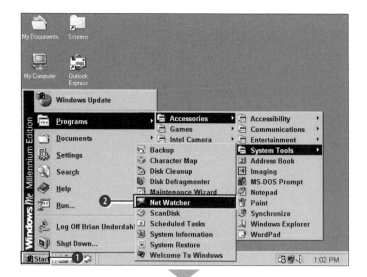

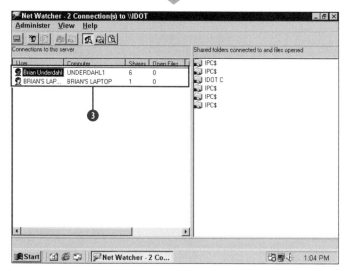

❶ Click the Start button.

❷ Select Programs ➪ Accessories ➪ System Tools ➪ Net Watcher.

❸ Select a user to view his or her connections.

CROSS-REFERENCE

See "Sharing Your Files" earlier in this chapter.

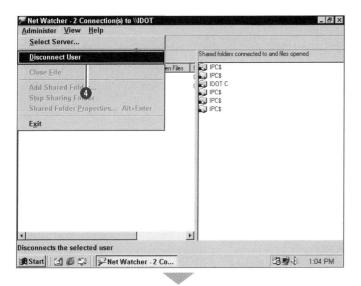

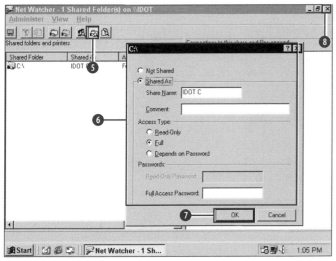

TAKE NOTE

USE CARE DISCONNECTING USERS

Even though you can disconnect network visitors without giving them any warning, it is generally not a good idea to do so. If you disconnect someone who has files open on your system, you could cause them to lose any unsaved work, you might damage the file they had open on your computer, and you run the risk of causing either their PC, your PC, or both to crash. It is usually far safer to ask them to disconnect from your computer so that they have the opportunity to close any files properly. Once they have disconnected, you can restrict network access for as long as necessary, and then re-enable that access when the restriction is no longer needed.

NET WATCHER MAY NOT BE INSTALLED

Net Watcher is not installed automatically when you install Windows Me. If Net Watcher is not available on your System Tools menu, you can find it in the System Tools category on the Windows Setup tab of the Add/Remove Programs Properties dialog box. You will probably need to insert your Windows Me CD-ROM to install Net Watcher.

④ Select Administer ⇨ Disconnect User to break their connection to your system.

⑤ Click the View Folders icon to control the sharing options.

⑥ Press Alt+Enter to display the properties dialog box for the folder and make any necessary adjustments.

⑦ Click OK to close the dialog box.

⑧ Click the Close button.

FIND IT ONLINE

For information on what a network can do for you, see http://www.3com.com/client/ipg/home/learn/intro/network.html.

Adding an Internet Connection

I f you aren't already connected to the Internet, adding an Internet connection is probably one of your top priorities. This is true whether you already have an Internet account and need to set it up on your Windows Me PC or if you are setting up your first Internet connection.

To connect to the Internet you need a physical connection to an Internet server, either via a modem or through your network. You also need an account that grants you Internet access. For dial-up connections— Internet connections through a device such as a modem— an *ISP* (Internet Service Provider) generally provides this account. You can choose any provider that meets your needs, including large ISPs such as Earthlink or a local service provider that you will find listed in the Internet category of your telephone directory.

In choosing an ISP, make certain that there is a local access number that you can use. Paying long-distance charges on top of your monthly access fees could result in huge bills very quickly. Also be sure to check the type of local access that is provided. You'll want fast access that is compatible with your modem. In some areas you can use 56K modems, ISDN or DSL connections, or even cable modems, but you'll need to check to see which service is available in your area. If your only option is to use a standard 56K modem, keep in mind that your connection speed will likely be quite a bit less than 56K. In reality, fewer than half of the phone lines in the country support 56K connections. Depending on your location, however, you may not have any other option.

❶ Click the Start button.

❷ Select Programs ➪ Accessories ➪ Communications ➪ Internet Connection Wizard.

❸ Select the appropriate option to suit your needs.

❹ Click Next to continue.

CROSS-REFERENCE

See "Using Internet Explorer" in Chapter 9.

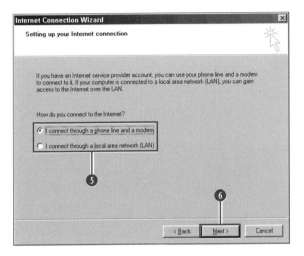

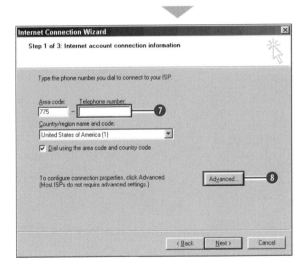

In most cases setting up a dial-up connection is very simple and straightforward. Although the example shown in the figures on these pages and the next two pages show you how to set the advanced connection options, you may not have to make any changes to these settings for most connections.

Continued

Continued

TAKE NOTE

▶ MAKING YOUR FIRST CONNECTION

Although the figures show how to set a manual connection to the Internet, the procedure is very similar if you are setting up a new account or if you choose to transfer your existing account to a new computer. In each case you must follow the prompts and answer a similar set of questions.

▶ WHY YOU NEED AN ISP

Although no one actually owns the Internet, to connect to the Internet you will probably need to use the services of an Internet Service Provider (ISP). An ISP provides the physical connection between the Internet and your PC. In most cases this connection is through your modem and phone line, but it may also be through an ISDN adapter, a DSL adapter, or through a cable modem. ISPs generally charge for the right to connect to the Internet through their equipment.

⑤ *Select your connection method.*

⑥ *Click Next to continue.*

⑦ *Enter the dial-up telephone number*

⑧ *Optionally, click the Advanced button to configure the advanced settings.*

FIND IT ONLINE

See **http://www.pageland.com/isp/frames/** for information on how to pick your Internet Service Provider.

Adding an Internet Connection
Continued

In addition to setting up the access number and any advanced settings that may be required for your account, you will need to enter your user name and password. In most cases this will not be the same user name and password that you use to log on to Windows Me. Your ISP may refer to your user name as your account name or your logon name.

When you enter your password, the password will not appear in the Password text box. You will see an asterisk in place of each character that you type, but because you cannot see what you are typing, it is easy to make a mistake. If you are unsure whether you typed in the correct password, reenter it to make certain it is correct. Both user names and passwords may be case sensitive. Entering either your user name or your password incorrectly can prevent you from logging on.

If you are concerned about security, you may not want to enter your password when you are setting up your Internet connection. If you do enter both your user name and password, anyone who uses your PC will be able to access your Internet account simply by opening Internet Explorer. Of course, if you do not enter your password it will be necessary to enter it manually when you wish to connect to the Internet. This will prevent your system from automatically opening your Internet connection and will effectively prevent other people from accessing the Internet through your PC unless you provide them with your password.

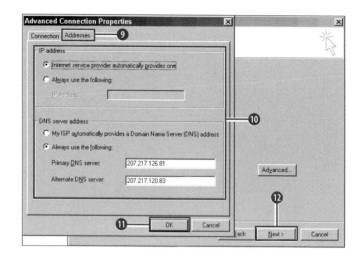

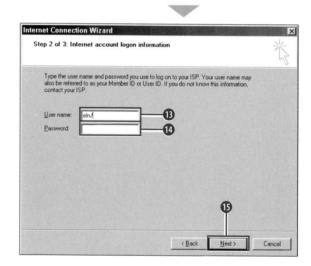

⑨ Click the Addresses tab.

⑩ Make any necessary IP or DNS address changes.

⑪ Click OK.

⑫ Click Next to continue.

⑬ Enter your Internet account user name.

⑭ Optionally, enter your Internet password.

⑮ Click Next to continue.

CROSS-REFERENCE

See "Visiting Web Sites" in Chapter 9.

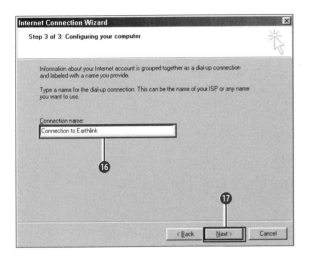

STATIC IP ADDRESSES

If you connect to the Internet through a dial-up connection you will probably be assigned a different IP address each time you log on to the Internet. As the first figure shows, you can also specify a specific IP address if one has been assigned by your ISP. The option to use a *static* IP address — one that is always the same — is generally needed only if your PC is acting as a Web server. If you have a Web page that is hosted on a server that is provided by your ISP, you do not need a static IP address.

DNS ADDRESSES

The second advanced address setting that you may need to configure is the DNS server address. *DNS servers* are the computers on the Internet that translate typed Web page addresses into series of numbers that are the true Web page addresses. Although DNS servers are normally accessed automatically, your ISP may specify addresses that you should use to access these servers. Using a specific DNS address may make accessing Web pages slightly faster and more reliable for some connections.

⑯ *Enter a name for this connection.*

⑰ *Click Next to continue.*

▶ *You may also be asked if you wish to set up an e-mail account.*

⑱ *Click the Finish button to complete the task.*

Sharing an Internet Connection

O
ne of the greatest benefits of having a home
network is that all of your PCs can share a single Internet connection. This can be a great
advantage if you happen to have a high speed — or
broadband — connection such as DSL, cable, or even
ISDN, but it is a great idea even if you use a dial-up modem. Because everyone on the network shares a single
Internet connection, you only need one connection and
one account for your whole network.

You may wonder if your Internet connection is actually fast enough to share. In reality, most of the time
your connection is probably sitting idle. Even when you
are actively browsing the Web, you're likely spending
quite a bit of that time just viewing a Web page that you
have downloaded. This usually means that even though
you are connected, no data is flowing across your connection. The only time you're likely to notice any slow-
down is if several people are downloading large files at
the same time. Otherwise you may not even realize that
anyone else is using the same connection.

It is important to understand that most ISPs enable
only a single logon at one time for each account. In
many cases they require that each user have their own
Internet access account. If you share your Internet connection with all of the PCs on your network you may be
technically violating your account agreement with your
ISP. But because you will only be using a single connection to access the Internet, your ISP will have no way to
determine how many users are accessing the connection
unless you tell them.

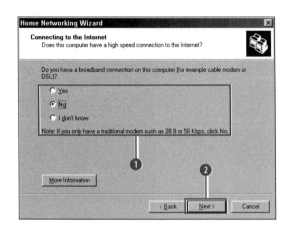

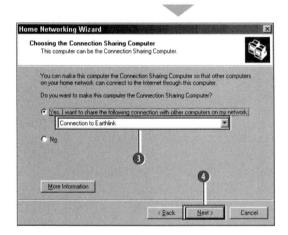

▶ *Select Internet Connection
Sharing in the Internet Tools
category on the Windows
Setup tab of the Add/Remove
Programs Properties
dialog box.*

▶ *When the Home Networking
Wizard appears, click Next to
continue.*

❶ *Select the type of connection
you use.*

❷ *Click Next to continue.*

❸ *Choose the connection to
share.*

❹ *Click Next to continue.*

CROSS-REFERENCE

See Chapter 9 for more information on using the
Internet.

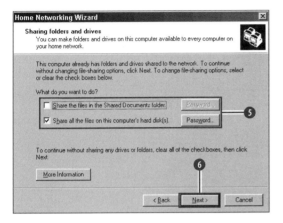

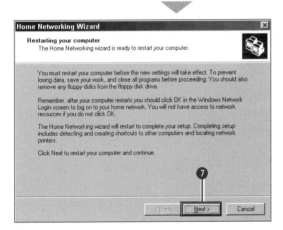

TAKE NOTE

HOW ICS WORKS

In order to share an Internet connection on your network, each of the computers that will use the shared connection must use the TCP/IP protocol on the network adapters that they use to access the network. When you enable connection sharing, each network adapter must be assigned a static IP address. This IP address is then used to send Web pages to the correct computer on your network. These IP addresses are used only on your local network, and they are not visible to computers that are not connected to the network. When you set up sharing on your Internet connection, your PC that is providing the Internet access to the network is automatically configured with the correct IP addresses. The remaining computers must be configured using the client disk that is produced when you set up Internet Connection Sharing.

USE YOUR BEST CONNECTION

If you have more than one type of Internet connection, make certain you use the PC with the fastest connection as the PC that provides Internet access to your network. This PC should also be running Windows Me.

⑤ *Select any sharing options.*

⑥ *Click Next to continue.*

▶ *Click Next on the following screen(s) to complete the wizard.*

⑦ *Click Next to restart your PC and continue.*

▶ *After your system restarts, Windows Me will create a client diskette you must use to set up your other PCs.*

FIND IT ONLINE

For more on sharing Internet connections, see **http://www.microsoft.com/windows98/USINGWINDOWS/WORK/ARTICLES/906JUN/SETOUR1.ASP**.

Personal Workbook

Q&A

1 How can you tell when you're seeing the name of a computer on the network?

_____

_____

_____

2 When you're trying to find a file, how much of the network can you search at any one time?

_____

_____

_____

3 Are folders that are contained within a shared folder on a network also shared on the network?

_____

_____

_____

4 What happens to your network places icons when the computers they refer to are no longer available?

_____

_____

_____

5 What connection speed is necessary if you want to share an Internet connection?

_____

_____

_____

6 Why does a network printer need drivers installed on PCs that aren't connected to the printer?

_____

_____

_____

7 How can you allow people access to master documents in a shared folder without allowing them to make changes?

_____

_____

_____

8 Who provides you with a connection to the Internet?

_____

_____

ANSWERS: PAGE 393

EXTRA PRACTICE

1 Find all the files with a .doc extension that are available in one of the shared folders on your network.

2 Figure out a method of enabling access to some of your document files without making all the files available on the network.

3 Open My Network Places and determine how many computers are on the network.

4 Look in your Printers folder and see which printers are shared on the network.

5 Create a new connection to the Internet.

6 Enable the other users on your network to share your Internet connection.

REAL-WORLD APPLICATIONS

✔ You're about to order a newer, faster computer to help you get more done. You network your new and old systems so that you have a backup system in the event of problems with the new computer.

✔ You install an ISDN line in your home and then allow the whole family to share the same Internet connection. This ends up saving you money because you don't need separate accounts for everyone.

✔ You want to help make your daughter's school assignments look neater. You buy a color inkjet printer and share it on the network so that everyone can have high-quality output.

Visual Quiz

How can you display a window like this one? What is the purpose of the Add Network Place icon?

_____

_____

_____

_____

_____

_____

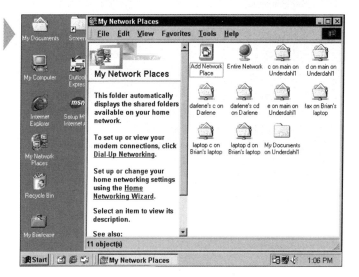

CHAPTER **8**

MASTER ▶ **Using the Accessibility Wizard**
THESE ▶ **Using the Magnifier**
SKILLS ▶ **Using the On-Screen Keyboard**
▶ **Changing the Accessibility Settings**

Using the Accessibility Options

Computers can be difficult for some people to use. Physical disabilities can turn using even the most carefully designed PC and software into a major undertaking. People with physical disabilities may feel left out if they don't possess excellent vision and great manual dexterity. To counteract this problem, Windows Me includes several tools designed to help people with physical limitations make effective use of their PC.

The Windows Me accessibility tools address the needs of people who have limited vision, hearing problems, or an inability to use a standard keyboard or mouse. This chapter shows you how to use these tools. You will learn how to start the tools as well as how to configure them so that they are of the most use when you need them.

The accessibility tools are useful for more than simply those people who have physical disabilities. These tools can be quite useful in many different circumstances. Almost everyone has encountered situations where a computer screen has been difficult to read due to poor lighting conditions or very small text. But quite aside from this obvious

case, the accessibility tools offer solutions to other problems, too. With a little imagination you can probably think of a number of innovative uses for these tools.

Even if you have no real need for the accessibility options yourself, you may know someone who could benefit from them. If so, it's important to remember that those who really need these tools might have a difficult time setting them up without a bit of assistance. By learning how these tools work you can be ready to provide that assistance if the need arises.

Just like any of the other Windows Me accessories, you will probably find that some of the accessibility tools are more useful to you than others. There is no reason you cannot simply use the tools you find helpful and ignore the others. Still, it can be very useful to know what is available so that you can gain maximum benefit from these options. It is also important to remember that the accessibility tools built into Windows Me are only a beginning, and that with the right combination of tools almost anyone can use a PC.

Using the Accessibility Wizard

In order to make the accessibility options as easy as possible to use, Windows Me includes the Accessibility Wizard to help you set up the various options. This wizard enables you to choose the correct options without giving the whole process a lot of advance thought or planning. You simply make a few easy choices and the Accessibility Wizard selects the options that seem appropriate based on your selections.

The Accessibility Wizard has several main options as shown in the figures. You can choose as many of the options as you need to configure your PC properly for your needs.

To access the features designed to assist users with vision limitations you select the *I am blind or have difficulty seeing things on screen* check box. When you select this option you have access to features such as higher contrast color schemes and larger text displays. In addition, you can choose the screen magnification tool if you need much greater magnification. The Magnifier greatly magnifies a portion of your screen as you move the mouse around your desktop, almost as if you were holding a large magnifying glass in front of the monitor.

If you have problems hearing the various audible prompts that Windows Me uses, you can select the *I am deaf or have difficulty hearing sounds from the computer* check box. When you select this option Windows Me augments the sounds that are used to signal system events with more visible onscreen alerts of these types of events. For example, Windows Me can flash a new warning message window several times to make certain that you notice the new message.

▶ From the Start menu select Programs ➪ Accessories ➪ Accessibility ➪ Accessibility Wizard.

❶ Click Next to continue.

❷ Choose the text size option that works the best for your needs.

❸ Click Next to continue.

CROSS-REFERENCE

See "Changing the Accessibility Settings" later in this chapter.

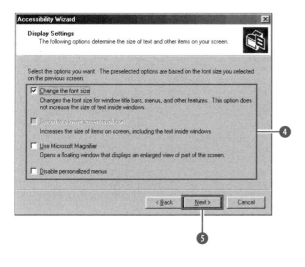

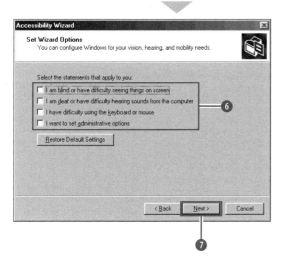

If you have difficulty with typing or the mouse, select the *I have difficulty using the keyboard or mouse* check box. This option enables you to use the On-Screen Keyboard or one of the options such as Sticky Keys that can make these devices a bit easier.

The administrative options enable you to fine-tune the accessibility tools. These settings can also be changed using the Accessibility icon in the Control Panel, as you'll see later in this chapter.

TAKE NOTE

▶ OPENING THE ACCESSIBILITY TOOLS

You can open the accessibility tools by clicking the Start button and then choosing Programs ⇨ Accessories ⇨ Accessibility to display a menu of the accessibility tools. Select the tool you wish to use from the list. You can also use the Accessibility Wizard or the Accessibility icon in the Control Panel to configure the accessibility tools to run automatically whenever your computer is started.

▶ USING THE ACCESSIBILITY TOOLS

Once the accessibility options have been enabled, Windows Me uses special keystroke sequences to start the tools. This makes it far easier to use these options, because you do not have to start a special program when you need to use them.

④ *Choose any of the display size options necessary to make your screen easier to see.*

▶ *The option to switch to a lower resolution is not available if your screen is already set for 640 × 480 resolution.*

⑤ *Click Next to continue.*

⑥ *Choose the areas where you would like Windows Me to make accessibility adjustments.*

⑦ *Click Next to continue.*

▶ *Follow the onscreen directions for the different options that you have selected.*

FIND IT ONLINE

To learn more about the accessibility options, see **http://www.microsoft.com/enable/microsoft/default.htm**.

Using the Magnifier

I f you have difficulty reading the Windows Me screen no matter how large the text size you select, you may want to try the Magnifier. The Magnifier acts like a magnifying glass to increase the size of anything that is displayed on your Windows Me screen. As you move the mouse around the screen, the Magnifier window displays the area around the mouse pointer. This enables you to simply move your mouse over something to view it in a much larger size. The Magnifier window can also follow the keyboard cursor when you are typing or making selections using the keyboard.

If necessary, you can choose from several different magnification power levels. Depending on your needs, you can select power settings up to nine times normal size. As you select higher magnifications, less of the Windows Me desktop will be visible in the Magnifier window, so you may also need to resize the Magnifier window to compensate.

In some ways you'll find that balancing the screen resolution setting with the size and magnification power of the Magnifier window is a delicate act. If you adjust the screen resolution to a higher setting, everything on your screen will be smaller, but there will be more room for the Magnifier window. This adjustment, however, will also mean that the items within the Magnifier window will appear somewhat smaller, so you may need to use a higher magnification level to comfortably view them. Setting the screen resolution to a lower setting has the opposite effect, and it also means that there will be less room left over outside the magnifier window.

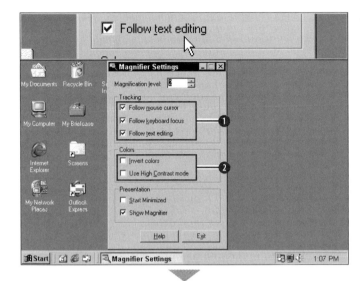

▶ From the Start menu select Programs ➪ Accessories ➪ Accessibility ➪ Magnifier.

❶ Choose the tracking options that you prefer.

❷ Choose the color and contrast options that work best for you.

❸ Use the Magnification level spin control to adjust the magnification power.

❹ Click the Minimize button to minimize the Magnifier controls.

CROSS-REFERENCE

See "Changing the Resolution" in Chapter 11.

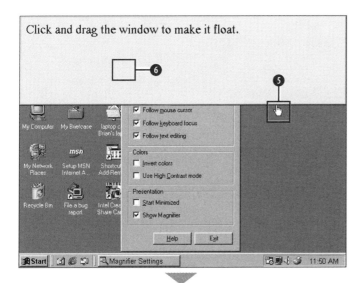

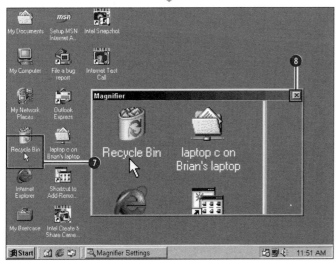

If you do need to resize the Magnifier window, there are two ways to do so. When the window is docked at the top of your screen, you can drag the lower edge of the window up or down to change its size. If you have undocked the window by dragging the whole window down onto your desktop, drag one of the corners to resize the window.

⑤ *Drag the lower edge of the Magnifier window to resize the window while leaving it docked at the top of the screen.*

⑥ *Alternatively, drag the window to undock it and move it to a new location on the screen.*

⑦ *Move the mouse pointer over the screen area that you would like to magnify.*

⑧ *Click the Close button to close the Magnifier.*

FIND IT ONLINE

To learn more about the Magnifier, see **http://support. microsoft.com/support/windows/inproducthelp98/ about_magnify.asp**.

Using the On-Screen Keyboard

I f you have trouble typing on a standard keyboard, you may want to give the On-Screen Keyboard a try. This is a keyboard that appears on the Windows Me screen and can be used with a mouse or another type of alternate pointing device. You don't need to be able to type on a standard keyboard to be able to use the On-Screen Keyboard.

The On-Screen Keyboard is intended as a virtual replacement for a physical keyboard so it works as much like a normal keyboard as possible. Typing on the On-Screen Keyboard only produces results if another Windows Me application is open and can accept keystrokes. You can use the On-Screen Keyboard to enter text into documents as well as into dialog boxes.

The Shift, Ctrl, and Alt keys act as toggles on the On-Screen Keyboard. That is, when any of these keys are selected, they remain active while you select another key. This enables you to easily use capital letters because selecting the Shift key causes the next character you select to be capitalized. You don't need to hold down the shift key while you type the letter you want capitalized. To help you see what is happening, the keys that appear on the On-Screen Keyboard always reflect the current Shift key state. That is, selecting Shift causes the keys to be displayed as uppercase characters. If you selected the Shift (or Ctrl or Alt) key in error, you can select it again to turn it off. As soon as you type another character the toggle keys return to their off position.

You will find several different appearance settings for the On-Screen Keyboard. You can choose an enhanced or a standard keyboard, a regular or block layout, and the

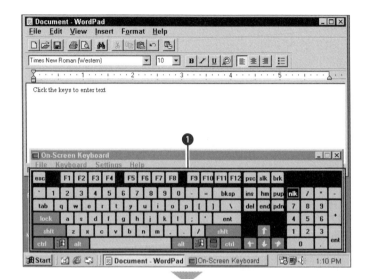

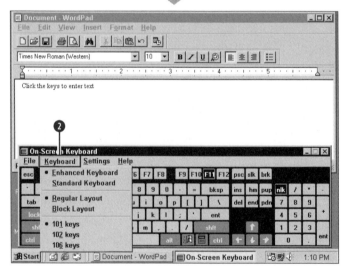

▶ From the Start menu select Programs ➪ Accessories ➪ Accessibility ➪ On-Screen Keyboard.

▶ Open the application that you wish to use with the On-Screen Keyboard.

❶ Select the keys on the On-Screen Keyboard to enter characters into the active application.

❷ Optionally, select Keyboard to choose the keyboard appearance and layout options as necessary.

CROSS-REFERENCE

See Chapter 12 for information on configuring the standard keyboard.

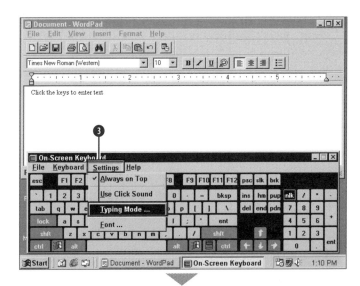

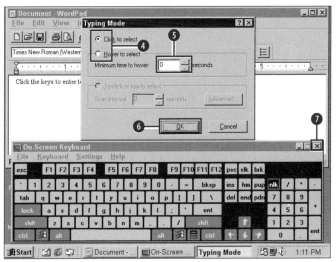

number of keys. The regular layout looks most like a real keyboard, but that layout might be somewhat difficult to use with a pointing device, because there are variable gaps between the various keys and keys of different sizes. Block layout uses uniform spacing and key sizes that can make using the On-Screen Keyboard far easier.

③ Optionally, select Settings ⇨ Typing Mode to adjust the typing method.

④ Select the typing mode as appropriate for your needs.

⑤ If you select hover mode, choose the hover time interval before characters are selected.

⑥ Click the OK button.

⑦ Click the Close to close On-Screen Keyboard.

FIND IT ONLINE

Visit **http://www.microsoft.com/enable/products/ default.htm** to learn about additional accessibility options.

Changing the Accessibility Settings

Windows Me includes a number of additional accessibility tools besides the ones that appear on the Programs ⇨ Accessories ⇨ Accessibility menu. These extra tools are generally simpler and more subtle than the ones on the Accessibility menu, but they can provide some valuable assistance for someone who needs only a little extra help with using a PC.

The additional accessibility tools include a number of useful options. The figures show you how to configure the keyboard-related accessibility options. The remaining options are covered in detail on the following two pages. The keyboard-related tools include the following:

StickyKeys, also known as *modifier keys*, enables a user to simulate the use of the Shift, Ctrl, and Alt keys in combination with another key. When StickyKeys is active, you can first press Shift, Ctrl, or Alt, release it, and then press the next key you would normally press at the same time. For example, rather than hold down Ctrl while you press A, you can press Ctrl, release it, and then press A to accomplish the same task. StickyKeys makes it possible to type and to use the menu shortcuts found in many programs even if you are able to press only one key at a time.

FilterKeys causes Windows Me to ignore keys you press in error or keys you hold down so long that they are repeated in error. You can tell Windows Me to ignore key repeat. In this way, no matter how long a key is held down it won't repeat. You can also choose to have Windows Me ignore repeated pressing of the same key unless there is a delay between pressing the keys.

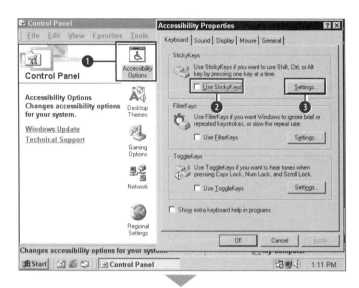

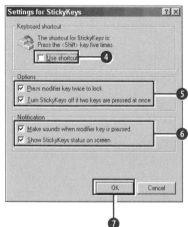

▶ Select Settings ⇨ Control Panel from the Start menu.

❶ Double-click the Accessibility Options icon.

❷ Click the Use StickyKeys check box to enable this option.

❸ Click here to configure StickyKeys.

❹ Click here to enable the shortcut.

❺ Select the desired StickyKeys options.

❻ Select the desired notification methods.

❼ Click OK to close the dialog box.

CROSS-REFERENCE

See "Using the On-Screen Keyboard" earlier in this chapter.

Using the Accessibility Options

CHAPTER
8

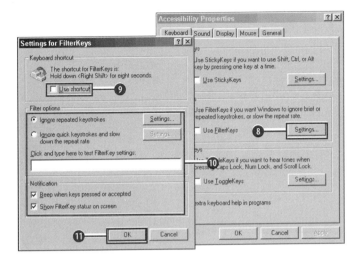

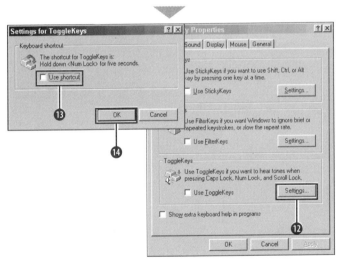

StickyKeys and FilterKeys can be a help to someone who has limited mobility or who types using a touch stick.

ToggleKeys plays sounds when the Caps Lock, Num Lock, or Scroll Lock keys are pressed. These keys can have an adverse effect on the way your PC operates, but if you have limited vision you might not realize that you had pressed them in error.

Continued

TAKE NOTE

TURNING ON THE KEYBOARD OPTIONS

The keyboard accessibility options use shortcuts to turn on the options. The figures show the shortcuts, such as pressing Shift five times to turn on the StickyKeys option.

ACCESSIBILITY USERS MAY NEED ASSISTANCE

If you assist someone who needs the accessibility options, be sure to take the time to fine-tune the settings to meet his or her needs. It may not occur to them to ask for assistance in adjusting these options for optimal performance, but a few extra minutes of setup time will pay many dividends. Be sure the user understands the full range of tools that Windows Me provides.

---

⑧ *Click here to configure FilterKeys.*

⑨ *Click here to enable the shortcut.*

⑩ *Select the FilterKeys and notification options.*

⑪ *Click OK to close the dialog box.*

⑫ *Click here to configure ToggleKeys.*

⑬ *Click here to enable the shortcut.*

⑭ *Click OK to close the dialog box.*

FIND IT ONLINE

See **http://support.microsoft.com/support/ windows/inproducthelp98/accessibility_options_ installs.asp** for more information.

179

Changing the Accessibility Settings

Continued

The additional accessibility options include a number of very useful items that go beyond enhancing the keyboard. There are also options for sound, the display, the mouse, and optional keyboard replacement devices. The figures on these pages can only give you an idea about what options are available.

You can use the sound options to assist Windows Me users who have a hearing impairment. These options supplement the sounds that Windows Me normally uses to advise you of system events. When *SoundSentry* is activated, rather than simply playing a sound, Windows Me will flash the title bar or window border to alert you of an event. *ShowSounds* displays text captions in addition to audible messages from your programs.

The display options use high-contrast color schemes to make the screen easier to read. You can choose the color scheme that is the easiest to read; the default high-contrast color scheme displays white lettering on a black background.

Users who have difficulty using a mouse may find that the *MouseKeys* option makes life simpler. When you enable this option, you can use the arrow keys on your numeric keypad to move the mouse pointer. To make the MouseKeys pointer work more like a real mouse pointer, you can press and hold Ctrl to speed up the movement or Shift to slow down the movement.

On the General options tab you'll find the option to allow the accessibility features to expire if they aren't used for a period of time. Because the accessibility options can be confusing to users who aren't familiar with them or who don't expect them, this option makes it

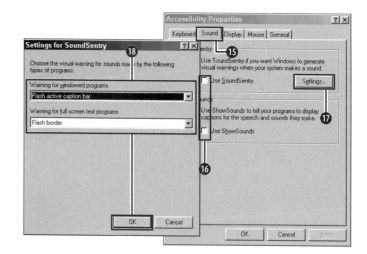

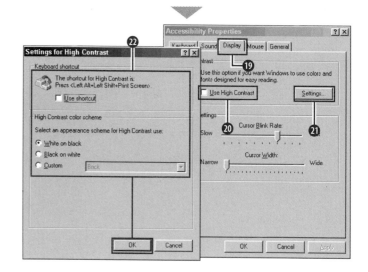

⓯ Click the Sound tab.

⓰ Select the sound options you wish to enable.

⓱ Click here to configure SoundSentry.

⓲ Configure the SoundSentry, and then click OK.

⓳ Click the Display tab.

⓴ Click here to enable the high-contrast display.

㉑ Click here to configure the high-contrast settings.

㉒ Select the options and click OK.

CROSS-REFERENCE

See "Using the Accessibility Wizard" earlier in this chapter.

Using the Accessibility Options

CHAPTER 8

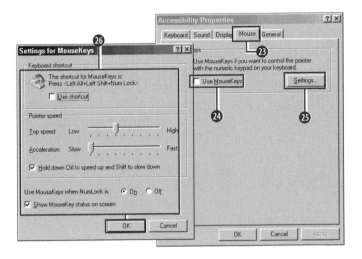

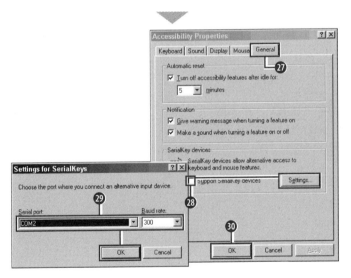

easier to share a PC in which the accessibility options have been activated. You can set the accessibility features to turn off after 5 to 30 minutes.

TAKE NOTE

▶ TALKING TO YOUR PC

Although we normally think of the keyboard as the way to input information into a computer, voice recognition is an alternative that may assist users who have difficulty using the keyboard. Windows Me does not offer any built-in voice recognition capabilities, but modern PCs are powerful enough to enable voice recognition software to do a creditable job. Dragon NaturallySpeaking (**http://www.dragonsys.com/**) is one example of this type of software that seems to work well, especially when used with the included high-quality headset.

▶ ALTERNATIVES TO THE KEYBOARD

Users who cannot use a standard keyboard or mouse can still use a Windows Me–based PC. *SerialKey* devices connect to the PC's serial port and enable the user to communicate with the system using specially adapted devices. For example, the Eyegaze device enables a user to interact with the computer completely through eye movements. Many other devices are available. See **http://www.lctinc.com/doc/egwin95.htm** for information on the Eyegaze system.

㉓ Click the Mouse tab.

㉔ Click here to enable MouseKeys.

㉕ Click here to configure MouseKeys.

㉖ Select the options and click OK.

㉗ Click the General tab.

㉘ Select the check box to enable SerialKey devices, and click the Settings button to configure your device.

㉙ Select the options and click OK.

㉚ Click OK to complete the task.

FIND IT ONLINE

For more documentation on configuring accessibility options, see **http://www.microsoft.com/enable/products/docs/default.htm**.

Personal Workbook

Q&A

1 How do you display and use the On-Screen Keyboard?

_____

_____

_____

2 What tool do you use to view screen contents at up to nine times normal size?

_____

_____

_____

3 What tool do you use to make dialog boxes flash when a sound prompt is issued by Windows Me?

_____

_____

_____

4 How can you make it possible to press the Shift, Ctrl, or Alt key first and then a second key without holding down the first key?

_____

_____

_____

5 How can you make Windows Me ignore keys that are held down too long?

_____

_____

_____

6 How long do the accessibility options normally remain active when the keyboard is idle?

_____

_____

_____

7 How can you make it possible to use the keyboard to move the mouse pointer?

_____

_____

_____

8 What shortcut can you use to turn on the StickyKeys option?

_____

_____

_____

ANSWERS: PAGE 394

EXTRA PRACTICE

1 Open the Magnifier and set the power to 3.

2 Move the Magnifier into a floating window at the lower right edge of your screen.

3 Open Notepad and use the On-Screen Keyboard to enter text.

4 Enable StickyKeys and practice pressing one key at a time.

5 Use SoundSentry to give you a visual warning when Windows Me plays sounds.

6 Set the accessibility options to turn off after 10 minutes.

REAL-WORLD APPLICATIONS

✔ You broke your arm skiing and find that it is quite difficult to type using one hand. You use the accessibility options to make the process a little easier.

✔ You need to help an elderly relative with impaired vision create a record of your family tree. You use the Magnifier to help them read the details as you enter them.

✔ You want to use your laptop PC on a field project. You use the Display options to make it easier to read the prompts in bright sunlight.

Visual Quiz

How can you display a window like this one? How can you increase the magnification to 8 power?

_____

_____

_____

_____

_____

Contents of 'Desktop'

Name

My Computer

Network Neigh

Internet Explore

Microsoft Outloo

Recycle Bin

My Briefcase

3252-9

3259-6

3261-8

3262-6

3281-2

3286-3

DE Phone List

Device Manager

In

Iomega Tools

PART

III

Harnessing the Internet

These days the Internet is everywhere. If you aren't yet using the Internet for research, e-mail, or just plain recreation, you soon will be. Windows Me makes it easy for you to connect to and use the Internet. In fact, you may start wondering where your Windows Me desktop ends and the Internet begins.

In this part you discover how to harness the power of the Internet on your Windows Me–based PC. You learn how to browse the Internet and find Web sites that interest you. You also learn how to send and receive e-mail, and how you can access areas such as Usenet newsgroups.

CHAPTER **9**

MASTER
THESE
SKILLS

▶ **Using Internet Explorer**

▶ **Visiting Web Sites**

▶ **Searching for Web Sites**

▶ **Saving Your Favorite Web Sites**

▶ **Offline Browsing**

▶ **Synchronizing Offline Content**

▶ **Organizing Your Favorites**

▶ **Configuring Internet Explorer**

▶ **Setting up MSN Messenger Service**

▶ **Sending Messages Using MSN Messenger Service**

Connecting to the Internet and the World Wide Web

The Internet is one of the most interesting phenomenons to ever hit the planet. In a few short years it has grown from a rather obscure network of a few government and university computers to a worldwide collection of millions of computers, and it has gained virtually unlimited possibilities. It has become almost impossible to turn on a news broadcast and not hear at least one Internet-related news story. It seems as though even people in the most remote regions of the earth have heard of the Internet. If you want to be a part of modern society it has become almost a necessity to be a part of the Internet.

In reality, what most people think of when they hear the word Internet is really only that part of the Internet known as the World Wide Web. The Web is the graphical portion of the Internet connected by millions upon millions of *links* — which are the addresses of other pages that you can visit by clicking. It is very easy to spend hours browsing the Web when you find yourself clicking some of those interesting looking links just to see where they may lead.

When you are browsing the Internet you are viewing *Web pages*. In most instances several Web pages are linked together to form a Web *site*. Web pages can contain text, graphics, sounds, and many other elements that provide visitors with a colorful and often quite entertaining view of information.

In Windows Me you don't need to look very far to find the software that enables you to view all of these Web pages. Internet Explorer is a *Web browser* that is tightly integrated into the Windows Me interface. In fact, you'll soon discover that when you're working in Windows Me, you can browse the Web just about as easily as you can browse your own computer or your local network. In some cases browsing the Web may even be easier!

As you read through this chapter, keep in mind that the Internet is constantly changing and evolving. Links that worked perfectly well this morning may be history by this afternoon. Keep your sense of adventure and you'll be rewarded with all sorts of interesting treats.

Using Internet Explorer

I nternet Explorer is a type of program that is known as a *Web browser*— a program that you use to view the countless documents that make up the Web. Web pages are documents that are created using *HTML*— HyperText Markup Language. A Web browser converts the HTML code into the graphical images that you see when you visit the page. Fortunately, you don't have to understand anything about HTML — all you have to do is start Internet Explorer and point it in the right direction.

Web pages typically include plenty of *links* that you can click to navigate your way to different Web pages. In fact, while you are surfing the Web, you're likely to do most things by clicking links or Internet Explorer toolbar buttons. Still, you can do a lot using the Internet Explorer menus. As an example, you can click the Print button to print the currently displayed Web page using the default printer settings. But if you wish to change any of the default print settings, you'll want to use the File ⇨ Print command instead of clicking the Print button.

You may soon discover that the Internet Explorer screen can look a bit cluttered with menus, toolbars, status bars, and so on. These features can make it difficult to view very much of a Web page — especially if your display is set to a low-resolution setting such as 640 × 480. You can do several things to increase the area used to display Web pages. You can drag the toolbars to new locations using the handle at the left edge of each

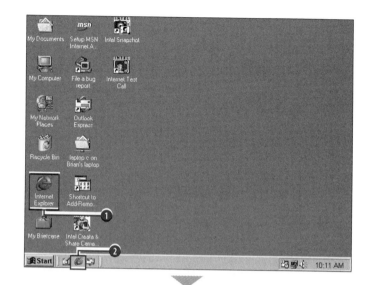

❶ Double-click the Internet Explorer icon on your desktop.

❷ Alternatively, click the Internet Explorer icon in the Quick Launch toolbar.

❸ Click the Back and Forward buttons to return to pages that you have just visited.

❹ If the page does not load correctly, try clicking the Refresh button to reload the page.

❺ If you want to print the page using the default settings, click the Print button.

CROSS-REFERENCE
See "Saving Your Favorite Web Sites" later in this chapter.

toolbar. You can stack more than one toolbar on the same row. You can even use the View menu options to remove some of these elements from the screen. Or you can press F11 to really maximize your browsing area.

TAKE NOTE

▶ STARTING INTERNET EXPLORER

You can use several methods to start Internet Explorer. The figures show the most common ones, but you can also start Internet Explorer in other ways, too. For example, if you click a Web page address link that appears in an e-mail message that someone sends you, Internet Explorer will likely open automatically so that you can view the Web page.

▶ USE THE ADDRESS TOOLBAR

The most direct route to a Web page is to right-click the Windows Me Taskbar and choose Toolbars ⇨ Address from the context menu. This will place an address box on the Taskbar. Type a Web page address into the address box, press Enter, and Internet Explorer will go directly to that page without first loading your home page. Close the Address toolbar once the page begins loading to regain the space.

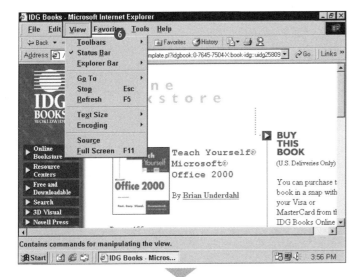

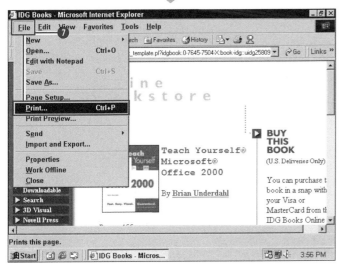

⑥ Open the View menu to select view options to suit your needs.

⑦ If you want to print the page and control the settings, select File ⇨ Print.

FIND IT ONLINE

Learn about Internet Explorer security issues at
**http://www.microsoft.com/windows/ie/security/
default.asp.**

Visiting Web Sites

One of the most confusing things you may encounter when you begin browsing the Web is the question of just how your computer can find all of those different Web pages. With Web pages literally scattered across millions of computers around the world, it seems like an almost impossible task. Indeed, finding specific Web pages probably would be impossible if it were not for the special type of address used to identify a Web page. That address is called the *Uniform Resource Locator* or URL. When you click a link or enter an address manually in the Address toolbar, Internet Explorer uses that address to send out a request across the Internet for a copy of the associated document file.

Each URL uses a standard format. It begins with a protocol identifier — such as http:// or https://. Next comes the domain or server name on which the page can be found, and then sometimes directory and file names. If no directory and file names are used, the server will send the default page (which is often index.html). A typical URL might look like this — http://www.idgbooks.com, although not all Web servers include the www portion of the address.

As you browse the Web you will probably notice that some Web pages may take a long time to load. This delay can be caused by overloaded servers or simply by a Web page that is very large and includes a lot of text and graphics. While Internet Explorer is waiting for a page to

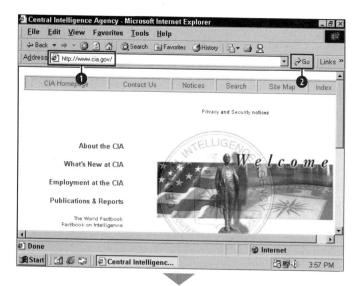

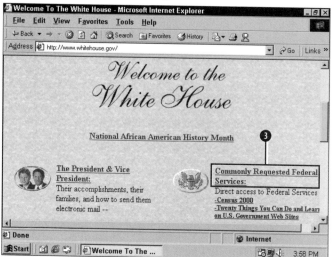

❶ Enter the address of a Web page that you wish to visit.

▶ If the address begins with http://, you don't have to include that part.

▶ If the main part of the address starts with www and ends with .com, type the single word and press Ctrl+Enter.

❷ Click the Go button.

❸ Click a link to view a different page.

CROSS-REFERENCE

See "Searching for Web Sites" later in this chapter.

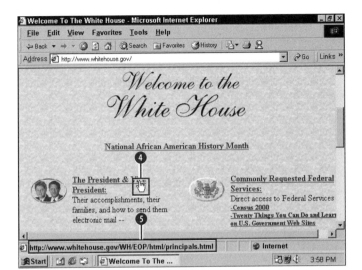

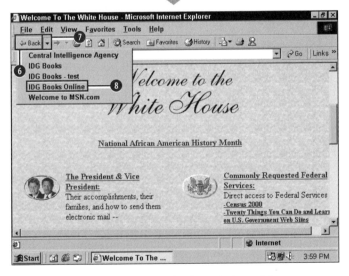

load, it displays a progress bar control in the status bar. To stop trying to load a slow page, click the Stop button on the browser bar. You may wish to try clicking the Refresh button after you click Stop. Sometimes a second request to load a page goes considerably faster — especially if loading the page seemed to be stalled the first time.

TAKE NOTE

USING LINKS

A *link* is text or a graphic that you can click to request the new page from the server. Links can be underlined text fields, graphical representations of buttons, banners, or anything else the page designer chooses. When you move the mouse cursor across a link, the cursor changes to a pointing finger, and the URL is displayed. Most Web pages include links you can click to view related pages.

GOING BACK

After you've visited several Web pages, you may find yourself wanting to return to a page that is several pages before the current page. Click the down-arrow next to the Back button to display a list of recently visited pages. Choose the page you want from the list. If the page you want has scrolled off the list, click the History button to display the complete list of pages that you have visited.

④ *Move the mouse pointer over a link to view the link's address.*

⑤ *When the pointer changes to a hand, view the link address here.*

⑥ *Click the Back button to return to the preceding page.*

⑦ *Alternatively, click the down-arrow to view the list of recently visited pages.*

⑧ *Click a page to return to that page.*

FIND IT ONLINE

See **http://home.netscape.com/smartupdate/ su1_ie30.html** for enhancements for Internet Explorer.

Searching for Web Sites

Almost anything that interests you is probably available somewhere on the Web. The problem is actually finding the Web sites that cover a particular topic. You certainly wouldn't be able to be very productive if you had to look for those Web sites yourself, as there are millions of pages on the Web. That's where *search engines*— special services that are available on the Web — come in handy. Search engines enable you to look for and find the Web pages that interest you.

In spite of what you might expect, using a search engine is generally free because advertising supports almost all search engines. A few specialized search engines charge for their services, but you are unlikely to encounter them unless you have search needs well beyond casual searching.

To use a search engine to find Web sites, you enter a *search string*— one or more words that define the content of the Web sites you'd like to see. If you enter more than one word in your search string, most search engines will look for any of the words. To find an exact phrase you can often enclose the phrase in quotation marks — although this does not work for every search engine. When you use quotation marks, most search engines will only show those sites in which the exact phrase was found.

If you do use quotation marks to specify a complete phrase, you probably won't find Web sites that contain all of your search words but not your exact phrase. To avoid this problem you may want to use *Boolean* search

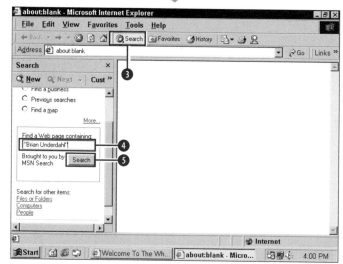

❶ Click the Start button.

❷ Select Search ➪ On the Internet.

❸ Alternatively, click the Search button if Internet Explorer is already open.

❹ Type your search phrase in the text box.

❺ Click the Search button to begin the search.

CROSS-REFERENCE

See Chapter 6 for more information on finding files on your computer.

techniques. A Boolean search is a much more sophisticated search method and will generally produce far better results when your search string includes more than one word.

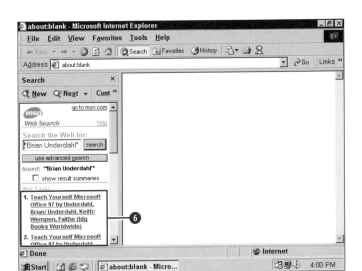

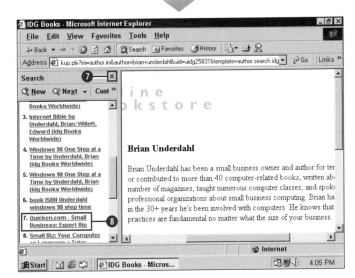

6 Click a link that appears to meet your needs.

7 Click the Close button to close the Search bar and maximize the browser window.

8 Alternatively, click another link to see if the site has the information you were looking for.

TAKE NOTE

▶ USE AN ADVANCED SEARCH

If your search doesn't produce the desired results, consider using some advanced search techniques. Most search engines offer advanced methods — such as Boolean searches — of searching for Web sites of interest. These advanced methods enable you to refine your search by specifically including or excluding a word, multiple words, or phrases in the search string. To access the advanced search capabilities, look for a button labeled "Advanced Search" or something similar.

▶ TRY SEVERAL SEARCH ENGINES

Each search engine uses somewhat different methods of categorizing Web sites, so you'll likely find that only some of them produce the results you want. If the first search engine that you try produces either no results or includes so many matches that you couldn't possibly visit all of them, try a different search engine. You may even find links at the bottom of a search engine's Web page that will run the same search on several other search engines.

FIND IT ONLINE

To download a tool that enables you to use many search engines at once, see **http://www.copernic.com**.

Saving Your Favorite Web Sites

Certain Web sites will soon become favorite sites that you go back to time after time. For example, if you engage in online investing, you will probably find yourself visiting your broker's Web site at least once a day. Or maybe you have a favorite Web site that gives you detailed weather information for a city where your favorite relatives live. Whatever your reason for returning to the same Web site regularly, you'll want an easier method of going to the site than always typing in the URL.

Of course, you have also probably discovered that it is easy to make a mistake when you are typing in URLs. Any typing error — no matter how small — will keep Internet Explorer from loading the correct Web page. Saving your favorite Web page links so that you can open those pages with a quick click is clearly far easier and less error prone.

Most of the time you will probably want to simply save a link to a Web page rather than saving the entire page on your PC. By saving just the link you are telling Internet Explorer to reload the page along with any updated content from the Web whenever you click the link. That way you can be certain that you are viewing the most recent contents of the page instead of possibly outdated material.

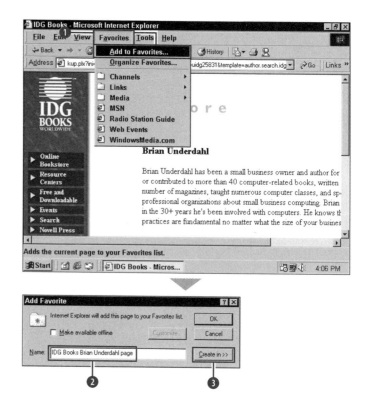

▶ If necessary, open a Web page that you wish to add to your list of favorite sites.

❶ Select Favorites ➪ Add to Favorites.

❷ Optionally, enter a new name for the page.

❸ If you wish to change the location where the link will be stored, click Create in.

CROSS-REFERENCE

See "Offline Browsing" next in this chapter.

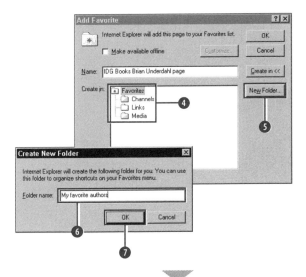

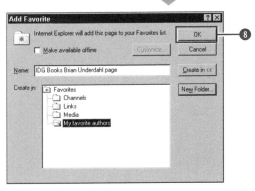

THE WEB IS ALWAYS CHANGING

On the Internet, change is the one constant that you can depend on. Your favorite Web pages can disappear as quickly as they appeared in the first place. If you attempt to visit one of the Web sites you saved in your favorites list, but you see only a message that the page cannot be found, it's likely that it has moved or no longer exists. Before you decide to delete the link, however, you may want to try the link later to see whether the message was only temporary.

RENAMING SAVED FAVORITES

When you save a Web page in your list of Favorites, Internet Explorer provides a default name for the page. This name may not appear anywhere on the Web page, so sometimes the default name can be a little confusing — especially when you want to use your Favorites list to visit the same site in the future. Internet Explorer is not just pulling some random name out of the air, however. The name that Internet Explorer suggests is the name that appears in the Internet Explorer title bar when you are visiting the Web page. The HTML `<title>` tag that is in the source code for the Web page dictates this name. You can change the suggested name into one that makes it easier for you to remember which link you saved.

④ Select the folder you prefer.

⑤ Alternatively, click New Folder to create a new folder.

⑥ Enter a name for the folder.

⑦ Click OK to continue.

⑧ Click OK to complete the task.

FIND IT ONLINE

See **http://www.lss.com.au/lss/windows/ft/ft_ins.htm** for a freeware utility that enables you to convert *Navigator* Bookmarks into *Internet Explorer* Favorites.

Offline Browsing

In addition to viewing Web pages online, you can choose to save those pages for offline browsing. Although you probably want to view most Web pages online, there may be some good reasons to view certain pages offline. If you pay for your connect time, offline browsing could save you a lot of money in connect time charges. If you are researching a project and most of the Web sites you use contain a lot of content that seldom changes, saving those pages for use offline makes a lot of sense, too. Finally, if a Web page contains important content that is likely to disappear when the Web page is next updated, saving the page for offline viewing enables you to make certain you don't lose that content.

If you choose to make a Web page available for offline viewing, Internet Explorer stores the entire page on your hard disk. This enables you to view the page again without first connecting to the Internet. This option also enables you to specify how many additional levels of linked pages to store. Saving the linked pages makes them available offline, too, but can use considerable disk space — especially if you choose to store more than one level of links. For example, if the page that you are saving is linked to 10 other pages and each of them links to 10 more pages, you'll actually be downloading and storing over 100 pages if you choose to save two link levels. Rather than storing the linked pages, you can click the links on the stored page to open your Internet connection and view the linked pages online.

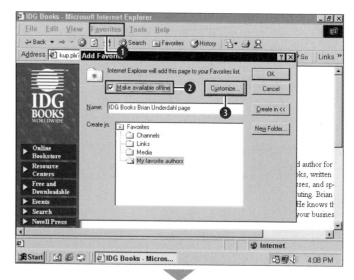

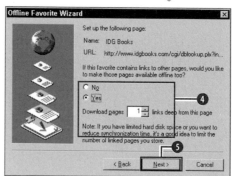

▶ If necessary, open a Web page that you wish to add to your list of favorite sites.

① Select Favorites ⇨ Add to Favorites.

② Click here to make the page available offline.

③ If you wish to change the offline options, click Customize.

▶ If the introductory page appears, click Next to continue.

④ Select the link level options you prefer.

⑤ Click Next to continue.

CROSS-REFERENCE

See "Synchronizing Offline Content" next in this chapter.

Connecting to the Internet and the World Wide Web

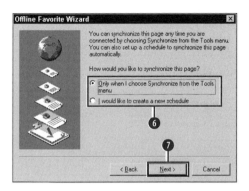

Internet Explorer offers two different options for saving your favorite Web sites. You can choose to simply save the URL or to save the entire page. If you choose to save the entire page for offline viewing, Internet Explorer will display the saved page without attempting to load it from the Internet.

TAKE NOTE

▶ HAVING IT BOTH WAYS

Pages you save for offline browsing can quickly get out of date. Unless you update the saved Web pages, you will not be able to see the latest content that is available online. You can, however, tell Internet Explorer to automatically update Web pages you save for offline browsing so that they will always have fairly recent content available. When you save a Web page for offline browsing, use the synchronization options to specify a schedule for updating the page.

▶ A CAUTION ABOUT PASSWORDS

If you save a Web page that requires a user name and password, Internet Explorer will save your user name and password information on your hard disk. Anyone who uses your PC will then be able to view that Web page even if they do not know your password.

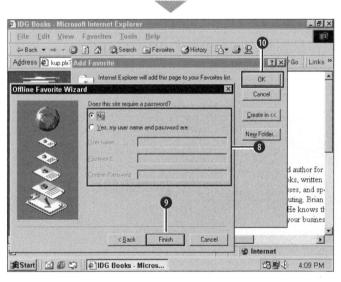

6 Choose the options for updating the page.

7 Click Next to continue.

8 If necessary, enter the correct password options.

9 Click Finish to continue.

10 Click OK to complete the task.

FIND IT ONLINE

See **http://www.microsoft.com/windows/ie/features/ offline.asp** for more on offline browsing.

Synchronizing Offline Content

I f you have saved Web pages on your hard disk so that you can view those pages offline, you have a static copy of that Web page. Any updates to the content of the online Web page won't be reflected in your copy unless you *synchronize* your offline pages with the online pages. Synchronizing your offline Web pages downloads the most recent changes to those pages.

You probably don't need to synchronize all of your offline Web pages on quite the same schedule. Some Web pages simply don't change all that often while others quickly become out of date. For example, if you save a Web page that deals with famous battles of the American Civil War for offline browsing, you probably won't need to update the page very often. On the other hand, a Web page that shows your local weather forecast probably needs to be updated at least daily if it is going to be of any value to you. You can use the Synchronization Settings dialog box to set up appropriate synchronization schedules for each of your offline Web pages.

You will probably want to view the synchronization results on the Results tab of the Synchronizing dialog box after your first few synchronization attempts. That way you can see if Internet Explorer has encountered any errors that you may need to deal with to ensure success in future attempts.

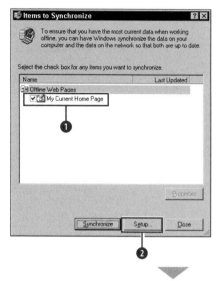

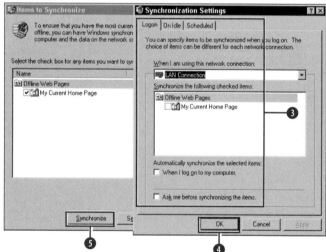

▶ Select Tools ⇨ Synchronize.

❶ Choose the items you wish to synchronize.

❷ Optionally, click Setup to change the synchronization schedule.

❸ Choose the synchronization settings appropriate for your needs.

❹ Click OK to continue.

❺ Click Synchronize to continue.

CROSS-REFERENCE
See "Offline Browsing" earlier in this chapter.

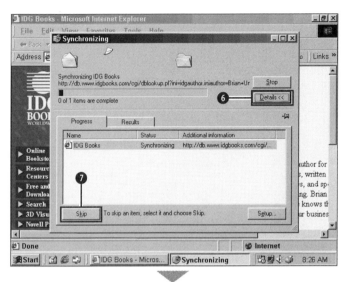

PREVENTING SYNCHRONIZATION

By default, all of the Web pages you have saved for offline browsing are updated whenever you select Tools ⇨ Synchronize and click the Synchronize button. While this is probably what you want for most offline Web pages, it may not be appropriate in all cases. For example, if you save a Web page for offline browsing because you know that the content will soon change and you want to keep a copy of the current content, synchronizing that page will likely replace the existing content that you wanted to save. To prevent an offline Web page from being updated with newer content, remove the check from that page in the Items to Synchronize dialog box. You may also want to save the Web page under a different name if retaining the existing content is really important to you.

SYNCHRONIZING WHILE IDLE

If you want your offline Web pages to be automatically updated when you aren't actively using your computer, use the settings on the On Idle tab of the Synchronization Settings dialog box. On this tab you can also click the Advanced button to specify how long your system should wait before considering your PC to be idle, and how often to synchronize the Web pages during idle periods. You can even choose to eliminate idle synchronization during those times when your system is running on batteries.

⑥ Click Details to view the synchronization progress information.

⑦ Click Skip to bypass an item.

⑧ Click the Results tab to view the synchronization report.

⑨ Click the Close button to complete the task.

Organizing Your Favorites

Saving your favorite Web site links so that you can easily go back to those sites in the future can really make Web browsing a lot more fun. Rather than trying to remember the Web site's URL, you simply choose the site from your Favorites list and off you go.

If you use the Favorites ➪ Add to Favorites command quite often you will soon find that your list of favorite Web sites could probably use some organization to make it easier for you to locate specific sites. Organizing your list of favorite Web sites isn't a lot different from organizing your My Documents folder. Just as you can organize your documents by creating extra folders under the My Documents folder, you can organize your favorite Web sites by creating new folders. In addition you can move, rename, or delete favorite links.

The folders that you create to organize your favorite Web sites appear in the Favorites menu as cascading menus. To view one of the saved links, choose it from the Favorites menu or one of the cascading menus. If you have a lot of favorite Web sites you can also create folders within folders for even more organization.

When you are creating folders to organize your Favorites menu, you may want to create a number of Web site categories. For example, you might create a folder to hold links to all of your favorite news Web sites. Another folder category might hold links to sites relating to your favorite hobby, or perhaps travel-related links so you can dream about your next vacation.

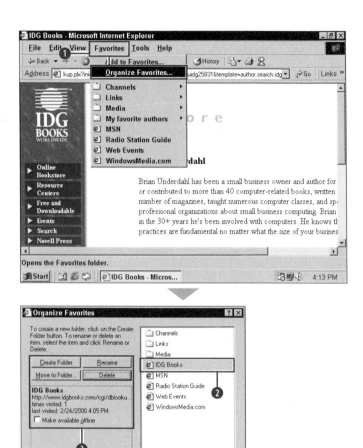

1 Select Favorites ➪ Organize Favorites.

2 To modify an item, first select it.

3 Select the appropriate options.

CROSS-REFERENCE

See "Organizing Your Documents" in Chapter 5.

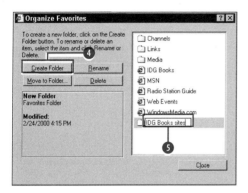

You can also delete links that you seldom use to help with the organization of your Favorites list. For example, if you find that you never use the links to various Microsoft sites that are automatically placed in your Favorites list, you can simply remove them. Alternatively, you may want to move them to an out-of-the-way folder.

TAKE NOTE

▶ DON'T USE WINDOWS EXPLORER

Although you can use Windows Explorer to organize your Favorites folder, the Organize Favorites dialog box shown in the figures is usually a better option. This dialog box has options specific to the Favorites list, and shows you information about how often and how recently you have visited each Web site. In addition, you can use this dialog box to specify that certain Web pages should be available for offline browsing and even modify the synchronization schedule for those pages.

▶ ADD ITEMS DIRECTLY TO FOLDERS

When you choose Favorites ⇨ Add to Favorites, one of the options in the Add Favorite dialog box is the Create In button. If you have created folders for organizing your favorite Web sites, you can add those links directly to the appropriate folder rather than moving them later.

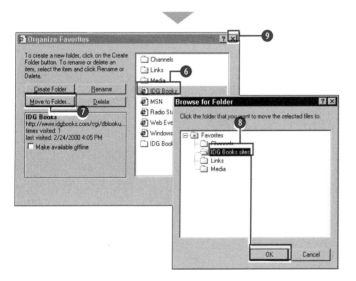

④ To create a folder, click the Create Folder button.

⑤ Enter a name for the new folder.

⑥ To move an item, first select it.

⑦ Click the Move to Folder button.

⑧ Choose the destination folder and click OK.

⑨ Click the Close button to complete the task.

FIND IT ONLINE

See **http://computingcentral.com/topics/ie4/** for answers to common questions about Internet Explorer.

Configuring Internet Explorer

Internet Explorer has a huge number of options that you can use to control just how the program functions. These options run the gamut from simple changes like choosing your start page to complex items such as setting up different security zones to protect yourself while you are browsing the Internet. The figures on these pages and the next two pages really only scratch the surface of all of the options that you can choose. You should use these examples to get you started on trying out the settings that look most interesting to you.

To give you an idea how some of the Internet Explorer settings might affect you, consider a few of the options you can access through the General tab of the Internet Options dialog box. If you need a little extra help viewing Web pages, the Colors, Fonts, and Accessibility options can make those pages much easier to see.

Next you might look at the options on the Security tab. If you are at all concerned about your safety as you browse the Web — perhaps because you are researching some questionable Web sites — you may want to change the setting for those sites from the minimal security offered by the Internet zone. When you choose one of the zones other than the Internet zone, you can click the Sites button to specify sites that belong in the selected zone. One of the side benefits of placing sites in the Restricted Sites zone is that *cookies* are disabled when the security level is set to high, as it is for this zone.

Continued

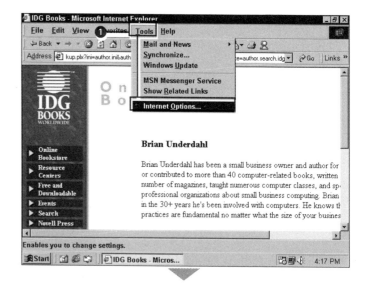

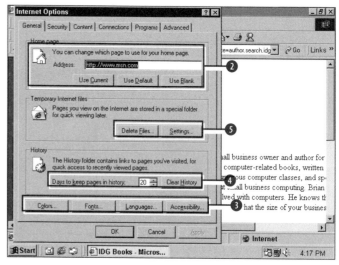

❶ Select Tools ➪ Internet Options.

▶ Alternatively, you can right-click the Internet Explorer icon on your desktop and choose Properties.

❷ Select the Internet Explorer start page options.

❸ Alternatively, use these buttons to control the appearance options.

❹ Use these options to control how long links remain in the History folder.

❺ Use these options if you wish to adjust the temporary file options

CROSS-REFERENCE

See "Visiting Web Sites" earlier in this chapter.

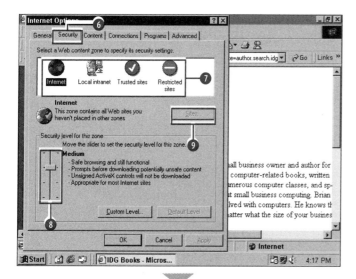

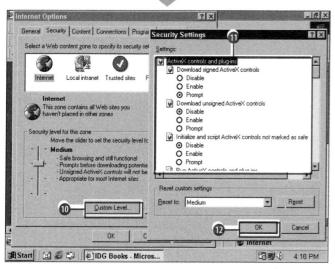

⑥ Click the Security tab.

⑦ Choose the zone to adjust.

⑧ Select the security level for the selected zone.

⑨ Click the Sites button to add sites to a security zone.

⑩ If you wish to change the security level, click Custom level.

⑪ Select the options you prefer.

⑫ Click OK to continue.

TAKE NOTE

CONTROL YOUR COOKIES

When you visit certain Web sites, those sites may use *cookies* to store information on your hard disk. Cookies are supposed to be text files, and they are only supposed to be accessible by the sites that sent them. Unfortunately, any Web site that is in the same *domain* as the one that sent the cookie can access that cookie on your machine, and ascertain information about your computer and your computer use habits. You may want to delete cookies from your computer to prevent unwanted access. To access the cookie settings, click the Custom Level button on the Security tab. Keep in mind, however, that some Web sites will not load unless your Web browser accepts cookies.

CUSTOM SECURITY OPTIONS

If you choose to set up a custom security level, you will have three options for most items — Disable, Enable, or Prompt. If you choose Prompt you will have to accept or reject each item every time it is part of a Web page. This can quickly become annoying, so it may be better to choose one of the other options, as you feel appropriate.

FIND IT ONLINE

See **http://www.adfilter.com/download/adfsetup. exe** for a shareware utility blocks advertising while you surf the Web.

Configuring Internet Explorer

Continued

In addition to the Internet Explorer options already shown on the previous pages, there are quite a few other options you can control.

On the Content tab you can use the Content Advisor to control the types of Web sites that can be visited on your PC. This option enables you to restrict access to sites that you find offensive. You can use the Certificates settings to control which certificates you will accept and to install your own personal certificates to confirm your identity (see the Take Note section). The Personal information settings make filling out forms easier.

The Connections tab enables you to configure the way you connect to the Internet. One of the options on this tab — LAN Settings — can be used to enable other computers on your network to share your Internet - connection.

You use the Programs tab to specify which application programs Internet Explorer should use for various tasks. Often you may find that there are several different programs installed on your system that can serve some of the same functions. This tab enables you to select the programs you prefer.

The Advanced tab has many different options that you can use to fine-tune Internet Explorer. Although many of these options are pretty much self-explanatory, some of them will require a little extra clarification if you are to understand their true purpose. The best way to determine what each option does is to click the question mark icon near the upper right corner of the Internet Options dialog box and then click the item that you want explained. If you still aren't positive about the best choice after reading an option's pop-up help message, it's probably safest to leave the option set to the default value.

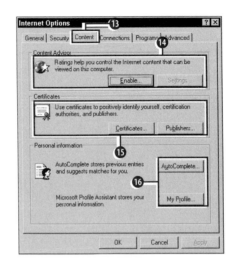

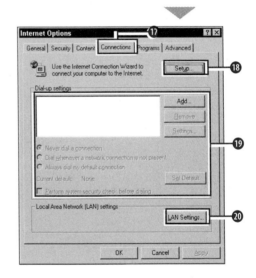

⑬ Click the Content tab.

⑭ If you wish to restrict Web content that can be viewed, use the Content Advisor options.

⑮ To obtain a certificate or view existing certificates, use these options.

⑯ Use these options if you want to change your personal information settings.

⑰ Click the Connections tab.

⑱ To create a new Internet connection, click the Setup button.

⑲ Use these options to adjust your existing connection.

⑳ If you want to adjust your network settings, click LAN Settings.

CROSS-REFERENCE

See Chapter 11 for information on changing the appearance of Windows Me.

204

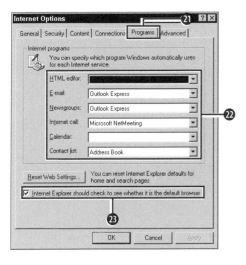

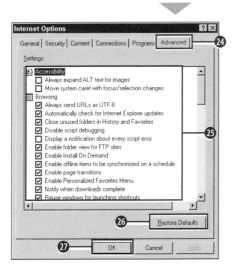

▶ ABOUT CERTIFICATES

Certificates are electronic identity codes that provide positive identification of people and content on the Internet. You can obtain a free or low-cost personal certificate from one of the *certificate authorities* by clicking the Certificates button and following the instructions. Having a personal certificate means that people with whom you exchange e-mail messages can be certain that messages actually were sent by you, and are therefore safe to open. In addition, files that are provided for download from various Web sites are often signed with commercial certificates. If you trust the company that holds the certificate, you should feel confident that a signed file is safe to download.

▶ BE CAREFUL ABOUT AUTOCOMPLETE

The Internet Explorer AutoComplete feature stores information that you enter into forms so that you don't have to type as much information when another form requests the same data. This feature can pose a security risk, because anyone who uses your PC could access your stored information. You may not want to use AutoComplete if you want to protect your credit card or other account information.

㉑ *Click the Programs tab.*

㉒ *If you wish to select a different program for one of these tasks, select it from the list boxes.*

㉓ *If you sometimes use a Web browser other than Internet Explorer, select this check box.*

㉔ *Click the Advanced tab.*

㉕ *Select the options that suit your needs.*

㉖ *To reset the defaults, click here.*

㉗ *Click the OK button to complete the task.*

Setting up MSN Messenger Service

MSN Messenger Service is an *instant messaging* service that enables you to communicate live over the Internet. Once you have MSN Messenger Service set up, you can designate other MSN Messenger Service users who you wish to communicate with. When they are online at the same time you are, you will both be notified and you can send messages instantly.

Instant messaging is somewhat similar to e-mail, but it is far more immediate. When you send an instant message it is immediately delivered to the other person. They don't have to open their e-mail program and check for new messages because instant messages appear in the MSN Messenger Service window as soon as you send them. Instant messaging is also similar to *chat*, but with instant messaging there is no need for you to go to a *chat room* to participate.

To set up MSN Messenger Service you must open a free account with one of the Microsoft Web-based e-mail services such as hotmail.com or passport.com. Although these services are free, you are required to use them on a regular basis if you want to keep the account open. You will be able to determine the current usage requirements by reading the welcome message after you sign up for a new account. If you don't already have a hotmail.com or passport.com account, you can sign up for the account as you are setting up MSN Messenger Service.

▶ Click the Start button and select Programs ⇨ Accessories ⇨ Communications ⇨ MSN Messenger Service.

❶ Click Next to continue.

❷ If you don't already have a hotmail.com or passport.com e-mail account, click here to set one up.

❸ Click Next to continue.

CROSS-REFERENCE

See "Sending Messages Using MSN Messenger Service" next in this chapter.

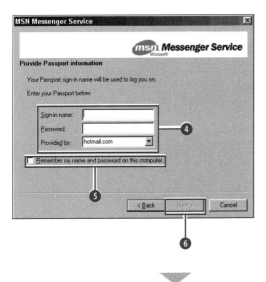

▶ INSTANT MESSAGING IS NOT UNIVERSAL

MSN Messenger Service is not the only instant messaging service that is available on the Internet. Some others include AOL Instant Messenger and ICQ. Unfortunately, AOL has taken steps to prevent MSN Messenger Service users from communicating with AOL Instant Messenger users. As a result, it is really only practical to communicate with other users who use the same instant messaging service that you use. It might be possible to sign up for more than one instant messaging service, but until the battles between the services are resolved, there is no way to determine which instant messaging services will be compatible.

▶ MSN MESSENGER SERVICE ICON

Once you set up MSN Messenger Service, an icon for the service will appear in your Windows Me system tray. You can click this icon to open MSN Messenger Service, to set your current logon status, or to send an instant message to one of your contacts. You can also tell when you are logged off MSN Messenger Service because the icon will have a red circle with an X. If you are logged off, other users will not be informed that you are available for messages even if you are connected to the Internet. You can click the icon and choose Log on to tell your friends that you are connected.

④ Enter your account information here.

⑤ Optionally, click here so you don't have to enter the information manually in the future.

⑥ Click Next to continue.

⑦ Click Finish to complete the task.

FIND IT ONLINE

See **http://messenger.msn.com/** to learn more about MSN Messenger Service.

Sending Messages Using MSN Messenger Service

Once you have set up your MSN Messenger Service account, you can begin to communicate in real time with your friends whenever they are connected to the Internet. They must also set up the MSN Messenger Service on their PC in order for you to communicate with each other, of course.

When you log on to the MSN Messenger Service, you will see a list of your contacts who are currently online and those who are not online. At first both lists will show "None" because you must add contacts to your list in order for them to appear. To add someone to your contact list you click the Add button and then enter their hotmail.com or passport.com e-mail address in the dialog box that appears. It may take a few minutes for a newly added contact to appear in your "Contacts Currently Online" list even if they are online.

If you don't wish to be disturbed, you can change your availability status by clicking the Status button and selecting one of the options from the menu. For example, you can indicate that you cannot respond to messages right now by selecting "On The Phone" so that your friends won't think you are simply ignoring them when they do send a message.

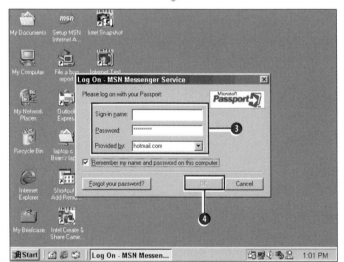

❶ Click the MSN Messenger Service icon.

❷ Select Log on from the menu.

❸ Enter your account information here.

❹ Click OK to continue.

CROSS-REFERENCE

See "Setting up MSN Messenger Service" earlier in this chapter.

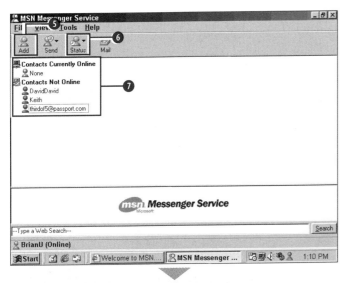

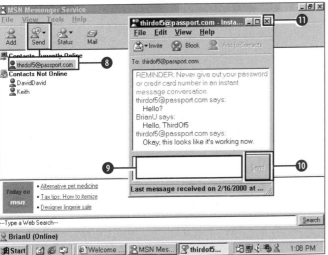

⑤ *Click here to add a new contact to the list.*

⑥ *Click here to change your availability status.*

⑦ *View the status of your contacts here.*

⑧ *Select an online contact and click Send to send them a message.*

⑨ *Type your message here.*

⑩ *Click Send to send your message.*

⑪ *Click the Close button to close the message window.*

TAKE NOTE

SET UP A SEPARATE ACCOUNT

You must have an e-mail account with hotmail.com or passport.com in order to use the MSN Messenger Service. There is, however, no requirement that you use the same account for e-mail and for the MSN Messenger Service. Because the account is free, you may want to set up a separate account that you use only for the MSN Messenger Service. That way you can more easily control your MSN Messenger Service and e-mail accounts, because you can make changes to one without affecting the other. If you do set up more than one account, be sure that you comply with the minimum usage requirements for keeping the accounts open. You can send yourself messages from time to time to generate the necessary usage.

ACCESS MSN MESSENGER SERVICE FROM INTERNET EXPLORER

If you are browsing the Web you can quickly access MSN Messenger Service by clicking the MSN Messenger Service icon on the Internet Explorer toolbar. You can then send and receive messages while you are browsing. You can even copy a URL from the Internet Explorer address box and paste it into a message if you want a friend to browse the same Web page that you are viewing. You can then use the MSN Messenger Service to discuss items on the Web page, such as an item you are considering buying online. This could be a good way to collaborate with someone else if you are buying gifts online.

FIND IT ONLINE

See the MSN Messenger Club at **http://communities. msn.com/MSNMessengerClub/home.htm**.

Personal Workbook

Q&A

1 How can you make certain that a search engine looks for two words that are together?

_____

_____

_____

2 What is a URL?

_____

_____

_____

3 What do both people need in order to use MSN Messenger Service?

_____

_____

_____

4 How can you make it possible to view a Web page without reconnecting to the Internet?

_____

_____

_____

5 How can you make certain that a Web page you visit won't send destructive content to your system?

_____

_____

_____

6 What option can you use to restrict which Web sites can be accessed from your PC?

_____

_____

_____

7 How can you create folders to store links to related Web sites?

_____

_____

_____

8 What button can you use to return to the last Web page you visited?

_____

_____

_____

ANSWERS: PAGE 395

EXTRA PRACTICE

1. Open Internet Explorer and go to **http://www.idgbooks.com**.

2. Click several links to open some different Web pages.

3. Use the Back button list to go back a couple of pages.

4. Save a Web page in your list of favorites.

5. Create a new folder to organize your favorites.

6. Send an instant message to a friend.

REAL-WORLD APPLICATIONS

✔ You are planning a trip so you search the Web to locate information about the events and lodging at a couple of possible destinations.

✔ You are working on a project that involves collaborating with someone at a distant location. You use MSN Messenger Service to communicate in real time.

✔ You have small children who use your PC for schoolwork. You use the Content Advisor to make certain they don't visit inappropriate sites when they are looking for information on the Web.

✔ You are researching your family tree. You search the Web for all references to your family name.

Visual Quiz

What must you do before you can view this window? What does the list of contacts tell you about their status?

_____

_____

_____

_____

_____

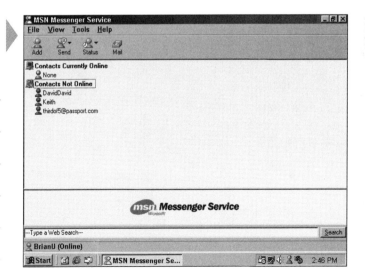

CHAPTER **10**

MASTER
THESE
SKILLS

▶ **Using the Windows Address Book**
▶ **Creating E-Mail Messages**
▶ **Attaching Files to E-Mail**
▶ **Sending E-Mail and Files**
▶ **Reading Your E-Mail**
▶ **Opening the Newsreader**
▶ **Finding Newsgroups**
▶ **Sorting Newsgroup Messages**
▶ **Posting Newsgroup Messages**
▶ **Configuring Outlook Express**

Handling E-Mail and News with Outlook Express

The Internet has many different uses, but one of the most important for many people is electronic mail — e-mail. In fact, some experts feel that e-mail has become the most popular form of communication in the world. Certainly anyone who uses e-mail can appreciate the speed, low cost, and convenience that e-mail provides — especially compared to more traditional methods of communication.

Consider a comparison between e-mail and telephone calls. You can send an e-mail message anywhere in the world without paying long distance charges and without worrying about time differences. The recipient can read your message at his or her convenience and send you a reply immediately — even if you happen to be sleeping when their part of the conversation is taking place. Of course, e-mail compares even more favorably against conventional mail sent through the postal system. Not only is e-mail cheaper, but also it has a delivery speed that no postal system could hope to match.

In this chapter you learn about the Windows Me application called Outlook Express. This program is a full-featured e-mail program, and it offers the bonus of being a great *newsreader*, too.

Newsreaders enable you to participate in *Newsgroups*— gatherings of people on the Internet who discuss topics that interest them. You can find thousands of newsgroups. Newsgroups are organized according to areas of interest, and each group contains so-called threads, which are topical sequences of messages. You can initiate a thread on a newsgroup, and you can add your own messages to the threads.

As an e-mail program, Outlook Express enables you to send and receive messages to anyone else who has an Internet e-mail account. You can then read, reply to, forward, and file your messages at your convenience.

To use Internet e-mail, you must have an account with a mail server, which your Internet Service Provider (ISP) usually provides. To use Internet news, you must have an account with a news server, which your ISP also usually provides. Be sure to set up these accounts before you begin the exercises in this chapter. Your ISP should be able to provide any necessary information to help you get these accounts set up.

Using the Windows Address Book

You probably have some sort of list of names, addresses, and telephone numbers that you use for daily communication. That is, you probably don't rely on remembering all of the addresses and phone numbers for everyone you know. The Windows Me Address Book serves the same function as these written address books, and it offers several advantages, too.

To send an e-mail message you must address the message properly. If you don't use a correct e-mail address, your messages either won't be delivered, or — maybe worse — they may be delivered to someone other than the person you intended. The Windows Me Address Book can serve as your e-mail "black book" so that you can be certain that all of your e-mail messages are properly addressed.

If you use Outlook Express to send and receive e-mail messages, you will find that the Windows Me Address Book is integrated into Outlook Express. But as the figures show, you can open the Windows Me Address Book separately if you want to work with the entries. You might find it easier, for example, to import a contact list from another program if Outlook Express isn't open at the time.

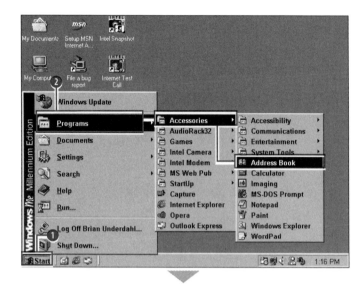

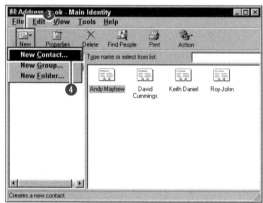

1. Click the Start button.
2. Select Programs ⇨ Accessories ⇨ Address Book.
3. Click the New button to display the drop-down menu.
4. Select New Contact to add a new person to your Address Book.

CROSS-REFERENCE

See "Creating E-Mail Messages" later in this chapter.

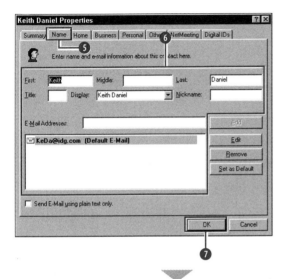

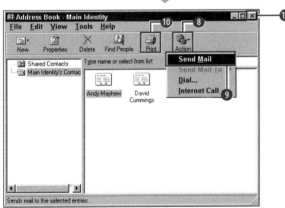

⑤ Click the Name tab.

⑥ Enter the contact information.

⑦ Click OK to continue.

⑧ Click the Action button to display the drop-down menu.

⑨ Click Send Mail to send an e-mail message to the selected contact.

⑩ Alternatively, click Print to print your contact list entries.

⑪ Click the Close button to complete the task.

CHOOSE YOUR FAVORITE VIEW

The Windows Me Address Book has several options on the View menu that you can use to control how your contacts appear in the list. In addition to the obvious settings for large or small icons, a simple list, or full details, you can use the View ➪ Sort By command to choose the order in which the items appear. You could, for example, choose to sort the list by last name rather than by first name. Or you might choose to sort by phone numbers to make it easier to see which of your customers are in a specific area code.

IMPORTING VCARDS

If someone sends you their contact information in the form of a vCard — an Internet standard for electronic business cards — you can easily import that information into your Windows Me Address Book. To do so, use the File ➪ Import ➪ Business Card (vCard) command. VCards make it very easy to share accurate contact information because you do not have to retype any information to add the contact to your Address Book. You can also export vCards using the File ➪ Export ➪ Business Card (vCard) command and then e-mail the vCard to someone else for their Address Book. Because vCards use a standard format, most modern e-mail programs can import and export vCard files to and from their Address Books. You may want to create a contact record for yourself in Outlook Express and export it to a vCard file to make it easy for people to add you to their Address Book.

FIND IT ONLINE

See **http://www.microsoft.com/ windows98/USING WINDOWS/COMMUNICATING/TIPS/OUTLOOK EXPRESS/ADDRESSBOOK/ADDRESS.ASP** for more info.

Creating E-Mail Messages

Creating e-mail messages really isn't much different than typing and mailing a letter. E-mail, of course, is quite a bit quicker, and it is very easy to include things such as digital images or other attachments. You can use Outlook Express to send and receive all of your e-mail in Windows Me.

The Outlook Express window has several important elements that you can use to work with your e-mail. For example, the Folders bar displays a list of your mail folders. The Inbox folder contains messages that Outlook Express has downloaded into your computer from the mail server. The Outbox folder contains messages that you have composed but that Outlook Express has not yet sent to the mail server. The Sent Items folder contains copies of the e-mail messages that have been sent to the mail server. The Deleted Items folder contains Dmessages that you have deleted from other folders. The Drafts folder is for storing messages that are in progress and that you are not ready to send.

Although Outlook Express enables you to format your message just as you would a word processor document, it may not always be safe to assume that the message recipient will see the formatting you've applied. If you must include formatting in your message, you may wish to create your message in your favorite word processor and send the message as a file attachment.

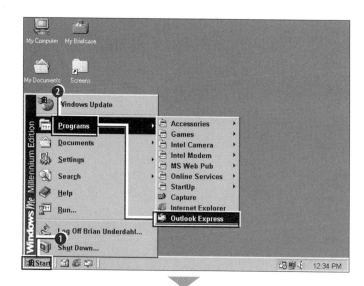

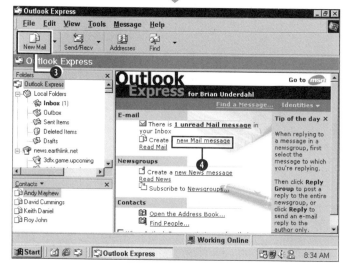

❶ Click the Start button.

❷ Select Programs ➪ Outlook Express.

❸ Click the New Mail button to begin composing a new message.

❹ Alternatively, click the new Mail message link.

CROSS-REFERENCE

See "Sending E-Mail and Files" later in this chapter.

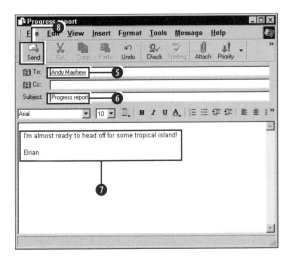

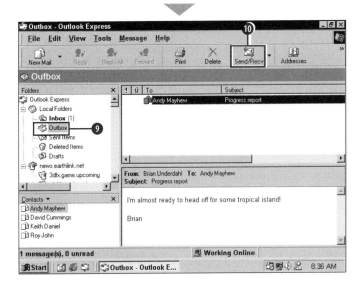

YOU MUST SET UP YOUR ACCOUNT

Before you can use Outlook Express for the first time, you must set up your e-mail account information. You will have to do this only once unless you change to a different e-mail account. If you entered your e-mail account information when you set up your Internet connection, Outlook Express will use the information you entered and will not prompt you to reenter the information. If you have not already entered the information you will have to step through a series of simple questions the first time you start Outlook Express. If you don't have all of the information to set up your e-mail account, ask your ISP to provide the details so that you can continue.

UNDERSTAND THE FOLDER DISPLAY

In Outlook Express, folder names sometimes appear in a bold font and are followed by a number in parenthesis. The bold font indicates that the folder contains unread messages, and the number in parentheses specifies how many unread messages are in the folder. Any Outlook Express folder can contain unread messages — if, for example, you delete messages without reading them, the Deleted Items folder would show how many unread messages it contained. If you want more room for reading messages, you may want to toggle the display of the Folders bar using the View ⇨ Layout command.

5 Enter the recipient e-mail address in the To box.

6 Enter a topic in the Subject box.

7 Enter the text of your message.

8 Click the Send button to place the new message into your Outbox and close the message editor.

9 Optionally, click the Outbox folder to view the outbound messages.

10 Depending on your settings, you may need to click the Send/Recv button to connect to the mail server.

217

Attaching Files to E-Mail

Although in most cases a simple text note may be all that is needed to put across your message, you'll probably find that *file attachments* are often a handy addition to some e-mail messages. File attachments can be any type of file — word processor document files, spreadsheet files, or graphics images.

When you send a file attachment along with an e-mail message, it's always wise to include both a descriptive subject line and a brief message explaining what you have sent. There are several reasons for this. Someone may not be willing to open a file and risk infecting their system with a computer virus. By adding a personal message you can offer some reassurance that your file attachment is safe. Also, mail systems sometimes mangle file attachments, so a message telling the recipient what you have sent can make it easier for them to sort out what was received.

When you send file attachments, it's always a good idea to be considerate of the intended recipient. Although you may have a fast Internet connection and may feel that a large graphic image is humorous, if the recipient is connecting via modem or has to pay for connect time, they may not share your sense of humor.

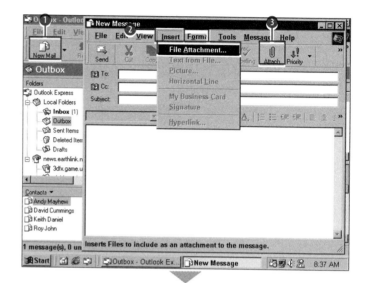

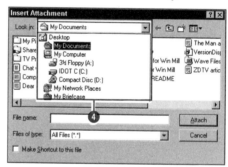

① Click the New Mail button.

② Select Insert ⇨ File Attachment.

③ Alternatively, click the Attach button.

④ Select the file location.

CROSS-REFERENCE

See "Creating E-Mail Messages" earlier in this chapter.

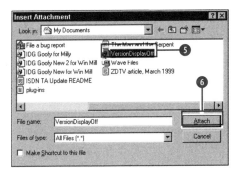

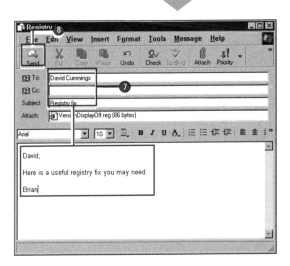

▶ WATCH FILE SIZES

One problem that you may encounter when sending file attachments is a limitation on the file size. Although it's not very common for your outgoing mail server to limit the sizes of files that you send, there are often limits on the sizes of files that people can receive. This limit may cause e-mail messages that contain file attachments to be returned to your Inbox — which can be especially frustrating if you are using a slow connection because you must not only wait while the message is sent but also while it is returned. You may want to check with the intended recipient before you send very large attachments.

▶ AVOID ATTACHMENT PROBLEMS

Unfortunately, not all mail systems are fully compatible. AOL, for example, uses a proprietary mail system that can cause recipients to be unable to open file attachments. If you have trouble sending file attachments to certain people, there are a couple of ways to avoid these problems. When you are composing a message you can select Format ⇨ Plain Text from the message editor menu to send the message in a format that should work for most recipients. Alternatively, you can use a utility such as WinZip to compress the file before you attach it to the message. In most cases recipients should be able to receive files compressed with WinZip without difficulties, and it may take far less time to send the message as well.

⑤ Select the file you wish to attach.

⑥ Click the Attach button to insert the file into the message.

⑦ Enter the address, subject, and text of your message.

▶ You can also enter the name of someone who is listed in your address book.

⑧ Click the Send button to complete the task.

FIND IT ONLINE

See **http://www.winzip.com** to download a trial version of WinZip.

Sending E-Mail and Files

The e-mail messages that you send must be sent from your computer to a mail server in order to actually get anywhere. When you place items in the Outlook Express Outbox, those items need to be transferred to the mail server provided by your ISP. Once the messages have been delivered to the mail server, they can be sent over the Internet to the recipient's mailbox.

Outlook Express can be configured several different ways. By default, Outlook Express checks for e-mail every 30 minutes whenever the program is running. It also automatically checks for incoming and outgoing messages when you first start the program. In addition, the default settings send any new messages you create immediately when you click the Send button in the message creation window. If you have changed any of the default settings, you can check for new messages and send any messages from your Outbox by clicking the Send/Recv button. You can also click this button to check for new mail even if you have not changed any of the default settings.

You can change the 30-minute interval or even disable the automatic e-mail checking if you like. Select Tools ➪ Options to display the Options dialog box. On the General tab, remove the check from the *Check for new messages every xx minute(s)* check box to disable automatic checking. To change the schedule, leave the check box selected and use the spin box to set the new interval. If Outlook Express is not checking for messages automatically and you want it to, make certain that this option is selected.

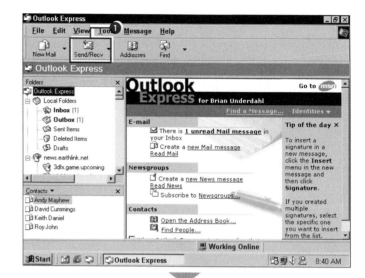

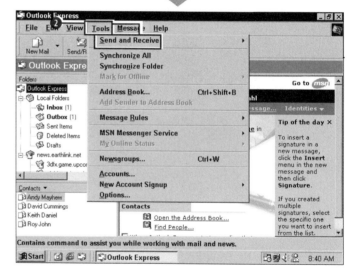

❶ Click the Send/Recv button.

❷ Alternatively, select Tools ➪ Send and Receive to open the Send and Receive menu.

CROSS-REFERENCE

See "Reading Your E-Mail" later in this chapter.

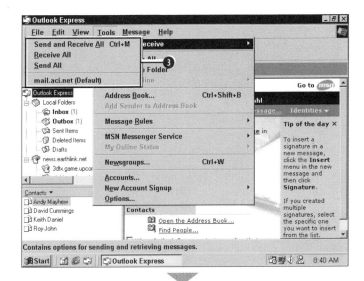

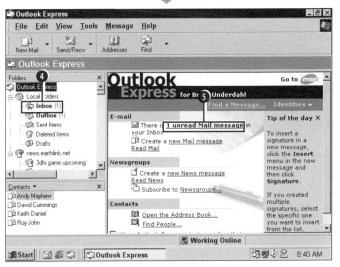

SEND MESSAGES WHEN YOU WANT

If you'd prefer to hold messages rather than have them sent as soon as you've composed them, select Tools ➪ Options and click the Send tab. Clear the "Send messages immediately" check box and click OK. You'll need to either send your messages manually or wait until the next scheduled connect time. Holding messages in the Outbox for a few minutes may be a good idea, especially for messages you may wish to reconsider. Once a message has been sent there's no way to retrieve it — there's no "Unsend" button.

TROUBLESHOOTING E-MAIL

If you are having trouble connecting to your mail server, you may need to do a little troubleshooting. One way to do this is to enable the command logging option that produces a log file that contains the dialog between your PC and the server. The log file is a text file named pop3.log. To enable logging, select Tools ➪ Options and click the Maintenance tab. Place a check in the Mail check box in the Troubleshooting section. Your ISP should be able to locate the trouble if you send them a copy of the log file along with a description of the problem you are having.

③ *Choose the mail handling option that suits your current needs.*

▶ *You could, for example, choose to receive all new messages without sending your outgoing messages immediately.*

④ *View the number of new messages here — click the Inbox folder icon to open the Inbox.*

⑤ *Alternatively, click this link to open the Inbox.*

Reading Your E-Mail

When you receive e-mail messages you will probably want to open and read them. In some cases you may want to reply to a message or you may want to forward that message to someone else. If the message contains any file attachments, you will probably want to save those attachments as well.

When someone sends you an e-mail message that has an attachment, Outlook Express uses a small paper-clip icon to indicate that the message has an attachment. If you want to open or save the attachment, you must view the message. Viewing a message in the message preview pane does not enable you to rename attachments when you save them. If a message has a graphics file attached, you can usually view the image in the preview pane.

When you open a message that includes a file attachment, the message window includes an Attach box for any file attachments. Each file attachment has its own icon in the Attach box.

After you've opened a message that contains file attachments, you can choose what to do with the attachments. The options vary according to the type of file that is attached, but two options are always available: opening or saving the file. If you choose to open the file, Windows Me attempts to determine the file type and use the appropriate method to open the file. If the file is a program, this means that Windows Me attempts to run the program. If the file is a data file or a document, Windows Me tries to open it in the associated

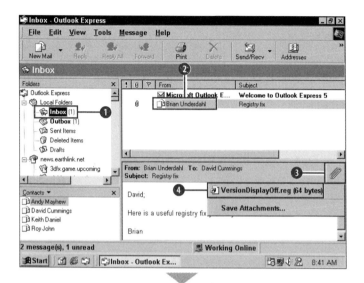

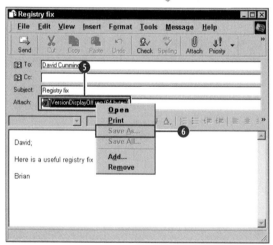

❶ Open the Inbox folder.

❷ Click a message to view it in the Preview pane.

❸ If the message contains an attachment, click the paper-clip icon to display the attachments context menu.

❹ Click here to open the attachment.

▶ Alternatively, double-click the message to open it.

❺ Right-click the attachment to display the context menu.

❻ Select Save As to display the Save Attachments dialog box.

CROSS-REFERENCE

See "Attaching Files to E-Mail" earlier in this chapter.

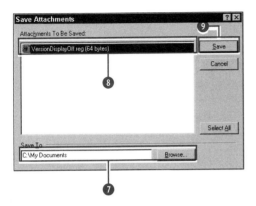

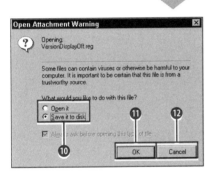

application. If you choose to save the file, Windows Me displays the Save Attachment As dialog box. Be sure to note the location where the file is saved so that you can find it later.

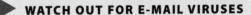

▶ WATCH OUT FOR E-MAIL VIRUSES

Recent news stories have made everyone aware of the danger of e-mail viruses. Viruses are typically programs that are attached to e-mail messages, and they spread by sending themselves to the people who are listed in your address book. If you open or run a file attachment that contains a virus, your PC is in danger. The best way to protect yourself against this threat is never to save or open file attachments unless you're certain you can trust the source and you were expecting a file. If you weren't expecting to receive a file, you may want to send a message to the sender asking them to confirm that they sent you the original message and the attachment.

▶ CLEAN OUT YOUR INBOX

If you receive a lot of messages it is a good idea to delete old messages when they are no longer needed. This is especially true if the messages contained attachments that you have saved. Otherwise your saved messages will continue to eat up your disk space.

⑦ Select the location to save the file.

⑧ Optionally, select the attachments to save.

⑨ Click the Save button.

⑩ If the Open Attachment Warning dialog box appears, choose to open or save the file.

⑪ Click OK to confirm the action.

⑫ Alternatively, click Cancel to skip opening or saving the file.

FIND IT ONLINE

To learn how to change the new mail notification sound, see **http://www.windows-help.net/windows98/oe-20.shtml**.

Opening the Newsreader

I n the last chapter you learned a little bit about one of the most popular parts of the Internet — the World Wide Web. So far in this chapter you've learned about another of the common uses of the Internet — sending and receiving e-mail messages. Now we turn to another very useful part of the Internet — Usenet newsgroups. These gatherings are giant discussion groups in which people from all around the world come together to discuss, argue, and dissect all manner of topics.

The people who frequent newsgroups represent an extremely broad range of personalities. In some newsgroups you'll find experts who can share information that you simply won't be able to find anywhere else. In others you'll find ordinary people who have come together to trade ideas about nearly any subject you can imagine. In almost any newsgroup you're also likely to run into self-styled "experts" who will do their best to either make you believe their latest conspiracy theory or rake you over the coals if you somehow offend them. To paraphrase an old saying, "let the newsgroup visitor beware" — not all of the information you'll see in a newsgroup is quite as reliable as you might hope.

Before you can use the Outlook Express newsreader, you must set up a news account. Typically your ISP will provide you with the name of their news server and any special information that you might need in order to access newsgroups.

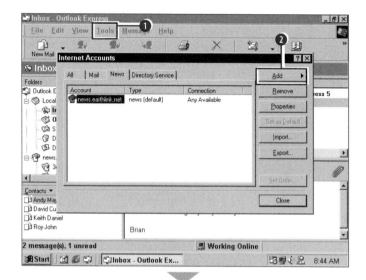

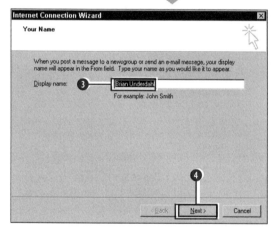

Continued

❶ Select Tools ➪ Accounts to open the Internet Accounts dialog box.

❷ Click the Add button and choose News.

❸ In the Internet Connection Wizard, enter the name that you wish to appear on any messages that you post.

❹ Click Next to continue.

CROSS-REFERENCE

See "Finding Newsgroups" later in this chapter.

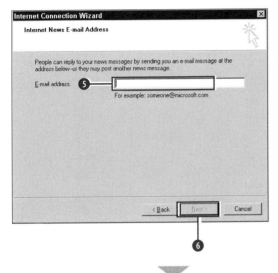

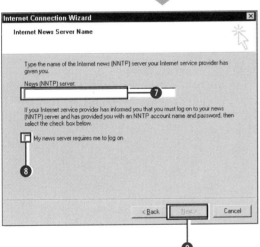

YOU MAY NEED A NEWSGROUP PASSWORD

The Internet holds literally thousands of newsgroups, and many of them cater to very extreme adult tastes. Not all of these newsgroups are really suitable for a general audience. Many ISPs limit the range of newsgroups that you can access unless you have specifically requested access to the adult-rated newsgroups. If your ISP has limits on general access to newsgroups, you may need a special logon name and password — which will be provided by your ISP — in order to access the restricted newsgroups.

CONSIDER A SECOND E-MAIL ACCOUNT

One of the biggest problems with posting messages on newsgroups is *spam* — unwanted junk e-mail that can end up clogging your inbox. Unfortunately there are people who use special software to scan newsgroups simply to find e-mail addresses. They then flood all of the addresses that they find with bulk e-mail messages advertising everything from get-rich-quick schemes to porno Web sites. In some cases they even sell lists of e-mail addresses to other bulk e-mailers. You may want to open one of the free Web-based e-mail accounts to use only for your newsgroup postings. That way you can close the account and move on to a different one if the spammers get your e-mail address from a newsgroup.

⑤ Enter the e-mail address that you wish to use for newsgroup purposes.

⑥ Click Next to continue.

⑦ Enter the name of the newsgroup server as provided by your ISP.

⑧ Optionally, click here if you must log on. You will also need to supply a name and password for the news server.

⑨ Click Next to continue.

FIND IT ONLINE

For information on how to open a Hotmail account, see
http://lc4.law5.hotmail.passport.com/cgi-bin/login.

Opening the Newsreader
Continued

Once you have set up your newsgroup server account, Outlook Express must download the list of newsgroups that are available on the server. Be prepared to wait several minutes for this process to complete — especially if you have a slow Internet connection. As you will soon discover, there are literally tens of thousands of newsgroups available on the typical newsgroup server. Fortunately you don't have to download the list each time you wish to visit the newsgroups. Outlook Express will keep a record of the existing newsgroups and in the future will only download any changes.

Newsgroup messages consist of *message headers* and the actual messages themselves. Message headers are the subject lines, and they are generally descriptive enough to enable you to figure out which messages look interesting enough to read.

When you select a newsgroup so that you can view the messages, Outlook Express doesn't really download all of the messages contained in the newsgroup. Rather it downloads the newest message headers so that you can choose the specific messages that you want to read. By default, Outlook Express downloads up to 300 message headers when you open a newsgroup.

As you browse through the available newsgroups you'll soon notice that most newsgroups contain a large number of messages that are unrelated to the newsgroup topic. Unfortunately, there isn't much you can do to avoid seeing these types of messages. As a rule, the best defense is to simply ignore them. The worst thing you can do is to respond. After the message originator has your e-mail address you're likely to be buried in unwanted junk e-mail.

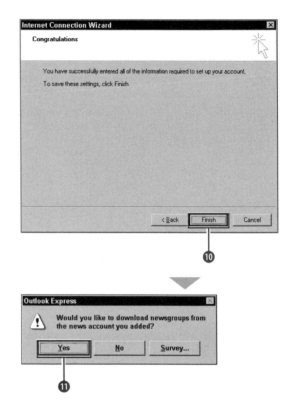

⑩ Click the Finish button to complete setting up your news account.

▶ Click the Close button in the Internet Accounts dialog box to continue.

⑪ Click the Yes button to begin the download of the newsgroup names.

▶ If you did not choose to download the newsgroups earlier, you may need to click the Read News link to begin the download.

CROSS-REFERENCE

See "Searching for Web Sites" in Chapter 9.

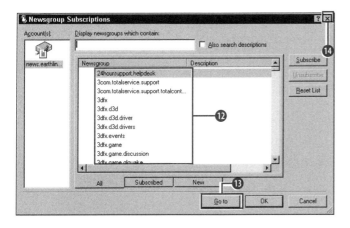

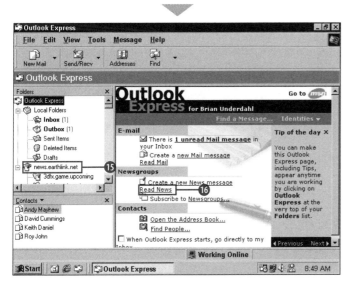

If you like, you have the option to *subscribe* to newsgroups. Subscribing to a newsgroup isn't the same as subscribing to a magazine; you don't pay for a subscription, and you aren't obligated to participate. Subscribing to a newsgroup simply tells Outlook Express that you want the newsgroup to appear in the folder list and that you always want the latest messages from that newsgroup available.

TAKE NOTE

▶ CONTROL NEWSGROUP OPTIONS

If you would rather download a different quantity of newsgroup headers instead of the default 300 headers, select Tools ⇨ Options and click the Read tab. In the News section of this tab you can specify the number of headers you would like downloaded whenever you enter a newsgroup. You can also use the *Mark all messages as read when exiting a newsgroup* check box to avoid having to consider old messages when you return to a newsgroup.

▶ AVOID FLAME WARS

Some pretty antisocial types inhabit certain newsgroups. These people will *flame* — insult — anyone who somehow offends them. If someone starts treating you abusively in a newsgroup, the best thing to do is to avoid them and don't start trading insults.

⑫ Select a newsgroup that you wish to view.

⑬ Click the Go to button to view the message headers for the selected newsgroup.

▶ When the message headers are displayed, click a header to view the message.

⑭ Click the Close button to close the dialog box.

⑮ To again view the list of newsgroups, click the newsgroup folder.

⑯ Alternatively, click the Read News link to view the list.

▶ You must select a newsgroup and connect to the Internet to view the messages.

FIND IT ONLINE

To learn how to set the mail server timeout, see http://www.windows-help.net/windows98/oe-12.shtml.

Finding Newsgroups

A typical news server may list many thousands of newsgroups — nearly 100,000 in some cases. Such numbers make it virtually impossible for anyone to manually look through the entire list of newsgroup names. You could spend days just looking through all of the names of the newsgroups and you still wouldn't know anything about the messages that were contained in more than a small handful of them. By the time you finished your search you'd be so confused you probably wouldn't remember more than a few of the interesting-sounding newsgroups. You need a better way to find specific newsgroups.

Newsgroup originators make an effort to indicate the newsgroup topic through keywords in the newsgroup name. For example, if a newsgroup includes the term "ms-windows" in its name, it's probably a pretty good guess that the newsgroup has something to do with a Microsoft Windows–related topic. Still, you need a way to narrow the list to include only those newsgroups with specific keywords in their titles. When you're looking for particular topics, you can have Outlook Express narrow the list by showing only those newsgroups with specified words in their names.

You can further refine your newsgroup search by searching the results for a second or even a third word. The figures show two methods of refining a search. You can search for a single term, subscribe to the resulting groups, and then search for the second term within the subscribed groups. Another way to reach this goal is by including all of the words in a single search phrase. All of the words you specify must be found in each newsgroup name that qualifies.

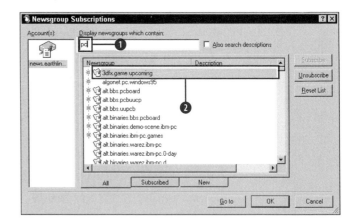

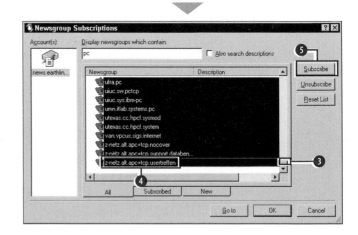

▶ Open a newsgroup list.

❶ Enter your first search phrase in the text box.

❷ Once Outlook Express narrows the list to those containing the phrase, click the first newsgroup in the list.

❸ Drag the scroll box down to the bottom of the scrollbar.

❹ Press and hold Shift as you click the last listed newsgroup.

❺ Click the Subscribe button to move the selected list to the Subscribed tab.

CROSS-REFERENCE

See Chapter 6 for more information on searching for files.

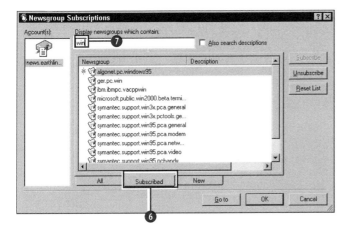

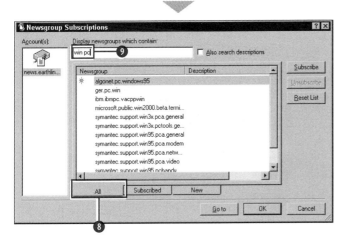

LOOKING FOR MESSAGES

The Outlook Express newsreader is handy but it is certainly not the most powerful tool for searching through newsgroup postings. You cannot, for example, look through a series of newsgroups to find every message on specific topics. If someone posts a message in a newsgroup that doesn't happen to be one of those you have selected, you probably won't ever see the message. Some other tools do a far better job of finding newsgroup messages than Outlook Express. One of these is Remarq, a service that indexes newsgroup messages. You can find Remarq at **http://www.remarq.com**.

CONSIDER A SEARCH TOOL

Locating interesting newsgroups can be a challenge — especially if you are interested in some particularly esoteric topics. If your newsgroup search doesn't seem to produce the desired results, you may need to consider alternative ways of locating the topic. One of the most effective ways to improve your results is to use Copernic, a tool you can download from **http://www.copernic.com**. One of the options in Copernic is to search for messages in newsgroups using several different message indexes.

⑥ Click the Subscribed tab.

⑦ Enter the second search phrase in the text box to further narrow the list.

▶ This step narrows the list to only show those newsgroups that include both phrases.

⑧ Alternatively, click the All tab to begin a new search using both phrases at once.

⑨ Enter both search phrases in the text box separated by spaces.

▶ Notice that the lists show the same results whether you enter the phrases together or in two steps.

▶ Notice also that the order of the phrases is unimportant.

Sorting Newsgroup Messages

When you find a newsgroup that looks interesting, the next step is to visit it so you can view the posted messages. Doing so will enable you to determine if you have actually found a useful and interesting newsgroup. You will be able to see, for example, if the newsgroup you selected contains messages with technical hints to help you solve a problem, or if the majority of the messages seem to be *off-topic* posts promoting porno Web sites and get-rich-quick schemes.

When you visit newsgroups you will discover that they often contain hundreds if not thousands of messages. While this means you will have plenty of chances to find something interesting, it also means that you may have a difficult time locating particular messages. You may want to sort the messages based on different criteria in order to better locate messages of interest.

When you are viewing the list of newsgroup messages, you will notice that some messages include a box containing a plus sign (+) directly in front of the subject. This box tells you that there are replies to the message. If you click the box, the replies will appear just below and slightly indented from the original message. Messages with associated replies are called *message threads* or sometimes just *threads*. Message threads are typically the most useful of newsgroup messages because they often include a question and a response. Viewing threads may save you the trouble of asking a question yourself.

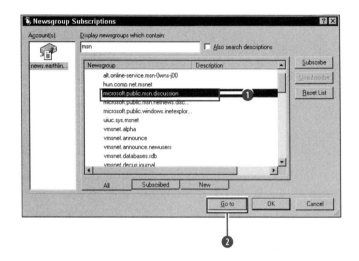

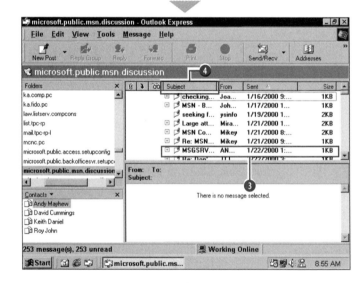

① Select a newsgroup whose messages you would like to view.

② Click the Go to button to display the newsgroup messages.

③ Select a message that you wish to view.

④ Alternatively, click the Subject column to sort the messages by subject.

CROSS-REFERENCE

See "Finding Newsgroups" earlier in this chapter.

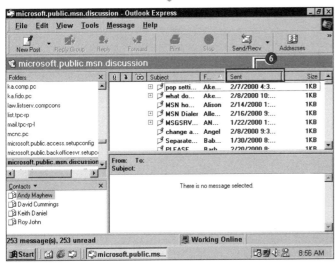

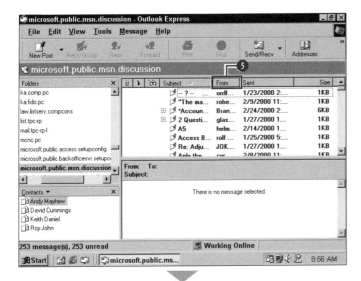

⑤ *To view messages from specific senders, click the From column to sort the messages by sender.*

⑥ *To view messages in descending date order, click the Sent column twice.*

▶ *Clicking any column header a second time reverses the sort order.*

TAKE NOTE

▶ IGNORE OFF-TOPIC MESSAGES

Most newsgroups are flooded with off-topic messages that have nothing to do with the stated focus of the newsgroup. Most often these messages will try to entice you to visit a Web site containing pornographic images or to respond to a pyramid-marketing scheme designed to cheat you out of your money. Although most newsgroup participants are greatly annoyed by these types of messages, the people who post them only need to get a few foolish people to respond in order to accomplish their goals. If you see messages that don't seem to fit the newsgroup topic, your best defense is to ignore them.

▶ LOOK FOR THE EXPERTS

Often one of the most effective methods of sorting messages is to sort them by the author of the posts. Many newsgroups are frequented by experts in the newsgroup topic, and those experts often provide valuable advice. If you sort the messages using the From column, you will be able to see all of the messages posted by particular people, and this may help you identify the people who most often are the sources of useful information.

FIND IT ONLINE

For information on filtering newsgroup messages, see
**http://www.windows-help.net/windows98/oe-04.
shtml.**

Posting Newsgroup Messages

Newsgroups can be a wonderful place to obtain useful information. They can also lead you so far astray that you will have no idea what is fact and what is simply fiction. It is important to keep this in mind before you begin posting your own messages to newsgroups — remember, not everyone who claims to be an expert really has a firm grasp of reality. Treat anything you read in newsgroup messages with a healthy amount of skepticism.

If you have something to contribute to a newsgroup — either useful information or a question that hasn't already been asked dozens of times, you can post a message to the newsgroup. Posting a newsgroup message is very similar to creating and sending an e-mail message, except that your message is sent to a group rather than to a specific person. Anyone who reads the newsgroup messages can also read your message. You will want to keep this very public nature of newsgroup messages in mind as you consider what types of personal information you might include in your messages.

As the figures show, you can also include attachments to your newsgroup messages. Attachments can be any type of file, but should only be files that you have the legal right to distribute. You could, for example, safely include an image you took with your digital camera in most cases. Posting a copy of someone else's work is a completely different matter, and could result in expensive legal problems.

In addition to posting new messages, you can post replies to existing messages. To do so, select the original message and click the Reply Group button.

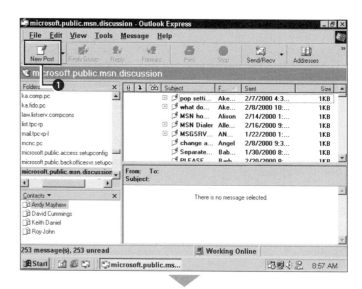

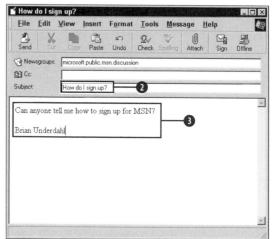

❶ Click the New Post button to begin creating a newsgroup message.

❷ Enter a message subject that describes your message.

❸ Enter the body of your message.

CROSS-REFERENCE

See "Sorting Newsgroup Messages" earlier in this chapter.

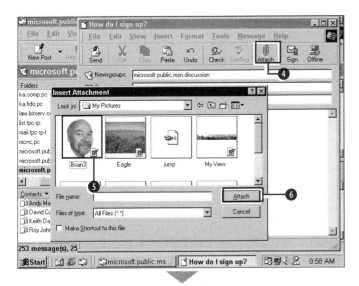

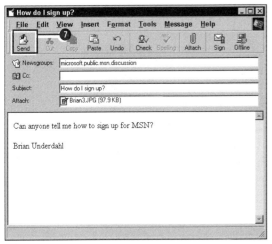

DON'T POST OFF-TOPIC MESSAGES

One of the easiest ways to make everyone in a newsgroup hate you is to post messages that don't have anything to do with the newsgroup topic. You may feel that everyone in the MSN discussion forum should know about the latest Elvis sighting, but it's unlikely that the other participants will share your enthusiasm. If you really feel strongly about a topic, look for the appropriate newsgroup and post your comments there.

LOOK BEFORE YOU LEAP

Newsgroups often have an extensive history of questions and comments about most subjects relating to the topic. New visitors seldom take advantage of this wealth of information and make themselves unwelcome by posting "newbie" questions — even though a few moments of searching the existing messages would provide quick answers. Needless to say, these types of posts are generally not greeted with positive responses. If you want the newsgroup regulars to help with a problem you are having, take the time to make certain that the question hasn't already been asked and answered.

④ If you wish to include an attachment, click the Attach button.

⑤ Select the file to attach.

⑥ Click Attach.

⑦ Click the Send button to send your message.

▶ Message posting may take some time — especially if the newsgroup controls which messages can be posted.

For information on using multiple accounts for newsgroup postings, see **http://www.windows-help. net/windows98/oe-05.shtml**.

Configuring Outlook Express

Outlook Express is a flexible program with plenty of options that you can adjust to make the program work the way you want it to. Until you play around with the Outlook Express options, you may not even realize many of the ways you can customize it.

Outlook Express has far too many options to cover here in a few figures. The figures do show you some of the more important configuration options. If you take a few minutes to understand these and then investigate the options that are not discussed, you'll be able to fine-tune the way Outlook Express works.

The options on the Send tab can be especially important to your satisfaction with Outlook Express. For example, if you make certain that the *Automatically put people I reply to in my Address Book* option is selected, you seldom have to add new e-mail addresses manually. If you have replied to someone in the past, Outlook Express will already know their e-mail address, and you can simply choose it from the Address Book by clicking the To button when you compose a new message.

If you sometimes forget to check for new e-mail messages, you can automate the process by using the *Check for new messages every xx minute(s)* option on the General tab of the Options dialog box. If you do select this option, be sure to also select the *Hang up after sending and receiving* check box on the Connection tab. Selecting both of these options will ensure that Outlook Express will regularly check for new messages but will not tie up your telephone line for long intervals.

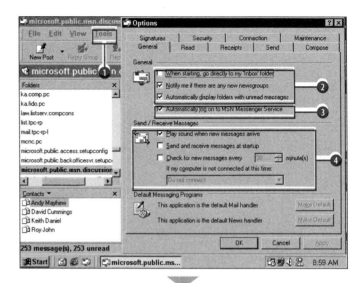

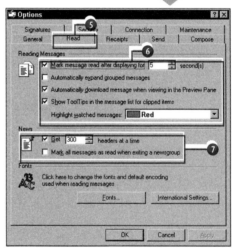

➊ Select Tools ➪ Options to open the Options dialog box.

➋ Select the startup options.

➌ Optionally, choose whether to automatically log on to the MSN Messenger Service.

➍ Choose the message sending and receiving options.

➎ Click the Read tab.

➏ Choose options for reading messages.

➐ Select your newsgroup settings.

CROSS-REFERENCE

See "Using the Windows Address Book" earlier in this chapter.

Be sure to check out the options on all of the tabs of the Options dialog box to see how you can customize Outlook Express.

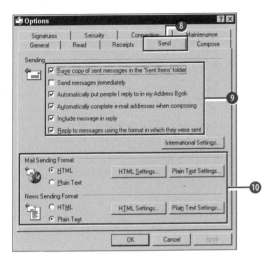

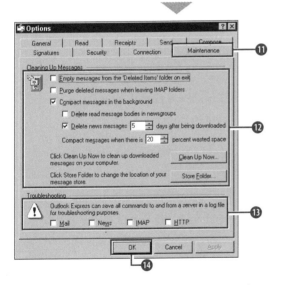

8 *Click the Send tab.*

9 *Decide which message sending options you prefer.*

10 *Select the formatting options for e-mail and news messages you send.*

11 *Click the Maintenance tab.*

12 *Select the options for removing old messages.*

13 *If necessary, select log files to create for troubleshooting purposes.*

14 *Click OK to close the dialog box and confirm your selections.*

TAKE NOTE

▶ INCLUDING THE ORIGINAL MESSAGE IN YOUR RESPONSE

To make certain you include someone's original text when you reply to a message, select the *Include message in reply* check box on the Send tab. If you consider that many people deal with dozens or even hundreds of e-mail messages in an average day, you can understand why including the original message is so important. If you don't include something that places your reply into the proper context, it's entirely possible that the recipient won't understand your reply.

▶ GETTING A NEW MAIL MESSAGE

Your PC can play a sound whenever new messages arrive. Be sure the *Play sound when new messages arrive* check box on the General tab is selected. You'll need to use the Sounds and Multimedia applet in Control Panel to assign a sound file to the New Mail Notification event as discussed in Chapter 12. You can even record your own unique sound file to use as the notification that you have new mail.

FIND IT ONLINE

To learn how to disable the screen that appears when you start Outlook Express, see **http://www. windows-help.net/windows98/oe-13.shtml**.

Personal Workbook

Q&A

1 Why do Outlook Express folder names sometimes appear in boldface?

_____

_____

_____

2 What do you need to do before you can save a file that came along with an e-mail message?

_____

_____

_____

3 Where do messages you've created wait until they're sent to the mail server?

_____

_____

_____

4 What is the meaning of the number in parentheses following an Outlook Express folder name?

_____

_____

_____

5 How can you find newsgroups that pertain to a specific subject?

_____

_____

_____

6 How can you stop an e-mail message from being delivered once it leaves your Outbox?

_____

_____

_____

7 What message format can you use to make certain that anyone can read your message?

_____

_____

_____

8 How often must you download the entire list of newsgroups?

_____

_____

_____

ANSWERS: PAGE 395

EXTRA PRACTICE

1. Locate newsgroups that discuss Windows Me.

2. Configure Outlook Express to check for mail every 10 minutes.

3. Create and send an e-mail message to a friend.

4. Attach several files to a message and send the message to your e-mail address.

5. When the new message arrives, open one of the attachments.

6. Subscribe to a newsgroup that relates to your favorite vacation activity.

REAL-WORLD APPLICATIONS

✔ You want to find out about relocating to a city halfway across the country. You send an e-mail message to a local real estate office to find out about homes that are available.

✔ You are having trouble finding the proper settings for your printer. You visit a newsgroup relating to your brand and search for messages that might indicate which settings you need to use.

✔ You are on a business trip and discover that you forgot an important file for tomorrow's presentation. You send an e-mail to the office and ask a coworker to attach the missing file to his or her reply.

✔ You are in charge of a family reunion. You send out e-mail messages to keep all of your relatives informed of the latest schedule updates.

Visual Quiz

How can you display this dialog box? If you want to place your outbound messages in the Outbox rather than sending them as soon as you've created them, what setting do you need to adjust?

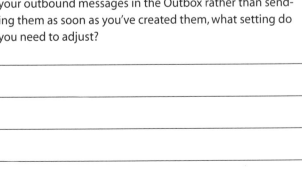

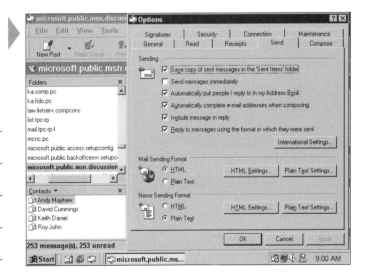

_____

_____

_____

_____

Contents of 'Desktop'

Name

My Computer

Network Neigh

Internet Explore

Microsoft Outloc

Recycle Bin

My Briefcase

3252-9

3259-6

3261-8

3262-6

3281-2

3286-3

DE Phone List

Device Manager

In

Iomega Tools

PART

IV

Customizing and Maintaining Windows Me

Just because Windows Me works pretty well right out of the box doesn't mean that you can't have a little fun by customizing the way it looks and works. In this part you see how you can really emphasize the "personal" part of personal computing. You also learn what you need to do to keep your Windows Me–based PC running at peak efficiency. You may be surprised at just how much you can do to make your computer even better than it already is.

CHAPTER **11**

MASTER
THESE
SKILLS

▶ **Configuring the Desktop**

▶ **Changing the Colors**

▶ **Changing the Resolution**

▶ **Setting the Refresh Rate**

▶ **Using a Screen Saver**

▶ **Using Desktop Themes**

▶ **Using Power Management**

▶ **Moving and Hiding the Taskbar**

▶ **Adding Toolbars to the Taskbar**

▶ **Controlling the Start Menu**

Changing the Look of Windows Me

In this chapter you learn how to have some fun with Windows Me by customizing its appearance. As you start playing around with some of the appearance options that are available, it will become clear that there is an amazing array of things you can do to change the look of Windows Me. While most of these changes are primarily cosmetic adjustments, others may make Windows Me easier to use. There are even some changes that can make Windows Me healthier to use. Of course, some of the changes may affect several of these aspects.

What sort of changes can you make to Windows Me? You can add an image or just a colorful pattern to your desktop. You can modify the colors used for virtually every element of your screen. You can change the screen resolution to squeeze more onto your screen or to make everything larger. You can reduce flickering on your monitor. You can add a screen saver to add some interest whenever you aren't using your PC. You can adjust the power saving features to save energy. You can modify the Taskbar. Finally, you can make a number of adjustments to your Start menu.

In short, you can modify the appearance of your Windows Me–based PC so that it really is personal and reflects your own tastes about how your screen should look. Your PC can and should be interesting to look at and pleasing to use.

As you modify the Windows Me appearance settings, most of the changes you will make won't affect how Windows Me functions. A few of the changes, though, can affect how a user must interact with Windows Me. For example, if you activate a screen saver and you specify a password, you must remember the password if you want to get back to Windows Me once the screen saver is running. If you move or hide the Taskbar, someone might shut down Windows Me incorrectly, perhaps causing you to lose any work you haven't saved. When in doubt, use caution with changes that make it difficult for someone to access the standard Windows Me screen elements. You want to make your PC easier to use, not harder.

Configuring the Desktop

If you want to make an easy change to Windows Me's appearance that has maximum visual impact, you can add a background image. Background images are commonly called *wallpaper*, and they add a unique touch that can change your desktop from boring to fancy. For example, if you work in a small cubicle with nothing to look at, you could add your favorite mountain or seashore image to brighten up your area.

When you add wallpaper to your Windows Me desktop, the image sits behind everything else on your desktop. You don't have to worry about hiding the icons when adding wallpaper. But even though your desktop wallpaper sits behind everything else, some images can make it difficult to see the desktop icons, especially if the wallpaper is loaded with a number of dark colors. If you encounter this type of problem with your favorite wallpaper, you may want to try centering the image rather than tiling or stretching it. Another possibility would be to use your favorite graphic editing program to lighten the image somewhat or perhaps to crop the image so that it uses less space on your desktop.

There are many good sources for image files that you can use as desktop wallpaper. You can, for example, download images you find on the Internet by right-clicking the image and choosing *Set as Wallpaper* or *Save Picture As* from the pop-up menu. If you choose *Save Picture As* you will have to use the Display Properties dialog box to later set the image as wallpaper. You can also use images from your digital camera or scanned copies of photographs as wallpaper. If you use your digital

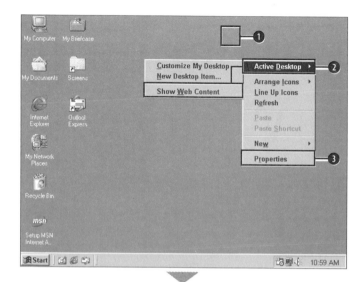

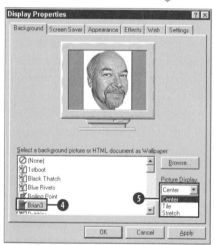

1 Right-click a blank space on the desktop to display the desktop context menu.

2 Select Active Desktop ➪ Show Web Content to enable JPEG images to be used as wallpaper.

3 Select Properties to open the Display Properties dialog box.

4 Choose an image to use as wallpaper.

5 Select the method of displaying the image from the drop-down Display list box.

CROSS-REFERENCE

See "Changing the Resolution" later in this chapter.

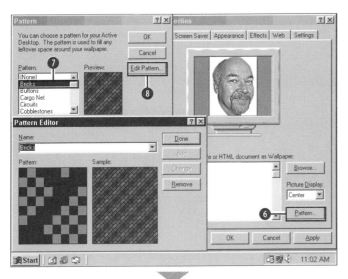

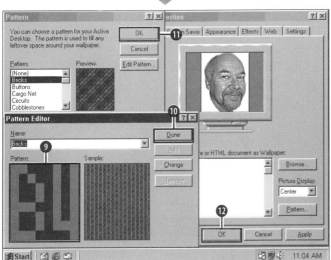

camera to create wallpaper images, you will generally have the best results if the original image has the same *pixel* size as your desktop. You will learn more about screen size later in this chapter.

TAKE NOTE

► ACCEPTABLE IMAGE FORMATS

You can use several different types of graphics files as background images. The Windows Bitmap (BMP) format is the easiest to use because it is automatically supported by Windows Me. If you decide to use a JPEG image, you must allow Windows Me to activate the Active Desktop in order to use JPEG images as wallpaper

► USE THE PROPER SIZE RATIO

Digital images that you download or create using your scanner likely won't have the same dimensions as your Windows Me desktop. You may end up with blank space around a desktop image, or the image may extend beyond the edges of the screen. Although Windows Me offers you the option to stretch the image to fit the desktop, this will produce distorted images unless the original image uses the same 4-wide by 3-high ratio as your screen.

⑥ *Alternatively, click the Pattern button to open the Pattern dialog box.*

⑦ *Choose a pattern from the list box.*

⑧ *Optionally, click the Edit Pattern button to edit the pattern.*

⑨ *Click individual squares in the Pattern box to change their color.*

⑩ *Click Done.*

⑪ *Click OK.*

⑫ *Click OK again to complete the task.*

FIND IT ONLINE

See **http://fdl.msn.com/pubshows/computingcentral/ pcutilities/walmagic.zip** to download a program that automatically changes your wallpaper.

Changing the Colors

If you want to make a really dramatic change to the appearance of Windows Me, you can change the colors used for the various elements of the screen. Almost every element on the Windows Me screen can be modified to use a different set of colors than the standard ones. Because most programs also use the colors that you select for Windows Me, changing the colors will have an effect even when the desktop is covered up.

In addition to going through and selecting your own set of colors, you can choose one of the optional color schemes that are included with Windows Me. The Scheme list box on the Appearance tab of the Display Properties dialog box enables you to choose from several different color schemes so you can see how changing the colors will affect the display without selecting individual colors for yourself. These color schemes may be a good choice— especially if you have special needs. For example, if you have difficulty viewing the screen, you may want to try using one of the high-contrast color schemes. These color schemes are designed to help make the screen much easier to view, especially in poor lighting conditions or for visually impaired users. You may need to experiment with the high-contrast color schemes to see which one works best for you.

When you are selecting a color scheme, choose contrasting colors for the text and background. If you pick text colors that are nearly the same as the background colors, you won't be able to see the text, and you may make it virtually impossible to use Windows Me. If you accidentally set your text colors this way, choose another

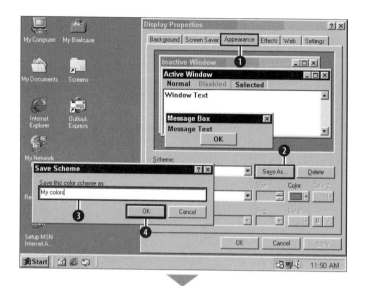

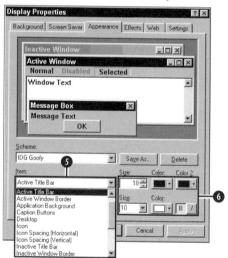

❶ Click the Appearance tab of the Display Properties dialog box.

❷ Click Save As if you wish to save your current color scheme before you make any changes.

❸ Enter a name for your current scheme.

❹ Click OK to continue.

❺ Choose a screen element from the Item list box to change its current color.

❻ Choose the color and size options for the selected element.

CROSS-REFERENCE

See "Using Dialog Boxes" in Chapter 4.

one of the Windows Me color schemes to reset the colors so that you can see message text.

It's usually best to avoid font changes. When you select alternate fonts you may see a drastic adverse affect on overall system performance. Stick with the default font selections to avoid this potential problem.

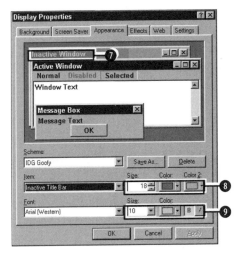

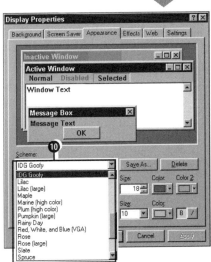

TAKE NOTE

SAVE YOUR EXISTING COLOR SCHEME

Be sure to use the Save As button before you begin making changes so you can return to your saved selections if you find that a new color scheme is not to your liking. Once you've created a new color scheme that you like, save the new scheme, too. Then you'll be able to return quickly to your scheme if someone else uses your PC and changes the color selections.

SOME PROGRAMS USE THEIR OWN COLOR SCHEMES

You may find that the colors and fonts that you select in the Display Properties dialog box don't have much effect on some of your applications. It's just a fact of life that certain programs have their own settings that are not controlled by Windows Me.

⑦ *Alternatively, click an item in the preview window to select it.*

⑧ *Choose the color and size options for the selected element.*

⑨ *If the selected element includes text, you can choose text options.*

⑩ *Alternatively, select a scheme from the Scheme list box.*

▶ *Click OK to complete the task.*

FIND IT ONLINE

Visit **http://www.desktopheaven.com/homepage. html** to download additional color schemes.

Changing the Resolution

Your monitor uses a series of very small dots to display the images that you see on your screen. The number of dots that can be displayed is measured in *pixels*— picture elements. This measurement is known as the *resolution* (or sometimes *screen resolution*) setting for your monitor, and is always expressed as a ratio of the number of horizontal and vertical pixels. In most cases there are several different resolution settings that you can choose, depending on the capabilities of your monitor and your video adapter. In this section you learn how to adjust your display resolution to suit your needs.

PC monitors typically use the same constant ratio of 4 horizontal pixels to 3 vertical pixels that is common to most television sets. Typical settings include 640 × 480, 800 × 600, 1,024 × 768, 1,280 × 1,024, or even 1,600 × 1,200 on very large monitors. In each case the first number is the number of horizontal pixels and the second is the number of vertical pixels.

Not all resolution settings will necessarily produce acceptable results. Higher resolutions make each item on your screen appear smaller, so too high a setting may make things too small to see without straining your eyesight.

When you change to a higher resolution, you may find that your PC cannot display as many colors as it can at lower resolutions. This is a function of the amount of memory in your display adapter and generally cannot be changed without replacing the adapter. Even so, a 2MB graphics card can display more than 65,000 colors at 1,024 × 768 resolution.

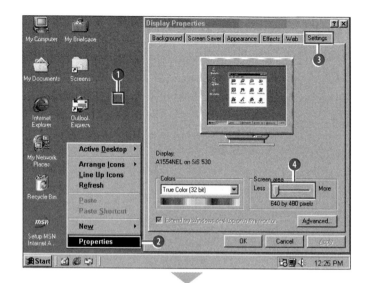

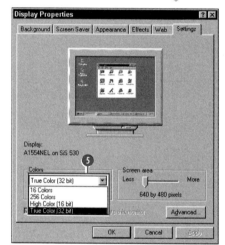

❶ Right-click a blank space on the desktop.

❷ Select Properties to open the Display Properties dialog box.

❸ Click the Settings tab.

❹ Drag the slider to the desired resolution setting.

❺ Select the number of colors to display.

▶ Choosing more colors may reduce your system's performance.

CROSS-REFERENCE

See "Setting the Refresh Rate" later in this chapter.

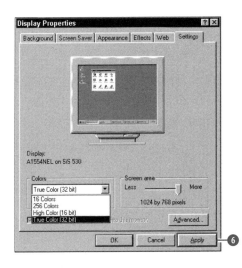

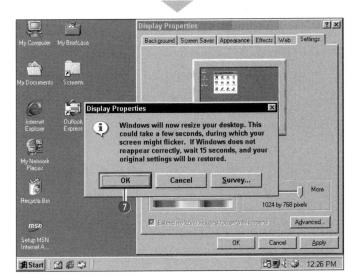

In most cases, 800 × 600 is the highest resolution setting recommended for 15-inch monitors. For 17-inch monitors 1,024 by 768 is the highest recommended setting. Choose a setting that is most comfortable to reduce the likelihood of eyestrain.

TAKE NOTE

▶ SOME SETTINGS MAY NOT WORK PROPERLY

Even if your monitor is a larger model you may discover that some resolution settings simply won't work for you. For example, at some settings you may discover that your screen takes on a strange appearance. The Windows Me desktop may not fill the screen, or the desktop may be too wide or too tall. If this happens, you may be able to adjust your monitor's controls to make the screen look normal.

▶ LCD RESOLUTION SETTINGS

If you own a laptop PC or have an LCD display on your desktop, you'll probably discover that although you can change the screen resolution, the screen will be almost unusable at anything other than the highest-resolution setting. The reason for this is that lower-resolution settings require that the image be stretched to fit the screen, and LCD screens typically don't display stretched images very well.

▶ *Notice that the number of colors and the screen area may conflict. You may need to compromise on fewer colors or lower resolution.*

❻ *Click Apply to continue.*

❼ *Click OK to try out your new settings.*

▶ *If your screen looks normal after it has been resized, click Yes to keep the new settings.*

▶ *If you do not confirm the new settings, your desktop will automatically return to the existing settings after 15 seconds.*

FIND IT ONLINE

To learn more about recommended resolution settings, see http://www.webopedia.com/Hardware/Monitors/refresh.html.

Setting the Refresh Rate

The image you see on your monitor may look like a steady image, but it is actually constantly being redrawn. The number of times per second that the image is redrawn is known as the *refresh rate*. If this rate is too low, your screen will seem to flicker and you may experience fatigue, eyestrain, and headaches. In very extreme cases monitor flicker may possibly trigger seizures in certain individuals.

You may not be able to notice any flicker, but that does not mean it isn't there. Screen flicker could be affecting you even if you don't see it. This is especially true if you have a lower-priced monitor, because manufacturers often use a lower setting to compensate for inferior equipment or design. It is generally recommended that you use a refresh rate setting of at least 70 *Hz* — 70 times per second. You should check this setting whenever you buy a new PC, change monitors, or install a new display adapter card.

Several factors influence the refresh rate settings that you can use. Your monitor generally supports only a limited range of refresh settings for each resolution and color depth setting, and your display adapter has certain refresh rates that it can supply. If Windows Me has a listing for your specific monitor manufacturer and model, it will typically show only refresh rates that are compatible with your monitor. If you are sure that Windows Me has correctly identified your monitor, you probably want to select the highest available refresh frequency setting. The highest safe setting will usually produce the best possible display on your screen.

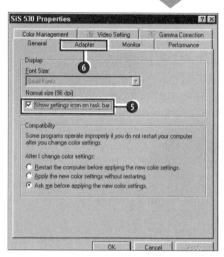

① Right-click a blank space on the desktop.

② Select Properties to open the Display Properties dialog box.

③ Click the Settings tab.

④ Click the Advanced button.

⑤ Click here to include the monitor settings icon in the system tray.

⑥ Click the Adapter tab.

CROSS-REFERENCE

See "Adding New Hardware" in Chapter 12.

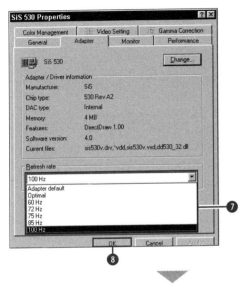

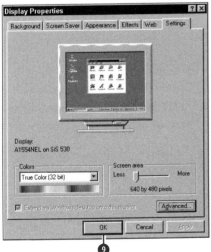

USE CAUTION

If you force the display adapter to choose a refresh rate that is too high for your monitor, you could damage your monitor. All monitors have maximum refresh rate settings that can be used, and these vary according to the screen resolution. If you select a refresh rate that is higher than what is specified in your owner's manual, you could do serious damage and will almost certainly void your warrantee. One way to avoid this dilemma is to accept the "optimal" refresh setting even though it may not result in the highest possible refresh rate. At least you can be confident that this setting should be safe if Windows Me has correctly identified your monitor.

LCD REFRESH SETTINGS

In most cases you cannot set the refresh rate for LCD screens such as those used on laptop PCs. LCD screens use a different method of displaying information than do CRT-based monitors, so refresh-induced flicker is typically not a problem with LCD screens. Some systems with LCD screens do have refresh rate settings, but these are generally only used when an external monitor is connected to the system.

7 *Select the refresh rate.*

8 *Click OK to continue.*

9 *Click OK to complete the task.*

FIND IT ONLINE

To learn more about flicker, see **http://www. zdwebopedia.com/TERM/s/screen_flicker.html**.

Using a Screen Saver

T̲he way things are named can sometimes imply that something serves a purpose even when it does not. This is the case with *screen savers*— which have nothing to do with protecting your monitor from damage. Modern monitors are immune to the type of damage that could burn a permanent image into early computer screens.

In reality, any screen saver you run on your Windows Me–based PC is there mostly for your enjoyment. Having a moving image on your screen when you aren't using your PC may not be high art, but it's probably more entertaining than seeing that report you're working on staring back at you.

You can specify a password that will be needed to return to your desktop once a screen saver has been activated, but in Windows Me this really offers almost no security. Even if you specify a password, someone would be able to simply turn off the power to your system and then restart to bypass your screen saver password. And because you can easily bypass the Windows Me logon password when restarting your system simply by pressing Esc, a password is almost worthless as a security measure. Your PC may offer the option of requiring a password to boot the system, but you will have to refer to your system documentation to learn about this option.

You can choose several different types of screen savers. You have many different options that you can configure, and these options vary according to the type of screen saver that you select. A purely graphical screen

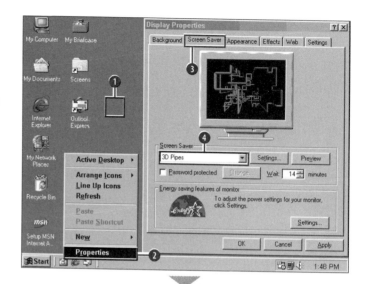

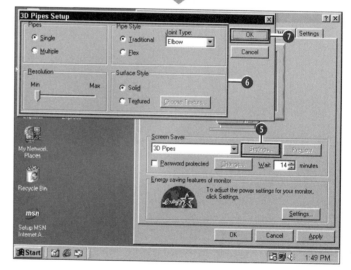

❶ Right-click a blank space on the desktop.

❷ Select Properties from the context menu to open the Display Properties dialog box.

❸ Click the Screen Saver tab.

❹ Select a screen saver from the list box.

❺ Optionally, click the Settings button to change how the screen saver operates.

❻ Select the options you prefer.

❼ Click OK to continue.

CROSS-REFERENCE

See "Using Power Management" later in this chapter.

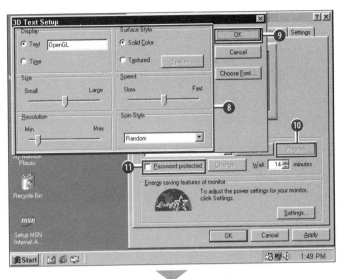

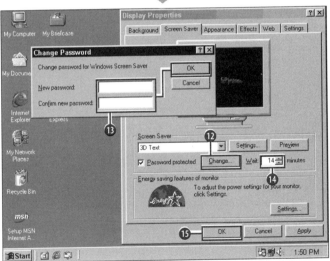

saver generally has settings that you can use to change the shapes, textures, and resolution settings. Screen savers that display text enable you to specify the text that is displayed, the format of the text, the speed that the text moves across your screen, and the motion.

TAKE NOTE

ADD A SCREEN SAVER TO YOUR DESKTOP

You can create a shortcut to your screen saver on your desktop so that you can instantly activate the screen saver by double-clicking the screen saver icon. To do so, open Windows Explorer and navigate to the \Windows\System folder. Change to Details view and look in the Type column for screen savers. Use your right mouse button to drag the screen saver to your desktop and choose *Create shortcut(s) here* from the context menu. Then when you plan to be away from your desk for a few moments you can start the screen saver immediately without waiting for the specified period.

SCREEN SAVERS ARE PROGRAMS

Screen savers are actually programs that run on your PC. If you want to use your own images in a screen saver, you can download screen saver programs from the Internet that enable you to select your favorite images to include in the display.

⑧ *If you selected a text-based screen saver, choose your text options.*

⑨ *Click OK to continue.*

⑩ *Optionally, click Preview to see the screen saver in full screen mode.*

⑪ *If you wish to use a password to close the screen saver, click here.*

⑫ *Click here to set a password.*

⑬ *Enter your password twice and click OK.*

⑭ *Specify the length of time before the screen saver activates.*

⑮ *Click OK to complete the task.*

FIND IT ONLINE

Find screen savers at **http://www. screensandthemes.com/**.

Using Desktop Themes

I f you would like a shortcut method of changing a whole range of Windows Me appearance options at once, desktop themes are for you. Desktop themes are complete collections of settings that include not only the appearance options you have seen so far but also such items as sounds, mouse pointers, and desktop icons.

When you choose one of the predefined desktop themes, you have the option to pick and choose which elements of the theme you would like to use. You could, for example, decide that you want the desktop wallpaper from one theme, the colors from another theme, mouse pointers from another, and sounds from yet another. Of course, you could end up with an awful looking mess, but that's up to you.

Even if you choose one desktop theme, there is no reason why you cannot change certain screen elements to suit your needs. You might find that you like almost everything about a particular theme but that the colors make everything on your monitor too hard to read. If so, you can apply the theme, make your own modifications, and then save your changes as a new theme.

One problem you may encounter after applying a theme is that each theme uses its own set of sounds for system events. In some cases you may find the new sound scheme distracting. If you saved your original sound scheme before applying the new theme you can reapply your favorite sound settings with a few clicks.

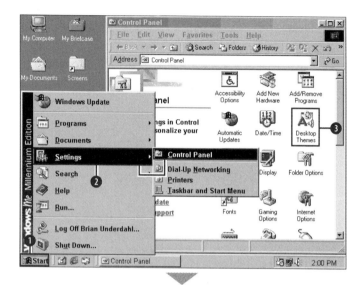

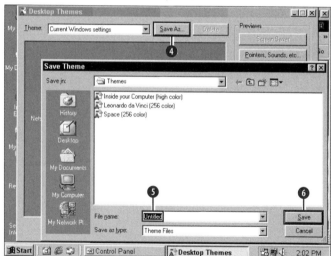

➊ Click the Start button.

➋ Select Settings ➪ Control Panel.

➌ Double-click the Desktop Themes icon.

➍ Optionally, click Save As to save your current settings.

➎ Type a name for your current settings.

➏ Click Save to continue.

CROSS-REFERENCE

See "Adding Sounds to Events" in Chapter 12.

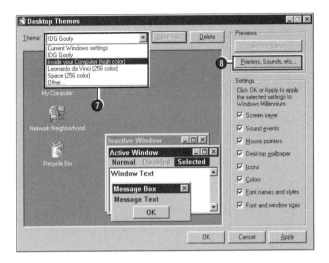

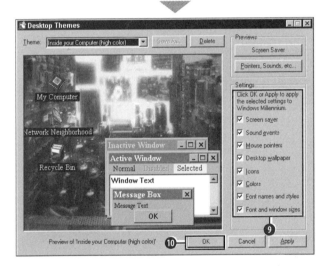

YOU MAY NEED TO INSTALL DESKTOP THEMES

If you don't find the Desktop Themes icon in your Control Panel, you will have to install the desktop themes before you can choose a new theme. To install the desktop themes, double-click the Add/Remove Programs icon in the Control Panel. Then click the Windows Setup tab and add a check to the Desktop Themes category. If you don't care to install the entire set of themes, click the Details button and choose the themes you want. Once you have completed the installation, you can reopen the Control Panel and open Desktop Themes. If the Desktop Themes icon does not appear immediately, press F5 to refresh the view and display the icon.

SAVE YOUR CURRENT SETTINGS

Applying a desktop theme changes almost every aspect of the Windows Me appearance settings. If you have created a group of settings that you prefer, be sure to save them as a new theme before applying any of the Windows Me themes. Because desktop themes include far more settings than those that are saved when you save a color scheme in the Display Properties dialog box, you must save your settings as a desktop theme or they will be lost when you apply one of the optional themes.

⑦ Select a theme from the drop-down box to preview the theme.

⑧ Optionally, click here to preview mouse pointers and sounds associated with this theme.

⑨ Optionally, choose theme elements to include.

⑩ Click OK to complete the task.

FIND IT ONLINE

See **http://fdl.msn.com/pubshows/computingcentral/ pcutilities/liver.zip** for a screen saver that can improve any desktop theme.

Using Power Management

Your PC is probably working even when you aren't using it. For example, if you use your computer to send and receive faxes, you probably leave your system powered on so that it will be ready if someone tries to send you a fax. Or you may have your PC set up to periodically check the mail server to see if anyone has sent you an e-mail message. Your PC has to be running to accomplish these tasks, but that doesn't mean that it has to waste a lot of energy to do so.

The one component of most computers that uses the most power is the monitor. Virtually all PCs come with monitors that can go into a very low power standby mode when they receive the appropriate signal from the computer. Automatically shutting down the monitor may save more than half the power otherwise consumed by your system.

Shutting down the other components of your PC after a specified time interval may save a small amount of power, but the amount that is saved is typically insignificant unless you are using a laptop PC that runs on batteries. If you set up your system to perform routine maintenance tasks automatically, your PC must be powered on at the time the tasks are scheduled. This is another good reason why you may want to leave your system running and use the power management options to minimize power consumption.

If you use both a screen saver and the energy saving features of your monitor, you may want to set the screen saver to display more quickly than the energy saving

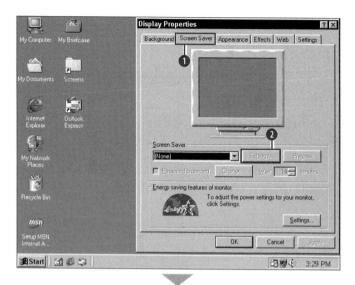

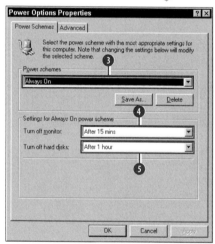

▶ Right-click a blank space on the desktop and select Properties to open the Display Properties dialog box.

❶ Click the Screen Saver tab.

❷ Click the Settings button.

▶ You can also use the Power Options icon in the Control Panel.

❸ Optionally, choose a power scheme that describes how you use your system.

❹ Select the length of time before the monitor goes into standby mode.

❺ Optionally, choose the length of time before your hard disks go into standby mode.

CROSS-REFERENCE

See "Using a Screen Saver" earlier in this chapter.

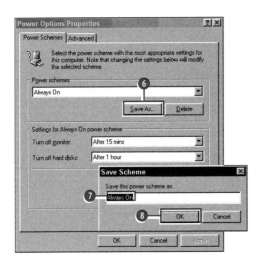

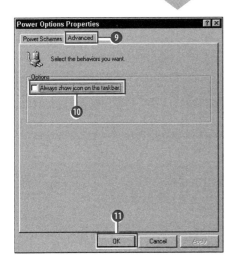

features. Otherwise, your monitor may turn off before the screen saver is ever displayed. You can use the power management options even if you do not use a screen saver.

TAKE NOTE

▶ INVEST IN A UPS

If you do leave your system on all the time, you may find an *uninterruptible power supply* — UPS — to be a good investment. These units maintain a steady supply of power to your PC even if the power from the wall outlet is disrupted. Of course, a UPS can offer excellent protection against loss of data when you are actively working with your system, too. Make certain your UPS is large enough to handle both your PC and monitor — especially the power surge that can occur when a monitor comes off standby. You should avoid plugging laser printers into the UPS.

▶ YOUR OPTIONS MAY VARY

Your power management options may not be the same as those shown in the figures. Laptop computers generally have more extensive power management options than do desktop systems. Even so, using the power management options that are available on your system is a good way to conserve energy.

⑥ To save your power scheme, click the Save As button.

⑦ Type a name for your settings.

⑧ Click OK.

⑨ Click the Advanced tab.

⑩ Optionally, click here to show the Power Options icon in the system tray.

⑪ Click OK to complete the task.

FIND IT ONLINE

See **http://www.apcc.com** for information on Windows Me–compatible UPS systems.

Moving and Hiding the Taskbar

Windows Me normally displays the *Taskbar* at the bottom of the screen. The Taskbar is a tool that makes it easy for you to see which programs are currently running, and to switch between those programs. If you prefer, you can move the Taskbar to another location, you can resize the Taskbar, or you can hide it when you need all of your available screen space as room to work. You can even make the Taskbar appear when a program has hidden it from you.

The Taskbar generally contains several different elements. The Start button displays the Start menu. The Quick Launch toolbar has icons to show the desktop, to start Internet Explorer and Outlook Express, and icons you may have added for quick access to your favorite programs. Next is an area that contains buttons for any programs that you currently have open. Finally, the system tray contains icons for system services such as the clock.

The program buttons that appear on the Taskbar shrink to accommodate the new buttons when you open additional programs. Eventually the buttons may be too cramped and you may not be able to figure out the function of each button. You can deal with this problem in several ways. You can drag the top edge of the Taskbar up to accommodate two or more rows of buttons — when you drag the Taskbar edge the Taskbar always resizes itself in full row increments. You can also dock the Taskbar along one of the sides of the screen, providing considerably more room for program buttons.

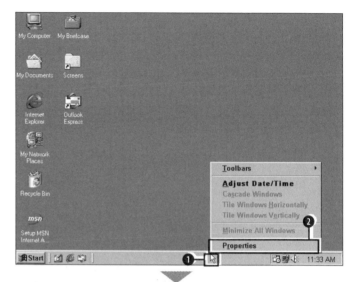

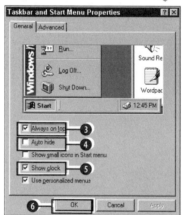

① Right-click a blank space on the Taskbar to display the context menu.

② Select Properties.

③ Optionally, select Always on top to reserve space for the Taskbar.

④ Select Auto hide if you want the Taskbar to disappear when you don't need it.

⑤ If you don't want to see the clock in the system tray, deselect this option.

⑥ Click OK to apply your changes.

CROSS-REFERENCE

See "Adding Toolbars to the Taskbar" later in this chapter.

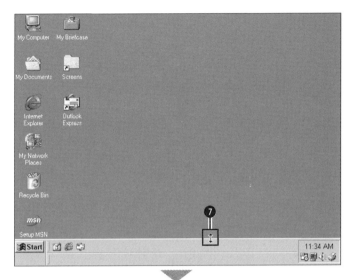

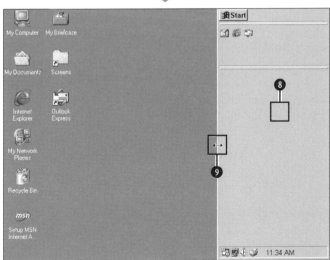

7 To resize the Taskbar, drag the edge.

8 To move the Taskbar, point to a blank spot on the Taskbar and drag it to one of the edges of the screen to dock it at that edge.

9 Drag the edge of the Taskbar if you want to adjust the size in the Taskbar's new location.

If the Taskbar is hidden, you can usually display it by moving the mouse pointer just past the bottom edge of the screen. If the Taskbar does not appear, try moving the mouse pointer just past the other edges of the screen until the Taskbar appears.

TAKE NOTE

▶ USING THE ALWAYS ON TOP OPTION

The Taskbar *Always on top* option reduces your workspace by reserving room for the Taskbar. If you deselect this option, programs can use the entire screen by covering part or all of the Taskbar. Deselecting this option also prevents you from displaying the Taskbar by moving the mouse off the edge of the screen. You should normally leave this option selected.

▶ ACCESSING THE TASKBAR

Programs sometimes hide the Taskbar to prevent you from doing anything else while they're running. This is most common with software installation programs. You may find times, however, when you need to do something else, such as explore your hard disk to find a place to install a program. When the Taskbar is hidden, press the Windows key or Ctrl+Esc to pop up the Start menu and display the Taskbar. This works no matter where the Taskbar is hiding.

FIND IT ONLINE

See **http://malektips.envprogramming.com/ 98taw0002.html** for information on using Taskbar buttons.

Adding Toolbars to the Taskbar

You can make the Windows Me Taskbar even more useful by adding new toolbars to the Taskbar. These toolbars provide several very useful functions that may surprise and please you.

You're probably already familiar with one of the Taskbar toolbars — the Quick Launch toolbar. This toolbar contains icons that you can click to quickly view your desktop, browse the Internet, or check your e-mail. You may even have added some of your own shortcuts to the Quick Launch toolbar. But the Quick Launch toolbar is only one of the toolbars that you can add to the Taskbar.

The Address toolbar is one of the most useful of the toolbars that you can add to the Taskbar. If you know the URL of a Web page you'd like to visit, the quickest way to go directly to the site is to add the Address toolbar to the Taskbar. You can then enter the URL into the Address bar. After you type the address and press Enter, Internet Explorer opens and takes you directly to the Web site, bypassing any start pages that Internet Explorer normally opens first.

The Links toolbar provides you with one-click access to the links on the Internet Explorer Links bar. By clicking one of the links you can quickly visit the associated Web site.

The Desktop toolbar enables you to access anything that appears on your Windows Me desktop. You don't have to minimize the open windows to click a desktop icon because all of those icons appear in the Desktop toolbar.

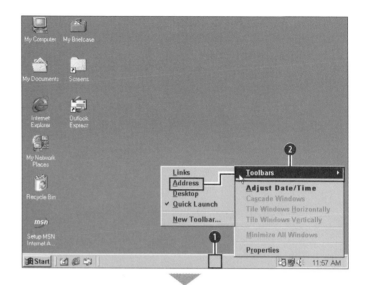

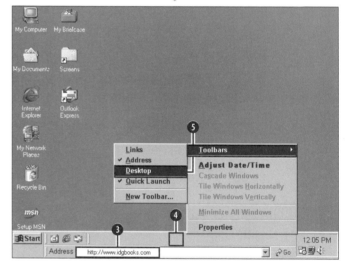

▶ You may wish to expand the Taskbar to two rows before you add new toolbars.

❶ Right-click a blank space on the Taskbar to display the context menu.

❷ Select Toolbars ➪ Address to add the Address toolbar to the Taskbar.

❸ To use the Address toolbar, enter a Web page address and press Enter.

❹ Right-click a blank space on the Taskbar to display the context menu.

❺ Select Toolbars ➪ Desktop to display the Desktop toolbar.

▶ You may wish to remove the Address toolbar.

CROSS-REFERENCE

See "Moving and Hiding the Taskbar" earlier in this chapter.

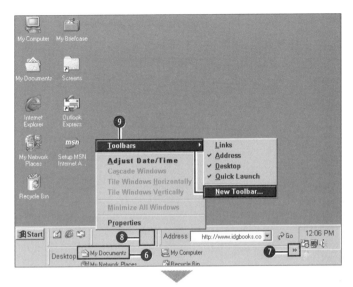

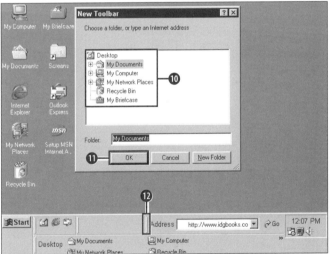

TAKE NOTE

CREATE YOUR OWN TOOLBARS

Adding a custom toolbar to the Taskbar may be the most useful addition of all. When you select Toolbars ⇨ New Toolbar from the Taskbar context menu, you can specify any folder as the source of the toolbar shortcuts. The folder you specify could be a document folder that you must access often, or you might want to create a new folder and add important shortcuts to that folder. When you select the new folder as the source for the new toolbar, all of the items in that folder will appear as icons on the new toolbar, thus providing you with quick access to the items. You could even create several different folders with shortcuts to programs and documents that relate to specific projects. This would enable you to have several custom toolbars for all of your projects.

MAKE ROOM FOR TOOLBARS

If you add toolbars to the Taskbar, you'll quickly discover that there really isn't room in a single row for program buttons and toolbars. Drag the top edge of the Taskbar up to add an additional row so that the new toolbars don't have to share a row with the buttons for your open programs.

⑥ Click an item to open it.

⑦ Alternatively, click the arrows to display the remaining items on the toolbar.

⑧ Right-click a blank space on the Taskbar to display the context menu.

⑨ Select Toolbars ⇨ New Toolbar.

⑩ Choose a folder to use as the source for the new toolbar.

⑪ Click OK to add the toolbar.

⑫ Optionally, drag a toolbar handle onto the desktop to make the toolbar into a floating toolbar.

FIND IT ONLINE

To create a Control Panel toolbar, see **http://malektips. envprogramming.com/98taw0003.html**.

Controlling the Start Menu

The Start menu is a useful tool. Through it you can open programs, access your recently used documents, and modify the way that your PC operates. In Windows Me the Start menu is also quite customizable. You can add items to it, control which items appear on it, and even control the Start Menu's ability to learn your working habits.

Windows Me keeps track of the items that you access on the Start menu as you use your PC. Eventually Windows Me shrinks the menus down and hides items you haven't used. You can still access these items by waiting until the full menu displays or by clicking the arrows at the bottom of the menu, but if you don't care to have menu items hidden, it is easy to make Windows Me display full menus. Simply deselect the *Use Personalized Menus* check box on the General tab of the Taskbar and Start Menu Properties dialog box.

Several different Start menu options enable you to expand the display of the Control Panel, Dial-Up Networking, My Documents, My Pictures, and the Printers folders. If you choose these options, you can view the contents of these folders as Start menu selections rather than first opening the folders. This enables you to choose an item that is contained in the Control Panel, for example, without first opening the Control Panel and then double-clicking the item you want.

Other options on the Advanced tab enable you to control whether certain items appear on the Start menu. You can, for example, choose to display the list of Internet Explorer Favorites to make it easier for you to

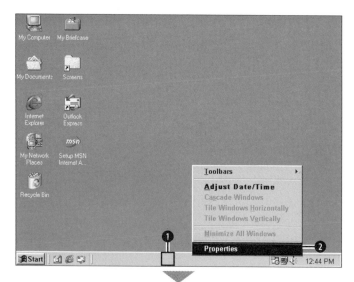

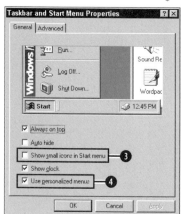

① *Right-click a blank space on the Taskbar to display the context menu.*

② *Select Properties.*

③ *Optionally, select Show small icons in Start menu to reduce the size of the Start menu.*

④ *Optionally, deselect Use personalized menus to prevent menu items from disappearing.*

CROSS-REFERENCE

See "Adding an Entry to the Start Menu" in Chapter 4.

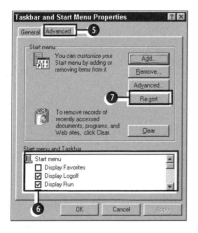

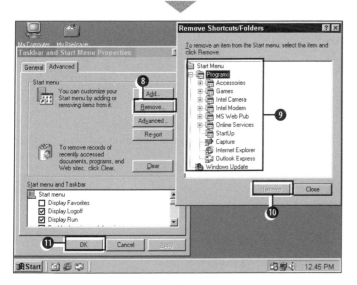

visit your favorite Web sites. You can also control whether someone can move or resize the Taskbar.

In addition to right-clicking the Taskbar and choosing Properties, you can also display the Taskbar and Start Menu Properties dialog box by double-clicking the Taskbar and Start Menu in the Control Panel.

TAKE NOTE

▶ SORTING YOUR MENUS

When you add items to the Start menu using the drag-and-drop methods you learned in Chapter 4, Windows Me assumes that you are intentionally reorganizing the menus and stops sorting the program and folder shortcuts that appear on the menus. This may be fine for a short time, but eventually you'll probably install some new programs, and those new items will not appear where you might expect in the menus. You can easily correct this by clicking the Re-sort button or by right-clicking the open menu and selecting Sort by Name.

▶ CLEAR YOUR DOCUMENTS LIST

You can quickly clear the items from your Documents list by clicking the Clear button on the Advanced tab of the Taskbar and Start Menu Properties dialog box. This will also remove the record of recently used programs and Web sites.

⑤ Click the Advanced tab.

⑥ Select the options you prefer.

⑦ Click Re-sort to place the Start menus back into alphabetical order.

⑧ To remove an item from the Start menu, click the Remove button.

⑨ Select the item to remove.

⑩ Click Remove.

⑪ Click OK to complete the task.

FIND IT ONLINE

For information on shortcuts, see **http://www. microsoft.com/Windows98/usingwindows/work/ articles/904Apr/Keyboardshortcuts.asp**.

Personal Workbook

Q&A

1 What will happen if you change the screen resolution setting but don't click the Yes button in the confirmation dialog box?

_____

_____

_____

2 How can you make a hidden Taskbar pop up without moving the mouse?

_____

_____

_____

3 How can you find a hidden Taskbar using the mouse?

_____

_____

_____

4 What do you need to activate before you can use a JPEG image as your desktop wallpaper?

_____

_____

_____

5 What can you do to restore order to the Start menu if items are no longer being sorted?

_____

_____

_____

6 How can you reduce the size of the icons on the Start menu?

_____

_____

_____

7 What is the fastest way to choose a desktop element on the Appearance tab of the Display Properties dialog box so that you can change the element's color?

_____

_____

_____

8 How can you view the items in the Control Panel folder without opening the folder?

_____

_____

ANSWERS: PAGE 396

EXTRA PRACTICE

1. Try out a different screen resolution setting.

2. Move the Taskbar to the left side of your screen.

3. Try one of the sample color schemes.

4. Sort your Start menu into alphabetical order.

5. Try several different refresh rates to see which produces the best display.

6. Add a toolbar that shows the contents of the My Documents folder to the Taskbar.

REAL-WORLD APPLICATIONS

✔ Your company has several PCs in public areas of your office. You add the company logo as wallpaper.

✔ You will be away from your desk for a few minutes, and you need to make certain that people won't be able to view the salary budget worksheet. You apply a password-protected screen saver to prevent unauthorized access.

✔ You have added several new programs to your PC, and your Start menu is a mess. You change to small icons and re-sort the menu to make your system easier to use.

✔ You use your PC a lot and have been experiencing headaches. You adjust your monitor refresh rate to correct the problem.

Visual Quiz

How can you display this dialog box? How do the controls on this tab interact?

_____

_____

_____

_____

_____

_____

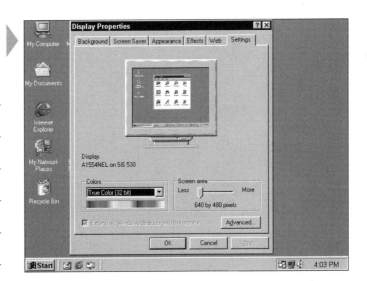

CHAPTER **12**

MASTER
THESE
SKILLS

▶ **Changing to a Single-Click Mouse**

▶ **Configuring Mouse Speed**

▶ **Configuring Keyboard Speed**

▶ **Adding Sounds to Events**

▶ **Adding New Hardware**

▶ **Setting the Gaming Options**

▶ **Using the Registry Editor**

▶ **Configuring for Multiple Users**

Changing How Windows Me Works

In this chapter you learn about making changes to the way Windows Me works. These types of changes can help make your PC work the way you want it to. Although these modifications typically aren't as noticeable as some of the visual changes covered in the last chapter, they can be just as important to your enjoyment of your system. Quite simply, if your PC is easier to use, you'll get more done with less fuss and bother.

You probably aren't interested in a total revamp of the way your computer currently works. Rather, you are more likely to want some small changes that simply make your system a little easier to use. If you change something so much that the difference jumps out at you, you've probably gone too far. Think of small adjustments and you'll get the idea of how much change is called for in most cases. Think of these changes as simple, subtle tweaks that give your computer a tune-up.

For example, if you are a very fast typist you might want to configure your keyboard for lightning-fast response. But if you're a hunt-and-peck typist, that setting could make your keyboard repeat characters too quickly, and you might want it to respond a little slower than normal.

If you have your PC automatically check for new e-mail messages every so often, you might want a sound file to play when a message arrives so you don't have to constantly check the screen. If you play games with your computer, you might want to tune up the gaming options to suit your style of play. In this chapter you learn how to deal with all these issues to make your Windows Me–based PC easier to use.

Most of the settings discussed in this chapter are accessed through the *Control Panel*. The Control Panel is the central location where you find the tools you need to configure and control nearly all aspects of how your PC runs under Windows Me.

Most of the changes discussed in this chapter pose no danger to your system. Be aware, however, that some tools — especially the Registry Editor — can cause major problems if you make changes just to see what will happen. When in doubt, don't change anything you don't understand.

Changing to a Single-Click Mouse

Using a mouse can be a little intimidating when you first start using a PC. Sometimes you have to click the left mouse button and other times the right button. Still other times you have to double-click or even hold down a button to accomplish your goal. And when you are browsing the Internet things can get even more confusing because a single click often works when you expect to have to double-click. One way to reduce this confusion a little may be to change the way your mouse works so that it always works pretty much the same.

The terms *single-click style* and *double-click style* indicate the two types of mouse behavior. In the single-click style, moving the mouse over an object selects the object, and a single click opens it. In the double-click style, a single click of the left mouse button selects an object, and a double-click opens it. When you're browsing the Web, moving your mouse over a link selects the link and a single click opens the link — in other words, Web browsing works in single-click style.

There are, however, big differences between browsing the Internet and working with your files and folders. For example, consider what it takes to select multiple files on your PC using single-click style. First, you move the mouse pointer over an object, and then you hold down either the Shift key or the Ctrl key depending on whether you wish to select a contiguous range or several individual items. Next, you move the mouse pointer to the next item you wish to select. If you don't want to

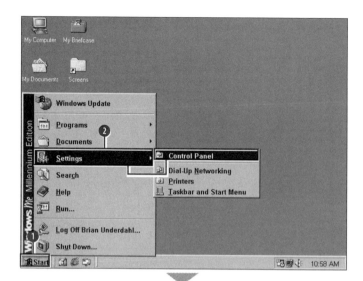

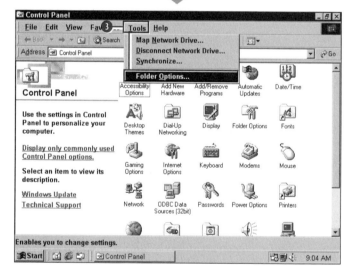

❶ Click the Start button.

❷ Select Settings ➪ Control Panel.

❸ Select Tools ➪ Folder Options to open the Folder Options dialog box.

CROSS-REFERENCE

See "Configuring Mouse Speed" later in this chapter.

select everything between the first and last item, the process gets a little tricky. You must move the mouse pointer carefully so that it touches only the items you want to select. If you select an item in error, move the mouse pointer onto the object and then away from it. You probably don't select multiple objects on a Web page, so you may not realize how difficult it can be to get in the habit of correctly selecting more than one object with a single-click style mouse.

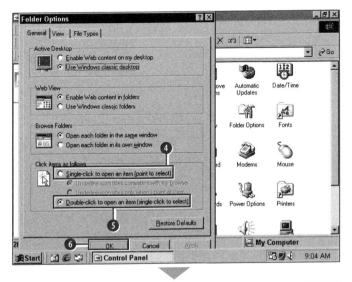

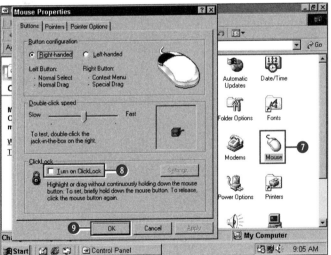

TAKE NOTE

TOUCH PADS CAN BE TRICKY

If you configure your mouse to use single clicking rather than double clicking, and you use a laptop PC with a touch pad, you may find that selecting items correctly is extremely tricky. Touch pads move the mouse pointer, but if you tap the touch pad, the tap is generally accepted as a click of the left mouse button.

USING CLICKLOCK

You may also wish to experiment with the ClickLock feature. When this feature is turned on, you don't have to hold down a mouse button while you highlight or drag objects. Instead you can hold down the button briefly, move the mouse, and click to release.

④ Select single-click to use single mouse clicks to open objects.

⑤ Alternatively, select double-click to use double mouse clicks to open objects.

⑥ Click OK to continue.

⑦ Optionally, double-click the Mouse icon.

⑧ If you to use the ClickLock feature, select this option.

⑨ Click OK to complete the task.

▶ You may wish to leave the Control Panel open if you are continuing in this chapter.

FIND IT ONLINE

For information on mouse utilities, see **http://www.winappslist.com/utilities/mouse_utilities.htm**.

Configuring Mouse Speed

Working in a graphical environment like Windows Me is very difficult without a properly functioning mouse. Fighting a mouse that seems unresponsive or one that reacts far too quickly can take all of the pleasure out of working with your computer. This situation can be especially true if you still are not comfortable using a mouse. In this section you learn how to correct these types of problems as well as how to choose different mouse pointers.

Your mouse has at least two buttons. You normally use the left button for selecting or opening things, and the right button to display those handy context menus. If you're left-handed you may find this button arrangement a little awkward, but there's an easy solution. You can quickly configure Windows Me to swap the functions of the two buttons so that using your mouse feels more natural to you.

If adjusting your mouse settings doesn't seem to help, you may have a different problem. Erratic mouse movement is most often the result of a dirty mouse or a worn out mouse pad. If you turn your mouse over you'll probably find that the mouse ball can be easily removed by turning a section of the mouse bottom. Once you have removed the ball, you can rinse it off in clean water and then dry it thoroughly. Also check the inside of the mouse for lint or dirt. Don't apply any liquids to the inside of the mouse, but you may want to blow out any dust before you replace the ball. Be sure that the door that holds the ball in place is turned to the proper position before you turn the mouse upright so you don't lose the ball.

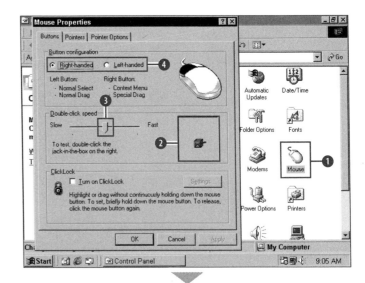

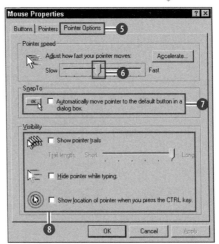

❶ Double-click the Mouse icon in the Control Panel.

❷ Double-click the test icon to test double-click speed.

❸ If necessary, drag the slider right or left to adjust the double-click speed.

❹ Optionally, choose the button configuration to suit your needs.

❺ Click the Pointer Options tab.

❻ Drag the slider right or left to adjust the mouse speed.

❼ If you want the pointer to jump to the default button, select this option.

❽ Select the visibility options you prefer.

CROSS-REFERENCE

See "Configuring Keyboard Speed" later in this chapter.

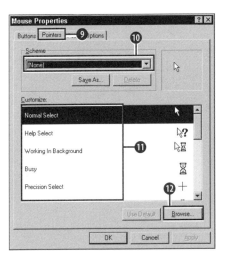

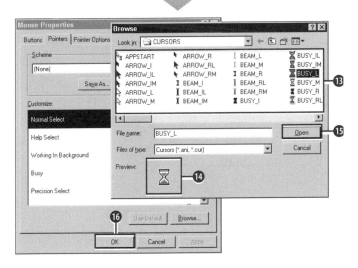

CHANGING THE MOUSE POINTERS

In addition to changing the way your mouse responds to movements and clicks, you can have a little fun with your mouse by selecting different pointers to replace the ones that Windows Me uses by default. You can even use *animated cursors* — mouse pointers that use animation to make the mouse pointer a bit more interesting. Animated cursors designed for Windows 95 or for Windows 98 will work fine in Windows Me.

FINDING THE MOUSE POINTER ON A LAPTOP

Finding the mouse pointer can sometimes be difficult — especially on some laptop PC screens. If you experience this problem you may want to try the pointer trail option. When you select this option, a series of pointers trail behind the mouse pointer as you move the mouse around on your screen, making it far easier to find the mouse pointer. You can also use the option that shows the mouse pointer location when you press Ctrl. These can be good options to use to help a new PC user learn to use a mouse.

⑨ Click the Pointers tab.

⑩ Optionally, choose one of the available mouse pointer schemes.

⑪ Select one of the mouse pointers to change.

⑫ Click the Browse button.

⑬ Choose one of the available mouse pointers.

⑭ Preview the pointer here.

⑮ Click Open to apply the new pointer.

⑯ Click OK to complete the task.

Configuring Keyboard Speed

Making certain that your keyboard is both comfortable and working properly is an important part of configuring your system to meet your needs. To that end, you can make several keyboard adjustments in Windows Me.

Keyboard speed can be a major factor in helping to make typing more efficient. The Keyboard Properties dialog box has two keyboard speed adjustments as well as a related visual adjustment.

The *repeat delay* is the measure of how long you must hold a key down before that character is repeated. Adjust this setting to the shortest delay that is compatible with your typing style.

The *repeat rate* is a measure of how many times per second characters are repeated once you've held the key down long enough to begin repeating characters. Adjust this setting to the rate that feels most comfortable.

The *cursor blink rate* setting controls how quickly the cursor blinks on and off. The rate you select is a matter of personal preference.

You can use the language settings to choose an alternative keyboard layout, such as one of the Dvorak keyboard layouts. Some people claim that typing on a Dvorak keyboard is faster than typing on a standard QWERTY keyboard layout, but this may depend on how you learned to type.

You can also choose additional language layouts by clicking the Add button on the Language tab. When you add a new language, you can also select the layout for the new language keyboard. In most cases you'll probably want to use the same type of layout for all of the

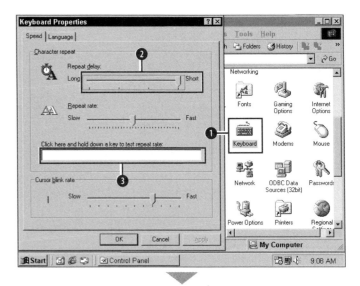

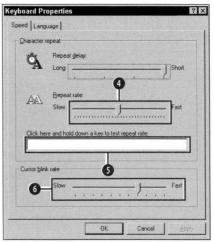

❶ Double-click the Keyboard icon in the Control Panel.

❷ Drag the Repeat delay slider left or right to test different settings.

❸ Click the test box and hold down a key to check the delay setting.

❹ Drag the Repeat rate slider left or right to test different settings.

❺ Click the test box and hold down a key to check the delay setting.

❻ Drag the slider right or left if you wish to adjust the cursor blink rate.

CROSS-REFERENCE

See Chapter 8 for information on the accessibility options.

languages. Once you have added new languages you can choose hot keys for switching between languages. The hot keys will have no effect until you install additional languages.

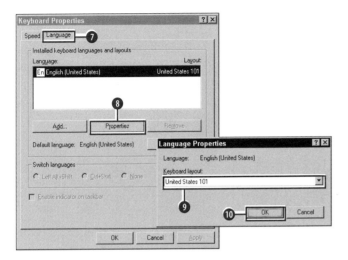

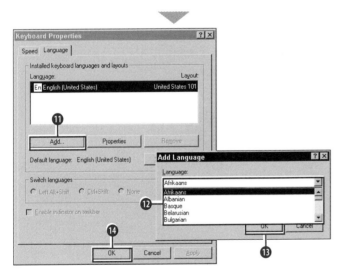

TAKE NOTE

▶ USING FOREIGN LANGUAGES

Foreign languages often include characters that are not shown on a standard keyboard. If you choose to add a new language, you'll find that typing those characters will be far easier. Of course, changing keyboard layouts won't actually move the keys on your keyboard. If you choose to use an alternative keyboard layout, remember that what is shown on the keys won't be the same characters that appear when you type.

▶ CLEANING YOUR KEYBOARD

After a time you may notice that your keyboard is starting to look a little dirty. If so, you are probably tempted to try cleaning the keys. Keyboards are generally pretty delicate and can be easily damaged through improper cleaning techniques. If you decide to clean your keyboard, start by shutting off your system. Use a vacuum cleaner to gently remove any dust and use a damp rag to lightly wipe the tops of the keys. Use plain water to lightly dampen the rag — solvents or too much water will damage your keyboard.

---

⑦ *Click the Language tab.*

⑧ *Click Properties if you wish to choose a new keyboard layout option.*

⑨ *Select your preferred keyboard layout.*

⑩ *Click the OK button.*

⑪ *Click the Add button if you wish to add additional languages.*

⑫ *Choose the new language.*

⑬ *Click OK*

⑭ *Click OK to complete the task.*

FIND IT ONLINE

To learn about Microsoft's line of keyboards, see
http://www.microsoft.com/products/hardware/keyboard/.

Adding Sounds to Events

Your computer uses various sounds to alert you to certain *system events*. These system events are common things such as opening Windows Me, displaying an error message, or emptying the Recycle Bin. In this section you learn how to control which sounds are associated with the various system events.

Most events do not normally have associated sounds. Adding sounds to every possible event would have your PC making sounds nearly all the time, and this could get very annoying quickly. You will probably want to use a certain amount of restraint in applying sounds to Windows Me system events.

Associating sounds with a majority of system events could be very useful in certain circumstances. The audible clues to system events could be very helpful if you have limited vision or when you need to be aware of events without looking at the screen. You could even record your own messages to help a new PC user learn how to use the system. If you do, remember to keep the sounds as short as possible to minimize file sizes.

If you start adding sounds to a number of events, you may discover that your system really doesn't sound good. The biggest factor on how good your PC's sounds will be is the set of speakers that you attach to your sound card. Manufacturers often include very cheap speakers with their systems, and these are usually barely more than usable. Upgrading to a decent set of speakers can make a huge difference in the sound quality. When buying new speakers, make certain that you purchase amplified speakers designed for use with computers.

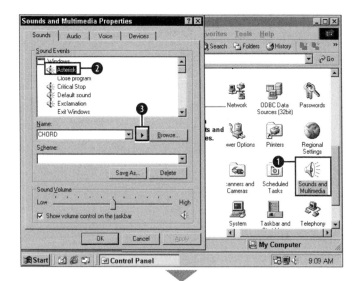

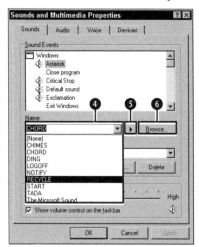

❶ Double-click the Sounds and Multimedia icon in the Control Panel.

❷ Select an event that has a speaker icon indicating that a sound has been assigned to the event.

❸ Click the Play button to play the sound.

❹ Optionally, select a new sound for the event.

❺ Click the Play button to play the new sound.

❻ Alternatively, click the Browse button to search for a different sound.

CROSS-REFERENCE

See "Recording Sounds" in Chapter 16.

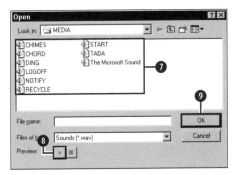

The speakers from an old stereo system probably won't be loud enough unless you connect the sound output of the PC to the auxiliary input of the stereo amplifier.

TAKE NOTE

▶ WAVE FILES

The only sounds that you can associate with events are *wave files* — digital recordings of actual sounds. You can record your own wave files or you can choose from the many thousands of existing wave files that you find either on your system or on the Internet. Wave files tend to be fairly large — especially if they were recorded at a high-quality level or in stereo. In most cases, however, even a low-quality wave sound is more than adequate to signal a system event. You don't really need a CD-quality recording. It's a far better idea to use short sound clips to signal events.

▶ CONSIDER THE DESKTOP THEMES

As an alternative to assigning sounds to events yourself, you may want to consider using desktop themes as discussed in Chapter 11. Each of the optional themes includes a broad set of interesting and sometimes humorous sounds that you can apply to a whole range of events without setting each sound individually.

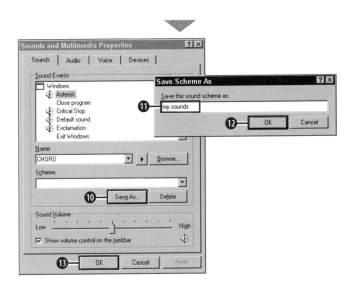

⑦ Select a sound file.

⑧ Click the Play button to hear a preview of the sound.

⑨ Click OK to assign the new sound and close the dialog box.

⑩ Optionally, click Save As to save your sound scheme.

⑪ Type a name for the sound scheme.

⑫ Click the OK button to close the dialog box.

⑬ Click OK to complete the task.

FIND IT ONLINE

See **http://www.winsite.com/info/pc/win95/sounds/andamb.exe** for a set of humorous sounds.

Adding New Hardware

Windows Me–based PCs are compatible with nearly all of the new types of hardware or peripherals that you might want to buy to expand your system. That almost universal compatibility is a huge advantage for PC users because they don't have to put up with a limited range of products when so many manufacturers support the Windows platform.

Adding new hardware to your Windows Me PC is fairly easy. Windows Me supports *plug and play*, so adding new hardware is often as simple as installing the new equipment and then starting Windows Me. In many cases Windows Me will recognize that the new piece of hardware has been installed and will automatically load the proper software to support it.

Because there are literally thousands of different types of hardware you can add to your PC, it's not really possible to show the entire process for every item you might want to add. Rather, this task provides an overview that shows several of the most important steps along the way.

When you install new hardware, Windows Me will eventually arrive at a point where you must choose which drivers to install. You will often have the option of choosing to use the driver that is supplied with Windows Me or to use a driver supplied on disk by the hardware manufacturer. Choosing the correct driver is very important, but your choice may not be an easy one. You can be certain that a driver that is supplied with Windows Me is Windows Me–compatible, but that driver may not always support the more advanced features of your hardware. The manufacturer-supplied driver will, of course, support every possible feature of the

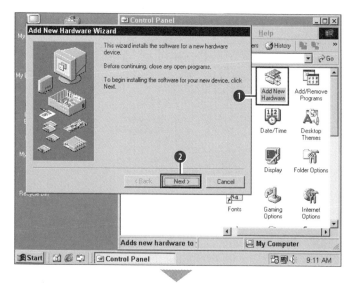

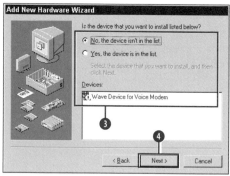

❶ Double-click the Add New Hardware icon in the Control Panel to open the Add New Hardware Wizard.

❷ Click Next to continue.

▶ Continue the installation process by reading the messages that appear and then clicking Next.

❸ If you see this message, choose the appropriate option.

❹ Click Next to continue.

CROSS-REFERENCE

See "Using Windows Update" in Chapter 14.

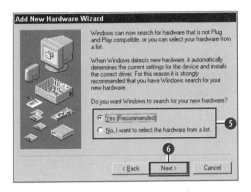

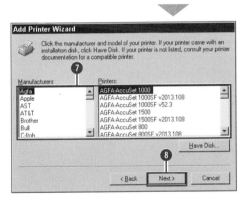

hardware, but may not work too well with Windows Me You may want to try the Windows Me–supplied drivers first. You can always update the drivers later if you discover that some important features are not supported.

TAKE NOTE

▶ LOADING DRIVERS

All versions of Windows use software known as *drivers* to support the various pieces of hardware that are installed on the system. This system of using drivers makes it possible for Windows Me to support many different types of hardware because the hardware manufacturer only has to supply a Windows Me–compatible driver in order for the peripheral to be usable by all of your application programs.

▶ USE WINDOWS UPDATE

The driver software that accompanies that new piece of hardware you just bought may not be the latest version. Once you've installed new hardware, it's a good idea to visit the Windows Me Update Web site to see whether newer versions of the driver are available. Click the Start button and then select Windows Update to check for newer drivers. You must have Internet access to use Windows Update.

⑤ *Select whether you want Windows Me to try and search for the new hardware.*

▶ *You may want to try Yes first, and try No if the search fails.*

⑥ *Click Next to continue.*

▶ *If Windows Me cannot find your new hardware, choose the type of hardware and click Next.*

⑦ *Choose the manufacturer and model.*

▶ *If you have a disk from the manufacturer, click Have Disk.*

⑧ *Click Next to continue.*

FIND IT ONLINE

To locate a driver, try **http://www.drivershq.com/**.

Setting the Gaming Options

I f you play any sort of action game with your PC, you know that controlling games using the keyboard or the mouse does not work very well. For any serious game playing you need a game controller such as a joystick. You may even want to have several different types of controllers for different types of games.

When you add a new game controller, choose the type of controller and characteristics carefully. Although Windows Me enables you to specify settings that do not match your controller's specifications, choosing the wrong type of controller could result in some pretty strange behavior when you try to play your favorite games.

If you have several game controllers, each should be assigned a different controller ID. This enables Windows Me to automatically use the correct movement controls when you change controllers.

In most cases leave the *Poll with interrupts enabled* option selected. You may find that your controller becomes unresponsive or at least responds poorly if this option is not selected.

Certain special types of game controller hardware may require nonstandard drivers in order to work properly. If your controller came with a disk from the manufacturer, you may need to select the proper *port driver* from the drop-down list box on the Controller IDs tab of the Gaming Options dialog box. The instruction sheet that came with your gaming controller should tell you if special drivers are necessary.

Some newer games support chatting with your opponent while you are playing games online. If you have one of these types of games installed on your PC, you

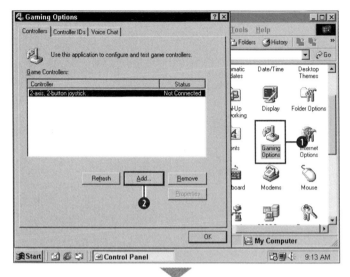

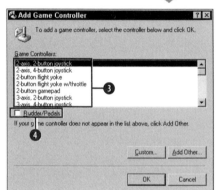

❶ Double-click the Gaming Options icon.

❷ Click Add to install a new game controller.

❸ Choose the controller type.

❹ Select this option if appropriate.

CROSS-REFERENCE

See "Playing Internet Games" in Chapter 17.

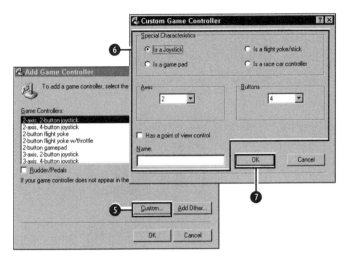

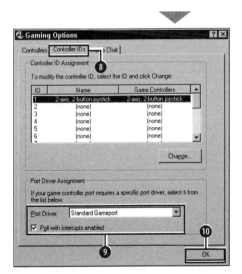

will find them listed on the Voice Chat tab of the Gaming Options dialog box. Microsoft's Flight Simulator and Combat Flight Simulator are two games that support this option.

CALIBRATING GAME CONTROLLERS

You may need to calibrate your game controller to make it work correctly. Once you have added a game controller, select it and click the Properties button on the Controllers tab of the Gaming Options dialog box. When the Properties dialog box opens, click the Settings tab and then the Calibrate button. Follow the instructions to test and calibrate each of the options available on your controller.

TROUBLESHOOTING GAME CONTROLLERS

If you are having problems making your game controller work correctly, try the Games & Multimedia Troubleshooter in the Windows Me help system. This troubleshooter will step you through a series of questions in an attempt to narrow the problem down and find a solution. To resolve the problems, make certain you note the exact error message that appears. Otherwise you may waste a lot of time, because "it doesn't work" is not one of the problems that the Windows Me troubleshooters are designed to resolve.

⑤ *Click Custom to change the characteristics of your controller.*

⑥ *Select the characteristics that match your controller.*

⑦ *Click OK to continue.*

⑧ *Click the Controller IDs tab.*

⑨ *Select any options necessary for your controller.*

⑩ *Click OK to complete the task.*

FIND IT ONLINE

To download the Tetris trial version game, see
http://www.microsoft.com/games/puzzle/.

277

Using the Registry Editor

This task covers a topic that must be approached with extreme care. If you are careless when editing the *registry* — a special database Windows Me uses to maintain system settings and to control how your system functions — you could make your system inoperable.

You can make many changes by editing the registry. In every case you'll be looking for a specific *key* — which is one of the values held in the registry. Different registry keys hold different types of values. Many of the keys hold complex numeric values, but some are like the key used in the example — they hold simple values.

The example used in this case shows you how to modify a registry key to control the display of the Windows Me version number on your desktop. Editing the registry is the only way you can control this option, so it is a good example of how you can use the registry to accomplish tasks that cannot be done any other way.

Most of the time when you use the registry editor you'll be making a change that does something more profound than simply displaying the version number on your desktop. Even so, the same procedures apply no matter what type of change you are making. First you must locate the correct key, and then you must change the correct item to show the new value. You must make certain that you enter the correct value for the item that you are changing.

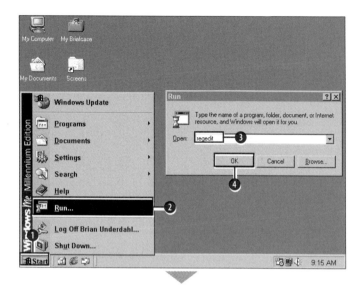

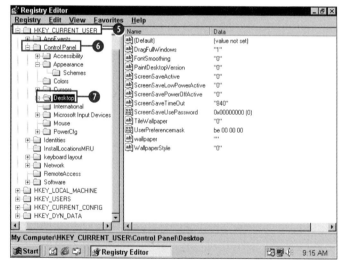

① *Click the Start button.*

② *Select Run.*

③ *Enter* **regedit** *in the text box.*

④ *Click OK to continue.*

▶ *You may need to expand the directories by clicking the plus signs next to the key options.*

⑤ *Click HKEY_CURRENT_USER to open this key.*

⑥ *Click Control Panel to open this key.*

⑦ *Click Desktop to open this key.*

CROSS-REFERENCE

See "Looking for Problems with Device Manager" in Chapter 14.

You can also use the Edit ⇨ Find command in the registry editor to locate specific values. It may take several minutes to find some items.

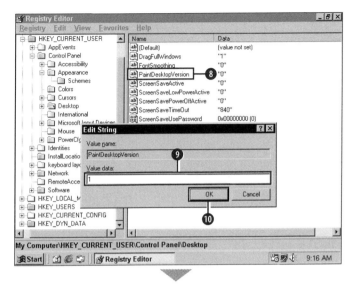

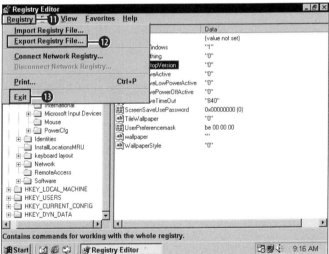

TAKE NOTE

▶ USE EXTREME CAUTION

Making changes to the Windows Me registry without using extreme caution can be very dangerous. You can render your system incapable of starting Windows Me if you start making changes at random. Whenever you are instructed to edit the registry, always make certain you are making the change to the correct location within the registry. Many different registry keys are quite similar — if you don't find the exact key you are looking for, don't assume that a similar appearing key is the one you want.

▶ SAVE REGISTRY KEYS

Before you make a change in the registry it's a good idea to save the section that you are about to change. That way you'll be able to reverse the change easily if necessary. To save a section of the registry, select the item you intend to change and then choose Registry ⇨ Export Registry File. Assign a meaningful name to the file so you will recognize it if you need it later. You can double-click a saved registry file to import it back into the registry.

⑧ *Double-click the value you want to change — PaintDesktopVersion in this case.*

⑨ *Enter the new value.*

⑩ *Click OK.*

⑪ *Click Registry.*

⑫ *Optionally, select Export Registry File to save the selected key.*

⑬ *Select Exit to close the registry editor.*

▶ *Your changes will not appear until you restart your computer.*

FIND IT ONLINE

To find out more about the registry, see
http://www.regedit.com/.

Configuring for Multiple Users

If you share a PC with other people, you have probably been annoyed at times when someone changed something on the system. After all, do you really want a picture of their cat as your desktop wallpaper? And what was wrong with those South Park sound effects you added anyway?

The solution may be to set up the PC with multiple user configurations. That way each person can have their own favorite working environment, and no one has to be offended by someone else's tastes.

Depending on how independent you would like each user to be, you can create separate versions of the desktop, the Start menu, the Favorites folder, downloaded Web pages, and even the My Documents folder for each person. Creating these items won't prevent someone from accessing items that belong to someone else, but it will make it harder to accidentally change someone else's settings.

One important point to remember about creating multiple user configurations is that you may not want to create individualized Start menus. If you do, programs you install will only appear on your Start menu, and other users will have a more difficult time sharing those programs. One solution is to install the shared programs before you create the multiple user profiles.

Each user must step through the process shown in the figures in order to create their separate configuration. If necessary, you can create all of the profiles yourself and then advise each user of their user name and, optionally, their password. See the Take Note section for more on passwords before you put too much trust in them, however.

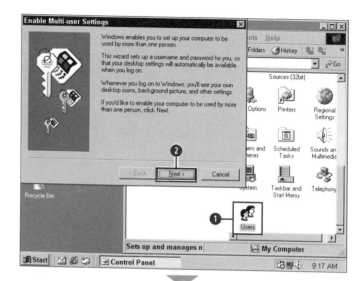

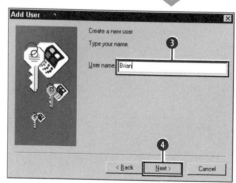

❶ Double-click the Users icon in the Control Panel.

❷ Click Next to continue.

❸ Enter the user name you want to use to log on to Windows Me.

❹ Click Next to continue.

CROSS-REFERENCE

See Chapter 11 for more information on configuring the appearance of Windows Me.

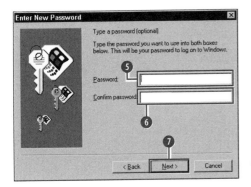

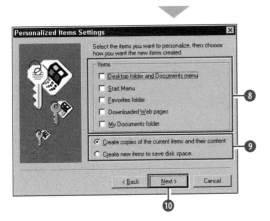

PASSWORDS PROVIDE LITTLE PROTECTION

If you use a stand-alone PC or one that is connected to a network made up entirely of Windows 95, Windows 98, or Windows Me–based PCs, the logon password you set offers little real protection. The reason for this is simple — there is no need to enter the password in order to start any of these versions of Windows. If you don't know the proper user name and password, you can easily bypass the logon prompt by pressing Esc. If your network is controlled by a PC running Windows NT 4 or Windows 2000, far more secure password protection of network resources can be available, provided that the network is properly configured.

MULTIPLE PERSONALITIES CAN BE USEFUL

Even if you don't share a PC with another person you may want to create multiple configurations. You might, for example, find that your laptop computer needs to be quiet and dignified appearing when you bring it along to important meetings, so you could create a separate user configuration with settings appropriate to that situation. You could then switch easily between your normal and meeting configurations simply by choosing the correct logon name.

⑤ Optionally, enter a password here.

⑥ If you entered a password, confirm it by reentering it here.

⑦ Click Next to continue.

⑧ Choose the items you wish to personalize.

⑨ Select the method for creating the personalized settings.

⑩ Click Next to continue.

▶ Click Finish to continue and restart your computer.

FIND IT ONLINE

To find out about a more secure way to create multiple users, see **http://www.sentry98.com/**.

Personal Workbook

Q&A

1 How can you change your keyboard layout?

_____

_____

_____

2 Where do you go to assign sounds to Windows Me events?

_____

_____

_____

3 What type of peripheral does Windows Me recognize automatically?

_____

_____

_____

4 What do you call mouse pointers that display a brief animation?

_____

_____

_____

5 What can you do to change the number of times keys repeat when they are held down?

_____

_____

_____

6 What type of sound files can you associate with system events?

_____

_____

_____

7 Where do you find most of the system configuration tools?

_____

_____

_____

8 How can you save a registry key so that it can be easily restored?

_____

_____

_____

ANSWERS: PAGE 397

EXTRA PRACTICE

1 Change the sound that plays when Windows Me starts.

2 Change your mouse to operate as a single-click mouse.

3 Set your keyboard repeat rate to the fastest position and see how quickly keys repeat.

4 Change your keyboard layout to one of the Dvorak layouts and try typing a letter.

5 Try one of the animated cursors.

6 Add a new printer.

REAL-WORLD APPLICATIONS

✔ You need to create a fancy document that has to be in your customer's office halfway across the country before the end of today, but you are sure that your customer does not have the correct software installed to open the document. You install the same brand and model of printer your customer owns and print the document to a file that you e-mail to the customer for printing.

✔ You are helping someone with limited vision set up their PC so that they can start a home business. You associate different sounds with all the important system events so that they can tell when something happens on their computer.

✔ You are having problems controlling your mouse. You change the mouse speed and acceleration settings so that the mouse moves more comfortably.

Visual Quiz

How can you display this dialog box? How can you tell which events have associated sounds? How can you hear the sounds?

_____

_____

_____

_____

_____

_____

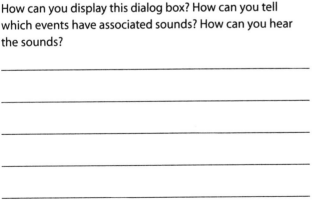
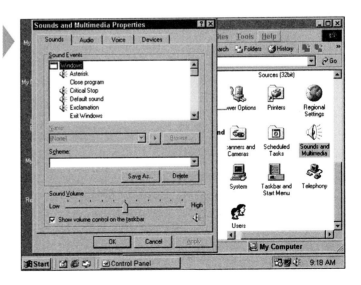

CHAPTER 13

MASTER
THESE
SKILLS

- ▶ Checking for Disk Errors
- ▶ Improving Disk Performance
- ▶ Using the Disk Cleanup Tool
- ▶ Backing Up Files
- ▶ Preparing for Disk Problems

Managing Your Disks

Without any doubt, your disk drives hold the most important thing there is on your PC — your data. Any other component of your system could fail and all you would be out would be the cost of replacing the item that failed. But if your disk drives have problems, you could lose many hours of work in an instant. Fortunately, disk drive failures are not a common problem with modern computers; but that doesn't mean you should ignore the possibility. In this chapter you learn how to take some steps to protect yourself from disk-related problems.

Windows Me includes several disk management tools that are designed to help you find and correct many disk-related problems. These tools include an error checker that you can use to make certain there are no physical or file system errors on your disks. Another tool improves system performance by making certain your files aren't fragmented and spread all over your disks in several pieces. A disk cleanup tool helps you to remove files that are simply wasting space and serving no real useful purpose. Finally, a backup program helps you to protect your valuable data by making archival copies of your important files.

Windows Me supports several different *file systems* — different methods of storing data on your disks. These include several versions of the *File Allocation Table* — FAT — file system for both hard disk and diskettes and also the *Compact Disc File System* — CDFS — for CD-ROMs. In addition, other file systems can be installed to deal with other types of storage media. The Windows Me disk management tools are designed to work exclusively with FAT-based file systems.

Although Windows Me supports several different file systems, there is no easy way in Windows Me to change back and forth between file systems. Some third-party partition management software is able to convert between different file systems, but because that is not a Windows Me feature, it will not be covered in this book. Also, because the FAT32 conversion tool is typically either not needed or is only run one time on most systems, it has been left out to leave room for more important topics.

Checking for Disk Errors

Y ou probably won't come across too many problems that give you the sinking feeling you get when your PC suddenly informs you that it cannot access that important document file that you need right now. And yet, that's exactly the situation you may face if your PC develops disk drive problems.

Most disk errors happen without too much warning. You could have problems right now and not even know it. Still, by using *Scandisk* to check for problems regularly, you can minimize the potential for losing important data.

You may encounter two primary types of disk errors. *File system* errors are the most common of these. Disk space is allocated using special information tables that are stored on the disk. Errors in these tables can result in space being marked as in use when in fact it should be free. Other, more serious file system errors can cause two or more files to be allocated to the same disk space.

Physical errors are places where the disk is physically unable to read or write reliably. All hard disks have some physical errors, but in most cases you won't be aware of them because hard drives automatically compensate for a certain number of physical errors. When the drive is initially prepared for use, any existing physical errors are mapped out and the drive skips the bad spots automatically. After the drive has been prepared, any new physical errors are called *bad sectors.* When you check for disk errors you can choose to scan for bad sectors so that they will not be used in the future.

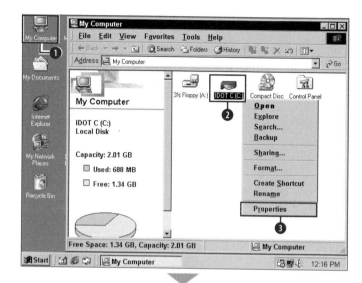

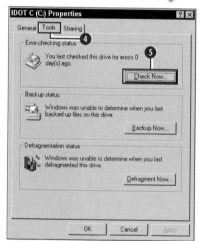

❶ Double-click the My Computer icon on your desktop.

❷ Right-click the drive you wish to check.

❸ Select Properties from the context menu to open the drive's Properties dialog box.

❹ Click the Tools tab.

❺ Click the Check Now button.

CROSS-REFERENCE

See "Improving Disk Performance" later in this chapter.

Any type of disk errors can cause serious problems. You can lose important files, or your entire system could lock up and refuse to function. Checking for disk errors can help you avoid many of these problems.

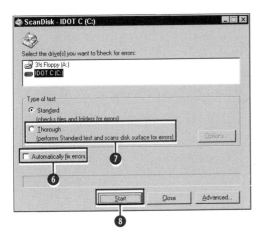

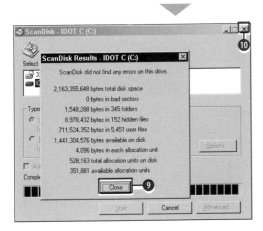

USE THE PROPER SHUTDOWN PROCEDURE

Many disk errors can be traced to a simple cause: PC users who don't bother to properly shut down their systems. Unless you use the Shut Down option on the Start menu, you may still have important files open when you turn off your PC. These open files can be corrupted, and the file system can easily lose track of the space allocated to the files. These types of errors can also result from power outages. You can avoid most power outage problems by plugging your PC into a UPS — Uninterruptible Power Supply.

CLOSE OTHER PROGRAMS

If other programs are running while you are checking for disk errors, Scandisk may need to restart when those programs write to the disk. You can usually avoid these types of conflicts by enabling Scandisk to run when no other programs are running. As you will see in Chapter 15, you can schedule Scandisk to run when you aren't using your system for other purposes.

⑥ Select this option to make sure that file system errors are corrected.

⑦ Select this option to scan for physical errors.

⑧ Click Start to begin the scan.

⑨ Click Close to continue.

⑩ Click the Close button to complete the task.

FIND IT ONLINE

For information on hard disk errors, see
http://support.microsoft.com/support/kb/ARTICLES/Q150/5/32.asp.

Improving Disk Performance

Your hard disk is one of the few predominantly mechanical devices that make up your computer. Any mechanical device is many times slower than purely electronic ones, so it follows that any problems with slow disk performance will have a fairly important impact on your overall system performance.

Disk performance can suffer due to *fragmentation*—files that are spread out in numerous pieces in various areas of the disk. Disk space fragmentation is easy to visualize if you think about the space in a shopping mall parking lot. If you arrange to meet a group of your friends at the mall early in the morning when the shops are just opening, it will probably be fairly easy for you to find a group of spaces where you can all park right next to each other. If you wait until later in the day, the lot will fill up and you'll all have to look for those random parking spots spread out around the lot.

Disk space allocation generally works pretty much like the parking spaces in the mall parking lot. Files that are created and saved first get the first available spaces. Later files use the spaces further out on the disk. But when a file is deleted from the disk, an open space is available for new files. If the next new file can fit into the opening, it is stored *contiguously*. But if the file is too large to fit into one space, it is fragmented into two or more pieces.

You may encounter problems with the disk defragmenter if you have other programs running while the disk is being defragmented. Whenever any data is written

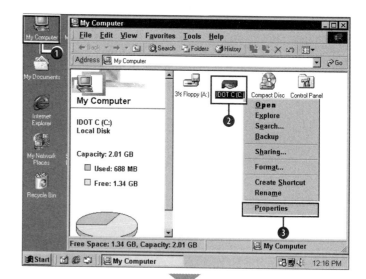

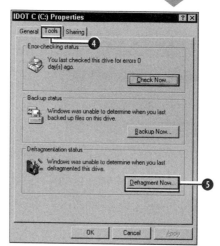

1. Double-click the My Computer icon on your desktop.

2. Right-click the drive you wish to check.

3. Select Properties from the context menu.

4. Click the Tools tab.

5. Click the Defragment Now button to begin defragmentation.

CROSS-REFERENCE

See "Using the Disk Cleanup Tool" later in this chapter.

to the disk, the disk defragmenter must stop what it is doing, and then check to see if the disk write has interfered with the defragmentation process. Even something as simple as your e-mail program can cause these problems — especially if you have the program set up to automatically check for new messages at specified intervals. If possible, stop all other programs when you run the disk defragmenter.

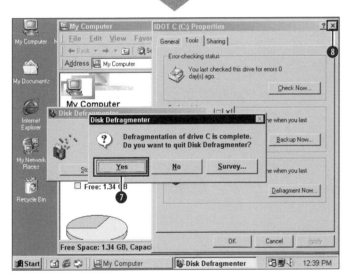

⑥ If you want to view the defragmentation details, click the Show Details button.

⑦ Click Yes to close Disk Defragmenter.

⑧ Click the Close button to complete the task.

TAKE NOTE

▶ DEFRAGMENT OFTEN

Defragmenting your hard disk can take a long time, but you can shorten the process by making certain you defragment often. If only a few files are fragmented, your hard disk can be defragmented in just a few minutes. If you wait until the fragmentation is severe, it may take considerably longer to complete.

▶ FREE SOME SPACE

Disk defragmentation can also take considerably longer if your hard disk is almost full. This can also prevent the defragmenter from doing as complete a job as it could if there is plenty of free space. Adequate free space provides room for moving files as the disk is defragmented.

FIND IT ONLINE

For more information see **http://www.microsoft.com/windows98/USINGWINDOWS/MAINTAINING/ARTICLES/811NOV/MNTFOUNDATION2A.ASP**.

Using the Disk Cleanup Tool

No disk drive has unlimited space. Eventually even the largest disk will become filled if you allow hundreds of useless files to simply waste space. All of those outdated files can reduce your PC's performance as well.

Windows Me provides a very useful tool to automate the process of removing those space-wasting files. The Disk Cleanup tool enables your computer to handle the process so you don't have to do it by hand.

A number of different types of files may be wasting your disk space. For example, temporary Internet files, which are stored on your hard disk so that Internet Explorer can later load those same Web pages more quickly, can eat up a lot of room. Also, files that you sent to the Recycle Bin may be using a lot of space, too. Of course, you can limit the amount of space wasted by Recycle Bin and temporary Internet files by properly configuring the Recycle Bin and Internet Explorer options. These subjects were covered in Chapters 6 and 9, respectively.

The Disk Cleanup tool can remove a number of other types of space-wasting files. You can view a description of each file type by selecting its type in the *Files to delete* list box. Depending on the type of file that you've selected, you may see a View Files button near the bottom of the dialog box. In most cases, viewing the files won't serve much purpose because it is often hard to determine whether a particular file is worth saving. When in doubt it may be safer to leave a file in place if you aren't sure of its purpose.

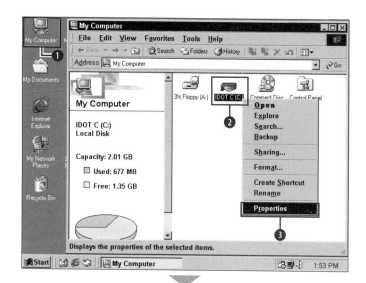

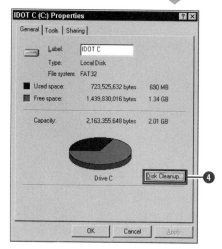

❶ Double-click the My Computer icon on your desktop.

❷ Right-click the drive you wish to check.

❸ Select Properties from the context menu.

❹ On the General tab, click the Disk Cleanup button.

CROSS-REFERENCE

See "Uninstalling Programs" in Chapter 4.

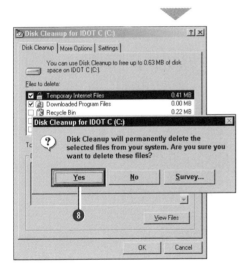

TAKE NOTE

▶ DO A MORE THOROUGH JOB

If you click the More Options tab of the Disk Cleanup dialog box, you will find additional ways to free disk space. You can choose to remove Windows Me components that you aren't using. You can also uninstall programs that you no longer need. You may find that you can free several hundred megabytes or more by junking old programs you don't use. This is especially true if the computer manufacturer installed a bunch of useless programs before you bought your PC.

▶ REMEMBER TO DEFRAGMENT AFTER CLEANUP

After you use the Disk Cleanup tool to remove unnecessary files, you should run the disk defragmentation tool so that your system makes better use of the available space. The disk defragmenter can do a better job of moving files into contiguous space if it has more free space to work with. In addition, defragmenting immediately after freeing up disk space makes it far less likely that new files you add later will have to be fragmented, because there will be more contiguous space in which to store them.

⑤ Select the types of files to remove.

⑥ If you want to look at the files first, click the View Files button.

⑦ Click the OK button to continue.

⑧ Click Yes to confirm that you wish to delete the files.

▶ The files you delete using the Disk Cleanup tool are permanently removed and cannot be recovered.

FIND IT ONLINE

To find disk cleanup utilities, see **http://www.zdnet.co. za/pcmag/pctech/download/swcol.cleanup.html**.

Backing Up Files

Power outages, computer viruses, disk failures, and simple human error are just a few of the many different types of problems that can all conspire to wipe out data that you really need. Backing up your files is the best way to protect yourself against losing your important data. Backing up your files can also be a fairly quick and easy process — especially if you understand what you are doing so you don't waste a lot of time backing up more than is necessary.

You can use many different types of media for backing up your files. You can back up your files to tape, to diskettes, to another hard drive, or to a network location. The basic procedure will be similar no matter what destination you choose. Of course, your choice of backup media will affect the process somewhat, because different types of media have different capacities. If you fill up the backup media you'll need to insert additional media to continue the backup.

Using the Backup program offers several advantages compared with simply copying your data to diskettes. Backup automatically spans diskettes (or other backup media), so when a diskette is full Backup will prompt you for an additional diskette. If you are attempting to back up your files by simply copying them to diskettes, you may have files that are too large for a single diskette.

You don't have to use the Backup Wizard to back up your files. You can cancel the Wizard and work directly with the Backup program. Using the Backup Wizard does insure that you select all of the necessary options before you begin the actual backup, however.

Continued

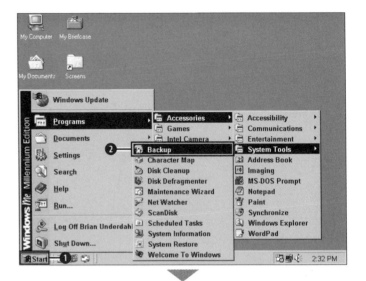

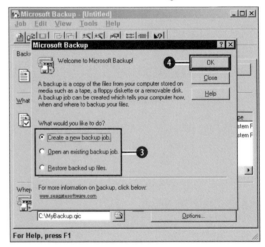

① Click the Start button.

② Select Programs ⇨ Accessories ⇨ System Tools ⇨ Backup.

▶ The backup wizard starts automatically.

③ Select the option that suits your needs.

④ Click OK to continue.

CROSS-REFERENCE

See " Using My Documents" in Chapter 1.

❺ *Select what you want to back up.*

❻ *Click Next to continue.*

❼ *Select the folders you wish to back up.*

❽ *Click the Next button to continue.*

Backing Up Files
Continued

When you select what you wish to back up, you can select entire drives or individual folders. You'll find that the backup selection windows look very similar to Windows Explorer with one important exception. Each folder in the backup selection windows has a check box just in front of the folder icon. To include an item in the backup, add a check to the item's check box. You can also click a computer or folder icon to open the folders so that you can make individual folder selections.

In most cases you will probably want to limit the backup to include only new and changed files. Windows Me keeps track of the files you have already backed up, so you can reduce the size of the backup by eliminating files that have not been changed.

Once you've selected the files to back up, you must select the backup destination. Generally, if you have a tape drive, it will be your first choice. Tape drives are made specifically for backing up files and can be the easiest backup media to use. A network drive can be another excellent backup destination — especially if you work in an office that has a file server on the network. Backing up to a network destination is usually quite fast and offers very good protection for your files. If you have a removable media drive such as a ZIP drive, that drive may also be a good choice for a backup destination. Diskettes are generally acceptable only for relatively small backups because using diskettes can involve a lot of disk swapping.

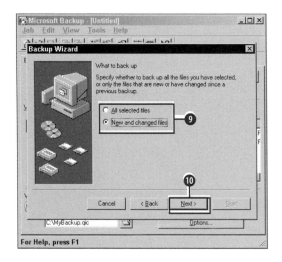

9 Choose which set of files you wish to back up.

10 Click Next to continue.

11 Choose the backup destination.

12 Click Next to continue.

CROSS-REFERENCE

See "Adding New Hardware" in Chapter 12.

You may be prompted to insert additional backup media during the backup. This is especially likely if you're backing up to diskettes. Be sure you have enough diskettes, tapes, or other backup media ready before you begin the backup. Format the media or erase any old files before you start the backup.

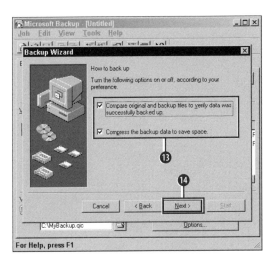

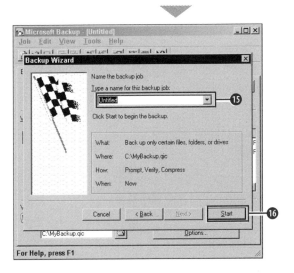

🔵 Optionally, choose additional backup options.

▶ It is usually best to select both of these options.

🔵 Click Next to continue.

🔵 Enter a name for the backup job.

🔵 Click the Start button to begin the backup.

TAKE NOTE

▶ CHOOSE A GOOD DESTINATION

Never choose a folder on your hard disk as the backup destination. Backups are intended to protect you against problems such as hard disk failures, so if you were to place your backups on your hard disk you would be losing that protection and wasting disk space. It's far better to simply limit the size of your backups by only backing up the files you really need, and then using diskettes as the backup media, rather than place backups on your hard disk.

▶ PROTECT YOUR BACKUPS

After you've gone to the trouble of backing up your important files, you may want to consider storing the backups someplace away from your computer. Backups are meant to protect you in the event of a disaster, and they can't do it if the same disaster destroys your backups.

FIND IT ONLINE

To find reviews of backup options, see
http://www.windrivers.com/wr/index.htm.

Preparing for Disk Problems

No one wants to have to deal with disk failures, but sometimes you may have no choice. If your PC won't start because it cannot access your hard drive, you don't want to discover that you aren't prepared.

Backing up your data files is very important. If you have a current backup you won't lose all of your work if your hard disk fails. But you need some additional protection against the possibility that a disk error might keep you from starting Windows Me. This sort of problem could be the result of a power failure at just the wrong time or even a computer virus that wipes out the partition information. Most of your hard disk may still be intact, but if you can't access it your data may be toast!

Windows Me uses a *Startup Disk* to start your computer when there is a hard disk problem that prevents your computer from booting. If your system will not start Windows Me, you can insert the Startup Disk in drive A and reboot. You will then need to use the command line options to recover from the error.

In some cases you may also be able to correct system problems by starting Windows Me in *safe mode*. This is a special operating mode that may enable your computer to start by bypassing all but the most basic Windows Me drivers and components. In safe mode you won't be able to use functions and services that were bypassed, but you may be able to solve many problems. For example, if your system won't restart after you add new hardware,

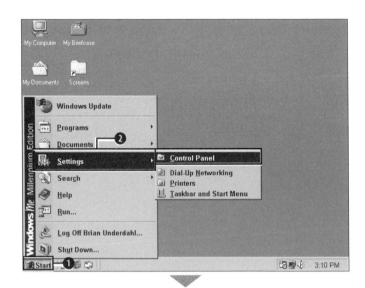

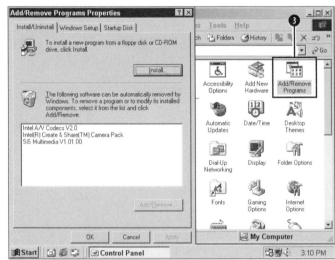

1 Click the Start button.

2 Select Settings ⇨ Control Panel.

3 Double-click the Add/Remove Programs icon to open the Add/Remove Programs Properties dialog box.

CROSS-REFERENCE

See "Looking for Problems with Device Manager" in Chapter 14.

you may be able to restart in safe mode and remove the offending item. Press F8 when your system begins loading Windows Me and choose Safe Mode to start in safe mode.

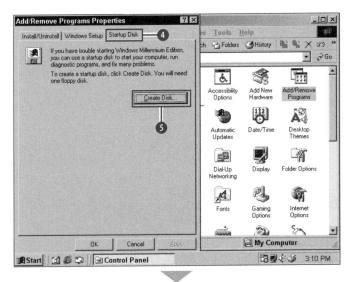

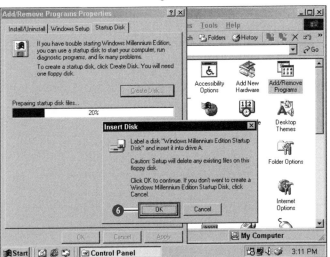

④ Click the Startup Disk tab.

⑤ Click Create Disk to continue.

⑥ Insert a blank diskette in drive A and click OK.

▶ You can create a Startup Disk in drive A only because you must be able to boot from the Startup Disk.

▶ Carefully label and store the Startup Disk.

FIND IT ONLINE

For a system troubleshooting utility, see
http://www.webroot.com/snap.htm.

Personal Workbook

Q&A

1 What tool can you use to remove old files that are no longer needed on your PC?

_____

_____

_____

2 What type of disk errors can prevent your PC from using specific places on your hard disk?

_____

_____

_____

3 What is the difference between contiguous and fragmented files?

_____

_____

_____

4 How can you reduce the size of backups and the time required to perform them?

_____

_____

_____

5 What will happen if you attempt to scan for errors on a disk that is in use?

_____

_____

_____

6 What do you call a diskette that enables you to boot in an emergency?

_____

_____

_____

7 What operating mode should you attempt to use first if Windows Me won't load?

_____

_____

_____

8 How can you free up additional space if the disk cleanup tool doesn't do as much as you'd like?

_____

_____

_____

ANSWERS: PAGE 398

EXTRA PRACTICE

1. Back up your My Documents folder.

2. Use the More Options tab on the Disk Cleanup dialog box to see how much additional disk space you can free by removing Windows Me components you don't use.

3. Run Disk Defragmenter and check to see which files are fragmented.

4. Print the list of fragmented files and compare it to the list after you run the disk defragmentation.

5. Check your hard disk for errors.

6. Create a Startup Disk and try booting from it.

REAL-WORLD APPLICATIONS

✔ Your PC has been in use for several months and is starting to run very slowly. You run the disk defragmenter to restore the performance so that you can keep the same system for a while longer.

✔ An earthquake shakes your office quite heavily. To make certain that your hard drive wasn't damaged you run the error checker and choose the option to look for physical errors.

✔ A computer virus strikes your system and prevents your system from booting. You use your Startup Disk to start your system so that you can use your antivirus program.

✔ You need to work on some very large video files but discover that you are low on disk space. You use the disk cleanup tool to free some space.

Visual Quiz

How can you display this dialog box? How can you tell when your hard disk was last defragmented? How can you check for disk errors?

_____

_____

_____

_____

_____

_____

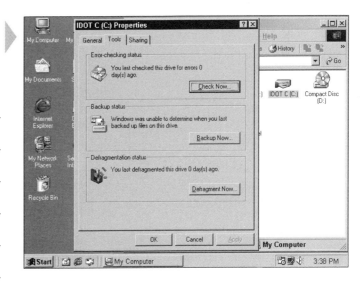

CHAPTER 14

MASTER
THESE
SKILLS

▶ **Using Windows Update**

▶ **Eliminating Problems with System Restore**

▶ **Tuning Up with the Maintenance Wizard**

▶ **Looking for Problems with Device Manager**

▶ **Viewing the System Monitor**

Maintaining Your System

Making certain that your PC is running its best is an important part of using your computer. A small amount of time and effort spent on simple maintenance will pay off in keeping minor problems from becoming major ones. In this chapter you learn how to use the Windows Me tools to keep your computer in top shape.

You don't need any special skills to properly maintain your computer, but there is one very important attribute that you should possess. When you are dealing with system problems — or trying to prevent them — it is important to take your time and understand what you are doing. This is not the place to barge ahead ignoring the text of any messages or warnings that may appear on your screen. If you don't fully understand a message, don't assume that it is meaningless. Take the time to read and understand what you are seeing.

You won't be using the tools covered in this chapter on a daily basis. These tools are primarily intended as problem solvers. They are the types of tools you hope you won't need, but that you will be glad you understand if you do need them.

The Microsoft Windows family of operating systems uses the *Windows Update* service to help users maintain their computers in peak operating condition. Windows Me introduces a unique new enhancement to Windows Update called *AutoUpdate*. Both of these services automatically download and install the latest updates to Windows Me. These updates may include drivers or security updates that can be vital to the health of your system. But these updates are only useful if you actually download and install them. It's easy to forget to visit the Windows Update Web site as often as you should, so Windows Me adds the AutoUpdate feature to make certain you are automatically notified when there is an important update that should be applied.

Before you begin the exercises it's important to inject a note of caution. Using any type of tool involves a certain amount of risk. The best way to prevent problems is to use common sense. If you don't know what you are doing, don't just blunder ahead with the "I wonder what will happen if I do this?" attitude. Caution is your best ally!

Using Windows Update

Windows Me is a complex array of different pieces of software that provides many important services on your PC. It is only natural that something as complex as Windows Me needs periodic updates to correct problems that have been discovered, to provide support for new types of hardware, and to address the newest security threats. Windows Me uses the Windows Update service to make certain that you have easy access to these updates.

You will usually find a number of available updates on the Windows Update Web site. You can select which of the updates you would like to download and install. You can also view the installation instructions for the software that you've selected. It's a good idea to print a copy of the instructions, especially if you're not completely sure you understand the entire download and update process.

In most cases you won't have to do anything special to install the software updates. Most updates install themselves automatically after they are downloaded. It may be necessary to restart your PC after the update has been installed, especially if the update changed critical system files. Most system files cannot be changed while they are in use, so the restart is required before the update will be completed.

After you click the Start Download button you'll see a dialog box that reports on both the download and the installation progress. You don't need to do anything while this dialog box is being displayed. Depending on the size of the updates you selected, the download could take several minutes to several hours, and it's best not to try to do anything else on your PC during this process.

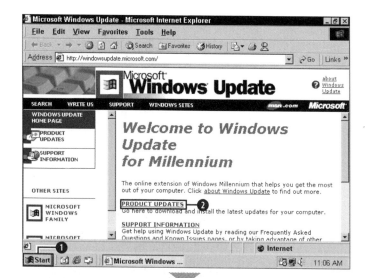

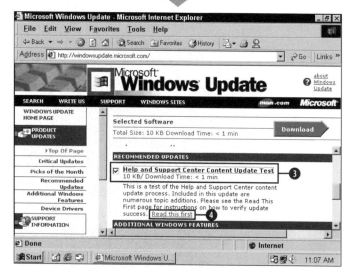

① Click the Start button and choose Windows Update.

② Once you have connected to the Web site, click the Product Updates link to continue.

③ Choose the updates to download and install.

④ Click the Read this first link to view the read me file.

CROSS-REFERENCE

See "Installing Programs" in Chapter 4.

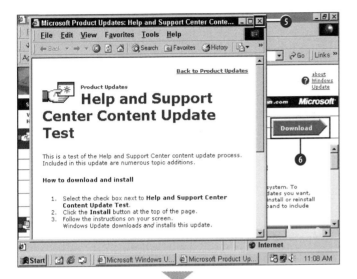

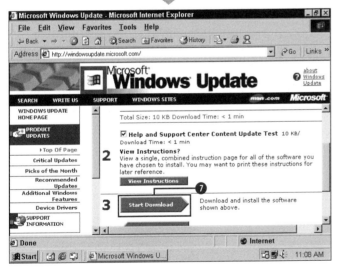

5 When you have finished
reading the information on
the update, click the Close
button.

6 Click the Download button
to continue.

7 When you have verified the
list of downloads, click the
Start Download button.

▶ Follow the onscreen
instructions to complete the
updates.

TAKE NOTE

▶ USING AUTOUPDATE

Because it can be difficult to remember to visit the
Windows Update Web site regularly, Windows Me includes a new feature called AutoUpdate. This is a tool
that automatically looks on the Windows Update
Web site for important updates you may need.
Depending on your settings, AutoUpdate can automatically download those updates or simply notify
you when updates are available. You can configure
the AutoUpdate feature by double-clicking the
Automatic Updates icon on the Control Panel. Then
choose the option that best suits your needs.
AutoUpdate never installs updates without first asking for your permission. If you decide against installing an update, you can go back later and change
your mind using the Restore Hidden Items button in
the Update Settings dialog box.

▶ UPDATES ARE FREE

If you are worried that obtaining updates for
Windows Me will cost a lot of money — don't be.
These updates are always free (unless you pay for
connect time, of course). Feel free to visit the
Windows Update Web site as often as you like. It
won't cost you anything except a few minutes of
your time to insure that your copy of Windows Me
is up-to-date.

FIND IT ONLINE

For information on critical update notification, see
http://www.microsoft.com/windows98/support/
critical/default.asp.

Eliminating Problems with System Restore

It's a fact that not all software is quite as perfect as we might like. That is one reason why using a computer is not always as enjoyable as it should be. Software that doesn't work correctly doesn't make anyone happy.

Sometimes installing a new program can cause your computer to start acting up. Maybe the new program simply doesn't work correctly, or maybe other things that were working suddenly stop working. Whatever the exact situation, you now have a problem.

You might think that because installing a program caused a problem you could get rid of the trouble by uninstalling the program. In some cases this procedure will work, but often it does not. In those instances you need a heavier-duty method of rolling your system back to a time when everything was working. In Windows Me, the System Restore tool provides that opportunity.

System Restore automatically creates *restore points* that you can use to restore your system if you have a problem that you feel may be related to some change that was made on your system. If you need to return to an earlier time, you can use System Restore to undo all of the changes that were made since a specified point in time. System Restore does not affect your data files, so any work that you have done should be unaffected when you restore. If you discover that restoring your system does not solve your problem, you can also undo the restoration.

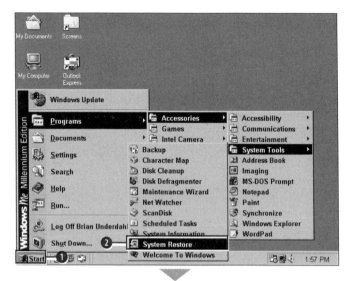

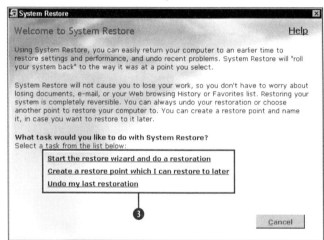

▶ Close any programs that may be running.

❶ Click the Start button.

❷ Select Programs ⇨ Accessories ⇨ System Tools ⇨ System Restore.

❸ Choose the System Restore option you wish to use. (To complete the following steps, choose the second option.)

▶ If you choose to do a restoration, you will have to select the correct restore point.

▶ In order to restore your system properly, you will have to restart your computer.

CROSS-REFERENCE

See "Using Windows Update" earlier in this chapter.

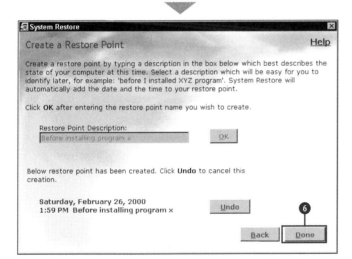

TAKE NOTE

PLACING THE BLAME IN THE RIGHT PLACE

When you start having problems with a piece of software that was working correctly, the problem is not likely being caused by that particular piece of software. Rather, the problem is more likely the result of some other software that you installed. The reason for this is simple — programmers often are too lazy to do things correctly. If a programmer is developing a piece of software that uses shared components — pieces of software that are shared by several programs — they are supposed to insure that their program works with the latest versions of those shared components. Unfortunately, programmers often take a shortcut and install an older version of shared components because they know those versions work with their software. If you have other programs that rely on these shared components, those other programs may quit working properly when the older component is incorrectly substituted for the newer one. Thus the lazy programmer has shifted the support burden to someone else rather than taking the time to design his or her own program correctly.

CREATE RESTORE POINTS

If you are going to install some new software or hardware, use System Restore to create a restore point just before you begin. That way you can restore if need be with minimum disruption to your system.

④ To create a restore point, enter a name for the point.

⑤ Click OK to create the restore point.

⑥ Click Done to close System Restore.

▶ Once you have created a restore point, it is safe to install a new program.

▶ You will probably want to create a new restore point just before each new program installation.

FIND IT ONLINE

For information on other problem-solving techniques, see **http://www.winmag.com/**.

Tuning Up with the Maintenance Wizard

You should perform a number of important routine maintenance tasks at regular intervals. These tasks can help keep your system running at peak efficiency, and they need to be run regularly to be most effective. The problem is that you probably either don't remember to run them as often as you should, or you just can't find a convenient time to run them. That's where the Windows Me Maintenance Wizard becomes so useful. The Maintenance Wizard enables you to schedule these tasks so that they run automatically at times when you aren't otherwise using your PC.

The Maintenance Wizard automatically schedules several different tasks. First, it schedules the Disk Defragmenter using an option to optimize the loading of your program files. You may forget to manually optimize the programs after you've added or removed programs from your system, so having this as a scheduled task helps keep your PC's performance at its peak. Next, the Maintenance Wizard schedules checks for and repairs of any disk errors. Because you may not always realize when an event has caused disk errors, scheduling this check on a regular basis helps prevent more serious problems. Finally, the Maintenance Wizard schedules the Disk Cleanup tool to remove unnecessary files from your hard disk.

After the Maintenance Wizard schedules the system maintenance events, be sure that you leave your system running at the scheduled time. If you prefer not to leave your computer on all the time, choose a maintenance schedule that enables the tasks to be performed at a time

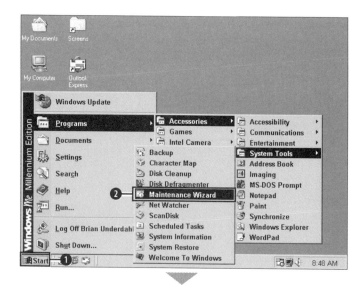

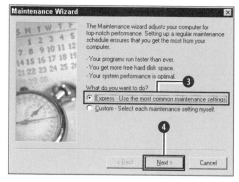

❶ Click the Start button.

❷ Select Programs ⇨ Accessories ⇨ System Tools ⇨ Maintenance Wizard.

❸ Choose the Express option to use the default settings.

❹ Click Next to continue.

CROSS-REFERENCE

See Chapter 15 for information on the Task Scheduler.

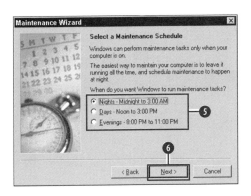

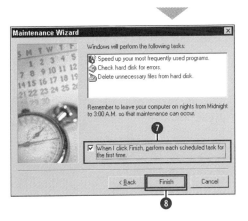

when you are comfortable leaving the system on, such as during lunch. If you select the custom setup rather than the express setup, you'll also be able to more closely control the task schedule. For even more control over the schedule, you can open the Scheduled Tasks folder after the Maintenance Wizard has created a schedule.

TAKE NOTE

▶ FIRST TIME SYSTEM MAINTENANCE

If you haven't performed any routine system maintenance in some time, some of the Maintenance Wizard scheduled tasks may take considerable time to complete the first time they are run. Although choosing the When I click Finish, perform each scheduled task for the first time option is a good way to make certain your system won't have problems when the tasks are run, selecting this option may tie up your PC for quite some time. Still, because you will probably see much improved system performance after the maintenance tasks are run, it may be worthwhile to choose the option if you can afford the time.

▶ SETTING YOUR OWN SCHEDULE

If you select the Custom radio button you'll have the option of selecting the settings for each of the routine maintenance items that the Maintenance Wizard schedules, and you can choose to eliminate one or more of them from the schedule.

⑤ *Choose the time schedule you prefer.*

⑥ *Click Next to continue.*

⑦ *Optionally, click here to run the tasks immediately.*

⑧ *Click Finish to complete the task.*

FIND IT ONLINE

For saving power when your computer is idle, see **http://www.microsoft.com/windows98/usingwindows/maintaining/tips/advanced/savepower.asp**.

Looking for Problems with Device Manager

Y our computer is made up of quite a few different components that all have to cooperate in order for the whole system to work together peacefully. Sometimes this may not work quite as well as it should, and this can cause conflicts when more than one device tries to use the same system resources. The Device Manager is a Windows Me tool that enables you to identify these types of problems, and usually to solve them as well.

Modern PCs and peripherals use a method known as *plug and play* to assign system resources. Older peripherals, such as scanner adapter cards, sound boards, or modems may not support plug and play (in that case they are called *legacy* devices), or they may require specific system resource allocations. If you encounter this problem you may be able to reserve certain resources using *bios setup options* or by using the Reserve Resources tab of the Computer Properties dialog box as shown in the figures. To use the bios setup options, you will need to reboot your system and press the correct key combination to enter your computer's bios setup screens.

If you can't resolve a resource conflict by selecting different device settings in Device Manager, you may be able to solve the problem by removing all the conflicting devices using the Uninstall option on each device's right-click context menu. Then shut your computer down, wait a few seconds, and restart it. Use the option to enter your system's bios setup and look for the setting to reset the plug and play resource table. This will be worded differently on different computers. When your operating system restarts, Windows Me should find the devices and try to assign them new, non-conflicting resources.

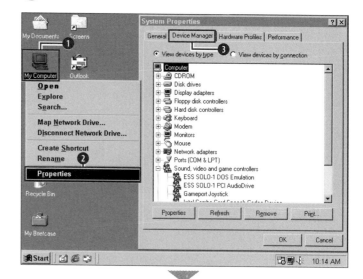

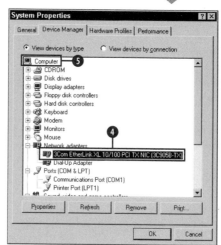

❶ Right-click the My Computer icon on your desktop.

❷ Select Properties to open the System Properties dialog box.

❸ Click the Device Manager tab.

❹ Double-click a device you wish to examine.

❺ Alternatively, double-click Computer to view resource allocations.

CROSS-REFERENCE

See "Adding New Hardware" in Chapter 12.

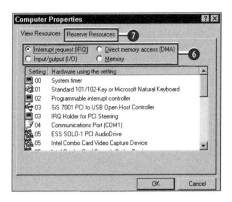

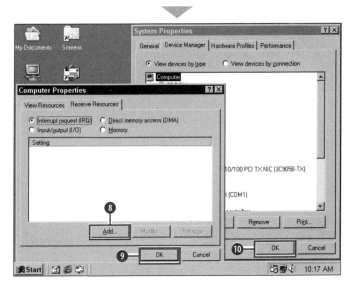

UNDERSTANDING DEVICE MANAGER

If some of the devices installed in your PC are experiencing a problem, Device Manager will use either a yellow exclamation point or a red X as markers to indicate the problem. Device Manager primarily looks for conflicts in which two or more devices are trying to use the same resources at the same time. These resources include interrupt requests (IRQs), input/output (I/O) addresses, direct memory access (DMA), and memory addresses. Most problems you'll encounter will be with IRQs. In some cases you can choose new, nonconflicting resource settings on the Resources tab of the device's Properties dialog box. Deselect the "Use automatic settings" check box and choose one of the optional configurations.

USE PCI OR USB DEVICES

Many of the conflicts that were a problem with older PCs have been reduced or eliminated in newer models through the use of PCI adapter cards and USB devices. If your computer supports the use of these types of devices, you can greatly reduce the number of problems you need to deal with by making certain you buy PCI or USB devices whenever possible.

⑥ In the Computer Properties dialog box, select the type of resource to view.

⑦ To reserve a resource for a legacy device, click the Reserve Resources tab.

⑧ Click Add to specify the resource you wish to reserve.

⑨ Click OK to close the Computer Properties dialog box.

⑩ Click OK to complete the task.

Viewing the System Monitor

I f you have ever wondered why your computer just doesn't seem to be quite as fast as you expect, the problem may be the number of demands that are being placed on the available resources. By using the Windows Me System Monitor, you can actually find out the specific processes that are using your computer's power and determine if it's possible to make some improvements — perhaps by adding additional memory, changing the location of shared network resources, or simply by taking better control of the programs that automatically run when you start your system.

When you first start the System Monitor, the display will show only information on the percentage of your system's processor power that is being used. To see additional information, you must add *counters* that display the information you are seeking. You can add several types of counters to the display. To be most useful, you probably want to add counters that display related types of information. For example, counters that display information on network traffic may help you understand if the network is having much effect on your computer's performance. Or you may choose to display several different items that relate to disk-related activity if you are attempting to diagnose disk performance problems.

Although you could choose to monitor dozens of different system processes, remember that simply monitoring those processes uses a certain amount of CPU time. Rather than taking a shotgun approach, try to narrow your focus and only monitor a few important processes. You may discover that you will need to add an additional item or two to the monitor list to get the true picture of

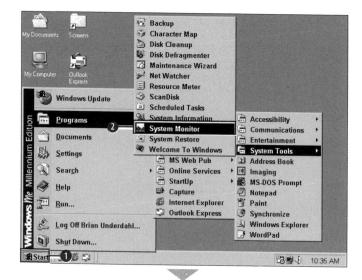

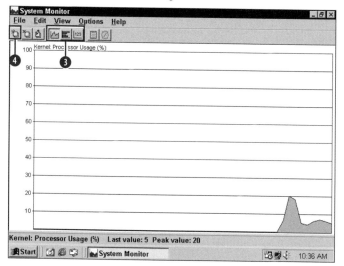

❶ Click the Start button.

❷ Select Programs ➪ Accessories ➪ System Tools ➪ System Monitor.

❸ Choose the display type by clicking one of these buttons.

❹ Click the Add button to add new counters to the display.

CROSS-REFERENCE

See Chapter 7 to learn more about networking issues.

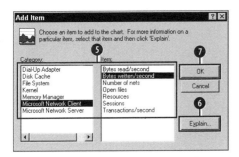

what is happening, but you may also discover that certain processes that you are monitoring are adding no real useful information.

You may need to use the Add/Remove Programs Properties dialog box to add the System Monitor.

TAKE NOTE

▶ **UNDERSTANDING THE COUNTERS**

While you are selecting counters to add to the display, you'll probably find it quite useful to click the Explain button that appears in the Add Item dialog box. When this button is clicked, a message box appears that describes each counter as you select it. These descriptions are especially useful if you aren't certain which counters will provide the details you need.

▶ **FINDING PERFORMANCE PROBLEMS**

One of the best ways to use the Performance Monitor is to look for bottlenecks — processes that are having a major adverse effect on system performance. For example, if you discover that some of the disk-related processes are using nearly all of their available resources while processor-related items have plenty of room to spare, it's a good guess that better hard disks will improve system performance more than a faster processor. Or if the memory usage statistics are constantly near the top of the scale, adding additional memory may boost your performance.

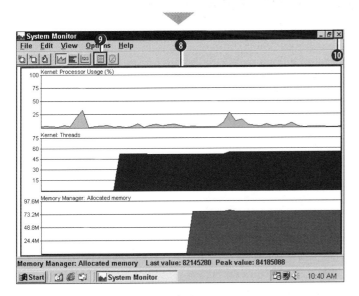

⑤ *Choose the counters here.*

⑥ *Click Explain to see a counter description.*

⑦ *Click OK to add a selected counter.*

⑧ *View the counters here.*

⑨ *Click here if you wish to create a log file from a counter.*

⑩ *Click Close to complete the task.*

FIND IT ONLINE

To download a screen saver that shows processor usage, see **http://www.smartline.ru/software/cpuss.zip**.

Personal Workbook

Q&A

1 What tool can you use to make certain your Windows Me system files are up-to-date?

_____

_____

_____

2 Where can you find out if your system has any resource conflict problems?

_____

_____

_____

3 Where can you look to see which IRQs are in use on your system?

_____

_____

_____

4 How can you eliminate a problem caused by installing a poorly designed program?

_____

_____

_____

5 What is the purpose of the Maintenance Wizard?

_____

_____

_____

6 How can you make certain your computer always has the latest updates without visiting the Windows Update Web site yourself?

_____

_____

_____

7 What do you call the items you add to the system monitor display?

_____

_____

_____

8 How can you make certain that you can roll back your computer to a specific point in time?

_____

_____

_____

ANSWERS: PAGE 399

EXTRA PRACTICE

1 Visit the Windows Update Web site.

2 Read the instructions for one of the available updates.

3 Create a restore point.

4 Use Device Manager to see if any of the devices on your system are reporting problems.

5 Look at the Reserve Resources tab to see if there are any reserved resources.

6 Use the System Monitor to see how many disk accesses occur when you open several different documents.

REAL-WORLD APPLICATIONS

✔ You want to improve the performance of your system so that you can wait another six months before you buy a new PC. You use the Maintenance Wizard to make certain your computer gets regular tune-ups.

✔ Your computer is connected to a network and you suspect that someone has been using your files and slowing your performance. You use the System Monitor to see if the network is creating performance problems.

✔ You need to test some beta software. You use System Restore to create a restore point so you can roll back your system if necessary.

✔ You always forget to check for updates. You use AutoUpdate to make certain your computer is updated when necessary.

Visual Quiz

How can you display this list in the Device Manager? What can you tell about the selected device?

_____

_____

_____

_____

_____

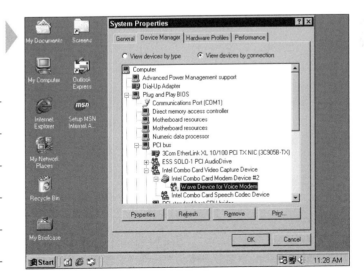

PART

V

Contents of 'Desktop'

Name

My Computer

Network Neigh

Internet Explore

Microsoft Outlook

Recycle Bin

My Briefcase

3252-9

3259-6

3261-8

3262-6

3281-2

3286-3

DE Phone List

Device Manager

In

Iomega Tools

Using Windows Me Accessories

Windows Me has a lot more to offer than you probably realize. In this part you learn about the extras that come along as part of Windows Me that can help you accomplish all sorts of really neat things. You learn how to schedule routine maintenance tasks so that Windows Me does most of the work for you and keeps your PC in top shape. You also learn how to play around with the multimedia capabilities in Windows Me and have some fun with the accessory applications.

CHAPTER **15**

MASTER ▶ **Setting Up Scheduled Tasks**
THESE
SKILLS ▶ **Modifying a Scheduled Task**
▶ **Administering Task Scheduler**

Using Task Scheduler

Using a computer should make your life easier and less complicated, but often it does exactly the opposite. For instance, making certain that your computer is properly maintained by running routine procedures that are designed to prevent problems and loss of performance should be easy, but can be time-consuming and difficult. If you have to do these things yourself, you have to remember to schedule your time around the computer's needs. But there is no reason why you can't simply tell your PC to do these sorts of things for itself and eliminate one more hassle from your life.

The Windows Me Task Scheduler is a program designed to enable you to move routine tasks from your to-do list into the computer's set of assigned duties. Once your PC is responsible for these tasks your life becomes a little simpler, because you no longer have to worry about making sure they are done.

Certain types of tasks such as routine system maintenance are typically handled by the Task Scheduler. This does not mean, however, that you cannot also add your own types of tasks to the schedule. To be useful as a scheduled task, the task must be one that can be completed without user intervention. For example, if you have an application that you can program to log on to your account at an online brokerage, download vital stock market information, analyze the information, and then let you know if you need to buy or sell some shares, then you have a good candidate for a scheduled task.

In this chapter you learn how to use the Task Scheduler to schedule routine tasks such as those you can schedule with the Maintenance Wizard. If you wish to schedule a different type of task, you will have to know how to set up the task so it can be run automatically once it has been started. Generally speaking this requires the use of macro programming, command line options, or perhaps some combination of the two. You need to refer to the documentation for the particular program you wish to automate in order to learn the details for creating automated tasks. In most cases programs that use automatically executing macros should be fairly easy to set up for automated tasks.

Setting Up Scheduled Tasks

reating a scheduled task can be a simple or a complex process — depending on how difficult it is to accomplish your goals by automating the task. If you are scheduling a program that is designed to be easily automated, you will have a much easier time than if you are trying to use a program that actively resists automation. For example, programs that use a macro programming language can generally accomplish complete tasks with little or no user intervention. But trying to automate the use of a program that has no such facility would be very difficult indeed.

The Windows Me Maintenance Wizard works by creating certain tasks within the Task Scheduler. Each of the items added by the Maintenance Wizard is actually a program that can be configured to do a complete job on its own once started. And the Task Scheduler is just the thing you need to start those jobs at specific times.

The Task Scheduler is always running in the background. The figures here show you how to start adding a scheduled task. The following two pages show you how to complete this exercise.

Continued

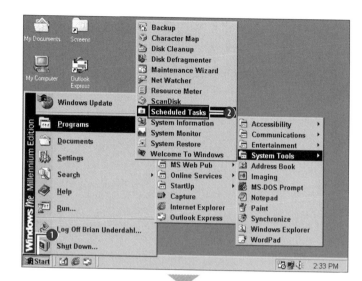

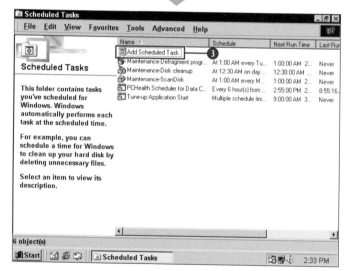

① Click the Start button.

② Select Programs ➪ Accessories ➪ System Tools ➪ Scheduled Tasks.

③ Double-click Add Scheduled Task to open the Scheduled Task Wizard.

CROSS-REFERENCE

See "Modifying a Scheduled Task" later in this chapter.

④

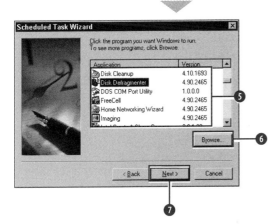

⑤

⑥

⑦

④ *Click Next to continue.*

⑤ *Select the program you wish to schedule.*

⑥ *Alternatively, click the Browse button to locate the program.*

⑦ *Click Next to continue.*

TAKE NOTE

▶ CREATING MACRO PROGRAMMING

You can schedule any type of task as long as you can automate it. The Windows Me tools for disk error checking and disk defragmentation are two good examples of programs that you can easily use, but what if you want to accomplish a project using a different application? In some cases you can automate a task by creating a *macro program* within an application. A macro program is simply a set of instructions that you create to tell the application how to perform a series of steps on its own. Most application programs that use macros provide a very simple means of creating macro programs — you can record them by stepping through the sequence of actions yourself. For example, in Microsoft Word, you can choose Tools ⇨ Macro ⇨ Record New Macro to create a macro program.

▶ VERIFY BEFORE YOU TRUST

If you add scheduled tasks other than the ones that the Maintenance Wizard creates, you should probably test those tasks to make certain they can run on their own without errors or user input. You might want to start by using the Run command from the Windows Me Start menu and entering the command line for running the task. If that works correctly, you might want to schedule the task to run while you wait and observe the process. If it is successful, reschedule the task for the correct time. This is especially important if the task could perform destructive actions such as deleting files.

FIND IT ONLINE

To learn how to distribute a task to multiple users, see
http://support.microsoft.com/support/kb/articles/
q217/0/06.asp.

Setting Up Scheduled Tasks

Continued

Once you have selected a program that you want to run as a scheduled task, your next step should be to decide when the task will run. Although the correct time to run a task may be obvious in many cases, you may need to give a bit of thought to determine the best time for other tasks. For example, logging on to the Internet and downloading your stock portfolio status probably won't do you a lot of good on the weekends when the markets are closed. Running routine maintenance tasks when you are likely to be using your PC would likewise be a poor scheduling choice.

In most cases you'll choose one of the first three options — daily, weekly, or monthly. In certain special cases you might choose one of the remaining options.

For example, choose the *One time only* option if you are testing a scheduled task. You could schedule the task to run once and then observe the results to see if the task needs any fine-tuning. The *When my computer starts* and *When I log on* options may be most useful for tasks you perform every time you use your PC. For example, if you always log on to the Internet and download the latest weather forecast, you might use one of these options. It's generally not a good idea to use these options to schedule a task — such as defragmenting your hard disk — that takes a long time to complete.

Your PC can run scheduled tasks only if the system is running at the scheduled time. If your system is off at the scheduled time, Windows Me will attempt to run the task as soon as possible after the scheduled time, but this may cause tasks to run while you are using your computer.

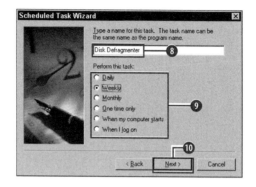

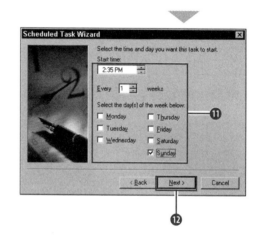

8 Optionally, enter a name for the task.

9 Select the task interval.

10 Click Next to continue.

11 Select the time options you prefer.

12 Click Next to continue.

CROSS-REFERENCE

See "Administering Task Scheduler" later in this chapter.

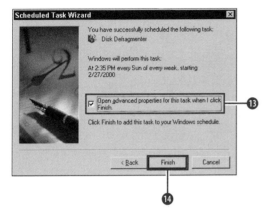

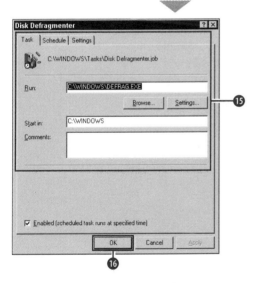

CUSTOMIZING EXISTING SCHEDULES

In addition to creating new tasks using the Scheduled Task Wizard, you can also use the Scheduled Tasks folder to adjust the schedule for existing tasks. If, as an example, you find that the Disk Defragmenter often is unable to complete the defragmentation before you want to use your PC, you may want to open the existing task and set it to begin at an earlier time. In fact, the easiest way to set up scheduled tasks is usually to set them up using the Maintenance Wizard and then fine-tune the schedule in the Scheduled Tasks folder.

SETTING UP YOUR OWN TASKS

If you want to add your own scheduled tasks using application programs other than the ones that can be scheduled using the Maintenance Wizard, you may want to visit the Microsoft Task Scheduler Web site at **http://support.microsoft.com/support/kb/articles/Q178/7/06.asp**. This Web site provides more specific information about how to schedule a program using command line options.

⑬ If you want to adjust the way the task runs, click here.

⑭ Click Finish to continue.

⑮ In the task's dialog box, choose your options to further configure the task.

⑯ Click OK to complete the task.

FIND IT ONLINE

To learn why ScanDisk may not always use the settings you prefer, see **http://support.microsoft.com/support/kb/articles/q179/3/69.asp**.

Modifying a Scheduled Task

Y ou shouldn't have to live with an inconvenient task schedule setup. If it turns out that the existing schedule doesn't quite work out for you, it is easy to adjust it. If, for example, you discover that ScanDisk is still running in the morning when you want to use your PC, you might want to have ScanDisk start an hour or two earlier so that it can finish before you arrive. You might also need to adjust the schedule if you find that certain tasks cannot be run on the same day without conflicting with each other. Or maybe it's just a case that you have changed your working hours and this requires a new task schedule.

When you are modifying a scheduled task, you primarily deal with the options on the Schedule and Setting tabs of the dialog box. The options contained on the Task tab are mainly used to set the parameters for the specific program you are running. For example, if you specify the name of the macro program file to open by including that name on the command line, you would specify the complete command line in the Run text box.

When you are adjusting a task schedule, you will encounter some options on the Settings tab that you haven't seen before. The *Scheduled Task Completed* section includes the option to delete the scheduled task after it completes. This section also enables you to limit the amount of time a task can run. The default is 72 hours, but you can set whatever limits you prefer. This option might be useful if you want to run a task fairly often but want it to end before you use your system for something else.

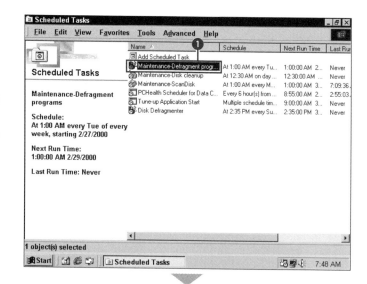

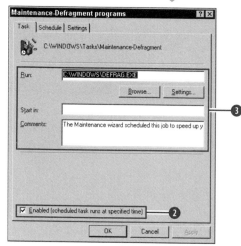

▶ Open the Scheduled Tasks folder if it is not already open.

❶ Double-click the task you wish to modify.

❷ Select this check box to enable the task or deselect it to disable the task.

❸ If you need to change any of the program settings, use these options.

CROSS-REFERENCE

See "Tuning Up with the Maintenance Wizard" in Chapter 14.

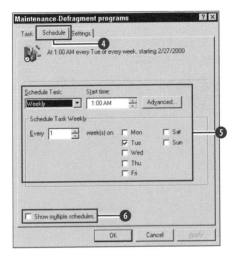

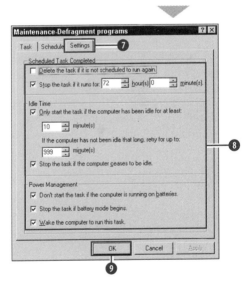

The *Idle Time* section delays or stops a task if you're using your system at the scheduled time. These options can help make scheduled tasks less obtrusive because they won't interfere with your use of your PC.

The *Power Management* settings are useful primarily on laptop systems where they can help save power by not enabling scheduled tasks to run when your computer is running on batteries. You also have the option to have your system wake up from hibernation to run the task.

④ Click the Schedule tab.

⑤ Select the schedule options you wish to use.

⑥ Click here if you wish to use more than one schedule.

⑦ Click the Settings tab.

⑧ Choose the appropriate settings for this task.

⑨ Click OK to complete the task.

FIND IT ONLINE

If Task Scheduler has problems starting a scheduled task, see **http://support.microsoft.com/support/kb/ articles/q178/6/91.asp**.

323

Administering Task Scheduler

The Task Scheduler is one of those parts of Windows Me that you will probably set up and then mostly ignore. Once your scheduled tasks seem to be running properly, you probably won't give too much thought to them. But if it is important that your scheduled tasks complete their missions successfully, you may want to learn how you can gain a bit more control over the whole process.

One of the important Task Scheduler administration tasks is verifying that your scheduled tasks actually ran and that they finished successfully. You can find out this information in two different ways. You can choose Advanced ⇨ Notify Me of Missed Tasks to be advised if a scheduled task did not run. Each time you select this option it changes from off to on or from on to off.

You can also choose to view the log that records the running of all scheduled events. By viewing this log you can determine whether the events you scheduled were completed successfully. If there were problems, you might need to suspend a task while you figure out how to correct the problem. You can also view the scheduled tasks log by opening SchedLog.txt in your Windows folder.

If you are notified of tasks that did not complete, be sure to examine the events log to learn more about the problem that prevented the tasks from completing. If the scheduled events log shows that certain tasks are consistently unable to complete successfully, you can look for additional clues within the log. You might find,

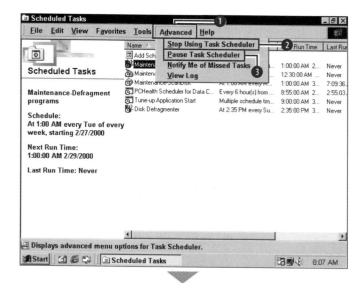

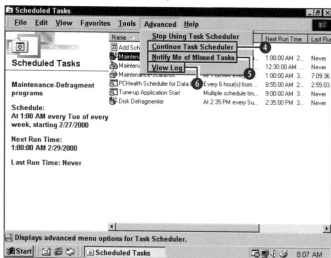

▶ Open the Scheduled Tasks folder if it is not already open.

❶ Click Advanced to open the menu.

❷ Select this option to stop the Task Scheduler.

❸ Select this option to pause Task Scheduler.

❹ If the Task Scheduler is paused, select this option to resume it.

❺ Select this option for notification of tasks that did not run.

❻ Select this option to view the log.

CROSS-REFERENCE

See Chapter 14 for more information on maintaining your computer.

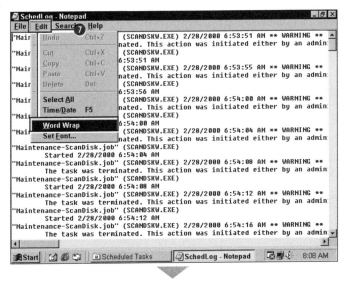

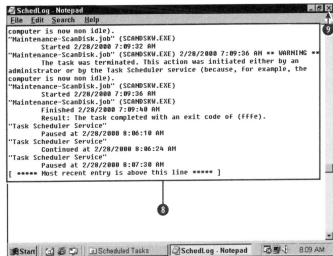

for example, that there is a conflict between two task schedules. If a scheduled task runs successfully but takes too long to complete, it might prevent a later task from completing.

TAKE NOTE

SUSPENDING SCHEDULED TASKS

You can temporarily suspend a scheduled task if you don't want it to run as scheduled. If you wish to pause all scheduled tasks, you can also temporarily stop the Task Scheduler. You may find that you need to do so if you wish to run certain critical functions that require all available processing power in order to be completed within a reasonable amount of time. For example, if you use a CD-R drive to create your own CDs, you may need to suspend all scheduled tasks to prevent problems during the CD-R creation process.

CLEAR THE TASK SCHEDULER LOG FILE

The Task Scheduler log file will continue to grow as long as Task Scheduler is running. You may wish to stop the Task Scheduler on occasion and use Notepad to remove the oldest entries from the file. Or you may want to delete the existing file after you have examined it. You can delete the file only if Task Scheduler is not running. You can, however, view the file anytime.

⑦ Select Edit ⇨ Word Wrap to make viewing the log easier.

⑧ Once you have opened the log, view the entries here.

⑨ Click the Close button to continue.

▶ Be sure to resume the Task Scheduler if it is paused.

FIND IT ONLINE

To download an alternate to Task Scheduler, see **http://www.sharewarejunkies.com/8ef3/ez_scheduler.htm**.

Personal Workbook

Q&A

1 How can you get an onscreen notification that advises you when a scheduled task did not run?

_____

_____

_____

2 How can you suspend a task?

_____

_____

_____

3 If you receive a notice that a task did not run, how can you find the problem?

_____

_____

_____

4 Why might you want to enter a descriptive name for a task?

_____

_____

_____

5 How can you specify that you wish to repeat a scheduled task twice daily?

_____

_____

_____

6 What setting can you use to automatically stop a task if you start to use your system?

_____

_____

_____

7 To be a good candidate for a scheduled task, what capability does a program need?

_____

_____

_____

8 How can you temporarily suspend all tasks?

_____

_____

_____

ANSWERS: PAGE 399

EXTRA PRACTICE

1 Add the Disk Defragmenter as a scheduled task.

2 Modify the schedule to run the task once a week.

3 Suspend the task.

4 View the event log to see which events have completed.

5 Resume the task, but change the schedule to every two weeks.

6 Pause the Task Scheduler.

REAL-WORLD APPLICATIONS

✔ You often use an application that creates hundreds of files and deletes other files. You schedule the Disk Defragmenter to run every other night to maintain system performance.

✔ You have a program that can check your stock market portfolio automatically. You schedule the program to run every weekday, one hour after the markets open.

✔ You browse the Internet quite often. You schedule the Disk Cleanup program to automatically remove all temporary Internet files every Friday just after you leave for the weekend. You also schedule the disk checking and defragmenting tasks to run over the weekend so that your system is running at top efficiency when you return to the office on Monday.

Visual Quiz

How can you display this dialog box? How can you make the task wait for 15 minutes after you stop using your system to begin the task?

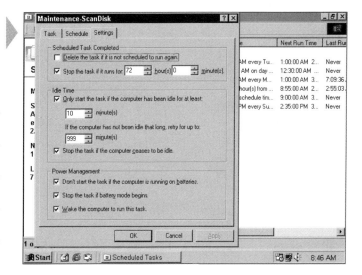

CHAPTER **16**

MASTER
THESE
SKILLS

▶ **Using Media Player for Sound**

▶ **Using Media Player for Video**

▶ **Playing Audio CDs**

▶ **Recording Sounds**

▶ **Using the Volume Controls**

▶ **Creating a Project in Movie Maker**

▶ **Recording a Movie in Movie Maker**

▶ **Editing Your Movie**

▶ **Saving a Movie Maker Project**

▶ **Configuring Multimedia**

▶ **Adding a Scanner or Camera**

Tools_30

Win32app

Playing Around with Multimedia

Using a Windows Me–based PC can be a lot of fun. One of the big reasons for this is the multimedia capability that is built into both your computer and into Windows Me. Computers are no longer boring boxes that just sit there waiting for you to type in a bunch of commands. Rather, they have become entertaining and even exciting to use in ways that people only dreamed about just a few years ago.

These days you'll find multimedia content used in many different ways in all sorts of places. Web pages, games, and even mainstream business applications often use multimedia features to enhance their impact. Many PC users are finding that they can use multimedia to take their documents out of the boring category and into the area of exciting presentations.

Windows Me supports a number of different types of multimedia content. The standard tools in Windows Me can play and even create a number of different audio and video formats. For example, you can play back sound files that are digital recordings of actual sounds. You can also play sound files that are closer to a musical score because your PC is actually creating the sounds using

the directions in the file. You can play video files that are simply recorded video clips, and you can play files that have an audio track synchronized with the video track. With Movie Maker you can even create your own video productions using your camcorder or other video source.

Multimedia encompasses a broad range of audio and video presentations. In this chapter we use a rather loose definition of multimedia that encompasses simple sound files as well as complex productions that include both video and audio tracks in a single file. The exact definition of multimedia isn't what is important — enjoying the benefits of having the multimedia capabilities of Windows Me is.

To use the multimedia capabilities, your computer needs to have sound, video, and music devices installed and properly configured. Every Windows Me system has at least some multimedia capability. To make full use of all of the possibilities may require you to do some upgrading — especially if you use an older PC that did not come fully equipped for a multimedia operating system like Windows Me.

Using Media Player for Sound

The most common type of multimedia file is a sound file. Windows Me uses an application called the *Media Player* to play back sounds as well as most other types of multimedia files.

Sound files come in two basic flavors — digital recordings and MIDI files. Digital recordings are actual recordings of sounds and, except for variations in speaker and sound card quality, they sound pretty much the same on any system. The most common type of digital recordings is a *wave* file — these use the .WAV file extension.

MIDI files are more like a musical score that tells your sound card how to synthesize a piece of music. That is, your sound card actually creates the music in much the same manner as an electronic organ might. MIDI files can sound quite different on different PCs. MIDI files generally use the .MID file extension.

Finding sound files to play in the Media Player is a simple task. You can find them not only on your hard drive but also on the installation CD-ROMs for most major office suites and other programs. Of course, the Internet is another good source of sound files. If you spend any time looking, you'll find there are more sound files than you could ever listen to.

To learn which types of sound files the Media Player can play, open the Media Player and select File ⇨ Open. Then click the Files of type list box and scroll through the list. Each file type includes a description of the type along with the supported file extensions. A few older

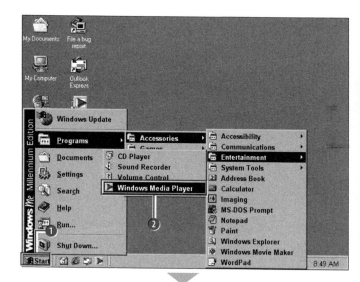

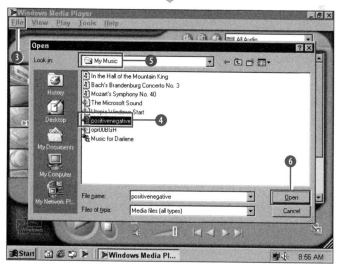

① Click the Start button.

② Select Programs ⇨ Accessories ⇨ Entertainment ⇨ Windows Media Player.

③ Select File ⇨ Open to display the Open dialog box.

④ Click the name of the sound file you wish to play.

⑤ Alternatively, click the Look in list box to locate the file.

⑥ Click Open to continue.

CROSS-REFERENCE

See "Using Media Player for Video" later in this chapter.

sound file formats aren't common enough to have much support these days, but with those exceptions aside, you'll likely find that Media Player can play virtually any sound file that you can find.

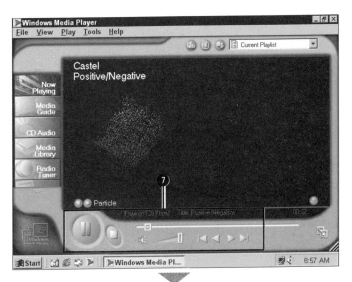

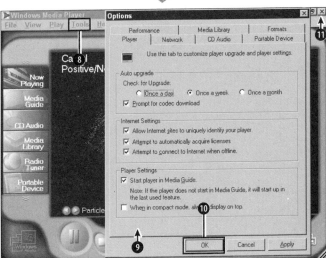

MEDIA PLAYER IS THE DEFAULT PLAYER

Windows Me associates the Media Player with several different types of multimedia files. If you double-click the most common types of multimedia files or click a Web link to a multimedia file, Windows Me will generally open Media Player to play the media clip. You can use other applications to play multimedia files, but Media Player is usually the easiest option to use because all you have to do is double-click the file you want to play.

MIDI VERSUS WAVE FILES

MIDI files are generally quite small compared to WAV sound files. MIDI sequences are limited to music, whereas wave sounds can be a recording of any type of sound, even human speech. You can record your own wave sound files easily using the tools that come with Windows Me. Creating your own MIDI files is far more difficult and requires specialized software that does not come with Windows Me.

⑦ Use these controls to control the playback.

▶ Hold the mouse pointer over a control to see a description.

⑧ Select Tools ⇨ Options to change the playback options.

⑨ Select the options you prefer.

⑩ Click OK to continue.

⑪ Click the Close button to complete the task.

FIND IT ONLINE

Visit the Media Player download page at
http://windowsmedia.microsoft.com/music/
downloads.asp.

Using Media Player for Video

The Windows Me Media Player can quite easily play several different types of video files in addition to various types of sound files. Playing video files may seem quite impressive compared to the far more boring things — such as writing letters or balancing your checkbook — that you probably do with your PC most of the time.

Media Player generally shows most videos in a small window rather than a full screen. There is a very good reason for this — a high-resolution, full-screen video presentation requires a substantial amount of data. Your PC monitor has a much higher resolution than a typical TV, and your computer screen is *refreshed* at a much higher rate than the typical TV screen, too. All of this greatly increases the rate that data must be supplied in order to view a video at full-screen. Even if your computer were fast enough to handle the high level of data flow, the file sizes would quickly get out of hand.

If you aren't happy with the size of the video window, you can try zooming it to see if the picture is acceptable. You can press Alt+Enter while the video is playing to expand the video to full-screen, or you can select one of the options on the View ⇨ Zoom menu. Remember, though, that the video will have the same actual resolution regardless of the zoom setting. If you make the video much larger than the default size, the video will appear quite blocky and out of focus.

The video files that Media Player supports may appear under several different names including Microsoft streaming media, video, MPEG movie, Indeo video,

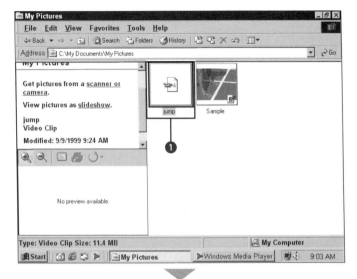

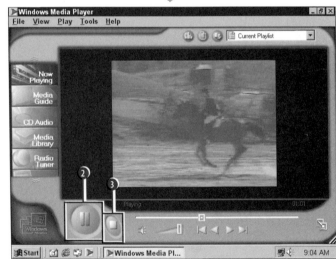

▶ Open the My Pictures folder — this is under your My Documents folder.

❶ Double-click a video file to open it in Media Player.

❷ Click here to pause the playback.

❸ Click here to stop the playback.

CROSS-REFERENCE

See "Using Media Player for Sound" earlier in this chapter.

QuickTime, and RealMedia. You don't need anything other than Media Player to view any of these types of video files no matter how they were created.

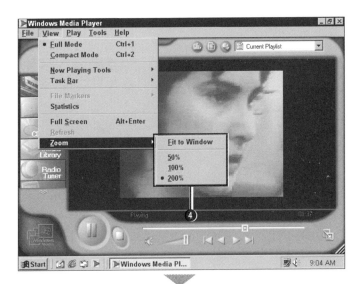

▶ VIDEO FILE SIZE CONSIDERATIONS

Video files generally take a lot of disk space. For example, a 90-second color video file with stereo sound may take over 11MB of space. Most video that is destined for viewing on a PC is intended to be viewed in a small window and not full-screen. Full-screen video files would take a prohibitive amount of disk space and a lot of computing power to display properly. Several methods are used to reduce the size of video files. Reducing the size of the video window is the most common step used. The *frame rate* — the number of images displayed per second — may also be reduced. As the number of frames per second drops, videos tend to become choppy-looking.

▶ CONSIDER YOUR BANDWIDTH

If you wish to use Media Player to view video files on the Internet, it's important to consider the speed of your Internet connection. You could easily spend an hour or more downloading a short video file that ends up not even worth watching.

④ *If you wish to change the playback window size, select View ⇨ Zoom and choose the size.*

▶ *Alternatively, press Alt+Enter to play the video full-screen.*

⑤ *To view the video file information, click the Media Library button.*

⑥ *Click the All Clips item under Video.*

⑦ *Click the Close button to complete the task.*

Playing Audio CDs

Y ou can use your PC's CD-ROM drive to play audio CDs on your computer. In fact, Windows Me incorporates an excellent audio CD player in the Media Player.

The Media Player was designed to function like a CD player that you might find in a typical home stereo system. You will find buttons for pausing and stopping a CD, as well as buttons that enable you to skip forward and back. You can choose what information you'd like to see on the display and even choose to play the tracks in random order or to preview each track for a few seconds. If the *play list* information is available, Media Player also shows the name of the album, artist, and current track.

Media Player stores the CD title, artist, and song list in a file on your system. When you download information on a new CD or edit the play list in the Media Player, the database file is updated. This enables you to correct any errors that might have been in the information that was downloaded from the Internet or to choose to play tracks in any order that you prefer. If Media Player is unable to locate the information about a CD, you can add the information yourself using the Edit Playlist button.

You'll find that the Media Player can be a lot of fun to watch, too. If you click the Now Playing button, you can choose the visualization that Media Player shows to accompany your music. Click the buttons at the lower left of the display window to choose the effect.

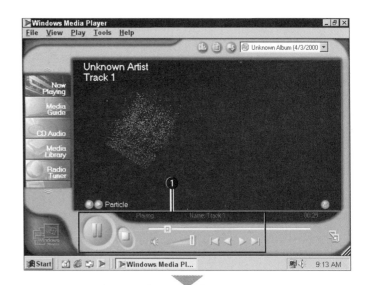

▶ Click the Start button and select Programs ⇨ Accessories ⇨ Entertainment ⇨ Windows Media Player.

▶ Alternatively, simply insert an audio CD in your CD-ROM drive to automatically start the CD Player.

❶ Use these controls to control the playback.

❷ Click the CD Audio button.

❸ If Media Player does not have the CD information, click Get Names to download the information from the Internet.

CROSS-REFERENCE

See "Configuring Multimedia" later in this chapter.

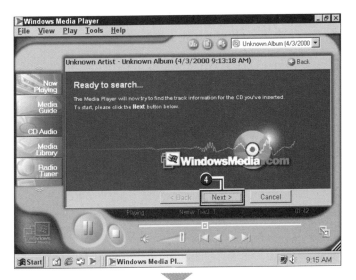

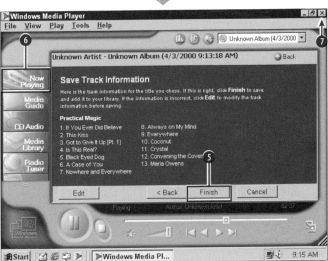

④ *Click Next to continue.*

▶ *You may need to enter information about the CD and click Next again to continue.*

⑤ *Once the information has been downloaded, click Finish to save the information.*

⑥ *If you wish to view the audio visualization effects, click the Now Playing button.*

⑦ *Click Close to complete the task.*

Recording Sounds

You can record your own sound files for use in Windows Me. In this section you learn how to use one of the Windows Me accessories — Sound Recorder — to record sounds that you can use to signal system events, to attach to an e-mail message, or even just for the fun of it.

You can record sounds from any source that is available on your system. In most cases you will probably use a microphone, but you can also record from the line input on your sound card and, depending on your equipment, maybe even from your CD drive. The procedure is pretty much the same no matter what source you use, so to keep things easy, this task assumes you are using a microphone.

When you make a recording you can choose from several different options that affect both the quality of the recording and the amount of disk space that it requires. Lower-quality recordings use less disk space and may be adequate for most purposes.

The settings that determine the recording quality level include the *sample rate* — the number of sound samples per second that are recorded; the *bit rate* — the number of volume levels that can be recorded; and the *format* — or type of compression.

In addition to choosing a quality level, Sound Recorder has some interesting features that you can use to modify sound files. For example, you can add an echo or reverse a sound so that it plays backwards. If the recording's volume isn't correct, you can adjust it up or down. If you want, you can change the speed, too. Each of these settings will have a rather major effect on the sound quality even if they are not normally thought of as recording-quality adjustments.

Continued

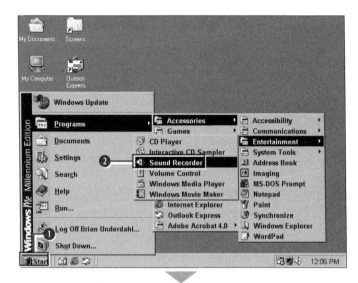

➊ Click the Start button.

➋ Select Programs ➪ Accessories ➪ Entertainment ➪ Sound Recorder.

➌ Select File ➪ Properties to set the recording properties before you begin recording.

CROSS-REFERENCE

See "Adding Sounds to Events" in Chapter 12.

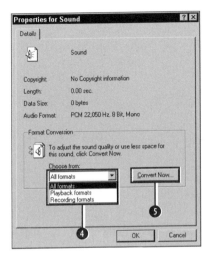

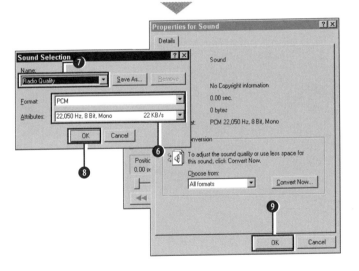

④ Choose the format type.

⑤ Optionally, click the Convert Now button to select the format settings.

⑥ Choose a format and attributes.

⑦ Alternatively, select one of the defined formats.

⑧ Click OK to close the dialog box.

⑨ Click OK to return to Sound Recorder.

FIND IT ONLINE

To find a number of sounds from a popular TV show, see **http://southland.hypermart.net/**.

Recording Sounds
Continued

If you have ever used a tape recorder, the Sound Recorder controls should seem quite familiar. You will see buttons for recording, playing back, fast forwarding, and rewinding. If you forget what any of the controls does, hold your mouse pointer over the button for a few seconds to see a description of the control.

You can have a little fun by using the selections on the Effects menu to modify sound files. Keep in mind, however, that it's pretty easy to add distortion as you are applying special effects to a sound file. Almost any special effect will modify the file in ways that degrade the sound output. If you don't care for the results after you have applied a special effect, select File ⇨ Revert to return to the last saved version of the file.

As an example of a little creative fun, you could use Effects ⇨ Reverse to reverse a recording so that it becomes unintelligible. If you send the reversed recording to someone, he or she would have to use his or her own copy of Sound Recorder to once again reverse the file and hear the message. This won't, of course, provide very much security, but it is an example of how you can have a little fun with the special effects.

You may discover that nothing is recorded when you click the record button. This is a fairly common problem that can have a couple of causes. First make certain that your microphone is plugged in correctly. If the microphone is plugged in correctly, check to make certain that the microphone input is enabled in the volume control. The Mute check box should not have a check

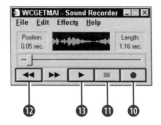

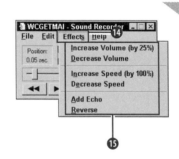

⓾ Click the Record button to begin recording.

⓫ Click the Stop button to end the recording.

⓬ Click the Rewind button to return to the beginning of the recording.

⓭ Click the Play button to hear the recording.

⓮ Select Effects to display the Effects menu.

⓯ Select an effect to apply to your recording.

▶ Click Play to hear the changes in the recording.

CROSS-REFERENCE

See "Using the Volume Controls" later in this chapter.

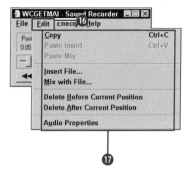

mark. If your volume control has a Select check box rather than a Mute check box, make certain the microphone is selected.

▶ **THE SOUND RECORDER DISPLAY**

Sound Recorder depicts the recorded sounds by varying the thickness of the line in the viewing window in the middle of the Sound Recorder window. Thicker lines indicate higher volume levels. The shape of the line is not an indicator of the frequencies that were recorded — only of the overall volume level.

▶ **EDITING SOUNDS**

You can use the Edit menu options to change the length of the recording or to mix two or more sound files together. For example, if you clicked the record button and waited a few seconds to begin speaking, you could move the position slider to the very beginning of your speech and then choose Edit ⇨ Delete Before Current Position to remove the silence at the beginning of the recording. You may need to play the recording several times to locate the correct point to begin your changes. You can also combine several short clips by using the Edit ⇨ Insert File command.

⑯ *Select Edit to display the Edit menu.*

⑰ *Select the action you wish to perform.*

▶ *Click Play again to hear the new changes.*

⑱ *Select File ⇨ Save As to save the file. You need to enter a name for the file.*

⑲ *Click the Close button to complete the task.*

Using the Volume Controls

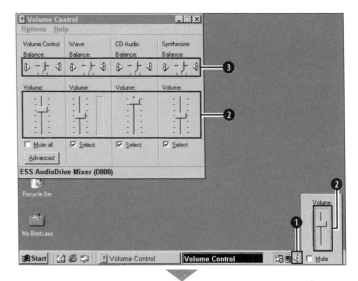

The different sound sources that are available on your PC probably produce widely varying volume levels. You may, for example, discover that wave sounds come blasting out of your speakers, but audio CDs play at such a low level that you can barely hear them. Or you may need to adjust the overall sound level at times to compensate for different conditions.

You can access the Windows Me volume controls by clicking the speaker icon in the system tray. This icon can be a little tricky to use at first because it reacts to both single and double mouse clicks. A single click opens a single volume control slider that adjusts the master volume level. A double click opens a much larger volume control with individual sliders for each sound source. The full volume control also includes sliders that you can use to adjust the left/right balance. Depending on your sound card, you may also be able to adjust the bass, treble, and loudness settings.

Once either volume control is displayed, you can adjust the volume by dragging the slider up or down. To turn the sounds off, click the Mute check box. Drag the horizontal sliders to adjust the left/right balance.

Most of the speakers that attach to PCs are *powered* speakers that include their own small amplifiers. You may need to experiment with the volume control settings to discover which settings produce the highest-quality sound. The amplifiers in some powered speakers may produce excess distortion if the volume level from your PC is too high or too low. Too low a volume level from your PC may also result in excessive hum from the speakers.

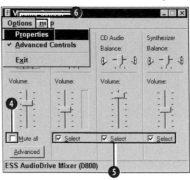

❶ Click the speaker button once for the small volume control or double-click for the full volume control.

❷ Drag these sliders to adjust volume.

❸ Drag these sliders to adjust balance.

❹ Select this check box to mute the sound.

❺ Select these check boxes to enable a specific sound source.

❻ To choose the controls, select Options ➪ Properties.

CROSS-REFERENCE

See "Playing Audio CDs" earlier in this chapter.

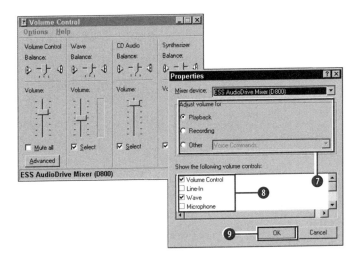

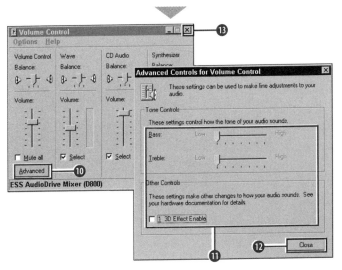

SOME COMPUTERS MAY HAVE TWO VOLUME CONTROLS

Some PCs have two different volume controls. In addition to the Windows Me volume controls shown on these pages, your PC may have a separate volume control that is adjusted by a special keystroke sequence or even special keys. To obtain adequate volume levels on a laptop, for example, in a noisy environment — such as in an automobile — you will probably have to adjust both sets of controls to their maximum levels.

MUTING AN INPUT

If you are using Sound Recorder or another application to record a sound file, you may discover that the sound file includes unexpected background noise. In many cases this unwanted noise comes from the other input sources that connect to your sound card. Each of the individual sound sources has a Mute check box that is intended to silence that sound source, but unfortunately many sound cards don't completely mute the sounds from a source even if this check box is selected. For the best results, reduce all unused sound sources to the lowest volume level in addition to selecting their Mute check boxes. Then adjust the remaining source to the proper level for recording.

⑦ Choose the set of controls you wish to use.

⑧ Choose the controls to appear on the full volume control.

⑨ Click OK to close the dialog box.

⑩ Click Advanced to adjust the tone and other settings.

⑪ Adjust the settings to suit your preferences.

⑫ Click Close.

⑬ Click the Close button to complete the task.

FIND IT ONLINE

For a program that will give you more control over sounds, see **http://www.goldwave.com/**.

Creating a Project in Movie Maker

W indows Me includes an exciting new multimedia tool that enables you to produce and edit your own video productions. Movie Maker is intended to enable anyone to have fun with creative uses of video.

Movie Maker automatically separates video files into individual *clips* that are basically scenes within your movie. When you import an existing video file, Movie Maker creates the series of clips as it imports the file. As you will learn later in this chapter, you can use these individual clips to edit your movie.

A Movie Maker *project* can be made up of video clips you import, video scenes you record, still images, and sounds. Once you have all of the elements of your project together, you can assemble them into a complete movie.

The Movie Maker window includes several different areas that you use as you are creating your project. A folder pane shows the project folders. Next to the folder pane is the thumbnails pane where you can see the individual clips. The viewer pane plays the currently selected clip or, if you have started assembling your movie, the current movie sequence. Near the bottom of the window is an area where you can assemble your clips on a *storyboard* or *timeline*— depending on how you prefer to work. Once you have created your movie, you can save it in a format that can be viewed by anyone who has Windows Media Player installed.

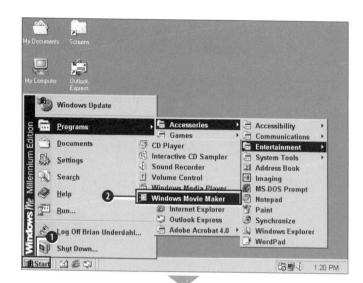

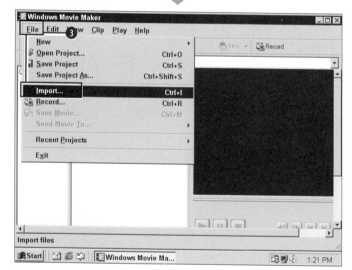

❶ Click the Start button.

❷ Select Programs ➪ Accessories ➪ Entertainment ➪ Windows Movie Maker.

❸ To import an existing video file, select File ➪ Import.

CROSS-REFERENCE

See "Recording a Movie in Movie Maker" later in this chapter.

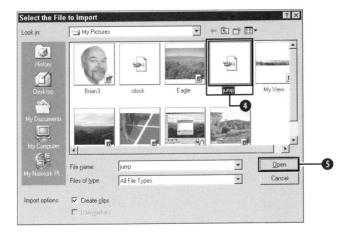

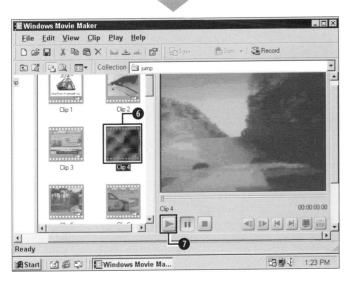

4 Select the file to import.

5 Click Open to begin importing the file.

▶ Wait while Movie Maker separates the file into clips.

6 To view a clip, select the clip in the thumbnails pane.

7 Click the Play button.

▶ Movie Maker automatically saves your project.

▶ YOU NEED A VIDEO CAPTUREDEVICE

Unless you simply want to work with existing video files that you obtain from other sources such as the Internet, you will need a video capture device to convert your videos into a format that can be used on your PC. Some of the newer digital camcorders can output video files directly to a PC, but to use an analog video source you will need a video capture board or a similar type of device installed in your computer. If you have a video camera such as the Intel Camera Pack or the 3Com Bigpicture Video Camera, or a video board such as an ATI All In Wonder installed in your system, you already have a video capture device.

▶ YOU NEED A LARGE HARD DISK

Video files take a lot of disk space. For example, the two-and-a-half-minute video file used in the example takes over 11MB of disk space even though the video plays in a 160×120 pixel window at 10 frames per second and uses 8-bit mono sound with an 11.25 kHz sample rate. If the video were recorded for full-screen 640×480 playback, the file size would be over 175MB. If the video were an hour in length, you would need over 4.2GB of disk space, and that's without increasing the frame rate or audio quality.

FIND IT ONLINE

See online movie reviews at
http://movies.eonline.com/?topmovies.

Recording a Movie in Movie Maker

If you have a video source attached to your PC, you can use Movie Maker to record your own video clips to add to your Movie Maker project. The video source could be a digital camera or even something like a VCR that is attached to a video capture device.

When you record a video file, it is always a good idea to keep your target audience in mind. You could choose to create your video clips using the highest possible quality setting, but you could easily end up with a file that takes hours for someone to download with their modem. This is an especially important point to remember if you are creating a movie to be viewed on a Web site — most people simply don't have access to high-speed Internet connections. You might want to create a couple of different versions of the same project. That way you could have a low-bandwidth version available for dial-up visitors, and a high-quality version available for people who have high-speed connections.

Once you have finished recording your video clip, you should view the results in Movie Maker. You can edit a clip to cut out unneeded sections at the beginning or end of a clip, but this may cause problems with any audio that was recorded as part of the same clip. You may want to consider recording your audio as a separate file so that you can build your movie by combining the video portions without regard to any audio considerations. You can then add your recorded audio as a separate part of the movie during the editing process. Don't be afraid to redo clips that don't work out quite right.

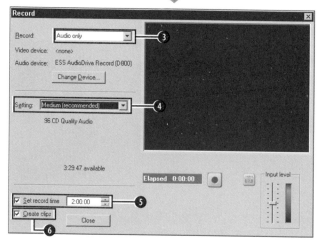

❶ Select File ➪ Record to open the Record dialog box.

❷ Alternatively, click the Record button.

❸ Choose what you want to record.

❹ Select the quality level for the recording.

❺ Choose the total length for the recording.

❻ To have Movie Maker automatically break your recording into scene clips, select this option.

CROSS-REFERENCE

See "Editing Your Movie" later in this chapter.

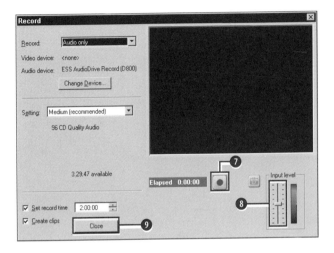

TAKE NOTE

▶ CONFIGURE YOUR CAPTURE HARDWARE

Before you can record your own video or audio clips you must have your video and/or audio capture hardware installed and correctly configured. Depending on the particular hardware you are using, this may require using a setup program supplied by the hardware manufacturer. Generally the configuration process will set the correct output level for your speakers, the input level for your microphone, and the proper frame rate and image size for your video device. These settings are very important because you want the highest possible quality, but you must be certain that your computer is powerful enough to process the data stream. If your computer isn't fast enough to keep up, your videos will be jerky or even completely unusable.

▶ CAPTURING AUDIO ONLY

If you don't have a video capture device, you can still use Movie Maker to record audio. Because you can use still images along with your audio files to create your movie, you can build a very impressive and interesting production using nothing more than a series of digital images and some recorded sounds.

⑦ Click here to begin recording.

⑧ If necessary, drag this slider to adjust the input level.

⑨ Click Close to close the dialog box.

⑩ To view your new recording, select it here.

⑪ Click the Play button to see the recording.

FIND IT ONLINE

To find fun video clips you can use for practice, see http://www.Volkswagen.org/media/.

Editing Your Movie

One of the most visible and important ways to make your movies more interesting is to edit the various scenes so that they blend into a real story. This can involve trimming down scenes to the most interesting parts, blending from one scene to another, and making certain the whole production flows together.

Movie Maker has two different views that you use to create and edit your movie. You start by using the *storyboard* to assemble the clips into the proper sequence. To add clips to the storyboard you simply drag them from the thumbnail pane and drop them where you would like them to appear on the storyboard. This makes it possible to show the clips in whatever order works best for your final production.

Once you have added the clips to the storyboard, you switch views to the *timeline* view. The timeline shows how long each clip runs, and where the movie switches from one clip to the next.

Most likely you will find that some clips include material that should be cut from the beginning or the end of the clip. For example, if your movie were to show someone arriving via airplane, you could probably cut a large portion of a clip showing them walking down the ramp. You use the timeline to review the assembled clips and then set *trim points* for the clips. These trim points tell Movie Maker where to begin or end playing the clip.

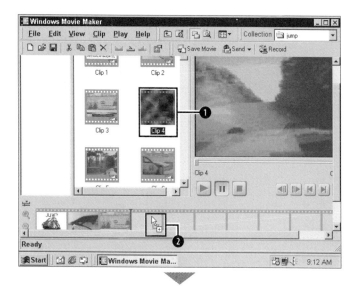

❶ Select a clip to add to the storyboard.

❷ Drag the clip to the point it should appear in your movie and release the mouse button.

❸ Click here to switch between storyboard and timeline view.

❹ Click these buttons to zoom in or out.

❺ Click here to record a narration track.

❻ Use this control to balance the sound tracks.

CROSS-REFERENCE

See "Dragging and Dropping Data" in Chapter 5.

ADD NARRATION AFTER ASSEMBLING THE CLIPS

Even though the various clips that make up your movie may include their own sounds, you may want to add a narration track once the clips have been assembled into a movie. The sounds that are part of each clip begin and end along with the clip, and the result can be a very choppy, broken up sound track. Professional movie producers always record the sound track separate from the video track because this enables the sound track to bridge scene changes. Your narration track can be something as simple as a spoken description of the activity, or it can be a completely scripted vocal track accompanied by background music.

BE PATIENT

It is important to be patient while you are assembling your movie. Some actions require your PC to manipulate a large amount of data, and this can cause your system to respond quite slowly — especially if your movie contains a large number of clips. Watch the mouse pointer for clues to see if your system needs a little extra time to complete an operation. For example, when you are dragging clips onto the storyboard, wait until the mouse pointer shows the plus sign as shown in the first figure before releasing the button to drop the clip.

⑦ Use this scroll bar to view the timeline.

⑧ Click here to preview your movie.

⑨ Select a clip to edit.

⑩ Use this slider to trim the beginning of the clip.

⑪ Use this slider to trim the end of the clip.

⑫ Click here to view the effect of the editing.

Saving a Movie Maker Project

Once you create your Movie Maker masterpiece you will want to be able to share it with other people. After all, why go to all that work and never have anyone see the results of your efforts?

Movie Maker automatically saves the clips that you import or record as a *collection*. This is essentially a folder under the My Pictures folder that contains all of the individual pieces that make up your movie. Even if you forget to save your movie project, all of the unedited pieces of the movie will be safely stored in the collection folder.

You can save your Movie Maker project a couple of different ways. If you want to be able to go back later and apply additional edits to your movie, select File ⇨ Save Project (or Save Project As) to keep all of your work in a format that enables further editing. When you have completed your edits, save the project as a Windows Media Audio/Video file using the File ⇨ Save Movie command. As the figures show, you can also save your movie directly to a Web server or to an e-mail message.

Once you name the movie file and click the Save button, Movie Maker will begin to assemble your movie. Depending on the complexity of your movie and the speed of your computer, this process may take several minutes. During this time Movie Maker is compressing the movie and creating the Windows Media Audio/Video file. Once the movie has been successfully saved, you can double-click the file to open it in Media Player.

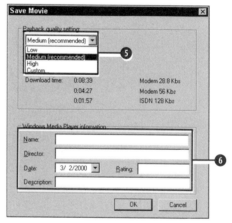

❶ Click File to open the File menu.

❷ Click Save Project to save the project for further editing.

❸ Alternatively, click here to send the movie file via e-mail or to your Web site.

❹ Click Save Movie to save your movie for viewing.

❺ Select the playback quality setting.

❻ Enter information about your movie here.

CROSS-REFERENCE

See Chapter 6 for more information on working with files.

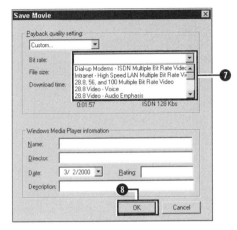

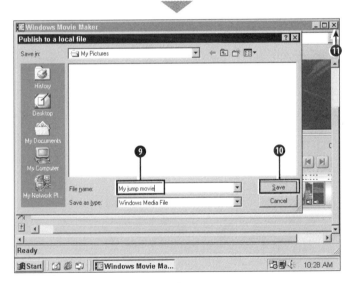

⑦ If you selected Custom, select the setting here.

⑧ Click OK to continue.

⑨ Enter a file name for your movie.

⑩ Click Save to save the movie file.

⑪ Click the Close button to complete the task.

TAKE NOTE

SAVE IN DIFFERENT QUALITY SETTINGS

When you create a movie in Movie Maker, the movie is always saved using an ASF file extension. This extension identifies a Windows Media Audio/Video file that is playable using Windows Media Player. Although you cannot save your movies in formats for use in other types of players, you can control the playback quality settings when you save the file. You might, for example, want to save the file in a high-quality version for playback direct from disk, and a lower-quality version for downloading from your Web site. This strategy enables people who use a dial-up connection to the Internet to view the movie even if it is not quite as nice as your high-quality version, which might take too long to download.

ADDING MOVIE INFORMATION

If you fill in the text boxes in the Windows Media Player information section of the Save Movie dialog box, Windows Media Player will display that information when someone plays your movie. The name you enter in the Name text box in this dialog box does not have to be the same as the file name you use when you save your movie.

FIND IT ONLINE

A fun diversion — the Mystery Science Theater 3000 Instant Movie Title Maker Machine at **http://www. geocities.com/Hollywood/Hills/3799/ MST3K.html**.

Configuring Multimedia

Windows Me has a very large number of multimedia configuration options that you can use to fine-tune virtually every aspect of your computer's multimedia capabilities. By using these options you can squeeze out as much or as little of the multimedia performance as you like. You can go for every bit of what is available or you can play it safe — it's your choice. Windows Me tends to be somewhat conservative in its default multimedia settings, so you may want to try adjusting the configuration to improve the performance of your multimedia devices.

To adjust your multimedia settings, use the Sounds and Multimedia Properties dialog box. This is the same dialog box you use to assign sounds to Windows Me system events.

A number of multimedia settings may be unfamiliar to you. For example, one of the figures shows the Speakers tab of the Advanced Audio Properties dialog box. Here you should select the configuration that most closely represents your speaker setup. This step is especially important if you have a very good set of speakers attached to your PC. Otherwise, Windows Me may not take advantage of all the advanced features built into your speaker system.

You'll also find performance settings for both playback and recording. The first type of setting is for *hardware acceleration.* This setting determines how much processing power is used to improve audio playback and recording features. Although the default setting uses partial hardware acceleration, you'll probably find that your system has no problems using full acceleration. Using a lower setting may be effective as a method of troubleshooting audio-related problems but results in poorer audio performance.

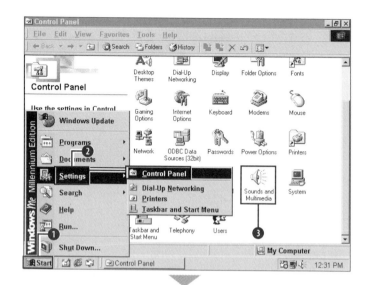

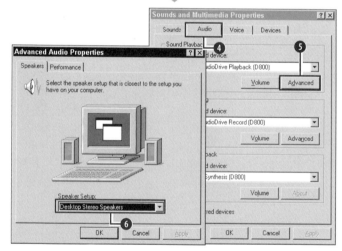

❶ Click the Start button.

❷ Select Settings ➪ Control Panel.

❸ Double-click the Sounds and Multimedia icon.

❹ Click the Audio tab.

❺ Click the Sound Playback Advanced button.

❻ Select your speaker setup in the Advanced Audio Properties dialog box.

CROSS-REFERENCE

See "Adding Sounds to Events" in Chapter 12.

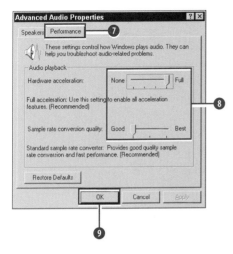

The second audio performance setting is the *sample rate conversion quality*. This setting determines the quality level of audio playback and recording. The default setting produces the lowest quality while imposing the smallest possible drain on system resources. If you prefer that your system sound as good as possible try one of the higher-quality settings.

You should experiment with these settings to find the best set for your needs. Faster computers are generally better able to handle the higher-quality settings at the right end of the two scales.

Continued

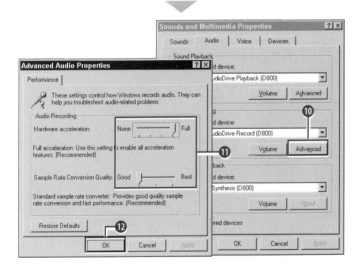

TAKE NOTE

SELECTING AUDIO DEVICES

If your system has more than one device that has audio capabilities installed, you may need to choose the correct device in each of the *Preferred device* list boxes. Windows Me may not know which you would prefer to use for multimedia purposes. You'll want to make certain the correct device is selected.

SET THE VOLUME

You may need to adjust each audio source to produce output levels that are more even. Click the Volume buttons in the Sounds and Multimedia Properties dialog box to open the full volume control, which has individual controls for each sound source.

⑦ *Click the Performance tab.*

⑧ *Select the playback settings you prefer.*

⑨ *Click the OK button.*

⑩ *Click the recording Advanced Properties button.*

⑪ *Select the recording settings you prefer.*

⑫ *Click the OK button.*

FIND IT ONLINE

To find shareware Windows multimedia applications, see **http://www.clicked.com/shareware/multimedia/index.html**.

Configuring Multimedia
Continued

Windows Me has some voice playback and capture capabilities built in as a part of its multimedia capabilities. You can use these capabilities in certain games as well as with voice recognition software to control your system. In addition, some voice recognition software can take dictation — often at a dictation speed much higher than your normal typing speed.

Windows Me uses the Sound Hardware Test Wizard to configure your system for voice playback and capture. To use this wizard you must have a microphone connected to your computer and be ready to read some text (any text will do) so that the wizard can analyze your sound levels.

To test your voice playback and capture capabilities, the wizard begins by checking your hardware to make certain that it can actually listen to your voice and play back sounds at the same time. Next, you must speak into your microphone while the wizard listens to your voice and adjusts the microphone sound level. Following this, you must adjust the playback and recording levels so you can hear your own voice but aren't plagued by echoes or feedback. See the Take Note section for a solution to excessive echo and feedback problems.

Once your system's voice capabilities have been configured, you can participate in voice chats over the Internet. As you will see in the next chapter, Windows Me includes several games that you can play against other people over the Internet. These games include voice chat capability so that you can speak with your opponent while you are playing. This can lend a whole new level of fun to using the Internet.

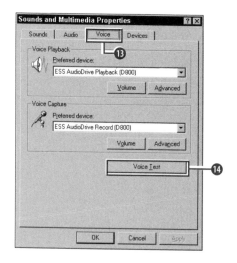

⑬ Click the Voice tab.

⑭ Click the Voice Test button to open the Sound Hardware Test Wizard.

⑮ Click the Next button to continue.

CROSS-REFERENCE

See "Playing Internet games" in Chapter 17.

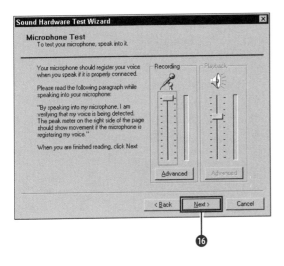

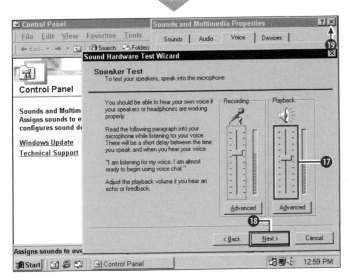

▶ Speak into your microphone as the wizard adjusts the microphone volume level.

⑯ Click Next to continue.

⑰ Speak into your microphone and adjust the playback volume level.

⑱ Click Next to continue.

▶ Click Finish on the final screen of the wizard.

⑲ Click the Close button to complete the task.

TAKE NOTE

FULL VERSUS HALF DUPLEX

In order to play sounds at the same time that Windows Me is listening to your voice, your computer must have *full-duplex* capability. This feature simply means that both the playback and recording hardware can be used at the same time. If only one of the sound capabilities can be used at one time, the hardware is said to have *half-duplex* capability. Examples of these capabilities include sound devices you are probably familiar with: telephones — which are generally full-duplex — and two-way radios — which are generally half-duplex.

USE A HEADSET TO REDUCE FEEDBACK

If you find that you hear excessive echo or feedback during the voice playback test, you can try to reduce these effects by reducing the playback volume. A more effective means of eliminating these effects may be to use a headset. In most cases a headset eliminates the problem because none of the sound from the earphones will be feeding back into your microphone. You will also find that using a headphone tends to keep the microphone at an even distance from your mouth, and this can make it far easier for someone you are chatting with to understand you.

FIND IT ONLINE

See the DirectPlay game rooms at
http://zone.msn.com/directplay/.

Adding a Scanner or Camera

If you want to use your own multimedia content on your PC, you will probably want to add a scanner or a camera to your system. Once you have added one or both of these items, you will be able to add images to your documents quite easily. Depending on the application you are using, your new scanner or camera may appear as one of the options on the menu. For example, if you are using Imaging, your scanner will be available on the File menu.

If your scanner or camera uses plug and play to identify itself to your computer, you may find that it has already been installed when you open the Scanners and Cameras folder. This is especially likely if your scanner or camera connects to your PC using the USB port. When a new device is plugged into a USB port, Windows Me identifies the device and automatically installs the necessary driver software for the device. These drivers remain installed even when you unplug the device, so you will not have to reinstall them in the future. You may need to insert your Windows Me CD-ROM to install the drivers when the device is first detected.

Depending on the equipment you are installing, you may need to insert a disk provided by the manufacturer or answer several questions during the installation. If you have a problem during the installation that prevents your equipment from functioning properly, it is usually best to open Device Manager, remove the equipment from the list, and restart your system before trying again.

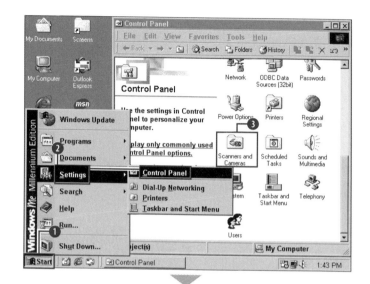

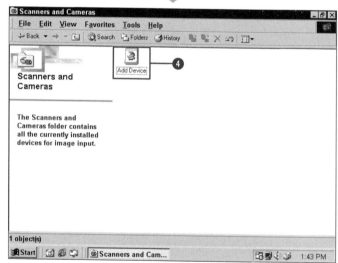

① Click the Start button.

② Select Settings ⇨ Control Panel.

③ Double-click the Scanners and Cameras icon.

④ Double-click the Add Device icon to start the Scanner and Camera Installation Wizard.

CROSS-REFERENCE

See "Looking for Problems with Device Manager" in Chapter 14.

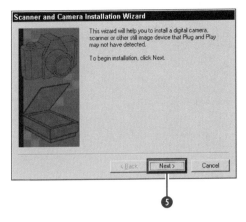

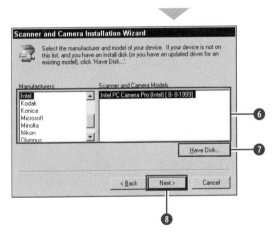

TAKE NOTE

▶ YOU MAY NEED SPECIAL SOFTWARE

Even though Windows Me supports many different scanners and cameras, you may discover that you must install the manufacturer's software in order to access all of the advanced features of your equipment. For example, the Windows Me default drivers may enable you to scan an image using certain preset image settings, but to exercise complete control you will need to use the software that came with your scanner. The Windows Me drivers might not support the full range of resolution settings or graphic enhancements that are offered by your equipment. However, using the Windows Me drivers may make using the equipment a bit more streamlined.

▶ KNOW YOUR PORTS

If you need to install a scanner or camera, you should know which port on your PC the unit is attached to. Typical cameras and scanners may attach to a serial (or COM) port, a parallel (or LPT) port, or a USB port. Some higher-end equipment may attach to a SCSI port or even a 1394 port. You should know which type of port your equipment uses so that you can specify the correct port during the installation.

⑤ Click Next to continue.

⑥ Select the manufacturer and model.

⑦ Alternatively, click Have Disk if you have a disk for your equipment.

⑧ Click Next to continue.

▶ Follow the on-screen prompts to complete the installation for your particular hardware.

FIND IT ONLINE

To find the newest multimedia applications, see
http://www.davecentral.com/multi.html.

Personal Workbook

Q&A

1 Which Windows Me tool would you use to record a voice message?

_____

_____

_____

2 What is the quickest method of displaying the full volume control?

_____

_____

_____

3 What type of file does the Sound Recorder produce?

_____

_____

_____

4 How can you make Media Player skip the same song on an audio CD every time you play the CD?

_____

_____

_____

5 Why are most video files shown in a small window?

_____

_____

_____

6 What do you call the tool you use to create Windows Media Audio/Video files?

_____

_____

_____

7 What type of files are actually instructions that are used to synthesize music on your PC?

_____

_____

_____

8 What does the thickness of the line that is displayed in the Sound Recorder represent?

_____

_____

_____

ANSWERS: PAGE 400

EXTRA PRACTICE

1 Open the full volume control and adjust each of the individual controls to suit your preferences.

2 Enter a play list for your favorite audio CD.

3 Play a sound file while you adjust the left/right speaker balance using the full volume control.

4 Play a video file and notice the difference as you select different zoom settings.

5 Record a message that tells you when new messages arrive.

6 Import a video file into Movie Maker and rearrange the clips.

REAL-WORLD APPLICATIONS

✔ You want to create a video presentation for your Web site to introduce your products. You use Movie Maker to blend together several different video clips along with your narration.

✔ You like to listen to a particular audio CD, but one of the tracks is damaged so it always skips whenever it is played. You edit the play list for the CD so the damaged track is automatically bypassed.

✔ You have the audio signal from your satellite receiver connected to your sound card so you can listen to a foreign broadcast while you work. You use the full volume control to adjust the line-in input so that the satellite sound is at the correct listening level.

Visual Quiz

How can you display this application? How can you tell how long the file will play? Can you tell what type of file is being played?

_____

_____

_____

_____

_____

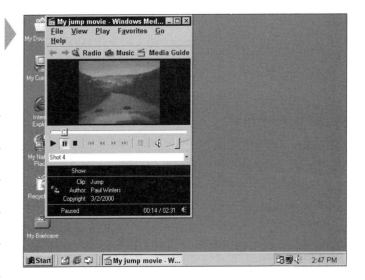

CHAPTER

MASTER THESE SKILLS

▶ Using the Calculator
▶ Using Character Map
▶ Using the Clipboard Viewer
▶ Using Notepad
▶ Creating Documents in WordPad
▶ Using Imaging for Windows
▶ Using Paint
▶ Playing Some Games
▶ Playing Internet Games
▶ Opening and Closing the MS-DOS Prompt Window
▶ Using the MS-DOS Prompt Window
▶ Getting Command Help

Using the Accessory Applications

The Windows Me accessory applications are small programs that do simple tasks with a minimum of fuss. None of these programs has a lot of excess baggage, so they tend to be very easy to use. In many cases the accessory programs are all you need to do a job that would be a waste of an expensive multipurpose program. As you'll discover, the Windows Me accessories are quite capable. They may not be as powerful as you might need for heavy-duty use, but they certainly do a very creditable job and suit your needs for occasional use.

All computers need software to enable them to do something useful. The Windows Me accessory applications are programs that lack a lot of the more complicated and advanced features of programs you might buy, but they are quite useful in their own way. For example, the Calculator accessory will not replace your favorite spreadsheet program, nor will the drawing tools in Paint rival those found in sophisticated graphics programs. But if all you need is to make some quick calculations or create a simple sign, you will find these Windows Me accessory programs handy. If you want to have a little fun, Windows Me includes a number of games — including several that you can play against opponents on the Internet. These games don't have all the sophistication you might find in a game you buy in a computer store, but they give you a chance to relax a little and enjoy yourself.

In addition to these types of programs that typically come to mind when you think of Windows Me accessories, this chapter also covers the *MS-DOS prompt* — otherwise known as the *command line*. Some people would say that the command line is a throwback to the early days of computing before graphical user interfaces (GUIs) took over. But it is just as valid to say that the command line provides you with a powerful tool that can be extremely important. Certain tasks are far simpler when the computer user has the ability to type in a single command that accomplishes more than dozens of mouse clicks ever could. You may never use the command line, but Windows Me provides it just in case you do need it.

Using the Calculator

The Windows Me Calculator is an onscreen version of a pocket calculator, but it can be far more convenient and useful than any pocket calculator you might own. Because the Calculator runs on your PC, it offers some unique advantages no stand-alone calculator can match.

The calculator keys work just the same as they do on a pocket calculator. The Backspace button removes the last digit you entered. The CE button clears the current entry from the display without modifying the current calculation. The C button zeros out the Calculator. You can enter numbers either by using your keyboard or by clicking the calculator keys with your mouse. If you want to use the keyboard you'll probably find it easier to use the numeric keypad; make certain the Num Lock indicator is lit.

When you store a value in the calculator's memory, an M appears in the gray box above the memory key column. The MC button resets memory to zero, and MR displays the value in memory. MS stores the value currently displayed into memory, and M+ adds the value currently displayed to the value that is in memory.

The scientific calculator includes several radio buttons that you can use to convert numbers to different numbering systems. For example, if the Dec radio button is selected, you can enter a base 10 number. To convert the number to a hexadecimal number, you can click the Hex button. When you choose a different numbering system, you may find that some of the keys will be grayed out to indicate that they are unavailable. For

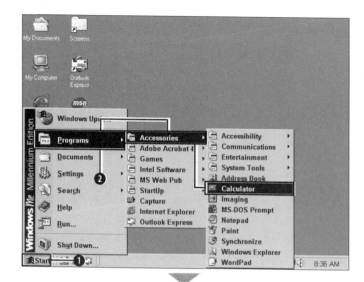

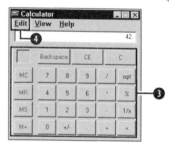

❶ Click the Start button.

❷ Select Programs ➪ Accessories ➪ Calculator.

❸ Enter your calculation using the onscreen keys or your keyboard.

❹ To copy or paste data, use the Edit menu.

CROSS-REFERENCE

See Chapter 5 for more information about using the Clipboard.

example, because binary numbers can only include 1s and 0s, all of the other number keys will be grayed out when you click the Bin button.

If you enter a formula using parenthesis to control the calculation order, the gray box above the right parenthesis button indicates the current nesting level.

TAKE NOTE

CHOOSING THE CALCULATOR MODE

The Windows Me Calculator has two different modes that can handle a broad range of computations. The standard mode is a simple calculator that includes basic capabilities such as add, subtract, multiply, and divide functions, a square root function, a percent function, a reciprocal function, and memory storage. If you need more advanced features such as base conversions, statistical functions, or logarithms, you can choose the scientific calculator. It has many additional functions like those you'd find on a sophisticated calculator used by a scientist or engineer.

SHARING RESULTS WITH OTHER APPLICATIONS

One of the big advantages of the onscreen calculator is that you can copy your results to the Clipboard and then paste them into a document. You can use Ctrl+C or Edit ⇨ Copy to copy the result to the Windows Me Clipboard. Then you can use Ctrl+V or Edit ⇨ Paste to paste the number into your document.

⑤ To choose a different view, click the View menu. (The following screen shows the scientific calculator.)

⑥ Select the type of calculator you wish to use.

⑦ To convert a number to a different base, use these options.

⑧ Click the Close button to complete the task.

FIND IT ONLINE

See **http://www.ucalc.com/ucalc.html** for an advanced Windows calculator.

Using Character Map

The Character Map is a program that enables you to enter any character into a document. You may not be aware that most character sets include far more than the characters you enter using your keyboard. The Character Map makes it possible to access additional characters with ease. This tool is especially useful if you need to enter foreign language characters into a document.

Your keyboard may have over 100 keys, but fewer than 80 of them are used for entering characters into your documents. A character set may have over 250 characters, so it is easy to see why the Character Map can be so useful. You might think of the Character Map as a tool for extending your keyboard and making it far more versatile. By using the Character Map you can easily choose any character you wish to insert into a document — no matter how difficult typing that character directly might be.

In addition to enabling you to enter foreign characters into your documents, the Character Map makes it easy to enter other types of characters. For example, if you need to create a document that uses *bullets,* you can easily choose any of the special characters that are generally contained in most character sets. You might choose uniquely shaped arrows or even sequentially numbered clock faces for special bullet points for a change of pace from the standard bullets that are used in most presentations.

You can also use the Character Map to insert standard typographic symbols such as the copyright symbol — © — or the registered trademark symbol — ® — into a document.

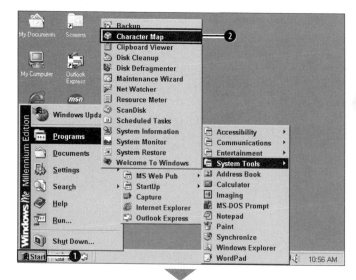

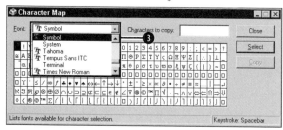

❶ Click the Start button.

❷ Select Programs ➪ Accessories ➪ System Tools ➪ Character Map.

❸ Choose the font you wish to use.

▶ Different fonts do not contain the same set of extended characters.

CROSS-REFERENCE

See Chapter 5 for more information about working with documents.

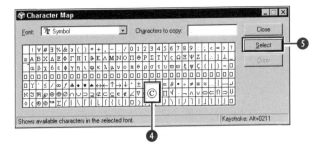

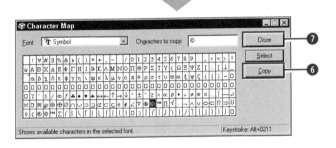

LEARN THE KEYSTROKES

Although the Character Map is quite handy for entering characters that you use occasionally, there is an easier way to enter characters that you use more often. When you select a character in the Character Map, the lower right portion of the Character Map window shows the keystroke combination that you can use to enter the character without opening the Character Map. To use these keystroke combinations, you hold down the Alt key and then enter the four-digit number code for the special character. Once you have entered the number, you release the Alt key to insert the character at the current cursor position.

USE THE CORRECT FONT

The special characters that you can enter using the Character Map or a keystroke combination can vary considerably in different fonts. It is important to make certain you have selected the correct font before you choose characters to insert in your document. Be especially careful about changing the document's font after you have inserted special characters — you may find that the special characters you inserted have been changed to completely different characters in the new font.

④ To view a magnified version of the character, click the character.

⑤ Double-click the character or click Select to select the character.

⑥ Click Copy to copy the selected characters to the Clipboard.

⑦ Click the Close button. Remember to paste the characters into your document.

FIND IT ONLINE

See **http://aritechdev.hypermart.net/ecm.htm** for a replacement Character Map with a larger display of sample characters.

Using the Clipboard Viewer

The Clipboard Viewer is a Windows Me accessory that enables you to view, save, and reload Clipboard contents. The Clipboard is the place where Windows Me temporarily stores items you have copied or cut from a document.

When you place an item on the Windows Me Clipboard, that item only remains on the Clipboard until another object is cut or copied to the Clipboard. If you cut something from a document, that object can be lost if you forget to paste it before you cut or copy another object. By using the Clipboard Viewer you can save the Clipboard contents in a file and later reopen those contents as necessary.

You may find that the Clipboard Viewer does not appear on your Start menu. The program is generally not installed by default, so you may have to use the Windows Setup tab of the Properties dialog box for Add/Remove Programs to install it. You will find the Clipboard Viewer in the System Tools category.

When you are viewing the Clipboard contents, you can see how the different available content formats appear by selecting a format from the Display menu. Choosing a different display format does not actually change the type of the data on the Clipboard — only the way it appears in the Clipboard Viewer. However, choosing a different display format can give you a better idea how the different options available on a program's Edit ⇨ Paste Special menu will affect the object when you add it to a new document. See the Take Note section for more information on content format.

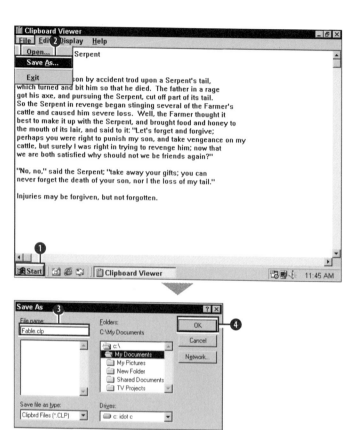

▶ Save some data to the Clipboard.

❶ Click the Start button and select Programs ⇨ Accessories ⇨ System Tools ⇨ Clipboard Viewer.

❷ Select File ⇨ Save As to save the Clipboard contents.

❸ Enter a name for the file.

❹ Click OK to save the file.

CROSS-REFERENCE

See "Cutting, Copying, and Pasting to the Clipboard" in Chapter 5.

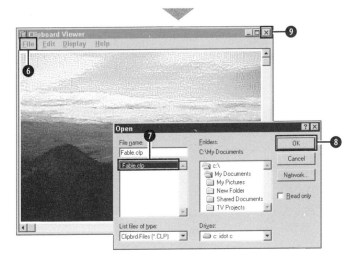

UNDERSTANDING CONTENT FORMAT

The Windows Me Clipboard stores any type of object that you cut or copy to it. Many Clipboard objects can exist in several different formats. These different formats are what make the Clipboard so useful. You might, for example, copy an image to the Clipboard from one program, and then paste the image into another program even though the two programs cannot share the image by opening the other's file type. In a certain sense, the Clipboard acts as a universal translator. When you paste an object into a document, the Clipboard automatically uses the most data-rich format available that is usable by the target program.

SHARING CLIPBOARD CONTENTS

If you need to share data with someone who does not have the same application program that you are using, one way to do so is to copy the data to your Clipboard, open Clipboard Viewer, save the Clipboard contents, and then send the CLP file to the other person. They can open your file in the Clipboard Viewer and then paste the contents into their document. Be sure you tell the other person that they will need to use the Clipboard Viewer to open the file.

⑤ *Copy some other data to the Clipboard and then click the Clipboard Viewer window.*

⑥ *Select File ⇨ Open to reopen the Clipboard contents you saved earlier.*

⑦ *Select the file to open.*

⑧ *Click OK to open the file.*

⑨ *Click the Close button to complete the task.*

FIND IT ONLINE

See **http://www.microsoft.com/com/resources/ netclip.asp** to learn about NetClip, a remote Clipboard Viewer.

Using Notepad

A number of types of files on your computer must always be plain text files. These include setup files that use the INF extension, log files that use the LOG extension, and MS-DOS batch files that use the BAT extension. These files cannot contain anything except plain text — otherwise they will be unusable. Notepad is the perfect editor for these types of files because it does not attempt to alter their format and always saves new files as plain text files. If you were to attempt to create one of these files in a word processor program such as WordPad or Microsoft Word, you would have to remember to specifically save the file as a plain text file.

You may discover that documents can be hard to read in Notepad because the lines are too wide for the Notepad window and you must scroll side to side to see everything. You can use the Edit ⇨ Word Wrap option to make the lines fit the width of the Notepad window. The paragraphs reform themselves as you change the size of the window. When Word Wrap is on, the horizontal scroll bar goes away and you can see text that would normally extend past the right side of the Notepad window. If you use word wrap to view a file that must remain as plain text and also must preserve the existing line layout, don't save the document while word wrap is selected.

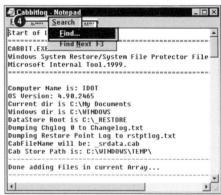

❶ Click the Start button and select Programs ⇨ Accessories ⇨ Notepad.

❷ Type your text in the document window.

❸ Select Edit ⇨ Word Wrap to wrap lines to the width of the Notepad window.

❹ To locate specific text, choose Search ⇨ Find.

CROSS-REFERENCE

See "Creating Documents in WordPad" later in this chapter.

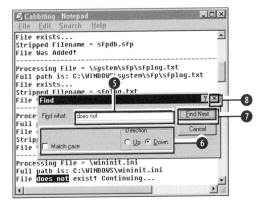

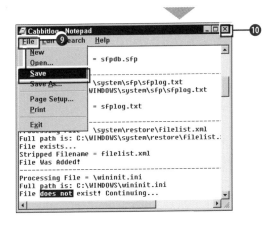

CHOOSING A FONT

The Notepad menu has a command that may confuse you. If you choose the Edit ➪ Set Font command to select a font and attributes to your Notepad document, those attributes only apply to the document while it is open in the current session. Font attributes are not saved with plain text documents. Also, the same formatting is applied to your entire document — you cannot make just one part of the document bold, for example. You can safely apply a font format change to any Notepad document, because Notepad will save the document as a plain text document without formatting.

PRINTING NOTEPAD DOCUMENTS

When you try to print text files in Notepad you may discover that short and long lines of text alternate in the printout. This problem is usually caused by the default margin settings Notepad uses. Often, text documents have too many characters per line to fit within the default margins, and this accounts for the odd appearance of the printouts. You can select File ➪ Page Setup to adjust the margins to enable the printed text to better fit the page. When you're changing margins, consider the capabilities of your printer. Many printers cannot print closer than 0.25 inches from the edge of the paper.

⑤ *Type the search phrase.*

⑥ *Select any appropriate search options.*

⑦ *Click Find Next.*

⑧ *Click the Close button to close the Find dialog box.*

⑨ *Select File ➪ Save to save your work.*

⑩ *Click the Close button to complete the task.*

Creating Documents in WordPad

Windows Me also includes an editor that is considerably more powerful than Notepad. WordPad is really just a simplified version of Microsoft Word that comes as one of the Windows Me accessories. WordPad will read, edit, and write WordPad documents in Word format as well as several other common document formats. WordPad also enables you to do many things you can't do in Notepad, such as apply text formatting as needed.

WordPad works much like any other word processor. As you type, you can tell your current position on the page using the ruler as a guideline. You can easily apply formatting using the toolbar buttons, and, unlike Notepad documents, you can format individual sections of the document as necessary. You can also use the View ⇨ Options command to select such options as the default measurement unit, the parts of WordPad that appear on your screen, word wrap settings, and the way WordPad selects a block of text when you manipulate it with your mouse.

WordPad doesn't save many of the document options, such as fonts and styles, that you may wish to use as the defaults for new documents. To make it easier to format new documents according to your preferences, you may want to set those options yourself when you begin a new document. If you press Ctrl+A to select the entire document, any changes you make will then apply to the entire document. You can later apply specific formatting changes to individual portions of your document as necessary.

Continued

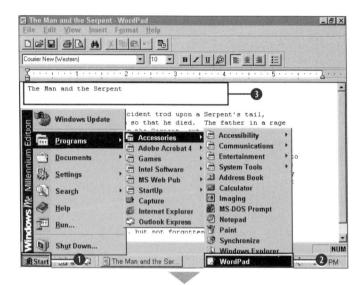

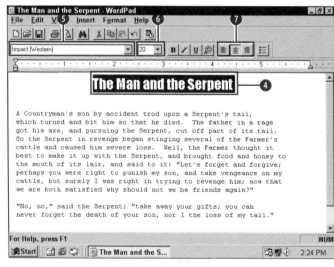

❶ Click the Start button.

❷ Select Programs ⇨ Accessories ⇨ WordPad.

❸ Type your text in the document window.

❹ To format the title, select the title line.

❺ Choose a font from this list box.

❻ Choose a font size.

❼ Select the appropriate alignment.

CROSS-REFERENCE

See Chapter 5 for information about printing documents.

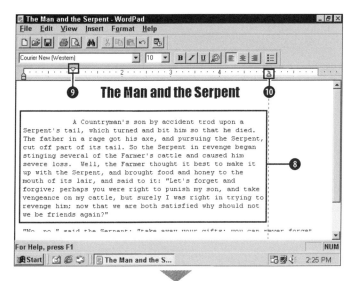

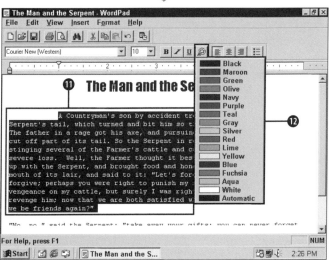

PROTECT YOURSELF FROM VIRUSES

Macro viruses have become a serious problem for anyone who shares Microsoft Word document files. One way to protect yourself from these problems is to use WordPad to open suspect documents. You can safely open any Word document in WordPad. Because WordPad does not execute macros, any macro viruses contained in the document will not be able to run when the document is open in WordPad. To be completely safe, you can copy the text from WordPad to the Clipboard, start a new WordPad document, and paste the text into the new document. When you save your new document, it will be completely virus free and safe to open in Word. Not only that, but also any formatting that was in the original document will be preserved.

OPENING WORD DOCUMENTS

Even if you use another more powerful word processor than WordPad, you may find that WordPad is a good option on occasion. For example, if you normally use a different word processor such as Word Pro or WordPerfect, WordPad may do a better job of correctly showing the formatting contained in a Word document. Different brands of word processing programs often have some difficulty maintaining document fidelity when opening a foreign document format.

⑧ *To change margin settings, click in the section you wish to change.*

⑨ *Move this marker to select a first line indent.*

⑩ *Move this marker to select a right margin.*

⑪ *To apply a formatting change such as text color, select the text you wish to change.*

⑫ *Click the color button and choose a text color.*

FIND IT ONLINE

Learn about UltraEdit-32, a more powerful editor, at http://www.ultraedit.com/.

Creating Documents in WordPad

Continued

Although no one would argue that WordPad has all the features of a full-blown word processor such as Microsoft Word, WordPad has many more capabilities than a simple text editor such as Notepad. In a WordPad document, you can use different fonts, font sizes, font styles, and even colors for the text. You can also embed objects such as bitmap images to enhance your WordPad document.

You can save WordPad documents in several different formats. By default, WordPad documents are saved in Word 6 format, but you can also select Rich Text Format (RTF), which preserves the text formatting you've applied. WordPad also offers several plain text formats that differ in the specific character sets used in the document. Unless you use accented characters such as those you might find in many European languages, any of the text formats work well.

You can insert objects into your WordPad documents. When you insert an object into a WordPad document, the appearance of WordPad may change while you're working with the object. To return WordPad to the normal appearance, click outside the object. If you choose to insert an object into a document, remember that many objects lose their effectiveness when the document is printed rather than being viewed on a computer screen. You can't, for example, effectively use an embedded sound file on a printed page!

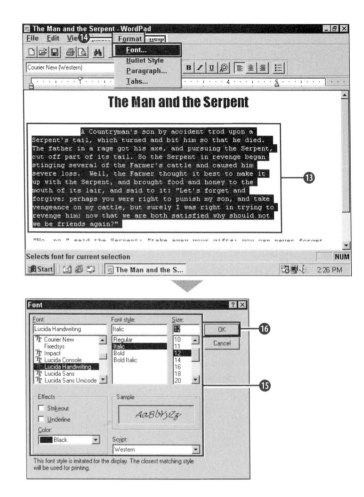

⑬ To format a block of text, select the block.

⑭ Select Format ⇨ Font to select the font formatting options.

⑮ Choose your format options.

⑯ Click OK to continue.

CROSS-REFERENCE

See Chapter 5 for more information about working with documents.

370

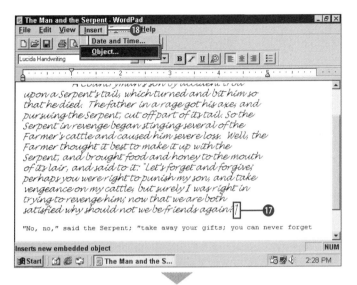

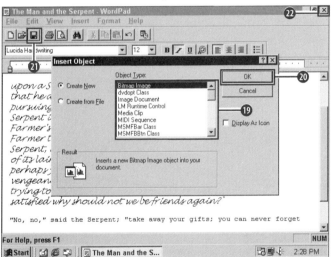

⑰ To insert an object into your document, click where you wish to place the object.

⑱ Select Insert ➪ Object.

⑲ Select the object.

⑳ Click OK to continue and follow the prompts to insert the type of object you selected.

㉑ Click Save to save your document.

㉒ Click the Close button to complete the task.

FIND IT ONLINE

For something a bit more powerful than WordPad, see
http://www.microsoft.com/works/.

Using Imaging for Windows

Imaging for Windows is a program that you can use to scan documents, view faxes, and even add your own comments to scanned documents or faxes. You'll find this accessory to be a useful addition to your Windows Me toolbox.

One problem you may encounter with the typical faxing software that comes with many scanners is that it can be difficult to assemble a multiple-page, scanned document into a fax. Sure, sending a single page is easy enough, but trying to add additional pages is often difficult or even impossible. You can find yourself sending a fax one page at a time, with each page requiring a separate phone call. Imaging enables you to add as many pages as you like before you send the fax, so you can easily send a multiple-page fax in one call.

When you send or receive faxes, you may want to add a response to something in the text. You can use the annotation tools to add lines, text, highlighting, or even a yellow sticky note to the image. The annotation toolbar has a number of interesting tools you can use to add your notes to an image. If you're not certain about the function of one of the buttons, move your mouse over the button. You'll see a description of the button in the status line. If you apply an annotation but don't like the results, you can remove the annotation. Imaging also enables you to use the Undo button to reverse the last thing you did, and the Redo button to redo the last thing that was undone. The Cut, Copy, and Paste buttons also work in the usual way when you have selected an annotation.

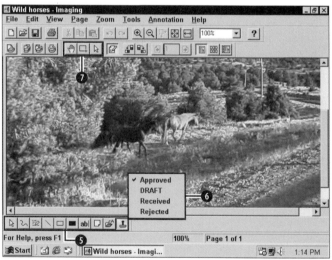

❶ Click the Start button and select Programs ➪ Accessories ➪ Imaging.

❷ Use these tools to scan an image.

❸ Use these tools to control the zoom.

❹ Use these tools to rotate the image.

❺ To add an annotation, select a tool.

❻ To use the rubber stamp annotation, select the type of stamp after you click the button.

❼ To select a part of the image, use these tools.

CROSS-REFERENCE

See "Using Paint" later in this chapter for more information about creating and modifying image files.

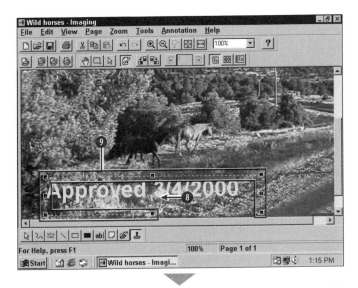

To scan an image directly into the Imaging application, you need to use a TWAIN image source. Usually this means using a scanner, but Imaging will use any available TWAIN image source. In addition to scanners, certain digital cameras and USB video cameras also function as TWAIN image sources. Select File ➪ Select Device to see which TWAIN image sources are installed on your system.

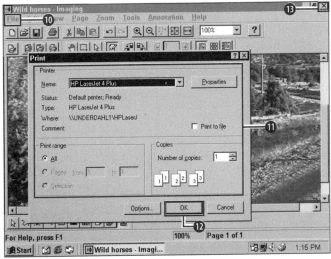

8 *Drag an annotation to place it where you want it.*

9 *Use the annotation's handles to resize the annotation.*

10 *To print or fax the image, select File ➪ Print.*

11 *Choose the destination and options.*

12 *Click OK.*

13 *After you save the image, click the Close button to complete the task.*

TAKE NOTE

▶ SENDING A FAX

Once you've scanned and annotated the images you want to send as a fax, you can use the File ➪ Print command to send a fax. Select FAX as your printer before you click the OK button in the Print dialog box. Remember to set the printer selection back to your normal system printer when you're finished sending the fax. You aren't limited to faxing from Imaging — you can print images on your normal printer, too.

▶ DATE STAMPING

Imaging makes it easy to add a date stamp to your annotations. Click the Rubber Stamp button and choose one of the rubber stamps. When you apply the rubber stamp to the image, the stamped message will include the current date.

FIND IT ONLINE

Download your trial of Imaging for Windows Professional Edition at **http://www.eastman software.com/products/wmx/pro/protrial.htm**.

Using Paint

The most common type of image you see on your computer screen is a *bitmap image*. These are the types of files that are created by scanners or digital cameras. Paint is a Windows Me accessory that you can use to create or modify these types of images. Although both Imaging and Paint work with these types of images, Paint enables you to create an image completely from scratch and to make changes that simply aren't possible in Imaging — such as spray painting over an area in an image.

To use the drawing tools, select the tool from the toolbox. The tools in the top row enable you to select a region on the screen. The eraser tool erases parts of the picture with the background color. You erase by dragging the mouse cursor across the picture. The Fill tool fills the portion of the picture that you point to with color. The Pick Color tool sets the foreground and background colors to the color in the picture that you click. The Magnifier tool zooms in on the picture to enable you to work with smaller details. The Pencil tool and the Brush tool draw as you drag the cursor around the screen. The Airbrush tool sprays a pattern as you drag the tool around the picture. The Text tool enables you to type text. The Line tool draws straight lines. The remaining Paint tools draw curves, rectangles, many-sided shapes, ellipses, and rounded rectangles.

If you begin modifying an image and then discover that you have made a major mistake, you can use the Edit ⇨ Undo command to undo the last drawing action

1 Click the Start button and select Programs ⇨ Accessories ⇨ Paint.

2 Use these tools to draw.

3 Select tool options that appear in this area as appropriate.

4 Use this box to select colors.

5 To change the zoom level, select View ⇨ Zoom and choose the level.

6 If you want to use custom colors, select Colors ⇨ Edit Colors.

CROSS-REFERENCE

See "Using Imaging for Windows" earlier in this chapter.

you performed. If you select the same command again, Paint will undo the previous action. You can continue selecting this command to undo several different actions, but remember that undo is sequential. You cannot keep your latest action while undoing the previous one.

If you want to match a color exactly, select the Pick Color tool and then click the right or left mouse button on a patch of the desired color. The Paint drawing tools will use the selected color as their right- or left-click color, respectively.

TAKE NOTE

SELECTING TOOL OPTIONS

Many of the tools have optional size or shape settings that you select in the area below the toolbox. As you select different tools, the options that are available for the selected tool appear in the box. Click the option you wish to use.

ALTERNATING COLORS

The colors that are used in your painting alternate between the foreground and background color as you switch between the right and left mouse buttons. This enables you to draw with either the foreground or background color simply by holding down the left or right mouse button as you draw.

7 Click Image to view the Image menu.

8 Use these options to apply special effects to the image.

9 Use this option to resize the image.

10 Click File to open the File menu.

11 Click Save to save the image.

12 Select one of these options if you want to use the image as your desktop wallpaper.

13 Click the Close button to complete the task.

FIND IT ONLINE

To view image files that Paint cannot open, download LView Pro 2.8 at **http://www.lview.com/**.

Playing Some Games

Windows Me includes a number of games that are intended to give you a little break from working with your PC. In this section we have a brief look at a few of the games that you can play against your computer. In the next section you learn about some games that you play against opponents over the Internet.

The figures show four of the games that are included with Windows Me. The games you can play against your computer include Classic Hearts, Classic Solitaire, FreeCell, Minesweeper, Pinball, and Spider Solitaire. To make certain I don't spoil your fun I'm not going to tell you too much about them, but just provide a brief description of each game.

Classic Hearts is a card game in which you attempt to make your opponents end up with higher point totals than you have. This is a game you can play against computer-generated opponents or against other computer users on your network.

Classic Solitaire is the standard solitaire card game. You can choose from several optional games to keep things interesting.

FreeCell is a solitaire card game that starts with eight piles of cards across the screen. Like any other solitaire game, the objective is to build complete same-suit stacks of cards.

Minesweeper is a game that has a number of mines hidden under the blocks that you click. When you reveal a safe spot, the numbers tell you how many mines are in adjacent blocks. Your goal is to reveal all the safe blocks without hitting a mine.

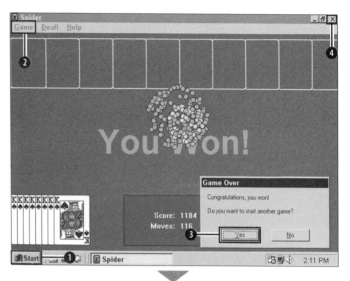

❶ Click the Start button and select Programs ➪ Games and choose your favorite.

❷ To play Spider Solitaire, select Game ➪ New Game to begin.

❸ Click Yes to begin a new game after you win.

❹ Click Close.

❺ To play 3D Pinball, press the Spacebar to launch the ball.

❻ Press Z to move the left flipper.

❼ Press / to move the right flipper.

CROSS-REFERENCE

See "Configuring Multimedia" in Chapter 16.

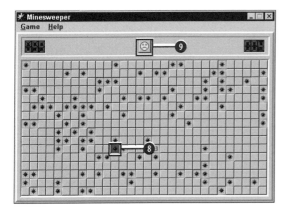

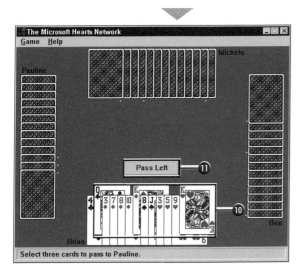

Pinball is an electronic version of the old arcade favorite pinball machines. When you fire your ball into play, your goal is to keep it in play and rack up points. You use the flippers to throw the ball back into the bumpers.

Spider Solitaire is yet another variation on the solitaire card game. This version may take some time to master, so you will probably want to start with the easier levels of play.

TAKE NOTE

LEARNING THE GAMES

One advantage to playing games on your PC is that the rules of the game are easy to find. Each of these games has a Help menu that can be an aid in learning how to play the game. Many of the games also include some assistance to help you "cheat" as you are learning how to play the games.

GAMES CAN BE NOISY

One of the problems with most of the Windows Me games is that they tend to have a lot of sound effects that can make it obvious to anyone within hearing distance that you are playing a game. If you want to play some games without attracting attention, you can silence your computer by clicking the Mute box on the volume control.

⑧ *To play Minesweeper, click blocks to expose their contents.*

▶ *Right-click blocks to mark mines. Right-click twice to place a question mark on a block.*

⑨ *Click here to begin a new game.*

⑩ *To play Hearts, select cards to pass.*

⑪ *Click Pass Left to send them to your opponent.*

▶ *You may want to limit yourself to a specified amount of play time!*

FIND IT ONLINE

See **http://www.thehellhole.com/downloads-/download.htm** for demo and shareware games.

Playing Internet Games

Playing games against your computer may be fun, but Windows Me offers another game-playing option you may enjoy even more. Windows Me includes five different games that you can play against live opponents over the Internet. These games use the MSN Gaming Zone server where people from all around the world can get together for a bit of online fun. You could end up playing checkers with someone from halfway around the world.

The Windows Me Internet games are generally fairly simple games, so almost any Internet connection should be fast enough. None of these games is the type of action game that requires fast response, so even a regular dial-up connection is adequate.

You probably want to set your screen resolution to at least 800 × 600 before you attempt to use the Internet games. Many of the games will not fit completely on your screen if your resolution is set to a lower setting, and the games lack the scroll bars that would enable you to see parts of the game that are off the screen.

If you need some extra help getting started using the Internet games, you may want to visit the DirectPlay Game Rooms Getting Started Web page at `http://zone.msn.com/directplay/start.asp`. Here you will find information on how the games work, how to configure your system for the best game play, and a number of other important details that can make your online gaming a whole lot more fun. You will also find out how you can participate in many more online games in addition to those included with Windows Me.

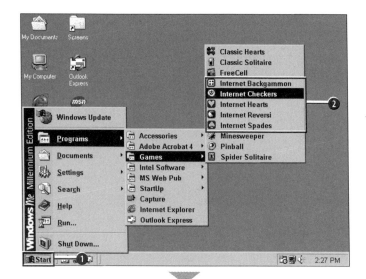

❶ Click the Start button.

❷ Select Programs ⇨ Games and choose your favorite Internet game.

❸ Click Play to begin a new game.

▶ If you are not already connected to the Internet, you may be prompted to connect.

CROSS-REFERENCE

See "Playing Some Games" earlier in this chapter.

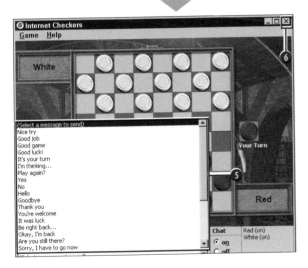

FINDING OPPONENTS

The MSN Gaming zone attempts to pair you with another opponent who plays at a comparable level with you. When you first log on to one of the Internet games, you will be considered a beginning player, so the MSN Gaming Zone will try to find another beginning-level player to be your opponent. As you continue to play the online games your player level will increase, and you will be matched against other more experienced players.

USING CHAT

Each of the Internet games has a *chat* feature so that the players can send each other comments during the game. If you have set up the voice capture and playback options using the Voice tab of the Sounds and Multimedia Properties dialog box, you may also be able to use the voice chat features. This will enable you to speak to your opponent rather than simply sending canned phrases from the text chat message list. If you use this feature, remember that it can be difficult to understand speech that is transmitted over your Internet connection. Try to speak clearly and keep your sense of humor — remember it's only a game!

④ *Click the game board to make your moves.*

⑤ *To send a message to your opponent, select it from the list.*

⑥ *Click Close to close the game.*

▶ *You may need to close your Internet connection when you finish.*

Opening and Closing the MS-DOS Prompt Window

If you are new to computers or have only used computers that don't enable the user to issue commands directly, you may not realize the power of the MS-DOS prompt. It's true that the Windows Me *graphical user interface* (GUI) will handle the computing needs of most users, but it's not possible to do everything by clicking a mouse. Accomplishing some tasks is too difficult or even impossible without access to the *command line,* the old standby from the earliest days of personal computing.

Almost anything that was possible to do from the command prompt on DOS-based PCs is still possible on a Windows Me PC. When you open the *MS-DOS Prompt window,* you can enter DOS commands.

The MS-DOS Prompt window can appear as an actual window, or it can be expanded to full-screen view. You can shrink the window down so much that it is virtually impossible to read any of the text in the window, or you can expand it to cover the entire screen. You can control the number of lines displayed in the window. You can also control the colors that are displayed in the window.

If you choose to run a DOS program, you must use a little bit of caution. To avoid losing data, you must shut down DOS programs properly. If the MS-DOS Prompt window shows the program name but does not show the "finished" message, choose the proper command from the program's menus to exit the program before you attempt to close the MS-DOS Prompt window. Otherwise, any files the program had open may be corrupted and you might lose data.

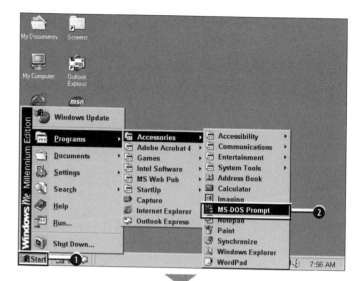

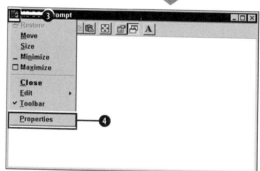

❶ Click the Start button.

❷ Select Programs ⇨ Accessories ⇨ MS-DOS Prompt.

❸ To adjust the window setting, click here to display the menu.

❹ Select Properties.

CROSS-REFERENCE

See "Using the MS-DOS Prompt window" next in this chapter.

Using the Accessory Applications

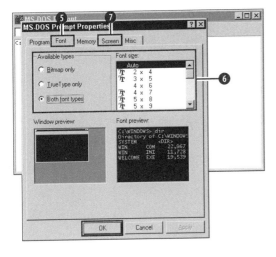

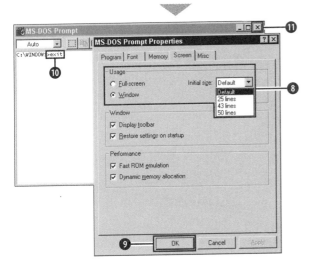

Also, be aware that some older DOS programs really weren't designed to run properly under Windows Me. In most cases this simply means that the program won't run or that it will have trouble identifying files due to long file names. You should not, however, attempt to run old utility programs that access your files or disks directly. In some cases these types of programs have the potential to damage your files.

TAKE NOTE

UNDERSTANDING THE MS-DOS PROMPT

To Windows Me, the MS-DOS Prompt window is simply another program that you can run on your PC. When you select Programs ➪ Accessories ➪ MS-DOS Prompt from the Start menu, you're actually running a program named Command.exe that is normally found in the C:\Windows folder. Command.exe is a special type of program, called a *command processor*, that executes the commands you enter at the command prompt.

CLOSING THE MS-DOS PROMPT WINDOW

When you're finished working in the MS-DOS Prompt window, close the window by typing **EXIT** and pressing Enter or by clicking the Close button in the upper right corner of the window. Be sure that any programs you are running are finished before you close the MS-DOS Prompt window.

⑤ Click the Font tab.

⑥ Select the font to use in the window.

⑦ Click the Screen tab.

⑧ Choose the window size settings.

⑨ Click OK and confirm how to apply your changes.

⑩ Type **exit** and press Enter to close the window.

⑪ Alternatively, click the Close button.

FIND IT ONLINE

For a more powerful command line, see
http://www.jpsoft.com/.

Using the MS-DOS Prompt Window

O nce you have opened the MS-DOS Prompt window, you have access to the *command line* — a place where you can type DOS commands. In the earlier example, you typed the EXIT command to close the command processor and the MS-DOS Prompt window. In this section you'll learn how to use other, more useful DOS commands.

If you've only used a GUI in the past, you may find that using DOS commands can be a little confusing. You may enter a command that you're certain is correct only to be greeted with the message "bad command or file name." This message is simply telling you that the command processor cannot find an internal command or a program that matches what you typed on the command line. This doesn't necessarily mean that what you typed was incorrect — only that the command processor cannot find something that matches it. You may need to give MS-DOS a little extra help as explained in the Take Note section.

Although the default size for the MS-DOS Prompt window — 25 rows high by 80 columns wide — is based on the traditional size of PC screens before GUIs became popular, there's no reason you cannot choose a size that better suits your needs. Increasing the size of the window may make it easier to use certain commands by reducing the amount of scrolling that is required.

One very handy trick to remember is that the MS-DOS Prompt window maintains a history of the commands that you have entered in the window. To recall the same

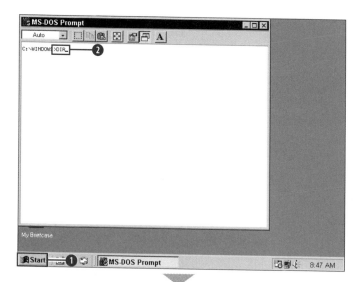

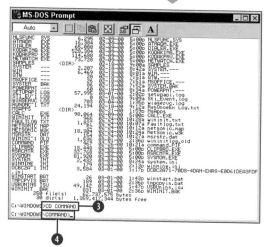

① If necessary, click the Start button and select Programs ⇨ Accessories ⇨ MS-DOS Prompt.

② Type your command on the command line and press Enter.

③ Enter a different command — such as this one to change directories.

④ View the outcome of the command — such as making a new directory the current directory.

CROSS-REFERENCE

See "Getting Command Help" later in this chapter.

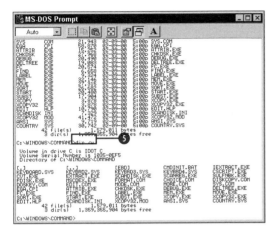

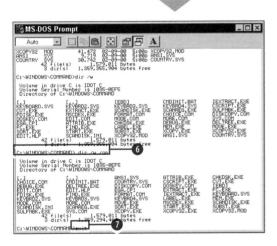

command you just used—perhaps to modify it and try again—press F3. You can also scroll back through the command buffer using the up and down arrow keys.

TAKE NOTE

SETTING THE PATH

One way to give the command processor the help it needs to find a program is to include the complete *path* to the program. For example, if Myprog.exe is in the C:\Allmine folder, you could enter the command as **C:\allmine\myprog** and press Enter. Sometimes this may not work because the program you want to run may not be able to find all its data files. In that case you'll need to use the CD—Change Directory—command to change to the program's folder before you execute the program. In this example you would first type **CD\allmine** and press Enter, and then type **myprog** and press Enter.

USING COMMANDS WITH SPACES

In Windows Me it is perfectly acceptable to include spaces in folder names, but this can cause problems at the command line because spaces are used to separate command line parameters. To enter a name that includes spaces, simply enclose the name in quotes, and MS-DOS will understand that the entire quoted string is a single name.

⑤ *Enter a new command followed by additional parameters and press Enter.*

▶ *Notice that you can type commands in upper- or lowercase.*

⑥ *You can use more than one parameter to further modify the command.*

▶ *In this case the second directory listing was sorted by name to make finding files easier.*

⑦ *Type **exit** and press Enter to close the window.*

FIND IT ONLINE

To learn how to start a program from the command prompt, see **http://support.microsoft.com/support/kb/articles/q126/4/10.asp**.

Getting Command Help

The biggest problem with using MS-DOS commands is that Windows Me does not include a comprehensive guide to those commands. As a result, if you aren't a DOS command expert it can be difficult and confusing to enter commands in the MS-DOS Prompt window. Using DOS commands is quite different from doing things using your mouse in the Windows Me GUI. Not only do you need to type the correct command, but also you may need to include a bunch of esoteric parameters to make the command function as you expect it to.

Windows Me does include help information for individual DOS commands. To access the help screens for a command you type the command name followed by **/?** on the command line and press Enter.

DOS commands must be typed correctly without any errors. It can be difficult to remember the exact syntax of DOS commands — especially commands that have a large set of possible parameters you can use. One way to make certain that you enter commands correctly is to make a printed copy of the command's help screens. As the figures show, you can redirect the output of DOS commands to your printer by adding > **PRN** to the end of the command line. When you press Enter this will cause the output that normally appears on the screen to be sent to your printer. You may need to manually select your printer's form feed after using this option — especially if you have a laser printer. You may also need to press Enter a time or two if the command prompt does not reappear immediately.

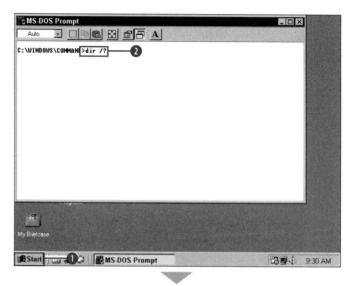

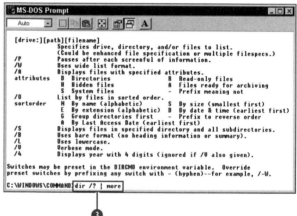

① If necessary, click the Start button and select Programs ⇨ Accessories ⇨ MS-DOS Prompt.

② Type **dir /?** on the command line and press Enter to display a list of DIR command options.

③ Add | **MORE** to the end of the command line to make the output display one page at a time.

▶ Help screens often include more information than you can see on one page.

CROSS-REFERENCE

See "Using the MS-DOS Prompt window" earlier in this chapter.

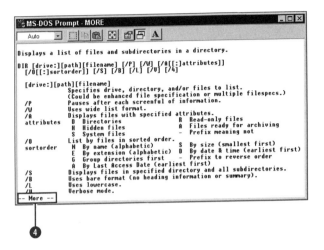

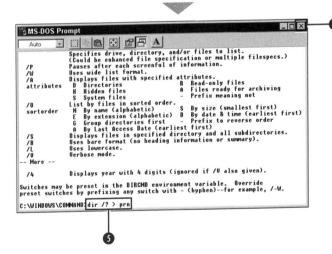

FINDING THE COMMANDS

In some ways defining the set of commands that make up MS-DOS is rather difficult. Windows Me no longer includes the HELP command that enabled you to see a list of the MS-DOS commands along with a brief description of each command. Sure, you can look for files with an EXE or COM extension in the C:\Windows and C:\Windows\Command directories, but this won't provide you with a listing of the *internal* commands that are included inside Command.com. If you are truly interested in knowing all of the commands that make up MS-DOS, you may want to consider buying a book such as *DOS For Dummies* from IDG Books Worldwide, Inc.

PAGING COMMAND OUTPUT

If you would rather view command help onscreen but find that the help screens scroll off the top of the MS-DOS Prompt window before you can read the entire text, you may want to view the text one page at a time. To do so you can *pipe* the output to the MORE command. You can do this by adding **| MORE** at the end of the command line. You may want to examine the MORE command help screens for more information on using this command.

④ Press Enter each time the MORE prompt appears to continue.

⑤ Add > **PRN** to the end of the command line to make a printed copy of the output.

⑥ Click the Close button to complete the task.

FIND IT ONLINE

For information about the DOS commands, see
http://www.computerhope.com/msdos.htm.

Personal Workbook

Q&A

1 What should you do if the MS-DOS Prompt window says "finished" in the title bar?

_____

_____

_____

2 What do you type to close the MS-DOS Prompt window?

_____

_____

_____

3 How can you transfer data between the calculator and other applications?

_____

_____

_____

4 What can you do if the lines of text in a Notepad document extend past the right edge of the window?

_____

_____

_____

5 How can you add a picture to a WordPad document?

_____

_____

_____

_____

6 How can you match a color exactly in Paint?

_____

_____

_____

7 What tool can you use to easily enter foreign characters into a document?

_____

_____

_____

8 Which tool can you use to assemble multiple scanned pages for a fax?

_____

_____

_____

ANSWERS: PAGE 401

EXTRA PRACTICE

1 Use the calculator to convert your age into a binary number.

2 Create a text file in Notepad.

3 Create a new Word format document in WordPad.

4 Add several different character formats to your document.

5 Open an image file in Imaging and add a date stamp.

6 Adjust the MS-DOS Prompt window to display 43 lines.

REAL-WORLD APPLICATIONS

✔ You receive a Word document that you suspect may be infected with a macro virus. You use WordPad to open the document and copy the text to a new document so that the virus won't infect your system.

✔ You need to send a multiple-page fax to someone overseas. You use Imaging to scan and assemble the pages so that you can transmit the entire fax in one piece to save on long-distance charges.

✔ You are writing a letter to an important potential client in a foreign country. You use Character Map to insert the correct characters into your document so that you can spell the client's name properly and show that you respect his or her customs and language.

Visual Quiz

How can you display this application? How can you tell the current zoom level? What button would you click to rotate the image 90 degrees clockwise?

_____

_____

_____

_____

_____

Personal Workbook
Answers

Chapter 1

See page 24

① **What are the three types of items that you will find on the Start menu?**

A: The Start menu includes three different kinds of items — commands, cascading menus, and items that display dialog boxes.

② **What do three periods following a menu item mean?**

A: Three dots (…) next to the label indicate menu selections that open dialog boxes.

③ **What happens when you click an item on the Start menu that has a small arrow next to the item?**

A: A small arrow next to the label indicates a cascading menu. These items display additional menus when you select them.

④ **What does a small arrow in the lower left corner of a desktop icon mean?**

A: A small arrow at the lower left corner of the icon indicates that the icon is a *shortcut* to the application or document.

⑤ **How can you make the icons on your desktop align automatically?**

A: If you right-click a blank spot on the desktop and select Arrange Icons ➪ Auto Arrange, the icons will snap into orderly rows and columns. Any new icons that are added to your desktop will also move into place automatically.

⑥ **What is the purpose of the My Network Places icon?**

A: The My Network Places icon provides quick access to the computers and printers that are available on your network.

⑦ **How can you quickly minimize all open windows to view your desktop?**

A: The Show Desktop tool button on the Quick Launch toolbar minimizes all open windows to buttons on the taskbar so that you can view the desktop.

⑧ **How can you quickly switch between two programs using your keyboard?**

A: You can quickly switch between two programs by pressing Alt+Tab.

Visual Quiz

Q: **How can you display this folder? What must you do to make the folder display the message shown here?**

A: Double-click the My computer icon to display the My Computer folder. Select the C drive to display the message.

Personal Workbook Answers

Chapter 2

See page 50

1 **How can you display your Start menu items when you open Windows Explorer?**

A: To display your Start menu, right-click the Start button and choose Explore.

2 **How can you run a program that doesn't appear on your Start menu?**

A: You can run programs by double-clicking their icon in Windows Explorer.

3 **What will happen if you click the History button?**

A: If you click the History button, the Folders Explorer Bar will be replaced by the History Explorer Bar.

4 **How can you preview the contents of graphics files without opening them?**

A: You can preview the contents of graphics files by selecting them in Windows Explorer.

5 **How can you make Windows Explorer display file previews in place of file type icons?**

A: To display previews of the file contents rather than file type icons, choose thumbnail view.

6 **How can you locate all of the Web pages you visited last week?**

A: To locate the Web pages you visited last week, click the Last Week folder in the history list.

7 **Which Windows Explorer toolbar can you use to listen to music over the Internet?**

A: You can use the Radio toolbar to listen to radio stations on the Internet.

8 **Which Windows Explorer toolbar can you use to visit the "Best of the Internet" Web site?**

A: You can use the Links toolbar to visit the "Best of the Internet" Web site.

Visual Quiz

Q: **How does this view differ from the standard Windows Explorer view, and how can you make Windows Explorer display image previews like this?**

A: This Windows Explorer view is different because thumbnail view was selected and the Explorer bars were closed to provide maximum room for the previews. You can choose Thumbnail from the drop-down View list and click the Explorer Bar Close button to make Windows Explorer look like this.

Chapter 3

See page 64

1 **How can you print a help topic?**

A: To print a help topic, first select the topic and then click the Print button.

2 **How can you copy a help topic?**

A: You can copy a help topic by selecting the topic text, right-clicking the selected text, and choosing Copy. You can then paste the text as needed.

3 **What is the Back button used for?**

A: The Back button enables you to return to the previous help topic easily.

4 **How can you find a topic the quickest way when you know the correct keyword?**

A: You can find topics quickly by typing the correct keyword in the index keyword box.

Personal Workbook Answers

5 How can you find a topic if your keyword is not indexed?

A: If your keyword does not appear in the index, type the keyword in the search box.

6 How can you toggle the display of the left side of the help window?

A: You can toggle the display of the left side by clicking the button just above the content area.

7 Which help system component is intended to step you through solutions to problems?

A: The troubleshooters step you through problem solutions.

8 How can you get more help if you can't find the answer in the Windows Me Help system?

A: You can get more help if you can't find the answer in the Windows Me Help system by using the resources on the Microsoft Support Web site.

Visual Quiz

Q: How would you display the topic shown in the figure? How would you print the topic?

A: To display this topic, open the help system index and scroll down. To print the topic, make certain the topic is displayed in the contents area and click Print.

Chapter 4

See page 92

1 If you have items you want to run automatically whenever you start Windows Me, where should you place them?

A: Place items in the Startup folder to make them run when you start Windows Me.

2 How many options can you select at the same time from a group of radio buttons?

A: You can select one option at a time from a group of radio buttons.

3 Which Control Panel icon do you use when you want to install a new program?

A: You use the Add/Remove Programs icon in Control Panel when you want to install a new program.

4 What does the size of the scroll box often indicate?

A: The size of the scroll box generally indicates the percentage of the document that is visible onscreen.

5 What dialog box can you use to shut down a program that has quit responding?

A: To shut down a program that has quit responding, press Ctrl+Alt+Del to display the Close Program dialog box.

6 What are desktop shortcuts?

A: Desktop shortcuts are icons on your desktop that open documents, Web sites, or programs.

7 What dialog box would you use to add Web TV for Windows to your PC?

A: To add Web TV for Windows, you would open the Add/Remove Programs dialog box, choose the Windows Setup tab, and select Web TV for Windows.

8 What will happen if you select No when Windows Me tells you that you are closing an application and haven't saved your work?

A: If you close a program without saving your work you will lose any unsaved changes.

391

Personal Workbook Answers

See page 120

See page 146

Visual Quiz

Q: How can you display this window? What can you tell about the installed status of the Accessories category?

A: Click the Start button, select Settings ⇨ Control Panel, and double-click the Add/Remove Programs icon. Click the Windows Setup tab. The Description box shows that 3 of the 7 Accessories are installed.

Chapter 5

1 What happens when you drag and drop data between two different documents without holding down any keys?

A: If you drag and drop data between two different documents, you will copy the data unless you hold down the Alt key to move the data.

2 What is likely to happen if you specify 0 margins for a document?

A: If you specify margins that are too small, some of your text will likely fall outside the printable area for your printer and will be cut off.

3 How can you control the format of data you paste from the Clipboard?

A: You can control the format of data you paste from the Clipboard by using the Edit ⇨ Paste Special command.

4 What command can you use to copy selected text to the Clipboard?

A: You can use Edit ⇨ Copy to copy selected text to the Clipboard.

5 What happens to data that you've copied to the Clipboard when you copy additional data to the Clipboard?

A: When you copy additional data to the Clipboard, the new data replaces existing data that you've copied to the Clipboard.

6 What is the best way to print multiple copies of the same document?

A: The best way to print multiple copies of the same document is to use the Number of copies spin control in the Print dialog box.

7 How can you temporarily pause printing?

A: To temporarily pause printing, double-click the printer in the Printers folder and choose Printer ⇨ Pause Printing.

8 If you are unable to open a document that appears on the Documents list, what might be the cause?

A: If you are unable to open a document that appears on the Documents list, the cause might be that the file has been deleted or moved.

Visual Quiz

Q: How can you display this dialog box? How can you change the number of copies to be printed?

A: Select File ⇨ Print to display the Print dialog box. Use the Number of copies spin box to set the number of copies to be printed.

Chapter 6

1 What will happen if you don't click the New button between searches?

A: If you don't click the New button between searches you will add new conditions to your previous search rather than create a totally new search.

Personal Workbook Answers

2 How can you specify that you want to limit your search to files larger than a certain size?

A: To specify that you want to limit your search to files larger than a certain size, click the Size check box and choose the size option that suits your needs.

3 How can you temporarily bypass the Recycle Bin and delete a file permanently?

A: You can temporarily bypass the Recycle Bin and delete a file permanently by holding down Shift as you delete a file.

4 Why is it more dangerous to delete files from diskettes than from hard disks?

A: It is more dangerous to delete files from diskettes than from hard disks because Windows Me does not provide a Recycle Bin for diskettes.

5 How can you change the Recycle Bin sort order?

A: You can change the Recycle Bin sort order by clicking one of the column headings to sort according to the values in that column.

6 What steps must you take before saving a search for future use?

A: Before saving a search for future use you must first run the search and then click in the Search Results pane.

7 How can you reuse a search you've saved?

A: To reuse a search you've saved, double-click the saved search in the My Documents folder and then click the Search Now button.

8 How can you find a file if all you know is two words that occur together somewhere in the file name?

A: You can find a file if all you know is two words that occur together somewhere in the file name by adding an asterisk before the first word, a question mark between the words, and an asterisk following the second word.

Visual Quiz

Q: How do you display this dialog box? Which part of the dialog box do you use to control how much disk space the Recycle Bin uses? What would you do if you didn't want to confirm that deleted items should go to the Recycle Bin?

A: Right-click the Recycle Bin and select Properties to display the dialog box. Use the slider to control the amount of space that is used. To bypass the prompt when you delete files, remove the check from the Display delete confirmation dialog check box.

Chapter 7

See page 168

1 How can you tell when you're seeing the name of a computer on the network?

A: Computer names on the network have two backslashes before the name.

2 When you're trying to find a file, how much of the network can you search at any one time?

A: When you're trying to find a file, you can search one computer at a time.

3 Are folders that are contained within a shared folder on a network also shared on the network?

A: When you share folders, any folders contained in the shared folders are also shared unless you specifically exclude them from sharing.

4 What happens to your network places icons when the computers they refer to are no longer available?

A: When the computers to which network places icons refer are no longer available, the icons remain, but clicking those icons will display a message telling you that the computer is not available.

Personal Workbook Answers

5 **What connection speed is necessary if you want to share an Internet connection?**

A: You can share an Internet connection no matter what its speed.

6 **Why does a network printer need drivers installed on PCs that aren't connected to the printer?**

A: A network printer needs drivers installed on PCs that aren't connected to the printer so that they can send the proper commands to use the printer.

7 **How can you allow people access to master documents in a shared folder without allowing them to make changes?**

A: You can allow people access to master documents in a shared folder without allowing them to make changes by granting read-only access to the folder.

8 **Who provides you with a connection to the Internet?**

A: An Internet Service Provider, or ISP, provides you with a connection to the Internet.

Visual Quiz

Q: How can you display a window like this one? What is the purpose of the Add Network Place icon?

A: To display this window, double-click the My Network Places icon on the desktop. The Add Network Place icon enables you to create shortcuts to shared folders on your network.

Chapter 8

See page 182

1 **How do you display and use the On-Screen Keyboard?**

A: To use the On-Screen Keyboard, you must open an application that will accept the keystrokes from the On-Screen Keyboard, and then click the keys on the On-Screen Keyboard.

2 **What tool do you use to view screen contents at up to nine times normal size?**

A: To view screen contents at up to nine times normal size you use the Magnifier.

3 **What tool do you use to make dialog boxes flash when a sound prompt is issued by Windows Me?**

A: To make dialog boxes flash when there is a sound prompt, you use the SoundSentry.

4 **How can you make it possible to press the Shift, Ctrl, or Alt key first and then a second key without holding down the first key?**

A: To make it possible to press the Shift, Ctrl, or Alt key first and then a second key without holding down the first key, enable the StickyKeys option.

5 **How can you make Windows Me ignore keys that are held down too long?**

A: To make Windows Me ignore keys that are held down too long, enable the FilterKeys option.

6 **How long do the accessibility options normally remain active when the keyboard is idle?**

A: The accessibility options normally remain active for five minutes when the keyboard is idle.

7 **How can you make it possible to use the keyboard to move the mouse pointer?**

A: You can use the keyboard to move the mouse pointer by enabling the MouseKeys option.

8 **What shortcut can you use to turn on the StickyKeys option?**

A: You can turn on the StickyKeys option by pressing the Shift key five times.

Personal Workbook Answers

Visual Quiz

Q: How can you display a window like this one? How can you increase the magnification to 8 power?

A: To display this window, click the Start button. Then select Programs ⇨ Accessories ⇨ Accessibility ⇨ Magnifier. Use the spin box to set the magnification level to 8 power.

Chapter 9

See page 210

1 How can you make certain that a search engine looks for two words that are together?

A: To make certain that a search engine looks for two words that are together, enclose the search phrase in quotes.

2 What is a URL?

A: A URL is a Uniform Resource Locator — another name for a Web page address.

3 What do both people need in order to use MSN Messenger Service?

A: In order to use MSN Messenger Service, everyone must have an e-mail account with hotmail.com or passport.com.

4 How can you make it possible to view a Web page without reconnecting to the Internet?

A: To make it possible to view a Web page without reconnecting to the Internet, select Favorites ⇨ Add to Favorites and make certain the Make available offline check box is selected.

5 How can you make certain that a Web page you visit won't send destructive content to your system?

A: To make certain that a Web page you visit won't send destructive content to your system, add that Web page to the Restricted security zone.

6 What option can you use to restrict which Web sites can be accessed from your PC?

A: To restrict which Web sites can be accessed from your PC, use the Content Advisor option on the Content tab of the Internet Options dialog box.

7 How can you create folders to store links to related Web sites?

A: You can create folders to store links to related Web sites by using the Favorites ⇨ Organize Favorites command and then selecting Create Folder.

8 What button can you use to return to the last Web page you visited?

A: You can return to the last Web page you visited by clicking the Back button.

Visual Quiz

Q: What must you do before you can view this window? What does the list of contacts tell you about their status?

A: To display this window, you must sign up for MSN Messenger Service, connect to the Internet, and log on to MSN Messenger Service. None of the contacts in the list are currently connected to the Internet.

Chapter 10

See page 236

1 Why do Outlook Express folder names sometimes appear in boldface?

A: Outlook Express folder names appear in boldface when they contain unread messages.

Personal Workbook Answers

❷ What do you need to do before you can save a file that came along with an e-mail message?

A: To save a file that came along with an e-mail message, you must either open the message and right-click the attachment or click the Attachment button in the Preview pane.

❸ Where do messages you've created wait until they're sent to the mail server?

A: Messages you've created wait in the Outbox folder until they're sent to the mail server.

❹ What is the meaning of the number in parentheses following an Outlook Express folder name?

A: The number in parentheses following an Outlook Express folder name indicates the number of unread messages in the folder.

❺ How can you find newsgroups that pertain to a specific subject?

A: To find newsgroups that pertain to a specific subject you can enter search phrases in the Newsgroup Subscriptions dialog box.

❻ How can you stop an e-mail message from being delivered once it leaves your Outbox?

A: In most cases you cannot stop an e-mail message from being delivered once it leaves your Outbox. Be sure you really want to send a message before you click Send.

❼ What message format can you use to make certain that anyone can read your message?

A: You can use the plain text message format to make certain that anyone can read your message.

❽ How often must you download the entire list of newsgroups?

A: You only need to download the entire list of newsgroups the first time you access the news server. Later you will only download updates to the list.

Visual Quiz

Q: How can you display this dialog box? If you want to place your outbound messages in the Outbox rather than sending them as soon as you've created them, what setting do you need to adjust?

A: To display this window, select Tools ➪ Options. To delay sending messages until you click the Send/Recv button, click the Send tab and remove the check from the *Send messages immediately* check box.

Chapter 11

See page 262

❶ What will happen if you change the screen resolution setting but don't click the Yes button in the confirmation dialog box?

A: If you change the screen resolution setting but don't click the Yes button, Windows Me will restore your previous setting after 15 seconds.

❷ How can you make a hidden Taskbar pop up without moving the mouse?

A: You can make a hidden Taskbar pop up without moving the mouse by pressing the Windows key or Ctrl+Esc.

❸ How can you find a hidden Taskbar using the mouse?

A: You can find a hidden Taskbar using the mouse by moving the mouse just past the edge of the screen where the Taskbar is hiding.

❹ What do you need to activate before you can use a JPEG image as your desktop wallpaper?

A: Before you can use a JPEG image as your desktop wallpaper, you need to activate the option to show Web content on your desktop.

Personal Workbook Answers

5 **What can you do to restore order to the Start menu if items are no longer being sorted?**

A: To restore order to the Start menu if items are no longer being sorted, click the Re-sort button on the Advanced tab of the Taskbar and Start Menu Properties dialog box.

6 **How can you reduce the size of the icons on the Start menu?**

A: To reduce the size of the icons on the Start menu, select the *Show small icons in Start menu* option on the General tab of the Taskbar and Start Menu Properties dialog box.

7 **What is the fastest way to choose a desktop element on the Appearance tab of the Display Properties dialog box so that you can change the element's color?**

A: The fastest way to choose a desktop element on the Appearance tab of the Display Properties dialog box so that you can change the element's color is to click the item in the preview window.

8 **How can you view the items in the Control Panel folder without opening the folder?**

A: You can view the items in the Control Panel folder without opening the folder by selecting the Expand Control Panel option on the Advanced tab of the Taskbar and Start Menu Properties dialog box.

Visual Quiz

Q: **How can you display this dialog box? How do the controls on this tab interact?**

A: To display this window, right-click a blank space on the desktop and choose Properties. Click the Settings tab to show these controls. The Colors and Screen area controls may interact if you try to choose a color setting and a resolution setting at the maximum end of the range — your display adapter may not support the highest number of colors at the highest resolution.

Chapter 12

See page 282

1 **How can you change your keyboard layout?**

A: You can change your keyboard layout using the Language tab of the Keyboard Properties dialog box.

2 **Where do you go to assign sounds to Windows Me events?**

A: You can assign sounds to Windows Me events using the Sounds and Multimedia dialog box.

3 **What type of peripheral does Windows Me recognize automatically?**

A: Windows Me automatically recognizes plug-and-play peripherals.

4 **What do you call mouse pointers that display a brief animation?**

A: Mouse pointers that show a brief animation are called animated cursors.

5 **What can you do to change the number of times keys repeat when they are held down?**

A: To change the number of times keys repeat when they are held down, change the repeat rate in the Keyboard Properties dialog box.

6 **What type of sound files can you associate with system events?**

A: You can associate wave sound files with system events.

7 **Where do you find most of the system configuration tools?**

A: You find most of the system configuration tools in the Control Panel.

Personal Workbook Answers

8 **How can you save a registry key so that it can be easily restored?**

A: You can save a registry key so that it can be easily restored by selecting Registry ⇨ Export Registry File.

Visual Quiz

Q: How can you display this dialog box? How can you tell which events have associated sounds? How can you hear the sounds?

A: To display this window, open the Control Panel and double-click the Sounds and Multimedia icon. Events that have sounds are indicated by a speaker icon. Click the Play button to hear a sound.

Chapter 13

See page 298

1 **What tool can you use to remove old files that are no longer needed on your PC?**

A: You can use the disk cleanup tool to remove old files that are no longer needed on your PC.

2 **What type of disk errors can prevent your PC from using specific places on your hard disk?**

A: Physical disk errors can prevent your PC from using specific places on your hard disk.

3 **What is the difference between contiguous and fragmented files?**

A: Contiguous files are located in one piece on your disk. Fragmented files are spread out in multiple pieces in various locations.

4 **How can you reduce the size of backups and the time required to perform them?**

A: To reduce the size of backups and the time required to perform them, you can limit your backups to include only your important data files — especially those with changes.

5 **What will happen if you attempt to scan for errors on a disk that is in use?**

A: If you attempt to scan for errors on a disk that is in use, Windows Me will continually restart the error scan. It is best to run this task when you are not doing other things with your PC.

6 **What do you call a diskette that enables you to boot in an emergency?**

A: You call a diskette that enables you to boot in an emergency a Startup Disk.

7 **What operating mode should you attempt to use first if Windows Me won't load?**

A: If Windows Me won't load, try to start your system in safe mode.

8 **How can you free up additional space if the disk cleanup tool doesn't do as much as you'd like?**

A: You can free up additional space by using the More Options tab and removing unneeded Windows Me components and unused programs.

Visual Quiz

Q: How can you display this dialog box? How can you tell when your hard disk was last defragmented? How can you check for disk errors?

A: To display this window, double-click the My Computer icon, right-click the drive C icon, and choose Properties. To see when a drive was last defragmented, look in the defragmentation status box. To check for disk errors, click Check Now.

Personal Workbook Answers

Chapter 14

See page 312

1 What tool can you use to make certain your Windows Me system files are up-to-date?

A: You can use Windows Update to make certain your Windows Me system files are up-to-date.

2 Where can you find out if your system has any resource conflict problems?

A: You can find out if your system has any resource conflict problems by opening the Device Manager and looking for problem markers.

3 Where can you look to see which IRQs are in use on your system?

A: You can look in the Device Manager to see which IRQs are in use on your system.

4 How can you eliminate a problem caused by installing a poorly designed program?

A: To eliminate a problem caused by installing a poorly designed program, use System Restore to roll back your system to a point before you installed the program.

5 What is the purpose of the Maintenance Wizard?

A: The Maintenance Wizard helps you schedule important routine system maintenance tasks that can help keep your system running correctly.

6 How can you make certain your computer always has the latest updates without visiting the Windows Update Web site yourself?

A: You can make certain your computer always has the latest updates without visiting the Windows Update Web site yourself by configuring the AutoUpdate feature using the Automatic Updates icon in Control Panel.

7 What do you call the items you add to the system monitor display?

A: The items you add to the system monitor display are called counters.

8 How can you make certain that you can roll back your computer to a specific point in time?

A: You can make certain that you can roll back your computer to a specific point in time by creating a restore point in System Restore.

Visual Quiz

Q: How can you display this list in the Device Manager? What can you tell about the selected device?

A: To display this list, click *View devices by connection* near the top of the Device Manager tab. The selected device has an exclamation point that indicates there is a problem with the device.

Chapter 15

See page 326

1 How can you get an onscreen notification that advises you when a scheduled task did not run?

A: You can get an onscreen notification that advises you when a scheduled task did not run by choosing Advanced ➪ Notify Me of Missed Tasks.

2 How can you suspend a task?

A: You can suspend a task by removing the check from the Enabled check box on the program's properties dialog box — which you can see by right-clicking the task and choosing Properties.

3 If you receive a notice that a task did not run, how can you find the problem?

A: If you receive a notice that a task did not run, you can find the problem by examining the log file.

Personal Workbook Answers

4 **Why might you want to enter a descriptive name for a task?**

A: You might want to enter a descriptive name for a task if you have more than one variation on the same task so that you can keep track of the different variations.

5 **How can you specify that you wish to repeat a scheduled task twice daily?**

A: You can specify that you wish to repeat a scheduled task twice daily by using the *Show multiple schedules* check box and setting up two different daily schedules.

6 **What setting can you use to automatically stop a task if you start to use your system?**

A: You can use the *Stop the task if the computer ceases to be idle* setting to automatically stop a task if you start to use your system.

7 **To be a good candidate for a scheduled task, what capability does a program need?**

A: To be a good candidate for a scheduled task, a program needs to be able to complete a task without human intervention.

8 **How can you temporarily suspend all tasks?**

A: You can temporarily suspend all tasks by selecting Advanced ⇨ Pause Task Scheduler.

Visual Quiz

Q: **How can you display this dialog box? How can you make the task wait for 15 minutes after you stop using your system to begin the task?**

A: To display this dialog box, double-click the task that you wish to modify. To make the task wait for 15 minutes after you stop using your system to begin the task, specify 15 in the *Only start the task if the computer has been idle for at least xx minutes* spin box.

Chapter 16

See page 356

1 **Which Windows Me tool would you use to record a voice message?**

A: You can use Sound Recorder to record a voice message.

2 **What is the quickest method of displaying the full volume control?**

A: You can display the full volume control by double-clicking the speaker icon in the system tray.

3 **What type of file does the Sound Recorder produce?**

A: The Sound Recorder produces wave (.WAV) files.

4 **How can you make Media Player skip the same song on an audio CD every time you play the CD?**

A: You can make Media Player skip the same song on an audio CD every time you play the CD by editing the play list.

5 **Why are most video files shown in a small window?**

A: Most video files are shown in a small window to reduce the size of the file.

6 **What do you call the tool you use to create Windows Media Audio/Video files?**

A: To create Windows Media Audio/Video files you use the Windows Movie Maker.

7 **What type of files are actually instructions that are used to synthesize music on your PC?**

A: MIDI files are instructions that are used to synthesize music on your PC.

8 **What does the thickness of the line that is displayed in the Sound Recorder represent?**

A: The thickness of the line that is displayed in the Sound Recorder represents the volume of the recorded sound at that position in the file.

Visual Quiz

Q: **How can you display this application? How can you tell how long the file will play? Can you tell what type of file is being played?**

A: To display the Media Player, double-click a multimedia file. The counter in the lower right corner of the Media Player shows the current position and the length of the file. A video file is being played — if a sound file were being played, no video would appear in the Media Player window.

Chapter 17

See page 386

1 **What should you do if the MS-DOS Prompt window says "finished" in the title bar?**

A: If the MS-DOS Prompt window says "finished" in the title bar, click the Close button to close the window.

2 **What do you type to close the MS-DOS Prompt window?**

A: You can close the MS-DOS Prompt window by typing EXIT.

3 **How can you transfer data between the calculator and other applications?**

A: You can transfer data between the calculator and other applications by copying and pasting.

4 **What can you do if the lines of text in a Notepad document extend past the right edge of the window?**

A: If the lines of text in a Notepad document extend past the right edge of the window, you can select Edit ⇨ Word Wrap to wrap the lines so you can see everything.

5 **How can you add a picture to a WordPad document?**

A: You can add a picture to a WordPad document by selecting Insert ⇨ Object and then choosing the type of object.

6 **How can you match a color exactly in Paint?**

A: You can match a color exactly in Paint by clicking the Pick Color tool on the color to make the color the left-click color.

7 **What tool can you use to easily enter foreign characters into a document?**

A: You can use the Character Map to easily enter foreign characters into a document.

8 **Which tool can you use to assemble multiple scanned pages for a fax?**

A: You can use Imaging to assemble multiple scanned pages for a fax.

Visual Quiz

Q: **How can you display this application? How can you tell the current zoom level? What button would you click to rotate the image 90 degrees clockwise?**

A: To display Imaging, click the Start button and choose Programs ⇨ Accessories ⇨ Imaging. The current zoom level is shown in the status bar and in the Zoom list box. Click the Rotate Right button to rotate the image 90 degrees clockwise.

Index

Index

Index

Index

Index

Index

Index

installing programs, 70-73
instant messaging service, 206-207
Intel Camera Pack, 343
interactive troubleshooters, 61
internal commands, 385
Internet
    access, 162
    account set up, 163
    address, 189
    advertising, 192
    connecting to, 149
    digital music files, 335
    display, improving, 188
    DNS address, 165
    favorites, 200
    games, 352, 378
    IP address, 165
    links, 187-188, 191
    offline viewing, 196
    overview, 63 70, 76
    password, 164
    search engine, 192-193
    speed, 190
    Uniform Resource Locator (URL), 190
    user name, 164
    voice chats, 352
    Web browser, 187-188
    Web pages, 187
Internet address, 47
Internet Connection Sharing, 167
Internet Explorer
    Advanced tab, 204
    application programs, 204
    AutoComplete, 205
    certificates, 204-205
    Connection tab, 204
    Content tab, 204
    favorites, 260
    menus, 188
    MSN Messenger Service, 209
    overview, 8, 164, 188, 256, 258
    Programs tab, 204
    restricting access, 204
    security zones, 202
    start page, 202
    viewing Web pages, 202
Internet Options dialog box, 202
Internet Options icon, 49
Internet Properties dialog box, 49
Internet Service Provider (ISP), 162-163, 166, 213
interrupt request (IRQ), 309
Invert Selection, 143
investments, 69, 80
IP address, static, 165
IRQ. *See* interrupt request (IRQ)
ISDN, 162, 166
ISDN adapter, 163
ISO-9660, 105
ISP. *See* Internet Service Provider (ISP)

J

joystick, 276
JPEG format, 17, 243
junk mail, 226

K

key, 278-279
keyboard, 86, 270, 276
keyboard commands, 84
Keyboard Properties dialog box, 270
keystroke combination, Character Map, 363
keywords, 228
knowledgebase, 62

Index

Index

Index

Continued

Index

Index

Index

Index

Index

Index